THE SMITHS

THE DAY I WAS THERE

Richard Houghton

www.thisdayinmusic.com

A catalogue record for this book is available from the British Library

ISBN: 978-1-9161156-6-8

Cover photo by Stephen Wright
https://www.smithsphotos.com
Front and back cover concept by Liz Sanchez
Cover design by Oliver Keen
Book design by Gary Bishop
Printed in the UK by Sound Performance

This Day In Music Books
2B Vantage Park
Washingley Road
Huntingdon
PE29 6SR

www.thisdayinmusic.com

Exclusive Distributors:
Music Sales Limited
14/15 Berners St
London
W1T 3JL

he Smith
THE WOODENTOPS
UCESTER LEISURE CEN
MONDAY 24th SEPTEMBER
DOORS OPEN 7.00pm
RDIFF UNIVE
SDAY 25t
Miserable Smiths top NME poll of most influen
Greater than Beatles
Happy now Morrissey
By Zoe Nauman
ALTHOUGH for many they are the best pop group of all time, the Beatles have only managed to come second in a poll of the most important
Charting the super
1 The Smiths
2 The Beatles
3 Stone Roses
4 David Bowie
5 Sex Pistols
26 Dexy's
27 Beast
28 T. Re
=28 Jes
30 Th
31 M
The Lansdowne Floris
CARD & FLOWER SHOP
17 19 HOLDENHURST ROAD
BOURNEMOUTH 23318
Don't mention it
DEAR MAILMAN,
I went to see the Sex Pistols at Manchester and they are the most exciting rock band to emerge since the New York Dolls. It puzzles me why bands like them don't get a mention in Record Mirror.
Steve Morrissey,
Stretford,
Manchester
● There you go, one free mention and that's yer lot.
SINGLE OF THE WEEK
THE SMITHS 'The Boy With The Thorn In His Side' (Rough Trade) Call me predictable, call me boring, call me sentimental – I don't care. The worries of the world float away as the new single from the ever lovable Smiths arrives on my desk. Still on Rough Trade, still adorning the covers with Morrissey's heroes (Truman Capote looking like Ernie Wise this time), and still making the most perfect pop music ever created. A light 'Williamesque' backing has Morrissey trilling and warbling his exquisite way around Johnny Marr's simple melodies. After the slip that 'Shakespeare's Sister' proved to be and the questionable decision to release 'That Joke Isn't Funny Anymore' – probably the only track on 'Meat Is Murder' that shouldn't have been a single – the group brush off the dust from a thousand gleeful cries of 'has beens' and resume normal service.
SMITHS
FORD CIVIC HALL
28TH FEBRUARY 7-30
"MEAT IS MURDER
Forte Promotions
SMITHS
Support June Bride
Doors
ew York Dolls and Patti Smith
some life pumping away in the
York, and they are the only ac
the N.Y. club scene worthy of any
e absolutely nothing to add that is of
nce and should be rightly filed and f

About the author

Like Johnny Marr, Richard Houghton supports Manchester City. Like both Johnny and Morrissey, he's a vegetarian. Living close to Morrissey's childhood home in Kings Road, Stretford, Richard shares his house with his girlfriend Kate, his pomapoo Sid and several scraps of Morrissey's shirts collected from different Moz solo gigs by his Smiths-loving family.

A number of Richard's books are published by This Day In Music Books, including *Sometimes These Words Just Don't Have To Be Said* about indie legends The Wedding Present (co-authored with David Gedge) and an official biography of Orchestral Manoeuvres in the Dark, *Pretending To See The Future*.

Richard has seen both Morrissey and Johnny Marr on stage, but never at the same time. He lives in hope.

Contents

1982 – The Early Gigs

1983 – On The College Circuit

1984 – Hatful of Hollow

1985 – Meat Is Murder

1986 – The Queen Is Dead

1987 – Strangeways and the Split

The Solo Years

Paying Tribute

Random Encounters

What Difference Does It Make?

Acknowledgements

INTRODUCTION

The impact of some bands is not measured by the number of albums they sold during their career or the size of the audiences they played to. Occasionally, the impression they leave on the musical world is best measured by the fervour of their fans. The Smiths are just such a band.

They burst onto a lifeless British music scene, groggy after the departure of punk and seemingly enraptured by the New Romantics and the hangover of disco. They gave spotty teenagers looking for their next guitar heroes something to get excited about after the demise of The Jam and The Clash. Britain in 1982 and 1983 had Margaret Thatcher, government spending cuts and looming industrial crisis in the shape of the impending miners strike.

Not that The Smiths sang directly about that. Their politics were more personal. It is this connection, through lyrics that were not being written by anyone else and with chiming guitar melodies that cut across the electro-pop filling the charts, that appealed to so many.

The Smiths spoke to and for those who felt outside of society. This is their story.

Richard Houghton
Manchester
August 2019

THE VINE

1981, SALE, MANCHESTER, UK

I WAS THERE: SIMON WOLSTENCROFT

The Vine pub in Sale, Greater Manchester is where the seeds of The Smiths were sown

I had a brief association with The Smiths, for better or worse! I was in a band with Ian Brown and John Squire. We would drink together in a pub called The Vine in Sale, a suburb of Manchester. Ian then went travelling around Europe before he and John became the Stone Roses. A mutual friend of Johnny Marr said that Johnny was looking for a drummer to start a new band, so I agreed to meet him in The Vine one night. Sure enough, he came along. And he was very, very cocksure. So I got to meet Johnny and he looked fantastic, with what he was wearing and his haircut. He was such a hustler. And he was such a funny guy, very quick-witted. He doesn't suffer fools.

We started to hang out at Andy Rourke's dad's house, in Sale, and started a band. Andy's dad was always away on business so Andy and his three brothers often had the run of the house. Their mother wasn't with them any more. It became a bit of a den of iniquity. We were listening to a lot of music and talking about forming this group called Freak Party - why Johnny chose that name I don't know - and me, Andy and Johnny started rehearsing at the house. Then we got a rehearsal room in the cellar of a carpet shop in Sale and then we started rehearsing in Ancoats. This was 1981, going into 1982.

We were all taking drugs - Andy and I more than Johnny - and all got arrested in the studio as we were auditioning singers for Freak Party. Johnny got arrested, fined and prosecuted and said to us, 'I can't hang around with you guys any more because I'm going to get into trouble.' So we didn't see him for two or three months. He moved out from Andy's, where he'd been sleeping in Andy's dad's bed with his girlfriend, Angie, and Andy and I carried on without him. We tried to audition three or four different singers but the final straw was the arrest of us all by the Serious Crime Squad in the studio. Johnny leaving finished Freak Party off.

Two or three months later, Johnny rang me out of the blue to say, 'I've met this guy, Stephen Morrissey. We've started a new band called The Smiths and we want you as the drummer.' My head wasn't really in a good place at the time with the drugs and everything, so I said, 'Oh, I don't know about that, Johnny.' He said, 'Come on, please give it a go at least. We're doing a demo recording at Decibelle Studios.' The studio owner was away in Paris on business and Johnny said, 'We've got the studio for nothing.'

I went along. Andy Rourke hadn't been asked to join the band. The engineer Dale (Hibbert), who had the key to the studio, was playing bass. It was me on drums, Johnny on guitar and Morrissey came along. But I didn't like the cut of his jib. He was what back in the day the *NME* was calling a shoe-gazer. I didn't like his style.

Because we'd been listening to jazz-funk and Grace Jones and Earth, Wind & Fire round at Andy's for the last six months, we wanted the band to sound a bit like that. Freak Party were very similar to A Certain Ratio, we were listening to the album *Sextet* over and over again with Andy playing all the bass lines off it and Johnny doing that Nile Rodgers-style guitar. I was hoping the band would sound like this when Morrissey came. But of course that wasn't to be.

There were a couple of songs recorded, including 'Suffer Little Children' about the Moors Murders, which was very morose and I just thought, 'Ugh, what is this?' So when Johnny told me the band was called The Smiths I said, 'It's a shit name.' It was very plain and boring. People had names like Freak Party or Depeche Mode - exotic sounding names.

We did the two tracks and I didn't really like it, so I said, 'Thanks Johnny, but I don't really want to do it.' According to Johnny in his book, he was offering me big bags of weed to do the gig, but I don't remember that. I just wasn't really interested at all. I said 'no' and that was basically the last time I played with them.

Another reason I didn't want to join The Smiths was because Andy had not been asked to play bass from the very beginning. I knew Andy a better bass player than Dale. If Andy had been in the band right from the word go, it might have all been different. It might have been me with a big mansion in Cheshire. But it just wasn't to be. They asked Andy to join pretty soon after that. Andy was my best mate and I was absolutely gutted and sank into a bit of a depression, self-medicating with the drugs. It was a pretty bad time really.

Simon Wolstencroft was Johnny Marr's first choice for drummer with The Smiths

Within about six months to a year they were riding high. The next thing you know they're on *Top of the Pops*. I learned to like them. With 'What Difference Does it Make?' I thought, 'Wow, this is pretty good, this one.' That was the first one that stood out for me. 'Hand in Glove' was a bit too indie and shambling for my liking.

I did used to go and see them on the early tours. One gig that stands out is at Cannock, in a marquee in Staffordshire. It was a very threatening atmosphere. I think they'd been in the paper already about the Moors Murders. And the association of Morrissey flailing flowers about. There weren't many people there but it was quite scary to be there, with all these little locals hanging about outside the marquee and looking very threatening.

I remember Brixton Fridge. That night, Seymour Stein from Columbia/Warner Brothers had flown over on Concorde just to see The Smiths. He was dressed up in this white flowing shirt with white trousers and white shoes. He looked like he had a lot of money, which of course he did! But Mike Joyce, made a couple of cock-ups on the drums that night. I drove Andy back home because I had driven down in my car and for a minute I thought I was going to get back in the band because Mike kept making these mistakes, which wouldn't have been very fair on Mike.

Andy and Johnny were trying to get me back in the band. But Joe Moss, the manager at the time, knew my history for dabbling in drugs and said, 'Whoa, whoa, whoa, we'd better not rock the boat at this stage'. Andy was having his own problems of course. By the morning time, we'd had an official statement off Joe Moss saying, 'We're going to stick with Mike' and that was the end of that.

Morrissey's a very charming guy. He didn't actually look me in the face during the recording. But he'd see me at the gigs and he'd say, 'Hello Simon. How are you? Lovely to see you.'

The Free Trade Hall in March 1984 is another gig I remember. I went to pick Morrissey and Sandie Shaw up off the train from London. They were going straight to the gig. Johnny must have said, 'Do you mind picking him up in case he gets lost?' I had a Triumph Dolomite. Sandie got in the back and Morrissey sat in the front. He was stroking the fake walnut dashboard and he said, 'This is a lovely car, Simon.' That was a good night.

By 1986, I'm in The Fall and we played the Festival of the Tenth Summer at the G-Mex in Manchester, which was packed out. The Smiths were on, as well as New Order, Orchestral Manoeuvres in the Dark, A Certain Ratio and others. One of my best memories is watching them there, with Morrissey waving the placard 'The Queen Is Dead' about on stage, to an ecstatic crowd. They just sounded so powerful, partly because of Johnny who is the finest guitarist of my generation.

Johnny asked me if Craig Gannon would join The Smiths when they wanted to double up and have two guitarists when they went to America. So I feel I was responsible for him getting the gig with The Smiths.

I was in and around the entourage right throughout the career of the band. I was there the night Andy got fired, after he got arrested. I remember the characters around the band, and the road crew going for sneaky McDonalds like naughty children so Morrissey wouldn't find out. Johnny bought into vegetarianism very early on in the band.

I'm still friends with Andy. I've been over to New York a couple of times to see him, and he comes over here maybe once a year so I always hook up with him. He's been there for over 10 years now. He's got another band.

I love Mike. He's a very, very funny guy. I bump into him from time to time if I'm out and about. Going back to the Seymour Stein night, I don't know where Mike got to hear about that. I think I mentioned it in my book.

I don't see Johnny a lot. I see him mostly driving around town now in a Bentley. When my book came out, I bumped into Johnny and he said, 'Si, I love your book. It's brilliant. I've read it. Thanks for saying nice things about me.' And he returned the favour in his book. He put a lovely picture in. So I'm really grateful to him for doing that.

I don't see Morrissey at all, although people see him in the Unicorn Deli in Chorlton when he's over here. After The Smiths split up, in 1989 I wrote to Morrissey asking 'Any chance of playing drums in your solo project?' He wrote me an amusing postcard saying, 'My hip-swivelling days are temporarily suspended. In the event of a thaw, I'll give you a ring. But is your P45 not spoken for? I thought you were in The Fall.' Which I was. But had he said, 'Yeah, come down to the studio next week,' I would probably have left The Fall and been off like a shot, because he was a household name by then.

I'm still playing. After The Fall I went with Ian Brown, my old schoolmate, for a couple of years in 1999/2000. Since then I've been in a few line-ups of different bands. I could have had a mansion and a Bentley but I've lived the dream too. I've been in a band touring the world. I've been very lucky with the bands I've been in. I don't feel totally hard done by. I got over it when I joined The Fall, because I didn't have time to think about what The Smiths were doing. Mark E Smith always used to take the piss, because they'd made it. He used to say, 'You're not like them, Simon.'

I am a fan, definitely. It was just that first impression that changed the course of my life in that room in Ancoats. It would have all been different had I said, 'Yeah, I'll stick with the band.'

THE RITZ

4 OCTOBER 1982, MANCHESTER, UK

Supporting Blue Rondo à la Turk, The Smiths' first live appearance was with a line up of Morrissey on vocals, Johnny Marr on guitar, Mike Joyce on drums and Dale Hibbert on bass. Morrissey's friend James Maker introduced the band and remained on stage throughout the performance as a dancer, apparently on a whim of Morrissey's.

James Maker: There were no instructions. I think it was generally accepted I would improvise... I was there to drink red wine, make extraneous hand gestures and keep well within the tight, chalked circle that Morrissey had drawn around me.

After the first gig Dale Hibbert was replaced by Andy Rourke.

Andy Rourke: I played my first gig in a tiny gay club called Manhattan Sound. I was very nervous. We all were. [Morrissey] had a pocket full of confetti and threw it over the audience, which none of us expected.

MANHATTAN SOUND

25 JANUARY 1983, MANCHESTER, UK

I WAS THERE: ANNE FORD

I was in my first year at university and I was a regular at the Manhattan, a basement club in Spring Gardens. Originally a cocktail/Stringfellows sort of place, with young women serving drinks dressed in tutus or something and not particularly a young persons club, it was taken over by a chap called Peter who later bought the Rembrandt. It wasn't really a live music venue and was fairly small. There was a separate room where films were sometimes shown on a screen. There was no stage as such. Acts performed on the dance floor.

There had been a few bands on, promoted by a couple of lads that came into the bar. I remember the poster going up behind the bar advertising The Smiths. It was the grey/lilac one that featured 'Hand in Glove'. The thing that struck me was their name. It was so different sounding compared with Joy Division, Duran Duran, Spandau Ballet, etc. We had no idea what sort of sound to expect.

There were about 40 people there. We were close to them as it was so small, Morrissey was Morrissey and did the flailing arms thing. The sound was great and different. They felt like they would stay around a bit and I think most people there liked them although I don't recall anyone having seen or heard of them before. I saw a few other acts there - Sade, who was called Pride at the time, performed with a sax player and was sexy, understated and fab. There was a bit of a scuffle right in front of her and she stopped singing and asked them to stop.

Two or three years later, I used to hang out at Corbiers and they had bands on – A Certain Ratio, Easterhouse. When that closed we used to walk over to Pierrot, off Cross Street. Pierrot also had the occasional band on. I hung out with the Diggle brothers and Craig Gannon, who had just joined The Smiths. I remember one time, when we wanted to carry on drinking mid week, we decided to walk over to the Man Alive club on Grosvenor Street. We walked in, they saw Craig and they started playing Smiths tunes, followed by Sandie Shaw.

Maker's services were dispensed with after two shows when it was agreed he was a distraction. The classic line up of Morrissey (vocals), Johnny Marr (guitar), Andy Rourke (bass) and Mike Joyce (drums) was now in place.

Sharing the bill with Factory Records funk band 52nd Street, The Smiths performed at The Hacienda on 4 February 1983, but left the stage to muted applause. Morrissey used flowers on stage for the first time.

Morrissey: We introduced them as an antidote to the Hacienda when we played there; it was so sterile and inhuman.

THE HACIENDA

4 FEBRUARY 1983, MANCHESTER, UK

I WAS THERE: DAVID MYERS

I saw their third ever gig at the Hacienda in Manchester in February 1983 and then their visit to Stoke Poly where I was a student not long after. Before all that, I bought my trousers from Johnny when he worked at X Clothes in Manchester.

Andy Rourke: It was a freezing cold, empty warehouse, showing weird films at the side of the stage.

Mike Joyce: We were supporting 52nd Street, and on the poster it said 'Smiths'. Morrissey came on and said, 'We are The Smiths, not Smiths... I remember watching the faces of the people at the front. It was just shock. 'What the hell is this?'

RAFTERS

21 FEBRUARY 1983, MANCHESTER, UK

I WAS THERE: SIMON DAVIES

I saw them a few times. The first time was at Rafters where they supported Richard Hell. As an aspiring guitarist at the time I knew it was game over after seeing Johnny. I'd just got my first car, a Triumph 1500, so it was a first drive into town. It wouldn't start after the gig and we were helped by a policeman, who took his helmet off to have a look in the bonnet. He then noticed my mate Ted jigging around with it on his head.

THE ROCK GARDEN

23 MARCH 1983, LONDON, UK

I WAS THERE: PHIL MCADAM, AGE 19

Like all my favourite bands I heard them via John Peel and read about them in *NME* or *Melody Maker*. I only saw them the once and I can't remember much about it. It was around the time of 'Hand in Glove' and before the first album came out. It was their first London show.

'HAND IN GLOVE'

RELEASED 13 MAY 1983

The Smiths first single release reached number 3 on the UK indie chart but only managed 124 on the UK singles chart. The sleeve carried the buttock-baring image of actor George O'Mara, chosen by Morrissey. When Andy Rourke's dad asked him why they'd chosen 'a bloke's bum' for the picture sleeve, 'I just didn't have an answer for him.'

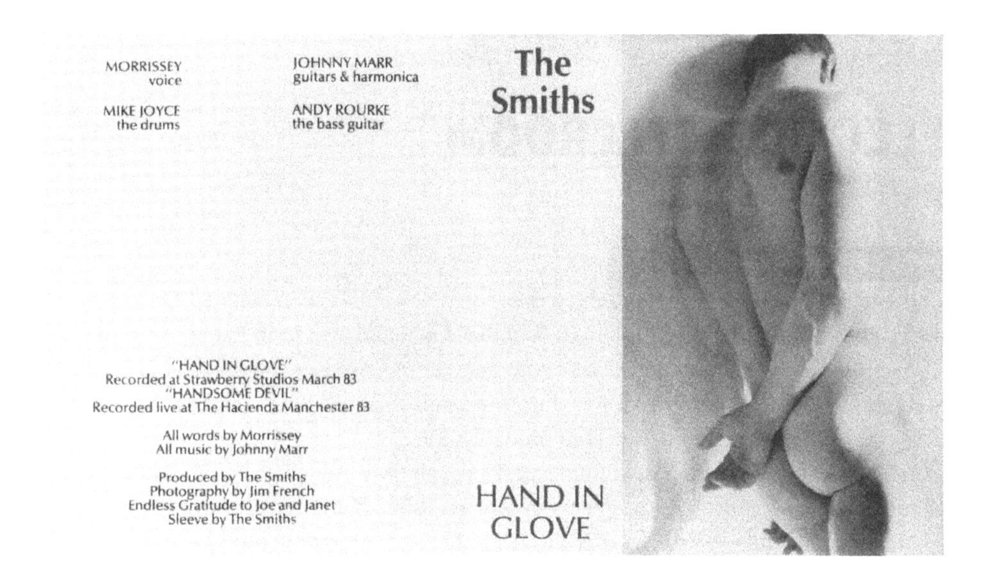

UNIVERSITY OF LONDON UNION

6 MAY 1983, LONDON, UK

I WAS THERE: STEVE CATTERALL

I first saw The Smiths at ULU. I first recorded them at the Brixton Ace in June. From the end of 1984 onwards I saw - and recorded - pretty much every Smiths show in the UK and Ireland. At the time I thought I'd take the opportunity to put down my memories of each show before I forgot them. Memory is a funny thing. Looking at those entries now, there are some I can't remember, and some I remember slightly differently. Recording the shows does give you a view, which is slightly set apart from the actual event sometimes. The Smiths hardly varied their set list from show to show on individual tours, which meant that shows did tend to blend into one another a bit. My favourite tour was probably the Scottish tour in 1985. I think they were at the top of their game at this period, and the tour was short enough and stopped in some out of the way places, such as the Shetland Islands, so that it never lost the initial energy.

PEEL SESSION, MAIDA VALE STUDIOS

18 MAY 1983, LONDON, UK

Broadcast on Radio 1's *John Peel Show* on 31 May 1983, the band went into the BBC's Maida Vale Studios and recorded their first session for legendary deejay John Peel, whose reputation for breaking bands in the UK stretched back to the Sixties and acts such as Pink Floyd and T.Rex. The band recorded four tracks – 'Handsome Devil', 'Reel Around the Fountain', 'Miserable Lie' and 'What Difference Does It Make?' – and the session was broadcast five further times in the following three years. Three of the four tracks, excluding 'Miserable Lie', were later released on *Hatful of Hollow.*

ELECTRIC BALLROOM

21 MAY 1983, LONDON, UK

I WAS THERE: GREG COTMORE

Context gives meaning, if only to the writer. I left New Zealand in early 1983 to follow my English-born girlfriend to London. Fool that I was and ever so in love, I saved up my wages from a deadbeat job and flew over to join her in Camden Town. Looking back at the young besotted idiot that I was, I'm sure I talked myself into believing she was pleased to see me. Maybe she was, but probably not.

Arriving in London was a daunting experience: all those people, all those buildings, all that history. Moreover, it wasn't easy getting established as job opportunities in Thatcher's England were not exactly throwing themselves at me. Consequently, I was somewhat miserly with what little money I had. Nevertheless, I still bought the *New Musical Express*, a regular read of mine since 1973. It was here that I saw an advertisement for The Fall playing at the Electric Ballroom in Camden. I don't remember noticing the name of the support band.

My girlfriend, not being a fan of The Fall, wasn't keen. Indeed, it was because of her that I had to leave The Fall's 1982 NZ Wellington gig before it ended, exiting mid-way through 'Tempo House'. I have remonstrated with myself for that stupid mistake ever since.

The idea of The Fall playing a gig within walking distance was a temptation I couldn't resist. So off I trotted to Rock On Records and bought my £3 ticket. I'm pretty sure it had the name of the support band printed on it, but again I paid no heed.

From the distance of 36 years, the night of the gig is memorable for two reasons. First, the stink and pall of smoke; cigarettes back then were not banned at concerts. I had to wave my hands about to see the stage, never mind breathe, and my jacket reeked of smoke for weeks afterwards. Second, the support band, the name of which I had dutifully ignored until now. They were, of course, The Smiths.

In 1983, I was still waiting for the music of the Eighties to happen; Duran Duran definitely were *not* the starting gun. By the end of The Smiths' short set, for me, the music of the Eighties had arrived.

Due to the passage of years, my memory of the setlist is somewhat vague. I remember the relentlessness of 'What Difference Does it Make?' and 'Hand in Glove', which had just been released as their debut single. One song is deeply etched into my brain; their performance of 'Reel Around the Fountain'. I was in awe of the majesty, mystery and magnitude of attitude. In that moment, I experienced my own pre-fame Beatles or Bowie moment. I knew that, in years to come, I would get a thrilling buzz to say, 'I saw The Smiths before they were big.' I did, and still do.

When The Fall came on, it was to the strains of 'Tempo House'. The smile on my face must have been insufferable.

I WAS THERE: PADDY SHENNAN, AGE 19

It's always a bonus when you enjoy a support band you had never previously seen or heard. I was vaguely aware of a new group from Manchester called The Smiths, possibly having seen them mentioned as the support in the gig listings in *NME*. The name would have intrigued me as my favourite band at that time - by a mile - was The Fall. Perhaps I imagined the name was a tribute - a Manchester band named in recognition of Mark E Smith.

Paddy Shennan thought The Smiths were a tribute band to The Fall's lead singer, Mark E Smith

I travelled from my home town of Preston to stay with a friend, Paul Platypus, who like me was an active participant in the underground cassette scene and who, like me, had compiled the Obscurist chart for *Sounds*.

This was The Smiths' seventh gig, and I recall watching their performance while sitting on the floor of the venue. Between songs I remember saying, 'Pretty good, aren't they?' I was impressed by their bright, clean sound, and their catchy songs. You could clearly hear the words, and they sounded intelligent and witty. I also recall thinking, 'That shades-wearing guitarist looks pretty cocky!' No offence, Johnny.

After the gig, Geoff Travis walked past me. Both bands, of course, were on his Rough Trade label, and Mark E Smith was later to complain about most of the company's resources being concentrated on The Smiths. Not at this point, though - The Fall were very much the bigger of the two bands.

But The Smiths were beginning to make their mark. When I got home I ordered their newly-released single, 'Hand in Glove', from Rough Trade's mail order business.

MINERS GALA, CANNOCK PARK

2 JUNE 1983, CANNOCK CHASE, UK

I WAS THERE: MICHAEL SMALLMAN

My love of music had me always on the lookout for exciting new bands. Most of my gig-going was centred on the Birmingham and Wolverhampton areas, but for favourite artists I would travel around the country. I was heavily into bands like Siouxsie and The Banshees, The Fall and Dead Kennedys, and consider myself very lucky to have seen them many times plus others such as Magazine. The Smiths hadn't really entered my list of 'bands I must see', but they were playing in my home-town of Cannock.

The Miners Gala had been taking place for many years. As a child it was one of the highlights of the year as there was so little to do in this quiet little mining town. In 1983, I remember an advert for it in the *Cannock Advertiser*. In small print, right at the very bottom of the page, it was announced that The Smiths would be playing live at the closing of the gala. I decided to join a few friends in the beer tent to watch the show. The gig was free entry, but strategically placed collection boxes were there for anyone wanting to make a donation to the miners' cause.

When I got to the park the large marquee where the bands would be performing was about a quarter full of people who were already well on the way to becoming blotto with booze. I joined my friends, who included members of local band Balaam and the Angel, and found a place to stand. The gala had been going on all day, with guest speakers including high up officials from the miners' union. This was the year before the great miners' strike of the Eighties and tensions were already running high as the threat of the closure of many of the areas surviving coal mines was ever present. A funfair was provided for children and several beer tents for the adults. A carnival queen would also have been crowned. Three bands would be providing the entertainment - A Dog Named Ego, Shambolic Climate and The Smiths.

A Dog Named Ego's set went by with little acknowledgement from the audience, who were mainly only interested in the seemingly never-ending flow of beer. Shambolic Climate were next and it was then that I noticed the first stirrings of the trouble that was to come later. The bass player had a habit of playing with his tongue stuck out and this did not go unnoticed by some unruly audience members, who spent most of the set mimicking him, leaping around in front of the stage with their tongues hanging out. It was starting to get ugly, but as soon as the band finished their set the ringleaders were back to the bar area. Most of the ringleaders were known to me – I used to go to school with several of them, whilst I was aware of others from local pubs. For the most part I had no problem with these people, but it became increasingly clear that the long day had induced their inner aggression and they were looking for an outlet to unleash it. The Smiths would, unfortunately, become that outlet.

The Smiths took to the stage at around 9pm. Morrissey introduced the band and opening number, 'You've Got Everything Now'. I was immediately struck by how professional they sounded in comparison to the opening acts. As the band continued, 'Handsome Devil' was next, proudly introduced by Morrissey as 'one side of a record we have out'. By now the drunken louts were starting to notice the band and were drifting back towards the stage area. The next song was introduced as a question to the now very vocal gathering – 'Can you accept yourselves?' The rowdy crowd were now throwing beer over each other and were getting dangerously close to the stage. At the end of the song, Morrissey stated, 'Obviously not. Oh well, what difference does it make?' It was clear now that what the gig most needed was security – but there was none. 'Reel Around the Fountain' was next and amazingly things seemed to settle down for the duration of the song. The next track was introduced as 'a brand new song called 'Wonderful Woman' and at this point the aggression boiled over and the louts decided that their idea of fun would be to spoil the event for the few of us that wanted to watch the band. Morrissey was ridiculed and called all manner of insulting names. The aggressors also turned on members of the audience. Despite pleas from the band to calm down, the wailing and screaming continued. The band pressed on by playing the other side of the single, 'Hand in Glove'. By now plastic glasses filled with beer were being lobbed around the marquee, aimed mainly at the audience. The band soldiered on through the song, bravely ignoring the hail of abuse aimed at them. Morrissey announced the song 'Miserable Lie' and was met with a hail of beer and homophobic abuse. After a few minutes, the band threw their arms up and abandoned the set – things had just got too dangerous for them to continue. It was quite obvious that they couldn't wait to get out of Cannock, and accompanied by a police escort they left.

It was such a shame, seeing the band perform for the first time was marred by a gathering of idiots. This was the first time The Smiths had played outside Manchester or London. After the set finished I grabbed a set list from the stage. I only wish I still had it. It showed that several more songs were due to be played, including 'I Don't Owe You Anything' and 'These Things Take Time'.

FIGHTING COCKS

3 JUNE 1983, MOSELEY, BIRMINGHAM, UK

I WAS THERE: CLIVE WHITTAKER

I can't remember whose idea it was to get into promoting. I can remember Brian Farley and I had given up with our own group and were sick of going to poorly run gigs in Birmingham. Brian - Wurz to his friends - wrote down an action plan which seemed to be pretty do-able and we started contacting venues and bands. After struggling to stop losing money elsewhere putting on bands that we liked, we fell into step and fetched up at the Fighting Cocks in the fall of '79. We had been getting demo tapes from a small ad Wurz put in the *NME*. Most of them were dire and it really was about showcasing the local talent, so we gave ourselves up to the arms of agents and agencies.

This is how we found ourselves working with Rough Trade who really were and probably still are the most ethical agency looking after their roster. The local music scene was buzzing with raw and practised talent and the likes of The Nightingales, Surprises Dangerous Girls and Crucial Music kept the venue afloat along with a collection of young people who were just starting out and a loose collective of bands that merged and demerged at alarming rates.

We named our outfit Nitelife and amongst us we designed printed and posted our print run of usually 100 posters a week. We rang the bands and agencies and tried to match the musical styles to give our young talented locals some good exposure other than to their own mates. They would fill the support slot of 8.30pm to 9pm-ish. The pubs shut at 10.30pm at first, moving to 11pm every Friday and Saturday night, so we had to get the main band off before last orders were called.

The crowds that came were many and varied. If a touring band had only a few reviews and a couple of plays by John Peel, some of the crowd would come from as far as Shrewsbury and Gloucester, the locals eschewing a lucky bet. Sometimes, if the weather was good, we would have a room full and be turning people away. It was all pot luck.

Sometimes we hit paydirt. Pairing a very young Benjamin Zephaniah with Crucial Music was fantastic, The Dancing Did with And Also The Trees was memorable, and any gig with The Nightingales and The Cravats brought in the serious moodies, like Adrian Goldberg. The Surprises and latterly The Ever Readies were always fun and good for our Christmas gigs. Attila the Stockbroker brought the young *NME* scribe Steven Wells aka Seething Wells for some good ranting poetry. Blurt blew the house down and Sisters of Mercy ground it into the dirt, but of course our piece de resistance, little noticed by many at the time, was The Smiths on their first tour after the release of 'Hand in Glove'.

Contrary to the hazy memory of many Moseleyites - who weren't there - only 70 people turned up which just paid the bills. This was to be one of the turning points of our journey at the Cocks as soon after our growing band of entrepreneurs fell out and split up, closing the doors for good in the winter of '83.

I WAS THERE: BRYAN FARLEY

My part in the Smiths' story is fairly insignificant. They had just started doing gigs outside Manchester and were signed to Rough Trade for bookings. I read a gig review in *Sounds* and decided to book them. My friend Clive and I were putting on bands, mainly pub gigs, in an upstairs room in a bog standard Mitchells and Butlers city pub called the Fighting Cocks in Moseley. We used to charge £1 entry and get loads of liggers. It's a very expensive, gentrified part of Birmingham now and the pub's still there, but unrecognisable from what it was.

Most cities have got rough areas and posh areas and King's Heath and in particular Moseley have always been very hippie-ish, very bomhemian, with lots of people in sandals and kaftans and dope smokers. There was a thriving music scene in most big cities around that time but in Birmingham it was largely ska and reggae influenced. There were a lot of reggae bands in Birmingham and The Specials and Selecter captured the imagination in nearby Coventry, so there was a lot of that sort of thing going on. There were a few goth bands but mainly they came from Leeds and places up north. And then there were a few indie outfits like Eyeless in Gaza and Felt and Fashion who hovered around the fringes of the indie chart on labels like Cherry Red. Quite a lot of them were Midlands-based.

There was a large multi-occupied detached Georgian house set in grounds in Edgbaston, which has since been pulled down. Lots of musical people used to move in and out of it, people who went on to form bands like The Beat and The Au Pairs and others of that ilk from the Birmingham area. Clive lived there, so he knew quite a few people, and he and I had been pals for a while and I was really into listening to music.

'Hand in Glove' had just come out on Rough Trade and I liked the single. I think Peel had played it. I read a review in *Sounds* of a concert in Manchester and thought they sounded really interesting, so I spoke to my contact at Rough Trade booking. I'd had one or two indie bands from Rough Trade previously that we'd put on for not much money. My contact at Rough Trade said, 'Yeah, they're looking for gigs outside of Manchester' so I booked them. I think the fee was £50. And we had to provide a case of Heineken and a large bunch of gladioli. That was the deal!

I did a recording at the time because we used to have a PA company that was really local to the pub do our sound system. Clive would hang microphones up from the rafters in the early days, and then we moved on to taping it off the mixing desk. I've got a pretty rough and ready recording of the show on an old EMI tape. But you can tell it's The Smiths.

Clive and I fitted together quite well. Clive was into the technical side of it – the PA, the silk screen printing which he had at home which he was a master of. We used to silk screen all the posters for our gigs, a very smelly, time consuming and dirty job. We used to print about 100 posters for each gig, throw away 40 that were not right and then fly post the rest around the centre of Birmingham, only to find two nights later that they'd been covered up by the heavy mob from London who did the corporate posting for the big venues.

Clive used to enjoy the ligging and the mixing with people. I enjoyed the booking. I used to book quite a lot of 'out there' bands. We did goth bands. We did reggae bands. If somebody rang me up and said, 'You can have this lot for 200 quid', we'd have to put them in a bigger venue to try and make money. I thought The Go-Betweens were wonderful. They were signed to Rough Trade and we had them on about three times.

We had a reasonable turn out for The Smiths. The venue only held 150. I've still got the original contract somewhere. I'm pretty sure we lost money on it. They became quite sought after quite quickly. People started writing good things about them. Suddenly it made a helluva difference to Rough Trade to have a Kylie Minogue-type act on their books as opposed to these touring indie bands who lost them shitloads of money every time they put a record out.

Mike Joyce: I remember we played in Birmingham at the Fighting Cocks very early on and there were about five people backstage. Morrissey told us, 'I don't want to be called Steve anymore, I want to be Morrissey'. So I was like, 'OK, fair enough.' After we'd done

the gig we were gonna have to drive back. I didn't have my watch on, so I thought, 'I'll ask Steve the time.' But then I thought, 'No it's not Steve is it, it's Morrissey?'
So I said, 'Morrissey, what time is it?' and he said, 'It's about quarter to 12, Joyce.'

BRIXTON ACE

29 JUNE 1983, LONDON, UK

I WAS THERE: DAVID MCLEAN

It was a converted cinema. The Smiths were sandwiched between leather-trousered goth bands The Sisters of Mercy, who were headlining, and Flesh For Lulu. An incongruous billing, but it was not unusual at the time to jumble bands up and which I liked. It's a pity it's not done today. It was still quite quiet when they came on but Morrissey seemed happy, saying something like, 'How kind of you all to abandon the pub for us.' I can only recall 'What Difference Does It Make?' from the short set they played - that and one of my friends passing out drunk mid-set - but I remember Morrissey dancing round the stage and waving those gladioli about.

UNIVERSITY OF WARWICK

30 JUNE 1983, COVENTRY, UK

I WAS THERE: SAM DEEMING

I saw one of their first gigs at Coventry College (University of Warwick). I loved them. Morrissey had his flowers swinging around. I've got photos but they are at my ex's house.

MIDNIGHT EXPRESS CLUB

1 JULY 1983, BOURNEMOUTH, UK

I WAS THERE: MICK TARRANT

I had an indie record shop called Armadillo Records in Bournemouth which started around '75 or '76 and which came up through the whole DIY punk ethic. Quite early on I ran into Geoff Travis from Rough Trade at a record wholesalers in Harrow Road in London called Lightning Records. Geoff overheard me asking, 'Have you got a copy of such and such?' and said, 'I can help you with that.' So I went back to Rough Trade's premises with him and got whatever I was looking for and a bunch more stuff I wanted. From then on I called there when I went on my buying trips to London and so built up a relationship with Rough Trade.

I sold a half share in the record shop to somebody who took on the running of it and started a small live music club with about 200 capacity. Because of the Rough Trade connection I started doing quite a few of their bands, The Smiths being one of them. By this time they had the record label and they started a booking agency. And, as I was known to them they started offering me bands. I put The Smiths on in July 1983. That same month I had The Cure in there, despite them being quite a big band by that time. It was quite fortuitous that in a 200 capacity club we had two of the biggest bands of the time.

They'd only had 'Hand in Glove' out and I quite liked the guitar sound on it. I knew Johnny Marr played a Rickenbacker. I was and still am a big fan of The Byrds, which formed a very important part of their sound. After they sound checked I fell into conversation with Johnny and had a drink and quite a long chat about The Byrds. He was a nice guy. Morrissey pretty much kept himself to himself.

A few in the audience were familiar with the single. They went down quite well. I think their fee was 150 or 200 quid and they didn't sell out. We got about 150 in.

On 4 July 1983, Morrissey was interviewed on BBC Radio 1's *David Jensen Show* by deejay David 'Kid' Jensen. Three tracks were recorded for the show – 'These Things Take Time', 'You've Got Everything Now' and 'Wonderful Woman.'

NIGHT MOVES

9 JULY 1983, GLASGOW, UK

I WAS THERE: JOE WHYTE, AGE 20

Joe Whyte was at the Glasgow Night Moves gig that has slipped from Smiths gig history

It's time this tale was told, dear readers. I swear I was there and all joking and Manchester Free Trade Hall punning aside, my memory remains relatively acute for the important parts of the gig.

This seems to be a mostly undocumented Smiths early show and there has been some dispute online about the circumstances and attendance at it. It also seems to have been reported as the 10th July, but I suspect that's incorrect.

There's actually a guy who tells the story in a Smiths forum of how his band supported that night (and of The Smiths replacing A Certain Ratio who'd cancelled) and of how the venue was mobbed. I can confirm from memory, albeit faded, that it certainly wasn't mobbed - there would have been around 40 people there. It was a Thursday night and I'm pretty sure it was the night of the General Election.

The Smiths had been on the *John Peel Show* a few nights earlier with presumably what would have been their first Peel session; Night Moves was a venue that attracted a fair crowd most weekend nights due to owner Willie Pott's policy of booking the movers and shakers of a pretty vibrant post-punk scene and the up-and-coming acts of the day. Remember, this is obviously pre-internet and music news was from the *NME* and the like, the radio and by word of mouth.

The reason that The Smiths gig was so empty, apart from them being not at all well known, was that this weekend was the start of the Glasgow Fair, a trades holiday that seems to have slipped into insignificance in the modern world. At that time, the city virtually emptied for a couple of weeks as people holidayed both abroad and in the well-worn stretches and lights of Blackpool and the like.

The gig was free entry, which wasn't unusual on a Thursday at Night Moves - this was perhaps one of my reasons for being there - and as mentioned, there were around 40 people who had climbed the three or four floors of winding stairs to the well-loved venue.

The odd thing is, being a pretty high tech venue for the time, the deejay would always video the performances as they were projected live onto TV screens above the bar and at the sides of the venue. Most bands would leave with a copy of their show and it's pretty bizarre that a copy of this one has never been heard of, far less seen. Perhaps, the deejay wasn't working that night, perhaps it wasn't filmed. Yet another mystery around a gig that seems to have pretty shadowy circumstances surrounding it. Glasgow also had a pretty avid bootlegging community and again it's odd that this one hasn't been recorded for posterity.

Johnny Marr has spoken about the gig, saying it was his first time north of the border in an interview with the *Daily Record* but his recollection of '11 people watching' is slightly underestimated.

The band, who I'd paid little attention to prior to this show, were tight and powerful and clearly much better musicians than much of their pre-indie/post-punk peers. I recall 'Suffer Little Children' being particularly potent as it slowed the set down for the first time. Of course, Marr's guitar playing was the focus for me - he switched between the Rickenbacker and a cream Telecaster and those water-falling arpeggios and jangling surges gave the band an edge that certainly made them stand out. The rhythm section was tight and taut; I remember Mike Joyce grinning happily from the drum riser and Andy Joyce looking pretty impassive and serious.

This next opinion is my favourite memory and just shows how one's 23-year old self is self-righteous and opinionated and often wrong. Watching The Smiths play, with Morrissey flailing around the stage flagellating himself with the microphone lead, I distinctly remember saying to myself, 'This band are great but they need to get shot of the singer.' The operatic falsetto parts of his singing were getting right on my nerves and his onstage fractured Romeo antics (which of course, we all grew to love) were grating on me. It was a short set, I don't recall them doing an encore, and was mostly made up of the songs from the first album. My friend Rob Christie remembers helping the band load out via the venue lift at the end of the night and recalls Morrissey not having much to say. If only it had stayed that way!

LYCEUM THEATRE

7 AUGUST 1983, LONDON, UK

I WAS THERE: SEAN NEYLON

In the early Eighties, I started going to Loughton College with two fellow Chelmsford school friends, John and Chris. It meant a free student pass for buses and trains and new friends in London where I could stay over. We were into the alternative end of alternative music - the industrial scene – and saw the likes of Cabaret Voltaire, Psychic TV, Einstürzende Neubauten and Test Dept as well as equally obscure artists like Artery and Danielle Dax. But we also liked Magazine, Echo and The Bunnymen, Bowie and The Cure. Liking similar bands was really handy - I got given the debut Bunnymen album and Bowie's *Low* by Chris (he also gave me *Heroes* but regretted it so took it back) and discovered the weird and wonderful world of Chrome when John gave me his *Red Exposure* album. With only Peel to listen to, if we didn't hear bands we wanted to on his show, we'd take a chance and buy the record we'd read about in *Melody Maker* or *NME* - not always with successful results.

We discussed going to see Howard Devoto (ex-Magazine) play at the Lyceum in London. SPK were supporting so it was all good. Myself and Chris, both still in Chelmsford (John had moved to London by now) decided that the decider would be whether or not we liked The Smiths, a band we were unfamiliar with, who were third on the bill. Peel was repeating their debut session a couple of days before. I remember the Peel session being energetic, lively and very different - almost monotone in the vocal delivery - to what we had all been listening to. The next day Chris called me up. We agreed it was pretty good, but the decider was the words and their humour! 'I look at yours, you laugh at mine….' and 'Let me get my hands on your mammary glands.'

The Lyceum was average sized and had an upstairs section at the back above the main floor with a bar and seating. It wasn't packed, so we got seating at the front of this section by the railings. One of the girls we were with, Julie, had my Cure button badge on which I'd lost at college that week. 'It fell off' she said, 'so I put it on!' I got it back and I sat down with a beer chatting to my pal Sarmad, who lived in Snaresbrook with his mum (who we all fancied, *Inbetweeners*-style) and who had a big spare room we stayed in after gigs. As we talked, the background music was shattered by the sharpest, loudest sound that made us both jump. It was the opening guitar chord from The Smiths. They were dressed like regular, slightly scruffy students and shambled about the stage. The sound was tight yet ramshackle and unfamiliar at this stage, and reminded me of a kind of modern take on rockabilly with that rhythm section. A few people danced, but not many - that sort of dance everyone did at the time, which seemed to consist of wandering about bumping gently into one another with flapping chicken arms and with hands folded in. It's quite telling looking back that I have absolutely no recollection of seeing SPK or Howard Devoto at the Lyceum, only The Smiths.

DINGWALLS

13 AUGUST 1983, NEWCASTLE-UPON-TYNE, UK

I WAS THERE: PHIL DUNN, AGE 18

I was born in Hartlepool. I was just too young for punk but got into new wave and people who were lyrically clever - like Elvis Costello, and Difford and Tilbrook from Squeeze - and had a bit of an edge to them and something to say. When Morrissey came

to the fore I was very interested in what he had to say.
'Hand in Glove' and 'This Charming Man' were the only songs I'd heard, at the alternative nights at the Gemini on a Thursday, Hartlepool's only nightclub.

We were 22 miles from Newcastle but there was no train back to Hartlepool after ten past ten. But a guy called John Little had a record shop called The Other Record Shop. He sold gig tickets as part of which you got the bus up and down. I got on the bus in Park Road outside the Park Hotel and almost everybody on with the exception of me was an art student from the local art college. There were a lot of faces from student night at the Gemini on the bus.

Dingwalls was a small venue and I'd already seen Orange Juice and New Order there. They didn't disappoint. It was crammed. There was a distinct buzz about the gig and the fact that they were going to be big. It was a case of 'get in to see these lads while they're playing at places like Dingwalls because they won't be playing places like this much longer.'

They hadn't been on *Top of the Pops* at this stage so I didn't know what to expect. It was the first time I'd ever seen anyone chucking flowers around and flowers sticking out of somebody's arse.

The next time I saw them was at Middlesbrough, which was closer to home, only six or seven miles. I remember looking at the gig listing in the *NME* and thinking, 'This guy (Morrissey) knows what he's doing because they're actually playing smaller places and going off the beaten track a little bit.'

GALA BALLROOM

19 AUGUST 1983, NORWICH, UK

I WAS THERE: DAVE GUTTRIDGE

Having heard 'Hand in Glove' on John Peel's show, I'd bought it and written to the address on the back of the sleeve to say how much I loved it, requesting a lyric sheet. I was knocked out to receive a letter back, partly handwritten by the singer and with the lyrics typed by the composer on the back of a photocopied promo picture.

Dave Gutteridge got a letter from Morrissey after he asked for a copy of the lyrics to Hand in Glove

I played bass in a Norwich band called 18 Yellow Roses, named after a Marty Robbins song recorded by Bobby Darin. Once I found out that The Smiths were coming to our favourite venue, my only mission was to get us the support slot. When I rang the venue manager, who didn't know me from Adam, he told me another Norwich group, The Gothic Girls, had been given the gig. Amazingly, I was able to convince him during this phone call that they were completely unsuitable and that we were the ideal act for the job. I was very close

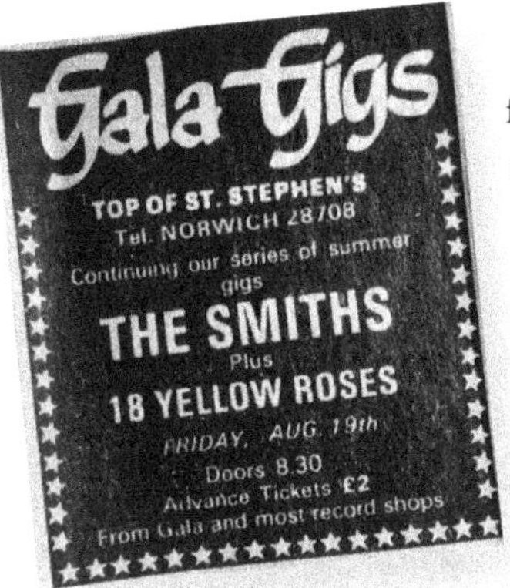

Dave Guttridge blagged his band a support slot with The Smiths

friends with The Gothic Girls, and even produced their first single, but I stand by my opinion and actions.

Lo and behold we were added to the bill. So, having been prompted by Morrissey, we turned up at the Gala for the sound check and presented him with 18 yellow roses. Not the ideal bouquet, due to the thorns. We were able to watch them set up and run through three or four songs for their soundcheck. As a Fall fan, I was delighted to be introduced to Grant Showbiz, who was their soundman. He ended up staying at our house after the gig as he wanted to visit Norwich's comic shops.

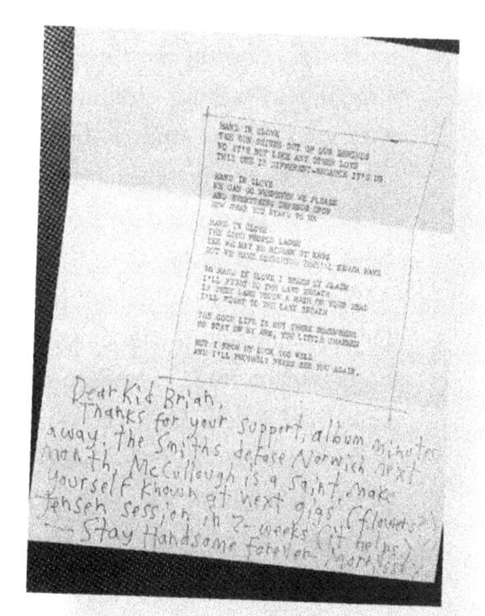
Dear Kid Brian,
Thanks for your support, album minutes away. The Smiths defuse Norwich next month. McCullough is a saint, make yourself known at next gigs (flowers?) Jensen session in 2 weeks (it helps) — Stay Handsome forever – Morrissey

The 'thank you' Morrissey sent Dave Guttridge for sending him a tape of the Gala show

The gig was one of the most exciting and powerful I ever witnessed at the Gala, about 40 minutes of raw romanticism with an energised and enthusiastic audience in very high spirits. The encore was a second rendition of 'What Difference Does It Make?' We asked them in the dressing room about the next single release and they were sure it would be 'Reel Around the Fountain'.

After the gig, as we were packing up, Andy and Johnny took me outside to show me their new touring van, a very basic Transit-type with a load of cushions for the band to relax on. I remember being quite taken aback by a couple of the band members smoking a joint backstage. I'd led a sheltered life!

I recorded both bands sets with a Panasonic Walkman - a much better recording than the one on YouTube - and sent a cassette to Morrissey, getting another nice reply. I've still got the poster for the gig, which is apparently pretty collectible, but it'll take a fair few quid to prise it out of my hands.

I WAS THERE: ANDREW HOOK, AGE 16

Post-punk, I wore black t-shirts, black jeans and desert boots. I'd been attending gigs sporadically for a couple of years - The Stranglers, Talk Talk, A Flock of Seagulls, Kissing The Pink. I was naïve. I was young. I had never been kissed.

I remember first hearing The Smiths at a friend's house - Steven Allen. I recall being struck by 'Reel Around the Fountain', particularly the line about falling out of bed twice.

Andrew Hook remembers the Gala being only half full

I always thought there was a lot of humour in Morrissey's lyrics, something that the music press who wanted to brand him as a miserablist didn't often understand. I assume Steven's older friend, Dave Foulkes, had taped a Peel session off the radio. There was a gig coming up. £2. Steven convinced me that we should go.

The Gala was a small venue, long since converted into a laser tag site. My memories of the venue are vague but I doubt the capacity was much over 200. I recall a low stage, situated in a corner. Myself, Steven and Dave milled about. We weren't drinkers. The venue was less than half full.

Andrew Hook's ticket for the Norwich Gala Ballroom gig

36 years later what do I remember of The Smiths? Much more than the local support band, 18 Yellow Roses, who were possibly Southern Death Cultish and who I never saw again. The Smiths were great. They laughed a lot. They played 12 songs. They ran out of material, reprising 'Hand in Glove' and 'Handsome Devil' as encores. There was a lot of intelligent energy. Morrissey had flowers stuffed down the back of his jeans. The music was fresh, was *now*. I was lyrically enchanted.

According to my five star gig-logging system of the time, I awarded this one four. On the way out I grabbed a handful of used tickets, managing to get my numbered one back, plus others that decades later I sold as memorabilia on eBay.

I was enamoured. I bought 'Hand in Glove', then 'This Charming Man' on 12 inch. Then suddenly – at school – everyone seemed to be into The Smiths. What difference did it make? I wasn't into popularity and I could feel my love draining. Musical snobbery taking hold.

I WAS THERE: JONTY YOUNG

Myself and Kenny Smith set off to celebrate his birthday on a Friday night out in Norwich. Somehow we had got our hands on a bottle of Malibu, not a particular favourite in a post-punk era but a means to an end. Our aim was simply to head to the Gala Ballroom to see an up-and-coming band from Manchester called The Smiths (no relation). The rules were the same then as they are today. Any band that has signed to Rough Trade were more than worth a listen, or in this case, a look.

The nearest pub en route to the venue was The Trowel and Hammer. We popped in for a couple of large pineapple juices, added lashings of our coconut-flavoured liqueur and came out very drunk about 8.45pm. We then stumbled to the Gala, no more than a few hundred yards away. Two things immediately struck us. The venue was by no means full, as it normally was on a Friday night, and a totally different crowd than usual but plenty of familiar faces from the flourishing Norwich music scene. Two free cans of warm Breaker later courtesy of the management, we installed ourselves in a prime position and viewing point.

Support on the night came from the Norwich-based 18 Yellow Roses, featuring Andy Hackett on guitar, now with Edwyn Collins and country outfit The Rockingbirds, and Dave Guttridge, the John Peel Archives photographer and BBC 6 Music regular, DJ78. All I can really remember about their set is they got a great reception from an excitable crowd and there was a trumpet involved. I knew for one thing I'd undoubtedly see them again.

As the lights dimmed for The Smiths, everyone pushed closer to the front. There seemed to be quite a buzz in the 300 strong crowd. After a few welcoming quips from Morrissey, the band launched into their first song. Some 60 seconds later, me and Kenny looked at each other and made faces of disappointment. Far too much jingly-jangly guitar for our liking. The second song was much better. Morrissey moved to the front of the stage with a bunch of flowers, which I now know to be gladioli, waving above his head. He was joined in the audience by two girls, in matching dresses giving out more gladioli to everyone looking their way. Me and Kenny, not quite of an age to appreciate gardening, threw ours unapologetically to the floor. This song was catchy though, especially the chorus, 'What difference does it maa-aaaa-aaake?'

By the third song they had really got going, as had the crowd and Morrissey, with his drawling vocals and lyrics, had made the stage his own. Next up was a series of what I believed to be unremarkable and slow songs. Just as I had started thinking that this lot had something, they totally lost me over the next 20 minutes or so. My firm belief was that only great bands could slip in a couple of slow songs and this was a Friday night after all. The rest of the set went in something of a blur.

For me, Johnny Marr's guitar was undoubtedly the highlight. Even at my most doubting moments, his effortless control of the strings was a joy to behold. The majority of the audience on the other hand, absolutely loved them. They had begged for an encore and then received two. That's unheard of for a band well outside of their comfort zone with one single to their name, which they played twice.

The next day was a hangover day. I woke up mulling the night before, cursing the taste of coconut and pineapple and thought to myself, 'I wonder if The Smiths will ever make it?' Some seven months later and two more singles down, The Smiths played to a baying sell out crowd of 1,500 at the University of East Anglia and the rest, as they say, is history.

I WAS THERE: ADRIAN LAST

They were the darlings of the music press at the time and played a memorable short set. It has stuck in my mind to this day, even though the music we heard that night was completely new to me. As I have never been a fan since bar the odd song they must have been doing something right that evening!

RADIO 1: DAVID JENSEN SESSION

25 AUGUST 1983, LONDON, UK

Broadcast on 5 September 1983, the band were back recording for Radio 1's *David Jensen Show.* 'Accept Yourself' (later to appear on *Hatful of Hollow*), 'I Don't Owe You Anything', 'Pretty Girls Make Graves' and Reel Around the Fountain' were recorded. After its initial airing, 'Reel Around the Fountain' was banned by the BBC and was not included in repeat airings of the session for two years.

PEEL SESSION, MAIDA VALE STUDIOS

14 SEPTEMBER 1983, LONDON, UK

Broadcast on the *John Peel Show* on 21 September 1983, the band returned to the BBC's Maida Vale Studios for their second Peel Session, recording 'This Charming Man', 'Back to the Old House', 'This Night Has Opened My Eyes' and 'Still Ill'. All four tracks were later released on *Hatful of Hollow.*

MOLES CLUB

16 SEPTEMBER 1983, BATH, UK

I WAS THERE: MARTIN WHITEHEAD

On the strength of nothing more than their first single, 'Hand in Glove', I wanted to interview The Smiths for my fanzine, *The Underground.* My usual method of turning up at the venue at sound check time when the band might be hanging around with time to spare worked again, and I got one of the best interviews of my fanzine career.

At the time I was struck by how unusual Morrissey's appearance was, a profile like a new moon, dominated by a pair of NHS specs. I was also impressed by how the pair complemented each other in the interview. When one was lost for a word the other took over the sentence. Both were very sure about what The Smiths was about and where they were going with the band, and their respective ideas were completely in tune with each other.

Some people have suggested that Morrissey's persona is adopted, a sham personality put on for publicity. One of the reasons I idolised The Smiths, apart from sweeping away the dark cloak of goth that hung over the land at the time, was that Morrissey seemed very genuinely and earnestly to believe he was on a divine mission to regain poop's high ground. At the time I predicted The Smiths would be the most important band since The Sex Pistols and I still largely stand by that.

I've never been totally fired up by Morrissey the way I was by The Smiths, but even now the echoes of what they did are still ringing in the charts. Johnny Marr put the guitar back on the instrumental agenda for all the post C86-ers and the band flew the flag for the indies and showed the world you didn't need black wigs and flour on your face to form a band. The Clash were lording it up in America, Strummer had become the irrelevant popstar he'd previously rallied against. We had four lads from Manchester with great songs and missionary zeal. Everything that has happened subsequently seems obvious in retrospect.

Moles Club back then could hold maybe 100 people. There wasn't even room for a stage. Despite that, the club was about two-thirds empty. Barely 30 people had turned up to see the most influential and iconic band of the decade. For me, this gave an opportunity to shoot some pictures to go with the interview. Five months later The Smiths played to a packed out main hall at Bristol University. I couldn't even get close to the stage, never mind the band.

FUTURAMA FESTIVAL, QUEENS HALL

17 SEPTEMBER 1983, LEEDS, UK

Scheduled to play as part of an all day line up, and billed below The Comsat Angels, The Armoury Show and headliners The Bay City Rollers, The Smiths cancelled, apparently because Morrissey didn't want to appear with the Shang-a-Lang lads. The crowd were also unimpressed by Edinburgh's finest, bottling them off stage.

GUM CLUB AT FERNANDO'S

23 SEPTEMBER 1983, BLACKBURN, UK

I WAS THERE: BRIAN FOSTER

I was the promoter of this gig in Blackburn with my friend Wayne. There were daffodils and arguments that night. My mam made Morrissey an omelette because he wouldn't eat fish and chips.

I WAS THERE: EMILY KELLY

It was a very small venue, not packed but also not empty. Brian, who organised the event, lectured in photography at Blackburn College. He was very into the band scene and was connected to the band James. I was studying graphic design at the college, which is how I knew him. Before the gig, I was bashing the cigarette machine trying to get the fags out, having paid for them. Johnny Marr came over and just put more money in, smiled and handed me the pack of John Players Blue. I thanked him. Morrissey was dressed in full flowery shirt mode and waving glads, which

Emily Kelly (left) with friend Jane saw The Smiths in front of an audience of no more than 50 people

he stuck in his pockets. It was so small I was able to stand right up to the space they were playing in. It was a lovely intimate gig, with fewer than 50 people there.

I WAS THERE: JOHN ROBINSON

A friend from Brinscall was bolstering his income whilst doing 'A' levels by working Saturdays at a now closed but then long established hardware store close to King George's Hall. He found out about some up-and-coming concerts at The Gum Club.

With him, I drove there in my mum's old Morris Marina on two occasions, firstly to see The Chameleons followed a week or so later by The Smiths. I was an apprenticed fabricator and thought The Smiths name had some association with forging (blacksmithing). Well, that was my first mistake!

John Robinson walked out on the Smiths gig at Blackburn's Gum Club

It was rented out and called The Gum Club by students from Blackburn College. The building front was rendered white with artificial Georgian windows facades and the club, upstairs on the first floor, held about 150 people and had a bar on one side with the bands set up in one corner. We were listening to post-punk music such as Death Cult, Bauhaus, Spear of Destiny, Killing Joke and Echo and The Bunnymen, so image was important. We came away from The Chameleons thinking their gig and the song 'Don't Fall' to be very good. But we left the Smiths' gig before the end as I couldn't believe the actions of the then-unknown singer with his dancing style, and the band looked pretty bland. My friend reminded me 25 years later that I shouted, 'No more!' after several songs. Shameful indeed and more than a little embarrassing knowing now what they made as a legacy. Obviously what did I - some Northern numpty from a backwater – know?

By the time I saw them again at Lancaster University in March 1984, everything had changed. They had already released two singles and a debut album and I was amazed what a contrast it was to the night at Blackburn. I'm fairly sure I didn't walk out on that one.

I WAS THERE: ALAN LEWIS

I was going to be a professional trumpet player. I went to the junior school of the Royal Northern College of Music from the age of about 15. When I was 18 I got a phone call from my cousin who ran a fanzine in Blackburn. A band called Some Now Are had won a competition to record with Peter Hook from New Order. I went and did a couple of records with them at Strawberry Studios and we recorded at Suite 16 in Rochdale. Our record 'The Truth' got five plays on Radio 1, three with Kid Jensen and two with John Peel. You can still find the seven-inch disc out there.

We ended up doing a support gig for a band called The Smiths at the Gum Club. Perhaps they were pretty well known if you read the *NME* or *Sounds*, but I didn't. I remember their long shirts and Morrissey twirling his daffodils around. I've seen conflicting accounts about the capacity. It wasn't a sell out. I would say the venue held about 300 to 400 and that there were between 140 and 150 people in there. There were no seats. We did a couple of sets and they played after us. I personally, have never been impressed by Morrissey and he didn't impress me that night. I didn't like the material. But I thought the guitarist was pretty good. He was clearly very talented. He looked down at his fingers all of the time. I don't know if he still does.They were clearly well rehearsed and accomplished at what they did.

I got offered a place at the Royal Northern College of Music to do classical trumpet studies but I had a place to study Law at Manchester University. I wanted to play in an orchestra but you're waiting for dead man's shoes, so I took the legal route. But I kept up playing on an amateur basis and won a lot of brass band trophies and did a lot of recording. You can hear me five times every day on a TV channel somewhere as I sat in with the Black Dyke Mills Band to record the theme music for *Ground Force*. I wish I was on royalties for that!

MOUNTFORD HALL, LIVERPOOL POLYTECHNIC

8 OCTOBER 1983, LIVERPOOL, UK

I WAS THERE: CATHY CASSIDY, AGE 19

I went with my boyfriend, now husband, Liam and that's us in the forefront of the drawing I did. We loved it. Liam found a pair of proper RayBans and I caught a thrown flower. I loved Morrissey at the time, loved the songs. I was an illustration student at the art college. Perfect music for its time.

Cathy Cassidy's illustration for 'Reel Around the Fountain'

BAR ONE, UNIVERSITY OF SHEFFIELD

17 OCTOBER 1983, SHEFFIELD, UK

I WAS THERE: DAVID HARRINGTON

It was 'intro week' of my first year at Uni. A London lad north of Watford for the first time, I was sharing a house with seven other first years, all from the Manchester area. Music became the main topic of conversation with John Peel our collective idol. One guy had taped a session by a band called The Smiths that the rest of us hadn't heard of. Coincidentally they were playing at the Uni that Friday evening.

Bar One wasn't exactly a music venue of note, more of a small basement student bar that I later found out even the students avoided. We turned up with low expectations together with 80 or 90 other bedraggled late teenagers. Bedraggled was the student look of the early to mid Eighties. I don't remember a support band but I'll never forget the first few minutes of a band that looked and sounded like nothing I'd seen before. The front man not only carried a bunch of gladioli, but whirled them around his head when he sang. We could hear every word he said and the melody from the guitar filled the air with a twangy, 'chang-chang' sort of sound. They were brilliant and everyone who attended that gig probably did exactly the same thing as me, which was to write multiple letters to their mates telling them of this new discovery. It was also a time when 'I saw them first' was an important part of musical appreciation.

I went on to see The Smiths several times and they were always fantastic live. Oh and I was lucky enough to catch Morrissey's beads when he threw them into the crowd. They were a proud possession for a couple of years until some drunken student stole them from my bedroom during a house party.

'THIS CHARMING MAN'

RELEASED 31 OCTOBER 1983

Topping the UK independent charts, 'This Charming Man' was the band's first UK Top 40 single, reaching number 25.

POLYTECHNIC

10 NOVEMBER 1983, PORTSMOUTH, UK

I WAS THERE: KATE ROSSI

I was in my late teens. They were just breaking. I went with my then boyfriend, Damien. I was there, but I was honestly so drunk I can't really remember much about it. I do remember the gladioli.

POLYTECHNIC

16 NOVEMBER 1983, LEICESTER, UK

I WAS THERE: IAN GELLING

I saw them at Leicester Poly and then at the De Montfort Hall in March 1984. They were fine gigs and Johnny Marr was marvellous. Moz is my most seen act after The Wedding Present. I've seen him walk off after a few tunes on a few occasions and I've turned up when he hasn't bothered to do so, even in the USA. I've even seen him feign death to avoid playing a cowshed of a leisure centre in Swindon. Around that there were numerous superb performances and some great nights. But Moz has pissed me off so much lately that I can't be arsed any more.

WESTFIELD COLLEGE

17 NOVEMBER 1983, LONDON, UK

I WAS THERE: PETER LINDSEY-JONES

They were booked to play the Student Union by an old friend of mine. They became famous between the booking and the gig and the campus was swamped with Smiths fans.

I WAS THERE: SEAN NEYLON

We must have really felt something from seeing them at the Lyceum and hearing that Peel session because a few months later we went to see them again at a gig at Westfield College. I think it was for Westfield students only, but we went anyway. This time it was just me and Chris, and so began an obsession that would last the band's entire career.

In my mind it was a bright warm sunny summer's day as we queued up through the grounds to get into the hall, but the internet tells me otherwise! Everyone was happy, everyone was friendly and smiling, there was excitement in the air and a feeling of genuine anticipation. Many of the girls wore flowers and beads were everywhere. I think I've given this queuing up a rather apt 'summer of love' vibe to my memory, hence thinking it was summer, because that's certainly how it felt.

Inside it was a standard college or school hall, and I remember being surprised at just how popular they had become in such a short time. 'This Charming Man' had come out two weeks before and the buzz had begun. At one point, I saw a gladioli being flung into the crowd by Morrissey. It was heading towards me but I couldn't free my hands from the throng in time and it struck me on the head.

It was one of the happiest gigs I've ever been to – there was just such a buzz about what was happening. Afterwards, the band came down with a couple of what looked like crates of beer. Me and Chris had to get back to Liverpool Street to get the last train to Chelmsford, so had to make a quick decision; chat to them or get back for the train? One of us said, 'No, we'll chat to them next time.' Of course we never did. Famous last words that we came to regret.

Even the staff got caught up in the happy atmosphere. Outside afterwards, I tried to prise open the notice board to get the gig ad - the 'Hand in Glove' poster with the time scribbled on in felt tip - as a souvenir and two of the young staff came over. I thought I was in trouble. 'Do you want the poster? Hold on I'll go and get the key.' He did and I got my souvenir. It's worth a fortune now and I've been trying to find it for the past year!

The buzz we'd felt at Westfield and the electricity between band and audience just grew as more and more people got to hear The Smiths. We'd never ever see them in such a small venue again. They were headline artists now. Another college friend, Rob, had repeatedly turned down the opportunity to come to see The Smiths. Then he heard 'This Charming Man' on the radio over breakfast and was gutted. 'I just thought they'd be another one of your noise bands like Cabaret Voltaire or something!' Now he's another Smiths convert!

I WAS THERE: DON PERRETTA

I was there, and wrote this review for *Smash Hits* magazine at the time:

The wonderful thing about college gigs is the sheer mixture of people who go to them. Tonight at Westfield College - a cross between a school dining hall and a gymnasium - is no exception. Standing side-by-side are trendies in long leather coats, punks in exhausted combat gear and even the odd long-haired hippie or two.

But all with something in common - they're all wearing flowers in their hair. You see, they've all come to see The Smiths which, of necessity nowadays, means a trip to the florist beforehand.

The atmosphere is very relaxed; the stage is small and bare, with a tiny PA and a mere five spots either side. It doesn't look like the setting for a band in the upper reaches of the chart, more like an amateur cabaret night in an old people's home. Still, nobody seems to mind.

A massive shower of carnations announces The Smiths' arrival on stage. The reaction is instantaneous - off the floor, up to the front and dance like a lunatic. The bobbing mass just below the stage laps up singer Morrissey's every gesture as he swings a huge bunch of flowers over his head, getting faster and faster until the stalks snap, sending yet another flurry of petals into the audience.

Johnny Marr's melodic but forceful guitar lines perfectly frame Morrissey's finely-textured voice to produce pop with a delicate passion. The intention is pretty simple - vibrant, optimistic, uplifting songs; a celebration of youth, love and having fun.

What a night - a floral riot, the sweet smell of success hanging in the air. And I even managed to catch a flower to take home with me.

It was a great gig. I think of it often as it was the first time I took my then girlfriend out with me on a 'working' night. She of course loved them and Morrissey in particular. She later named our cat after him. We married three years later and we referenced that night often, even to our kids who must have got bored to death by it. Sadly, she passed away in 2010. I can't listen to The Smiths without thinking of her. So it's bitter sweet. But still a great night.

STUDENT REFECTORY, EDGE HILL COLLEGE

18 NOVEMBER 1983, ORMSKIRK, UK

I WAS THERE: LOUISE BENNETT

Yes I saw The Smiths at Edge Hill in 1983. Amazing gig but I was slightly drunk!

I WAS THERE, JEREMY KIDD, RED GUITARS VOCALIST

'I need advice, I need advice, I've got my balls trapped in a vice...' we'd croon to each other in the van as we criss-crossed Britain in the wake of The Smiths during the winter of 1983 and the spring of '84. It was clear that something special was going on from our first gig supporting them at Edge Hill College in Ormskirk. When we arrived in mid-afternoon for the sound-check there was already a buzz about the place, and there were loads of people hanging around just trying to catch a glimpse of the headliners.

I grew up obsessed with The Beatles but too young to actually participate in Beatlemania. I had to be satisfied with listening to the records and watching them on telly or at the cinema. Of course The Smiths weren't The Beatles, but there were parallels. For me 'This Charming Man' was their 'She Loves You' and when Morrissey sang, 'Do not go to them, let them come to you, just like I do' or 'I never had a job because I never wanted one', I thought it was the equivalent of Lennon asking the people in the cheap seats at the Royal Variety Show to clap along and the others to 'just rattle your jewellery'. Not to mention the fact that in those days Johnny Marr was wearing a Rickenbacker and sporting a mop top.

Johnny and Steven - both great craftsmen, very skilful. And I can't say the so-called plagiarism ever bothered me. It was just the vernacular out of which they grew and above which they soared with exhilarating frequency. I reckon I witnessed getting on for ten per cent of all the Smiths live shows, and from backstage to boot, and I have to say it was privilege.

I WAS THERE: LOU DUFFY-HOWARD, RED GUITARS BASSIST

It was producer John Porter who introduced us to The Smiths. We recorded a John Peel session with him at Maida Vale studios in August '83 and he'd just recorded The Smiths. He spotted something in common between Hal's African guitar riffs in 'Marimba Jive' and Johnny's guitar intro in 'This Charming Man'. I couldn't hear the similarity at the time.

We chatted to them and their manager back then, Joe Moss, swapping cassettes and playing a couple of gigs with them at the end of the year, one at a college in Lancashire and one at the Electric Ballroom.

Jeremy Kidd (left) and Lou Duffy-Howard of The Red Guitars

Red Guitars had a handful of singles in the indie charts and we were preparing to record an album for release on our own label, Self Drive. The Smiths album - produced by John Porter - was due to come out and they invited us to support them on their first UK tour, without a buy-on which was brilliant. We played around 20 shows with them and during the course of the tour 'This Charming Man' hit the charts so the gigs were packed and we all had a blast. We were very different bands but got on well and it was interesting to watch them play every night and see the set develop. One time we turned up to do our sound check and when they saw us they started to jam out one of our songs, 'Heartbeat Go'. That was cool. Morrissey kept himself to himself a lot of the time but one of my daughter Christa's earliest memories is that he gave her a piece of chewing gum. She was only about three, too young to know what it was. I think she just ate it.

Both bands kept in touch with John Porter who took us to record in the legendary Matrix Studio in Bloomsbury. We went in to record some demos and he played us an early version of 'How Soon Is Now?' he was working on. It sounded fantastic and still stands out to me as the best of their songs.

I WAS THERE: DEREK MOIR, AGE 17

Derek Moir saw The Smiths several times

We lived in Perth, a town of 50,000 with a strong underground scene, and had been hanging with the punk/post punk crew, but felt we had missed seeing all those bands in their prime and were really passionate about making sure that we didn't miss the next wave of brilliance. We had heard 'Hand in Glove' and taped the first two Peel sessions. We read that they were playing in Ormskirk, outside Liverpool, so skived off work or college and drove down from Scotland without tickets.

Four of us set off early on the Friday. My mate had a run down Chrysler Sunbeam, more rust than orange. We called in sick and set off early to get to Ormskirk - where the fuck was that? The car overheated once or twice but got us over the border. As we entered Ormskirk we got lost, as you did in the pre-satnav world, and stopped at a bar to ask for directions. Everyone told us that we were mad and that the gig was sold out. Nevertheless a very kind, ie. pissed and off-duty, policeman offered to take us to the college where the gig was, despite his indicators not working. He did the old 'hands out of the window' 1932 thing as he took us to the venue and dropped us off.

They were playing in a college dining hall. The dinner ladies told us, 'Ohhh, you won't get in - it's sold out,' but sneaked us in through the dining room partition. The Red Guitars were sound checking. The Smiths were watching it and Grant Showbiz was doing the sound. I got the job of going up to Grant and telling him our story. He was amazed we had travelled so far. The Smiths - Johnny, Andy and Mike - were amazed as well and invited us to stay for the gig, but we had to work for it. The bar was in a separate building to the gig, so we got the job of fetching booze and fags. Great fun, especially when we were trailing these back as The Alarm were being refused entry!

We asked if we could record the gig on our boom box and they were very happy for us to do so - it was recorded from the drum riser but it's great. Our mate's family had just moved down to Ormskirk and put us up for the night. The Smiths letting us stay for the sound check was like Christmas!

TOP OF THE POPS

24 NOVEMBER 1983, LONDON, UK

The Smiths appeared on the BBC TV's legendary pop programme for the first time, performing 'This Charming Man'. Forced to mime, Morrissey sang into a bouquet of gladioli. Afterwards, the band caught a train home to Manchester for a gig at the Haçienda.

Johnny Marr: At the time, there'd been this question of whether it was cool to go on *Top of the Pops*, probably from The Clash refusing to do it. But we were a new generation and it felt like there were new rules.... Plus, when the members of The Smiths were children, *Top of the Pops* was one of the most important days of the week. Suddenly we found ourselves on it. Previously, we'd been synonymous with the John Peel show, and suddenly that culture was on *Top of the Pops* – John Peel started to present it, and it was a new phase: post-punk going mainstream.

Everyone remembers the flowers Morrissey took on to the show. I'd been very aware of how powerful *Top of the Pops* could be visually, from my childhood watching T. Rex. We'd first used gladioli onstage at the Hacienda about a year before, to counteract the all-encompassing austere aesthetic of Factory Records. People assumed it was an Oscar Wilde homage but that was a bonus. The flowers made the stage very treacherous if you were wearing moccasins, but they became emblematic, iconic. After that we tried to make every TV appearance a spectacle – Morrissey pulling off his shirt and having things written on his chest, the hearing aid.

HACIENDA

24 NOVEMBER 1983, MANCHESTER, UK

I WAS THERE: CHRIS PARKER

I first heard The Smiths sometime in 1983, probably on John Peel's show. They immediately felt like a very personal find - my band, from my town. Being in at the start felt important, without even knowing what it was the start of. Getting records on the day of release was always vital, if you didn't want someone else casually telling you how ace something was an, 'Hadn't you heard this new band/song yet? You're not a proper fan then....'

This was special though. 'Hand in Glove'. The sun shines out of our behinds. A naked man on the sleeve, looking half-ashamed, half-oblivious. What an introduction to everything that followed. There were rumours Morrissey had been in another group from round our way (Wythenshawe): Ed Banger and the Nosebleeds. I didn't know if that was true (Google later killed that wonderment), but even a hinted at local connection was good enough back then.

I couldn't have been, or looked less, like Morrissey if I'd tried. He was cool. I looked like a teenage Ned Flanders: long-haired, sporting Wrangler denim and sibling cast-off corduroy, or big baggy jumpers and drainpipe jeans, or even my dad's stuff from the Fifties, just to look different. But not the way he did. I'd have to change. It got me beaten up by drunk United fans some time later, but that just made me love them, and Manchester City, all the more.

Before 1983, I'd been into heavy rock (brothers) and punk (schoolmates). I'd seen Led Zeppelin, Black Sabbath, The Jam, The Damned, all before I was 18. But I'd missed out on Sore Throat and various reggae and ska bands because I was too scared to risk missing the all-nighter back from the clubs in Moss Side and having to walk all the way back to Benchill. Not when you dressed like I did. There's a big difference between defiance and idiocy.

Then John Peel happened and Factory happened and sticking to genres seemed pointless; suddenly there was just great music of all kinds, or stuff you turned off. When The Smiths arrived out of nowhere, I wasn't going to miss out again. I'd bought two tickets well in advance, proudly brandishing my pink and yellow striped Hacienda membership card, Ned portrait and all, at the box office as proof of cool entitlement, though it was clear anyone could buy them without one.

On the day, I was at the tail-end of splitting up with the girl who the second ticket was intended for. We decided to be adult about it and go together anyway, the way teenagers imagine being adult works. Besides, she loved them just as much; well, almost. Later, 'How quickly would I die, if I jumped…' reminded me of her dramatic frailty, then if not now.

That Thursday early evening was typical. You always watched *Top of the Pops*, if only to criticise who was on. But then, there they were, in amongst a load of average other stuff, waving flowers about and singing the best song of the year. Hearing them on the radio was one thing, but seeing them on telly…. I couldn't believe it, not least because I thought *Top of the Pops* was made in London. Maybe they'd cancelled the gig? Or was it recorded? No idea, then or now. But it was a lovely taste of things, hopefully, to come.

There was no way to find out then, short of ringing the club, and we didn't have a phone. Besides, going into town was always an adventure in those days. So, dressed half-rocker,

The Smiths played Manchester's Hacienda on 24 November 1983

half-punk, I called for the girl and we got the bus into town, the 102 from Hall Lane in Baguley. We sat on the top deck, at the front. She'd seen *Top of the Pops* too, so any awkwardness was warded off by the excitement of that performance and the thrill of the gig to come. No heavy words lightly thrown, just giddy chat and not-talking about tomorrow.

I remember town that evening as drizzly and cold, not icy, but grim. Manchester often seemed like that. But Manchester then wasn't like now, not buzzing and busy and with options galore, nor was it quite the grimy Seventies either. We got off near The Ritz to walk back down the road and straight away there was a sense of something. We heard the queue before we saw it. The shivers that shook us weren't from the cold. This was going to be something else. No-one complained about the wait to get in.

I was used to the girder chic of the club's insides, but it was her first time and she thought it was fascinating and cool and brilliant. Drinks weren't cheap, so we made do with just a couple, though getting served was a chore for someone who still never catches a bartender's eye. We stood near the back and people-watched and drank and chatted, with a view of the stage over to the left and the entrance back over to the right. And we waited. You run out of things to say in the end and I, and I suspect she, just wanted the gig to get going. Sometimes bands don't turn up, do they? Surely not for a home tie? Then James came on.

And James were superb. We liked what we knew of them before that, but now we loved them. They lit the fuse. The singer's shocking, epileptic jarring dances, tiring just to watch, sparked a mosh of at first reluctant then embracing madness. 'Hymns From A Village'. Some people left straight after, obviously not mithered about seeing the headliners. That struck me as odd at the time, like leaving a match before the end, but people still do. The Smiths had better be good to outdo this, mind, we said, half expectant, half fearful.

They were. After a long wait when we thought they might not show up, with people around us saying they definitely wouldn't and that was why others had already left, and you looked to the people at the front for a sign that they'd seen or heard something or someone, but there was nothing to indicate one way or another, it was getting late, we were thinking about last buses and maybe a taxi, or a train and a long walk, or....

That split second before a band comes on, the lights are out, and there's a swell and a surge and you know something's about to happen, something you knew was going to happen anyway but that creates a sensation you never experience doing anything else in life. We felt it, looked at each other, grinned and laughed. And on they came. Can a band save a relationship? Did either of us want it saving? These things take time.

They crashed into the first song and the place went mental. Everyone sang, everyone knew the words, everyone was Morrissey. You handsome devil. There were flowers everywhere, just like the ones on *TOTP*. Apart from my mum, I didn't know anyone who knew what gladioli were, but now everyone knew. They took each single one of us and made us as one, flowers in hand, chucked or plucked from the stage and strewn and caught with glee. Not sunny Sixties San Francisco, just a rainy winter's night in Eighties Manchester.

We bounced about, sang along, got close enough to get some flowers. Then slower songs brought the mood down. People swayed, but sang less. They were controlling things. Or maybe they didn't have enough bouncy songs written yet. But it was a reminder. They might be young and cool and different, but they sang about pain and bad things as well as joy and not caring. Bad Manchester things, good Manchester things, all full of universal truths. You don't want that in the middle of a performance like that, but you accept it. And something else is going to happen, soon, you can feel it. They'll get us bouncing again.

They do. 'Hand in Glove'. The sun shines out of our behinds. With flowers in. Tight songs, tightly played. Two encores, two song repeats. By their choice or demands from us? 'Haven't they already done this one?' 'Who cares!?' Then before you know it, it's over and the lights go up and suddenly it's just a bright warehouse full of sweaty, ecstatic, buzz-deaf kids. Children of a revolution? Nothing could be the same again now, surely. Maybe everything from now on would be always this good.

Going home, we sat on the back seat, downstairs. We didn't stop talking all the way to Baguley. About the gig, the band, the songs, the flowers she still had in her hand, bedraggled a bit now but proof that it wasn't a dream, was real, had all happened, just as we were describing. But not about us.

I dropped her off and headed for the subway under the motorway, running through it as fast as I could to the light at the end, dodging the broken glass underfoot. Liking the same band, even that band, isn't enough. All the better for her – she's got everything now. So have I and I went to see her that night. Betrayal is part of The Smiths as well, isn't it?

A few years later, I was in St Ann's Square, outside a clothes shop where my new love was browsing. Looking towards the Royal Exchange steps, a tall man was gangly-gracefully walking in the direction of the church. People around stopped. Watched. Pointed. Isn't that...? What's he doing here...? What's he doing...? Let the people stare, he really didn't care. He was just walking along. Like a normal person. Like someone who looks like Morrissey. Whose words have become part of your own vocabulary, of how you describe and frame your life story. I was looking for a band and then I found a band.

Of all the bands I've ever seen, or wanted to, they were and are number one. And I'm glad they never re-formed; that Morrissey went his own way; that there were acrimony and accusations; that what remains of them is the love of a clutch of fantastic music and lyrics, no filler, nothing forced, all instantly recognisable. It's what you want from a great band. Half a lifetime later, I'm still boasting about seeing them. Pathetic really. And brilliant.

I WAS THERE: CATH COLLINS, AGE 17

I was a fan before they were on *Top of the Pops*. Before they were big. I was going to Xaverian College in Manchester, and we used to go to the Hacienda. I remember being in the park and having a tape recorder and somebody playing it. You know when you're all in the park and being cool? Someone played 'Hand in Glove' and I thought, 'Flipping heck' and 'Oh my god.' Then 'This Charming Man' came out and that Hacienda gig was a massive homecoming, because they'd been on tour. The Hacienda was absolutely rammed. It was a really brilliant gig, the best of all the gigs I've ever seen. I saw them at Glastonbury too. But I didn't see them again after that. You know when you think, 'Oh, they've gone a bit big?' It's not in a conscious way but suddenly it's outside of your own then.

In 1986, we were in the Seymour, one of those humongous old fashioned pubs. It's not there now but it was on the corner of Upper Chorlton Road in Manchester so about half a mile from Morrissey's childhood home. This chap who was part of the group I was sat in the pub with said, 'Do you want to come back to mine for a drink?' So we went back to his house, a council house, and he made us tea and toast. The walls were lined with gold and silver discs. He was playing us videos of Morrissey being interviewed but not just the parts that were broadcast. He had the full tape before it was edited, including Morrissey being miked up beforehand and unmiked after. It was Morrissey's dad. I was having tea and toast with Morrissey's dad!

Mike Joyce: By the third Hacienda gig I remember Interflora bringing 30 boxes of gladioli at that gig. The place just stank. By this time we were being mobbed. The height of the stage was perfect for people to use other people as a stepping-stone to get on stage. It was absolutely insane.

The Smiths' appearance at Derby's Assembly Rooms was filmed for BBC Television's *Old Grey Whistle Test*. It served to bring the band to a wider audience.

ASSEMBLY ROOMS

6 DECEMBER 1983, DERBY, UK

I WAS THERE: LYNNE DICKENS, AGE 20

I saw The Smiths at the Assembly Rooms before they were really well known, performing for *The Old Grey Whistle Test.* I think it was free. My boyfriend at the time, now my husband, bought a Smiths LP and I liked them straight away. I think a lot of people who went to that gig just went because it was free. I saw them again in Nottingham for *The Queen Is Dead* tour. They were absolutely brilliant on both occasions. They really played to the crowd. I was gutted when they split up.

I WAS THERE: THOMAS JONES

We got free tickets for the filming for *Whistle Test* and, as four lads from the sticks - well, Crewe - we didn't know much about the band except for the two singles to date and snatches we'd heard on John Peel. 'This Charming Man' had been on *Top of the Pops* a week or so before and that was our Road to Damascus moment. Everyone at school the next day was saying, 'Did you see that?'

The Assembly Rooms were decked out in flowers and people were throwing them at the stage and each other even before the band took the stage with 'Handsome Devil', Morrissey brandishing a bunch of gladioli. The band later went on record as saying this gig was a low-light for them as their hardcore Manchester fans didn't land tickets. All I know is that the whole room seemed to fall under their spell and by the time of the stage invasion, during 'You've Got Everything Now', it was beautiful pandemonium. I ended up standing a couple of feet from Johnny, next to his Fender Twin Reverb amp, and I well remember the slightly nonplussed mascara'd scowl at the chaos that was unfolding.

A particular highlight was the breakneck 'Miserable Lie'. Morrissey had been hit in the eye with a flower in the intro after 'Please stay with your own kind' and the remaining three had to count the bars and go into the fast section without any vocal cues. He returned to sing the song - with extra venom - and concluded with, 'I need advice....AND SO DO YOU!'

Other highlights were Marr's subtly overdriven Rickenbacker 330, surely the definitive early-Smiths guitar sound, and a beautifully delicate 'This Night Has Opened My Eyes' with a few lyrical improvisations, such as 'I'm never happy and I'm never sad'.

The TV transmission stopped at the end of the stage invasion on 'You've Got Everything Now', but I'm fairly certain that they played another two songs. I remember Morrissey pleading, 'Civility, please' as everyone was ushered off the stage. As for us four, on Derby station we pledged to sell the keyboard and become a guitar band ourselves but, to coin a phrase, the world never listened.

DINING HALL, TRINITY COLLEGE DUBLIN XMAS BALL

9 DECEMBER 1983, DUBLIN IRELAND

I WAS THERE: DECLAN HASSETT

I saw them a few times but most memorably their first gig in Dublin. They played in Trinity College and The Blades supported. They played 'Hand in Glove' and 'This Charming Man' twice as their encore and most memorably I met my wife for the first time. My three kids, all now in their twenties, are fans.

I WAS THERE: MILL BUTLER, AGE 20

It was their first Dublin gig. I was roadie for The Blades downstairs - I still am – and watched The Smiths whole sound check. We finished just in time to catch them play.

NEW YEARS EVE 1983

The Smiths made a brief one-show-only trip to the United States.

DANCETERIA

31 DECEMBER 1983, NEW YORK, NEW YORK

Johnny Marr: We had to play at midnight and we went to this club, Danceteria, which was this pretty trendy hip predominantly hip-hop club, or electro as it was then. We went and played on New Year's Eve at our very first American show. It was a little bit of a weird show for us. We didn't have too great a time. We had some sound problems and we were just trashed (from jetlag). Supporting us was the girl who worked on the coat check and we didn't really pay too much attention to her but it was Madonna. She played for about 20 minutes before we went on. I think she went down pretty well.

1984

'WHAT DIFFERENCE DOES IT MAKE?'

RELEASED 16 JANUARY 1984

'What Difference Does It Make?' climbed to number 12 in the UK Top 40, with Morrissey briefly on the picture sleeve until actor Terence Stamp consented to his image being used. Actor Albert Finney and footballer George Best both declined similar advances from La Moz.

CITY HALL

31 JANUARY 1984, SHEFFIELD, UK

I WAS THERE: ADRIAN KEELING

I was probably 15 and a fan of pop when I first saw The Smiths doing 'This Charming Man' on *Top of the Pops*. I thought, 'This is something different. They look a bit weird, I'll try and watch this and see if I can expand my horizons.' Weird wasn't my thing so unbelievably it didn't grab me.

My parents were members of a society called the Independent Order of Foresters that put on social events and raised money for charity. I was in the Young Foresters and one of the things we did was go to a gig once a year. In 1984, we booked to see OMD at Sheffield City Hall, but they cancelled and we booked The Smiths instead. By this time 'What Difference Does it Make?' was in the charts and I did like that - it did grab me - so I bought the album and played it to death. The gig at the City Hall though was something else. I remember a very bright light behind Morrissey at times, making it look like the sun was shining out of his behind. Pity it doesn't anymore, but I digress.

NORTH STAFFS POLYTECHNIC

1 FEBRUARY 1984, STOKE-ON-TRENT, UK

I WAS THERE: GARY DONALD

The guys had just made it into the charts and were either just about to or had just done *Top of the Pops*. I was part of the student union team manning the door and doing security at front of stage. It was a brilliant night, with possibly 400 to 500 there. It was packed. Morrissey was chilling out in the bar in his long brown raincoat, cool as fuck. Gladioli were in full swing. Although the memory is a bit hazy now, I do remember 'This Charming Man' being played. Before the show, I stopped a fella at the door and asked him for his ticket. He replied, 'Nah, but I've got one of these', holding up his guitar. I had just asked Johnny Marr for his ticket!

I WAS THERE: GLYN WADE

I saw them three times. The first time was at this gig. It was packed. They had broken big since the gig was announced but I managed to get to the front. Big mistake! The stage was about shin-high and I spent the whole gig crushed against it, unable to move as swathes of people pushed against me. Flowers were spinning but it was hard to concentrate as I was in so much pain. My shins were bruised for days afterwards but – hey - I saw The Smiths at one of the smallest ever venues!

UNIVERSITY OF WARWICK

2 FEBRUARY 1984, COVENTRY, UK

I WAS THERE: RICHARD DYER

The Smiths has just come to our attention among my student friends at Warwick through the release of 'Hand in Glove' and 'This Charming Man'. Marr's jangling, hypnotic guitar and Morrissey's sexually ambiguous literary-referenced lyrics and monotone crooning set them apart from many of the new wave post punk indie bands of the time.

Richard Dyer (right) saw The Smiths at Warwick Uni

Tickets for the Warwick concert went on sale in January and sold out almost immediately. I worked the student union bars and theatres in the evenings to supplement my postgrad grant and jumped at the chance to work at the concert. I was right on the small stage with the band, stage right, facing the crowd, as The Smiths unceremoniously strolled on. Marr and Rourke plugged in their guitars and Joyce sat at the small drum kit. Morrissey followed, clutching huge red gladioli, white shirt open to the waist, bouffant hair.

Warwick was an easy audience that loved to dance, so the energy was instant. I jigged along at the side of the stage, next to Andy Rourke, hypnotized by the proximity of the band, the immediacy of all the previously unheard tunes and Morrissey's self-absorbed arrogant posturing. Once all the gladioli were tossed to the crowd, the band skipped off. We got only 30 minutes of fast melodic tunes, which was probably all they had written at that point. No encore, they were off to London. I was left with jangling ears and a red gladiolus, aware that something special had happened, but not quite knowing how special. A couple of weeks later, The Smiths' first album was released. I like to think that the fiver I earned that night at the concert was the fiver I used to buy the album. I am sure that the playlist that night was the album, in its entirety, short and sweet.

I WAS THERE: IAN GREEN

I saw The Smiths at the University of Warwick in February and on 10th March at Lanchester Polytechnic, both in Coventry. Whoever arranged the tour may have thought one was in Warwick and one was Lancaster - a regular mistake. They had a backdrop of the 'What Difference Does It Make?' cover and Morrissey waving gladioli around and them all being trampled underfoot afterwards.

I first heard the band when John Peel played 'Hand in Glove' as a new release on his show and I bought it from HMV in Hertford Street, Coventry the next day. It stuck out as sounding a bit Sixties with the harmonica riff and the chord sequence. I wasn't a fan of the single that elevated them, 'This Charming Man', but was excited by their first Peel session - especially the stunning 'Reel Around the Fountain'. I remember discussing it avidly with friends a day or so later. We picked up on all the 'kitchen sink' film references as there was a revival of interest in them as a sort of bookend or mirror to the grim, bleak and desperate feeling of early Eighties Britain. One was the country in its ascendancy, the other one the fag end of the engineering industry.

They were compared to a UK version of REM, who I also saw in 1984, probably due to both having enigmatic frontmen and guitarists who used Rickenbackers as much as their melodic pop music.

I WAS THERE: NICK WATT

In sixth form at school, I was one of those kids who would turn up at gigs and always manage to squirrel my way backstage. If I wanted something, I was pretty shameless in ringing people up and asking for it. I was one of the first people ever to study media studies at A level and I wanted to film a band. The only band that interested me at that time were The Human League. I didn't know how to get hold of Bob Last, who was their manager, but I knew Geoff Travis at Rough Trade probably would. So I contacted Geoff and through that I got to know Geoff a little bit. I used to write to him.

I was at Coventry Poly, which was down the road in the centre of town. One of the reasons I'd gone to Coventry was because of The Specials and the whole Two-Tone thing. I hadn't done as well in my A levels as I hoped I might and basically I had various polys that had offered me a place and Coventry was a pretty good place to get to see a lot of bands. Within the first couple of weeks I saw U2, Echo and The Bunnymen and The Dead Kennedys.

But I realised I was studying the wrong degree and I was trying to get onto a radio journalism course at London University. Part of the deal was you had to interview a local politician or somebody equivalent. I thought, 'Well, I don't really want to interview a politician. I'd rather be interviewing bands.'

I thought, 'The Smiths are getting pretty interesting.' This was still early days - I don't think the album was out at that stage, and this was their first proper tour - so I persuaded Geoff to get me an interview with Morrissey and Marr at Warwick University.

I bowled up on the night of the gig. I'd been told to turn up backstage before the concert and I'd get my interview. I walked into the dressing room. Johnny was dancing around. He was always a very lively character. Morrissey was lying flat on his back on the floor of the dressing room and he had a parka over the top of him with the hood over his head. He looked like he had no interest in actually moving. I don't know whether he just didn't want to do an interview or whatever. Obviously I wasn't anybody. But I did write it up for the college magazine.

Johnny turned round and said to me, 'Oh, you're Geoff's friend, aren't you?' and he let me interview him. He was fantastic. He gave me a heck of a lot of time. Bruce Kent, who had been the Archbishop of Canterbury, had just resigned to become head of CND and he'd done a rally at Warwick that day. So the first question I asked Johnny was about politics. I'd read most of the stuff that had been written about them in the music press and politics hadn't really been anything people had picked on with them. So I sat there and we talked a bit about politics and we talked a bit about The Smiths. I've still got the tape of the interview in the loft, I think. At the end of it I said, 'Okay, what's your favourite record of the moment? What track are you listening to the most?'

He said, 'Oh, it's a really old song. Do you know 'Walk Away Renee'?' I said, 'Well, it depends which version you're talking about.' He looked at me and went, 'Well, The Four

Tops of course.' I said, 'Yes, it's a brilliant song' and, being a bit of a clever clogs I said, 'Do you actually know who wrote it?' He said, 'I'm assuming Holland-Dozier-Holland or one of the classic Motown writers' and I said, 'No, you're a million miles off.' And he went, 'Okay, smart arse. Who was it?' I said, 'Have you ever heard of a band called The Left Banke?' And he went, 'Left who?' I said, 'Next time I see you, I'll give you a copy of the record.'

I was doing a bit of Ents at the time at Coventry Poly and the Head of Ents was a real goth, so we had Spear of Destiny, The Mission, most of the goth bands. And I persuaded him and Mike Hinc at Rough Trade to book them for the Poly. And when they turned up after the gig I wandered into the dressing room and handed Johnny a seven inch reissue of 'Walk Away Renee' by The Left Banke in this lovely gatefold sleeve. He was running around the dressing room going, 'Look, look, look!' We still didn't get a heck of a lot of response out of Morrissey.

OXFORD ROAD SHOW

10 FEBRUARY 1984, MANCHESTER, UK

I WAS THERE: KARREN ABLAZE

We were supposed to be interviewing The Smiths after their appearance on the BBC television programme *Oxford Road Show* on 10 February 1984 and although Andy Rourke said he'd make sure our names were put on the guest list, the receptionist refused to let us in. instead we spent an hour standing outside the doors until Johnny Marr came out to sign autographs. He was very helpful and he took us inside to do the interview but half the group had gone home so there wasn't much point. Well thanks, Andy!

LYCEUM THEATRE

12 FEBRUARY 1984, LONDON, UK

I WAS THERE: CHRIS MADDEN

Hearing 'Hand in Glove' on John Peel piqued my interest. I've still got that on a seven inch single and it's an amazing record. But 'This Charming Man' was doubly amazing - amazing guitar music with a lyrical sensibility and really different from what I'd been listening to before. I can remember being at the school disco and going out with mates who were rude boys and punks. At 14, 15, 16 I was a headbanger - a heavy metal kid - only it was called heavy rock then. The New Wave of British Heavy Metal (NWOBHM) was starting to be a thing. But our mates were into all sorts of stuff and it was a really brilliantly visceral shared experience. So I was going to see Thin Lizzy, Queen and Motorhead but also The Smiths, Aztec Camera, Orange Juice and Black Uhuru with Sly and Robbie. That was from the influence of mates who just wore slightly different clothes and who bought into an identity. My identity really began to evolve and change when The Smiths came along. I took signifiers from Morrissey and Marr and started to develop a style of my own. What an amazing time to be alive.

My mum and dad were very young when they had me, in their teens, so I came from a household steeped in listening to music - Motown, Stax, Zeppelin, Floyd. Thin Lizzy were the big one for my dad, and the Beatles and the Stones. The Smiths were something completely different. I was 17 or 18 and I just found them utterly entrancing, totally beguiling. I found my band in that moment.

I was very, very lucky to see them quite a few times. The first time was around the time 'What Difference Does it Make?' came out. They played at the Lyceum with The Redskins and Billy Bragg. I was doing a graphics diploma at Bradford College and we went on a graphics course on a trip down to London. We took the train down to London on the Sunday, went straight to the hotel and me and my mate Gary threw our bags in the room and bombed down to the Lyceum in the middle of the afternoon.

It was a sold out gig but I really wanted to see them. We were dead lucky - as we were walking down the street without tickets, on the other side of the street were Johnny Marr, Mike Joyce and Andy Rourke. So we wandered over and said, 'We've come down from Bradford to see you' - which was a slight variation on the truth – 'and there's no tickets left.' And Johnny Marr said, 'Don't worry, lads.'

We just walked in with them and watched the sound check. Johnny said, 'Look we haven't got any room on the guest list. But I reckon if you hide in the toilets you'll be okay.' So we went and hid in the toilets after the sound check and then the doors were opened and we watched the gig.

I WAS THERE: EVE WENTWORTH

I'm American, but I was doing a year abroad and saw them live a couple times when I was a university student in London. I'd seen a short film of them singing 'This Charming Man' on some music show, maybe *The Tube* on Channel 4 or something on BBC2. I picked up the album as soon as it was out and wanted to see them live.

Back then you got concert info on the radio or in papers like the *NME* or *Melody Maker* or in *Time Out*. I'd heard they were touring and I was excited to see Billy Bragg was also on the bill. He was playing a lot of gigs around the time of *Life's a Riot with Spy vs. Spy* in 1983, so I'd already seen him a few times. He was still busking on occasion with his busted old guitar and that backpack amp thing he used to do.

My first Smiths gig was at the Lyceum. The Smiths were headlining and the opening acts were The Redskins and Billy Bragg who had had actually been playing outside the venue before the show. When he took the stage after The Redskins he thanked those who'd tossed money in his case outside. I think the amount he mentioned was '27 quid' but don't quote me on that - it's been a while! The crowd was laughing because some clearly hadn't realised he was on the bill and not just some funny, mouthy guy with a guitar entertaining bored concert goers queuing up outside.

When The Smiths finally came on (ah, young and pretty Morrissey and cool Johnny Marr, be still my twentysomething heart) the crowd roared. There were flowers in Morrissey's back trouser pocket and eventually some got tossed into the crowd. Or maybe some originated in the crowd, who knows? There were definitely flowers flying around at some point. The sound was decent, the crowd was loving it and it was a fun though not terribly long set. So much lovely guitar jangle. I remember I had some kind of lecture or school thing the next day and my ears were still ringing.

I WAS THERE: MICHAEL FARRAGHER, AGE 19

I discovered them through hearing 'Hand in Glove' on John Peel and Kid Jensen. They were playing it fairly regularly when it came out. I thought, 'That's an interesting record.' And I remember being in my bedroom and Peel having The Smiths 'in session'. I was just dumbstruck. I was hugely into The Jam before that and then The Smiths just appeared. Even before I'd seen The Smiths live or seen a picture of The Smiths or heard Morrissey speaking, I knew from hearing their session tracks that this was a band I could really get into. The lyrics were just completely different to any other band.

Morrissey photographed by Michael Farragher

I tried to get to see them towards the end of '83 when they were playing in London but I couldn't get a ticket. I was almost the same age as The Smiths themselves, apart from Morrissey. My sister Rita, who's 18 months younger than me, had the same feeling. We were into a lot of different music but we both got into The Smiths. I got into them first and then she became obsessed with them as well. We were extremely close and we went to a lot of gigs together anyway. We first got to see them at the Lyceum. It was only a very short gig and they were only on stage for about 45 minutes because Morrissey wasn't well but that sealed it for me. By this time I was buying all the music papers - *NME, Melody Maker, Record Mirror* - Morrissey was on everything at that point. The music press was in love with The Smiths.

UNIVERSITY OF EAST ANGLIA

14 FEBRUARY 1984, NORWICH, UK

I WAS THERE: NEIL KIMBERLEY

I'm pretty sure the first time I heard The Smiths was in the autumn of my first year at the University of East Anglia in Norwich. We were listening to old Doors albums, dancing to New Order and being inspired by U2. Then The Smiths changed everything. Looking back, I'm not sure whether it was the jangly guitars, the angst or the sense of humour. But as for so many others, The Smiths spoke to me. I began to get obsessed and inspired.

When we came back from Christmas holidays, UEA - the best college for gigs announced that despite the closure of the LCR (the Lower Common Room - the big concert venue) for refurbishment, the university would host a gig by The Smiths. I had already been working as a stage-hand, so getting a ticket to the show was not an issue. But I was attempting to become a host on the UEA's Nexus TV, and thought it might be a cool thing to interview The Smiths on Nexus. Having no idea how to make this happen, I went to see the master of all gigs at UEA – Nick Rayns. He listened to what I wanted to do and gave me the name of Scott Piering at Rough Trade Records. And he said, 'There is no way they will do this.'

This was way before mobile phones and even phones in individual rooms, so I went to Nexus and used the office phone to call Scott Piering. Every day. For two weeks. He finally picked up the phone and we talked for 15 minutes, and I pitched him on an interview. To my surprise he said, 'Okay' and I nearly fell over. I was to go to their dressing room at 5pm and would have Morrissey for 30 minutes. There followed two weeks of panic as I found a cameraman and thought of questions.

The big day came and at 5pm it was apparent all was not well. Morrissey was nowhere to be found. Apparently he was 'under the weather'. But Johnny Marr stepped up. The rest is a bit of a blur. I walked him up to the Nexus studio where we chatted on camera for 20 minutes. He was energetic and funny - and made my job really easy. We talked about Manchester, Joy Division, guitar sounds, their writing process – and the aspirations of The Smiths. We continued to laugh and talk on the short walk back to the dressing room. Then he said, 'Fancy a drink? We never finish our rider', and so I was ushered into the room and introduced to Mike and Andy and saw the world's largest supply of gladioli and other flora laid out on a table. Where was Morrissey? The management was flustered. The rest of the band was used to it.

In later years, I would find out that renowned photographer Paul Slattery photographed the room. Back in 1984 it seemed big and glamorous. Today it all looks a bit naff.

Morrissey finally showed up and the band performed a 45-minute set. The stage was mobbed as the band, were in their flower-whipping, jangly heyday. In later years I would see them multiple times in the US where the shows were amazing. But back in 1984, I was just happy to see the amazing Smiths songs live. After the show, I got the chance to have a few beers with the band and some other fans. I even got to meet and talk for five minutes with Morrissey. I fawned horribly but he was funny, thoughtful and patient. I was truly meeting a hero, and he was all I hoped he would be. The evening ended and I took a bus home, not quite sure that I had been so close to my heroes for a couple of hours. From today it is a distant dream.

I WAS THERE: PAUL GRIGSON, AGE 18

My mate who worked in Backs Records in Norwich told me I would like this group. He was so right with their first album, which is still one of my favourites, especially 'Reel

Around the Fountain'. I was there with my best friend, Lynn, and brother Colin. It was Morrissey at his best, with gladioli everywhere, and one girl decided to give me a horrendous love bite in reaction to 'This Charming Man'.

I WAS THERE: ANDREW HOOK

There was a second Norwich gig, Valentine's Day 1984, almost exactly six months since the Gala, at the University of East Anglia. The venue was in the process of being refurbished and the stage was temporarily in the foyer, so the capacity might have been less than the usual 1,200. Either way it was full, no longer intimate. There was a queue. Everyone held gladioli. Everyone sang along. It seemed as though I was now part of a club and I didn't want to be a member. They played 11 songs. None of them twice. Morrissey hurled flowers into the crowd. I still have a stem.

Andrew Hook's 1984 ticket

Red Guitars supported that evening. I was blown away, felt they were the better band. I saw Red Guitars twice more that year, but I didn't cross paths again with a Smith until a Morrissey gig in Auckland, New Zealand on 8 September 1991. He didn't play any Smiths' songs. The gig was surprisingly good, although the backing band looked to be the same age as when I'd first seen The Smiths, back on that August evening when I was only 16.

I WAS THERE: NEIL WARD, AGE 17

After a foggy drive over from West Norfolk, I set foot on the UEA campus for the first time that night. The Smiths had broken onto the national scene in late 1983. Their first two singles – 'Hand in Glove' and 'This Charming Man' - were a breath of fresh air, with Johnny Marr's exquisite guitar bringing to life Morrissey's radical lyrics. They had taken *Top of the Pops* by storm with an iconic performance of 'This Charming Man' on 24th November. Beginning the New Year as the hottest new band in an age, they embarked on a 32-date tour to promote their eponymously titled first album.

On 14th February they rolled into Norwich. Because the LCR was being refurbished, unusually the gig was held in the Foyer of Union House. A stage was constructed under the balcony, and the crowd packed the Foyer and filled the main staircase, straining to get a good view of the spectacle to come. After The Red Guitars finished their support slot, the atmosphere of anticipation became spine-tingling. As the lights dimmed, roadies tossed several armfuls of gladioli into the crowd. Amidst a euphoric storm of flowers and leaves, The Smiths took the stage.

The set that foggy February night contained much of the first album, which was released just six days later. 'Still Ill', 'Pretty Girls Make Graves' and the new single, 'What Difference Does it Make?' were highlights, with Morrissey pirouetting around the stage, gladioli aloft. They also played 'Heaven Knows I'm Miserable Now', their next single, and a new track – 'Barbarism Begins at Home' - which appeared on their second album, *Meat Is Murder*. Morrissey kicked off the encore of 'You've Got Everything Now' by saying, 'Thank you Norwich, you're very convivial people' and more flowers were strewn around with joyful abandon. I was wide-eyed at the front, and when Morrissey left the stage casting off his necklaces into the crowd I managed to grasp a fistful of his beads, which I still have to this day. The crowd slowly shuffled off, gradually revealing a mass of mulched foliage all over the floor. Inspired, I set about growing a quiff straight away, which I carefully maintained for the rest of the decade.

I was thrilled to see this mesmerising new band so close up in an intimate venue. As a 17-year old King's Lynn A-level student, little did I know that decades later I would be working at UEA.

ROCK CITY

15 FEBRUARY 1984, NOTTINGHAM, UK

I WAS THERE: DEAN DRAKE

'That bloke looks like you, Morrissey,' said Andy.

Dean Drake was mistaken for Morrissey

I was and still am such a big Smiths fan. I was such a Smiths fan that I even looked like a young Morrissey with quiff and all and have on three occasions been told I looked like him. I was mistaken for him in a bar in Bingham and on that occasion I of course played along with it but left quickly to keep the illusion going!

When a friend announced that she had two tickets to go and see The Smiths on their debut tour in Nottingham I jumped at the chance. We travelled from Leicester. When we got to the gig, the atmosphere was amazing and the set list - although short - was played like the album. It was fabulous! I'm not a big crowd fan, so we stood around at the back of the gig enjoying the magic and watched the fans go mad for a piece of his shirt at the end.

After the concert, I was buzzing and suggested we go around the back of the building to see if we could see the band leave. As we got around the back there were only a dozen people milling around and a coach parked up close to the building. As we approached the small crowd, a door opened to my left and some bloke barged into me. I gasped, 'Hey, steady on mate!' (This was Leicester talk). It was only Mike Joyce, followed by Andy Rourke (best bass player in the world), then Johnny Marr and then the man himself - Mozzer!

They ran on to the coach one by one and the coach's engine started up. We were at the front right hand side window of the coach behind the driver's seat, and Moz sat down on the right hand side at the front right next to me. The band were clearly fired up and already had beers in their hands. Mike was already seated on the left side and Johnny was stood in the aisle.

Andy was looking at me and I could see him say to Moz, 'Hey, that bloke looks like you!' Moz turned and looked at me and smiled. I put my hand up to the window and he did the same - tap, tap on the window from both sides before the coach was on its way. I will never forget it!

I still follow Morrisey and I am friends with his current writer and guitarist Boz Boorer and his wife Lyn. Alas, I never made any further contact with Mozzer but Boz is a close second. Moz is always welcome for a cup of tea though!

LEICESTER UNIVERSITY

16 FEBRUARY 1984, LEICESTER, UK

I WAS THERE: LEE THACKER

I saw The Smiths in concert three times between 1984 and 1985. I'd heard (and taped) 'Hand In Glove' and 'Handsome Devil' from John Peel's Festive Fifty in 1983 as well as the band's first Peel Session and loved what I heard. A live gig was also aired on national television around the same time and I was equally impressed by what I saw, especially the quiff-sporting individual who swung a bouquet of flowers around on stage and sang about things that actually meant something to me about my life. The stage invasion at the end of this performance was the cherry on the cake – I couldn't wait to see them play live. I ordered the 'Hand In Glove' and 'This Charming Man' seven-inch singles from Rough Trade and still treasure them both to this day.

In early 1984, an advert in the *Leicester Mercury* newspaper announced the band's forthcoming appearance at Leicester University and I immediately bought a ticket. I also did a drawing of the band in black marker pen on a plain white t-shirt (which I copied from a photo in the *NME*) and wore it to the gig. It was a great show despite the fact nobody attempted to clamber onto the stage. I sweated so much from dancing that the freshly applied marker pen ran and I had to redraw it!

The band's debut album was released a few days later. One of my friends bought it (I had no funds back then) and I listened to it round his house whilst he transferred it onto cassette tape for me. What a disappointment. Their live sound had been reduced to what sounded to me like watered down and under-produced versions of their songs. The piano on 'Reel Around the Fountain' (a song which sounded perfect in the Peel session version) and the flat delivery of 'Miserable Lie' (another song which sounded perfect on the Peel session version) was the last straw and I didn't actually purchase a copy of the album until the band had split up.

UNIVERSITY OF ESSEX

18 FEBRUARY 1984, COLCHESTER, UK

I WAS THERE: JO COOPER

Jo Cooper at Colchester Uni with Johnny

This was my fifth Smiths gig. I had been lucky enough to meet them in January 1984 at a *Top of the Pops* rehearsal so went to the gig hoping to meet them again. My friend Emma, who was like a big sister, managed to talk her dad into giving us a lift there from London and he waited patiently in the car until the end.

We met them – which I was very excited about – especially to meet Johnny Marr. He gave us 'This Charming Man' t-shirts and I still have mine, although it's not in great condition!

The gig was great – packed – and I was at the front on Johnny's side. The gig became more lively and the student audience began to mosh, I started to levitate up the barrier and someone's feet ended up under mine. The foam covering the metal barrier in front of the stage came off and I eventually ended up half way over it. Johnny noticed and asked his guitar tech, Phil, to pull me over the barrier. I watched the rest of the gig from the wings.

I really enjoyed it – a small venue, close to the band, with a very tight lively performance in their more 'punk/folk' days. Nothing beat the feeling of seeing The Smiths live, and I was totally immersed in how different they looked, sounded and presented themselves, and how they connected with those of us who were struggling to find our place in the world.

After the gig, we waited to speak to Johnny and I managed to get a photo with him but there were a few people waiting and he was trying to avoid being smooched by a drunk female student and dashed off without saying goodbye. Emma and I walked across a muddy, grassy grounds back to her dad's car for the journey home.

I saw Johnny four days later at the Reading University gig and he said he had got into their blue tour van with Phil and tried to look for us. At the Reading gig, I was given a copy of their debut album, fully signed – and with the aqua font, not that that meant anything - so that made up for it!

I WAS THERE: KIRSTIE GORMAN, AGE 18

On *Top of the Pops* The Smiths looked like four people on a stage who had never met before and paid each other almost no attention but - my god - the music! They made my palms tingle with excited electricity. I had a Saturday job in a shoe shop and spent everything I earned on fags, vodka and music. I bought a lot of Smiths music. I began to wear my school jumper hanging off one shoulder and walked about sighing like it was just too much like hard work for an aesthete such as me. Rather than giving me admiring glances, people kept asking if I was okay.

I was already spiking my hair but started to favour black frayed clothes, massive tweed overcoats and pale make up. I wore black lipstick and eye makeup and so much mascara a child on a train said, 'Mummy, that girl has spider eyes.' One day I was so surprised by something that when my wide eyes blinked I left one false lash stuck to my eyebrow. I was such a beautiful creature that the poor bloke in Parrot Records had no option but to give me publicity posters, some of which I still have. I've a feeling, 'If you give her stuff she goes away' might have been muttered every time I shuffled in.

So where else was I going to spend my 18th birthday than with The Smiths? On 18th February 1984 I queued with four friends; three with tickets and one without. Amanda South nee Ormerod, a school friend, was there with her boyfriend and future husband Mike South. She remembers buying the 'This Charming Man' single in Boots and we never knew why they insisted on stamping the sleeves of everything they sold. We talked about the gig recently and she said, How Soon Is Now?' riff? That takes me back to my local, smoke-filled pub.' All very lovely but she also said she's 'very embarrassed' that she and Mike preferred The Red Guitars. She said Morrissey was 'to type, as in being rather remote.' Well, what's wrong with that? Cathryn Bower, also a school friend, was there to see The Smiths and definitely rated them on the night.

The non-ticket holder was Neil Gosling. I'd met him at a party and we had a lovely friendship that involved lots of music, making mix tapes and getting high on gloss fumes while I painted a monochrome homage to Edvard Munch's 'Scream' on the back of his bedroom door. The Smiths and The Birthday Party played on a loop punctuated by his mum's head round the door asking, 'Do you eat bacon/chicken/sausage rolls? That's not meat is it?'

I lived over 20 miles away so Dad dropped us off unfashionably early and came back to meet us. I ran between my mate without the ticket and my mates who wanted to get in and down the front. If I didn't leave a gig with bruised ribs it didn't count. Neil got a ticket for the extortionate price of £4.25.

We made it downstairs and began filling up on pints and vodka and orange. The union at Essex Uni was an odd shape, a long space with the stage in the furthest two thirds. The ceiling was covered in eggbox shaped panels and during the main act the sweat would condense on the ceiling and drip on the crowd.

I shoved forward though until I was two people away from the stage for The Smiths. It was so hot that layers were lifted up over heads and tied around waists. Denim and plaid, crushed together trying to find space to flail and express. Me lifted off my feet and feeling my boots being prised off. Elbows hitting my cheeks and my toes crushed under the crowd. I was five foot four and at risk of drowning in the tidal wave of limbs. Neil got hold of my arm and stood me back upright. Then Morrissey took his shirt off and began to helicopter it round his head. Neil predicted what I'd do and took hold of my collar. I jumped, straining to reach Morrissey's pale blue shirt as he let it go. I felt the material graze my finger tips and with a last stretch hooked the cotton and pulled it toward me. But a man taller than me or Neil leant over our shoulders and snatched it from my hands. 'Yoink,' I think it's pronounced.

As the crowd dispersed under the harsh lights that clearly said, 'Stop shouting, they're not coming back on stage', we kicked our way through plastic glasses and bottles until we stood together for the obligatory debrief. I looked at Manda and Mike differently that day 35 years ago when she said she'd preferred the support. But we've worked through it and are still friends now. Cathryn and I are also friends and music is still important to us all. I lost touch with Neil after a boyfriend of mine got jealous and treated my friend appallingly. But if you ask my mum what she remembers about my 18th birthday it will be making me, Neil and Dad cocoa when we got back from the gig and Neil raising his forehead from the kitchen table to say, 'It were 'ot, weren't?' And he was right.

I WAS THERE: LORRAINE CATER

They only played a very short set. My friends and I were disappointed because we wanted more. It was the time of the gladioli, which were being thrown from the stage. I have several favourite tracks – 'There is a Light That Never Goes Out', 'Asleep' and 'Panic' just to name a few. They were prolific but, like all good things, they come to an end. I love it that The Smiths live on.

THE SMITHS DEBUT ALBUM

RELEASED 20 FEBRUARY 1984

The debut album by the band was released by Rough Trade. It debuted at number two on the UK album charts.

TOWN HALL

21 FEBRUARY 1984,
BOURNEMOUTH, UK

I WASN'T THERE: GAVIN UNDERHILL

I never saw The Smiths when they performed at the Midnight Express in Bournemouth. Unlike most of the local music scene, mainly current or ex-art students, I wasn't very impressed with their singles apart from 'This Charming Man'. I thought

The Smiths Debut Album

they were a bit of a hype and it was pretty clear to me from the second hit onwards that Morrissey was a one-trick pony.

The following year the guys who had run the by then defunct Midnight booked them to perform for a much larger audience at the local town hall, as befitting their new status as Blighty's favourite indie band as opposed to them being the latest hipsters on the street. A mutual acquaintance asked me if I was interested in working security on behalf of the promoters, but as it wasn't a paid gig I declined.

I used to hang out in a second-hand record shop in Manchester about 15 years ago, and the owner somehow managed to get hold of a job lot of a set of badges that Morrissey had custom made as a 'gift' for punters when he did a gig at the MEN Arena around that time. They were apparently placed on each seat and had various pics of him on them, each showing the date and venue, with the legend 'he stole our hearts away'. The guy tried to shift them on eBay, but I don't think he managed to sell very many and it wouldn't surprise me if he still has a few left hanging around even now.

I WAS THERE: MICK TARRANT

When they started to break Rough Trade offered them to all the people who put them on first time round and I had a good relationship with Rough Trade so I got offered them again.

As a concert venue it actually wasn't bad, with a good stage and dressing rooms and a big standing area. There wasn't a permanent bar but in an ante room off the main auditorium they brought in a portable bar

THE MIDNIGHT EXPRESS
present
THE SMITHS
plus SUPPORT
GRAND HALL rear of TOWN HALL
St. Stephen's Road, Bournemouth
TUESDAY, 21st FEBRUARY, 1984
8.00 p.m. till late
Bar
Advance Ticket £3.00
On the Night £3.50
Right of admission reserved
№ 446

ALL TRADE BOOKING
137 BLENHEIM CRESCENT, LONDON W11 2EQ
TELEPHONE: 01 - 221 2761 – 229 - 5736 – 221 - 2126

THE SMITHS _RIDER (2)

4. A minimum of six strong humpers must be provided to carry in and help assemble PA, lights and other equipment.These persons must also be available to breakdown and carry out/ load the same euipment after the performance.They are to be under the direction of the Smith's tour manager.

5. The band's representative agent must be consulted in the booking of any and all supporting acts as the Smiths reserve the right to determine supports.The promoter guarantees to provide an immediate and unconditional release from this contract for television,radio,or promotional purposes.

6. The promoter shall provide at no charge to the artist on termination of soundcheck.
a. Tea,coffee,biscuits and six cans of lager on the arrival of the PA crew at the venue.
b. Tea,coffee and biscuits on arrival of the band at the venue.
c. Good quality hot meals for ten people(2 vegetarian,8 non vegetarian).
3 x 75 cl bottles of Soave,3 x 75 cl bottles of Valpolicella,18 large cans of German Pilsner lager,a good and varied selection of fresh fruit,40 Marlborough cigarettes.

7. A selection of flowers to the approximate retail value of £50 sterling,including gladioli.(No roses or other flowers with thorns,please)

8. The promoter will also provide at no charge to the artist 2 x 6ft x 4 ft drum risers,approximatly 2ft high.

9. The artists reserve the right to select their own choice of music both prior to and after their performance.

10. The above constitutes the sole and complete and binding agreement between promoter/ management and artist(The Smiths) any deviation from contract or rider will result in cancellation of performance and payment of the artist in full.

SIGNED AND AGREED ON BEHALF OF THE MANAGEMENT/PROMOTER..............................

DATE..............................

The Smiths rider for their Bournemouth Town Hall show included £50 worth of flowers for the night. And it was pretty cheap to hire - only 60 or 70 quid. I put on loads of stuff there. But you had to employ your own staff and you got no proceeds from the bar. If you hired the bar, you got 20 per cent off the booking fee because they'd make money from the beer they sold.

That gig was a completely different kettle of fish from the Midnight Express Club. It was sold out completely in advance. The capacity was about 800 but on the night there were so many people without tickets hoping there'd be some left and wanting to get in that the people with tickets couldn't get to the door. We had this press of people against the doors and I could see the glass in the entrance doors bowing under their weight. I thought, 'Any minute now the glass is going to break and people are going to come tumbling through.' I could imagine the headlines in the local paper: 'Local promoter in fracas at sold out punk gig.'

Two guys from Bournemouth Borough Council were there to oversee it and I said, 'Look it's sold out but I've got to sell tickets and let these people in otherwise the people with tickets aren't going to get in.' And they went with it, which was the most sensible thing to do. So on the night we probably had 900 in there. It was a huge place and by putting a few extra in there, there was no danger of people dying in the crush. It was just the most sensible thing to do on the night.

It was quite an odd atmosphere. 'This Charming Man' was out and was obviously a big seller but I forget what big waves they were making. People were initially in awe but the audience warmed to them. I still have the contract. I also have the receipt for Morrissey's flowers. Part of the rider was 'fifty quid's worth of flowers and no thorns' which was the gladioli. That was a lot to spend on flowers and nearly as much as hiring the venue.

It was a runaway success, although as a promoter in situations like that it's a lot of stress. You've got to constantly be going round checking you've got someone on the fire doors making sure that people don't open them and let a bunch more people in. You've got the local council on your case. You don't really have any time to enjoy it because it passes in a blur. I can't remember at any time standing there and watching a couple of numbers.

I packed up promoting soon after that. The club closed because it needed a lot of structural work doing to comply with fire regulations. It was doing okay but we weren't making a huge amount of money. We didn't have big reserves of cash where we could afford to do structural alterations.

A year or so after doing The Smiths, I was not doing much of anything and one day I was looking after a stall in Camden Market for a friend who sold old brass light fittings and stuff. Johnny passed by with his girlfriend and either Andy or Mike. Johnny spotted me. He remembered me from the gigs and said, 'Christ you've got some strings to your bow.' They were a proper big act by this time so it was quite nice and humble of him to stop and chat.

UNIVERSITY OF READING

22 FEBRUARY 1984, READING, UK

Nick Deaves saw The Smiths at Reading Uni

I WAS THERE: NICK DEAVES, AGE 21

For a music-mad 21 year old, moving from Reading, where nothing really happened apart from the yearly festival, to London was a dream come true. I always had to come to town to see anyone. I'd come across The Smiths in the *NME* and bought 'Hand in Glove'. As I arrived in London, 'This Charming Man' was released and I bought every version I could find – the seven inch, the 12 inch. The song summed up my life, being a new kid on the block in the big city, as did many of the songs to come. This was my band.

The Lyceum was a regular Sunday night haunt with great four band line-ups. I can't really remember too much about the gig. I think the excitement took over. But in a matter of days I saw them again at Reading University. Most university gigs were closed shop affairs but this must have been open to the public. I took two friends from home who were armed with flowers, which I wasn't sure about, being a serious music fan - or snob! The gig wasn't that well attended but it gave me the chance to be right at the front. It was a fast and furious beer-soaked set.

I WAS THERE: STANLEY NORTH

I saw them three times – at Reading University in 1984, at Reading Hexagon in 1985 and at Brixton in 1986. In 1983 I went on my own as no mates were interested. They were by 1985 though!

UNIVERSITY OF SWANSEA

23 FEBRUARY 1984, SWANSEA, UK

I WAS THERE: JAYNE ALLEN, AGE 16

I met them the day after the gig and they all signed my album at the Dragon Hotel. It was the first album they had seen that had been bought (Morrissey told me it was the first one he had seen). I shared a pint of milk with Mike Joyce and still have one of his drum sticks from the gig. I can't find the other one.

Jayne Allen got the band's autographs on her copy of the debut album - the first one they'd seen

COCKCROFT HALL, BRIGHTON POLYTECHNIC

25 FEBRUARY 1984, BRIGHTON, UK

Sean Baldwin was at the Brighton Poly gig

I WAS THERE: SÉAN BALDWIN, AGE 15

I discovered The Smiths through the alternative media available: namely listening to the John Peel show whilst doing my homework, reading the *NME* and rifling through record shops. I remember buying a seven-inch double A-side promo of 'Still Ill' and 'You've Got Everything Now' from Max Records in Eastbourne. I was an early adopter of the Morrissey look and dug out my old NHS specs from the days I wore them back up north. No one else dressed like that at school and no one else sounded like The Smiths. It was like they'd created their very own genre. And, of course, they spoke to me in a way that no other music of the time managed to do.

On its release I bought 'This Charming Man' on seven inch from Virgin in Brighton and later on that day I went to a party in Burgess Hill. It was full of people from school I didn't identify with. I drank too much and someone pushed me in the swimming pool. This just made me feel like more of an outsider - having been displaced from living up north when my parents split up - and my bond with the band only strengthened.

I went to see them play at Cockcroft Hall, Moulsecoomb, Brighton with Nick Myall, a friend from school. We got to the gig early so we could get right up the front. I remember nothing about the support band, The Telephone Boxes, but the music on the PA before The Smiths arrived on stage was memorable because it was played on repeat. The band were on quite late so this Frank Chickens track seemed to play so many times that to this day I can still hear it in my head.

The gig was thrilling. Wild, passionate, a crush and gladioli everywhere. The band were excellent and far more powerful than I was expecting, Morrissey waving his shirt and flowers, whipping the crowd into a greater frenzy, leaning into the monitor, chin and quiff jutting provocatively into the melee. It was all a blur and a squash and I don't remember many details except that Johnny Marr was playing right in front of us. At one point he stood on my hand, which didn't matter because a) he was only wearing suede moccasins, b) he mouthed 'sorry' after he did so and c) it was Johnny fucking Marr!

I never bumped into Moz but I often think that maybe as a kid our paths might have crossed. I used to live in Kenwood Road, Stretford in the mid-seventies, just round the corner from King's Road, where he lived. I was always cycling about Longford Park and hanging around newsagents and - who knows? maybe we brushed past one another as he was buying a music mag and I was getting a comic and some sweets. My family were great friends with another family called the Morrisseys (no relation) and this only compounded the feeling later on that I 'knew' him. Oh Manchester, so much to answer for!

I WAS THERE: NICK MYALL

A dark and cold winter's night in February 1984 added to the atmosphere as I set off from home for my first ever Smiths gig. It was only my second ever gig, having seen The Jam a couple of years before so it was a big night. I got the train down to the Poly's Cockcroft Hall, a favourite venue for indie and post punk bands. Me and my mate from school, Sean Baldwin, had been buzzing about 'This Charming Man' and 'What Difference Does it Make?' so we had to be there. We were still too young for beers in the bar so just watched the gathering crowd of indie kids, goths, punks, etc. As it turned out, for several hours as the band were determined to keep us waiting while they had a night out in Brighton. At last they took to the stage, Morrissey in his trademark tatty faded jeans, charity shop shirt, NHS specs, hearing aid and of course half a bush hanging out of his back pocket.

The whole of the first album was knocked out with effortless style with 'Miserable Lie', 'Reel Around the Fountain', 'You've Got Everything Now' and the singles forming some of the many high points. Sean and I were right up against the stage and the buzz coming off the band and back from the audience was massive, as it always was at a Smiths gig, with Morrissey passing round a carton of juice to the crowd. They were rockier than I'd expected and of course Johnny Marr's guitar playing was superb, him not even looking at the fretboard on his Rickenbacker as he sailed through a classic early Smiths set. After a triumphant gig it was back home to dreary Haywards Heath on the rattling BR train and off to school in the morning where we agreed it was a fantastic night. It remains one of my best gigs. How couldn't it?

I WAS THERE: STEVE FANNING

They were delayed by about two hours. I found out years later, from their promoter Josh Dean, that he had taken them into Kemp Town for a meal, which ran over somewhat – and not a vegetarian meal, he hastened to inform me. When they finally came on stage the excitement was at fever pitch and they went on to smash the place much to our young and eager ears delight.

Morrissey was in full gladioli mode and I had to chuckle with my friend who I had gone to the gig with, called Merran Wrigley. She turned to me and said, 'What is Johnny Marr doing up on the stage? I know him, he went to school with me in Manchester.' She had no idea that he was the guitarist in The Smiths. Another friend met them backstage afterwards. He was wearing a Sisters of Mercy t-shirt and regaled me with tales of Morrissey completely ripping him apart as a consequence.

It was the one and only time I ever saw The Smiths but it is indelibly imprinted on my memory.

UNIVERSITY OF KENT AT CANTERBURY

27 FEBRUARY 1984, CANTERBURY, UK

I WAS THERE: LUKA VERCAUTEREN

I was abused from the ages of four to 13 by my alcoholic father and mother. I was placed in a home for children with bad parents and at 14 placed in a foster home where I was not so well. I started the search for who I was. Like so many, punk grew in me. I remember hearing 'What Difference Does it Make?' on the radio and I immediately loved it. I began searching for Smiths t-shirts and badges. The first time I saw them was in Canterbury in 1984, and later I saw them in Belgium and the Netherlands. The Smiths saved my life - the music, the lyrics, their way of doing things. 'How Soon Is Now?' is still my favourite.

The Smiths saved Luka Vercauteren's life (left)

VICTORIA HALL

28 FEBRUARY 1984, HANLEY, UK

I WAS THERE: GLYN WADE

I just got near the front for this one and managed to catch a necklace and some flowers that Morrissey dropped and threw into the audience. Being tall helped with the necklace, but then what to do with it as people clawed to try and get it? So I shoved it into my underpants. Luckily the clawing stopped, as it could have been quite painful! There were flowers everywhere so catching a few daffodil heads was easier. I still have them in a book somewhere, as I do the necklace.

Glyn Wade shoved Morrissey's necklace down his underpants - Morrissey wasn't wearing it

UNIVERSITY OF LEEDS

29 FEBRUARY 1984, LEEDS, UK

I WAS THERE: MARCUS AMBLER

I saw The Smiths in Leeds. They were supported by The Red Guitars. I've still got my ticket - it's number 001341.

QUEEN MARGARET UNION

2 MARCH 1984, GLASGOW, UK

I WAS THERE: GERRY O'CONNOR, AGE 17

I saw The Smiths every time they played Glasgow and also had a ticket for the Albert Hall but sadly did not go. I went to all the gigs with friends. I bought every release on the day it came out and bought the seven and 12 inch singles. I bought the 'What Difference Does It Make?' single again because the cover changed from Terence Stamp to Morrissey. I jumped up on the stage twice at QMU and at the first Barrowland gig.

DUNDEE UNIVERSITY

3 MARCH 1984, DUNDEE, UK

I WAS THERE: ALAN CORMACK, AGE 16

I'd been listening to John Peel since I was about 10, in 1978, so thought I was fairly good at picking up new stuff. But for some reason I never actually heard The Smiths on Peel. I'd somehow missed the nights they were on. I heard them through a friend's brother who came home one day with 'This Charming Man'. We put it on and listened to it over and over and over again. And also the B-side, 'Jeanne', which was brilliant but it didn't sound like 'This Charming Man'. Then it was a case of going back and checking out 'Hand in Glove' and stuff like that. The only way I could find out about them was through *NME*, *Melody Maker* or *Sounds* or what was getting played on Peel.

When the first album came out, I thought Morrissey was speaking directly to me. I always thought of myself as being a bit different to everybody else. Nobody else at school was into indie, alternative music. The closest it got to alternative for people was Simple Minds, which was pretty bad. Morrissey was talking about isolation and being different and stuff. That really spoke to me.

We saw that they were playing Dundee University. I went with my friend, Craig McNeil, whose brother had introduced us to The Smiths. Getting into Dundee University was a bit of a trial because you had to be signed in and, being still at school and under age, this was going to be doubly difficult. But somehow we managed it.

The support band was The Red Guitars. The Tube had done a documentary on Hull and they were on it, performing 'Good Technology', so waiting to see The Red Guitars and knowing one of their songs was a bonus.

Back then Dundee had a bit of a pyschobilly group that went around, quite scary-looking guys with big flat tops, who were into The Meteors, The Guana Batz, King Kurt and all that kind of stuff. You actually ran the risk, if you weren't a flat top, of getting a bit of a filling in from these guys. They used to go to the university discos on a Saturday night. They were all at the Smiths gig. I remember eyeing these guys and thinking, 'I need to keep out of the way of them because I don't want any hassle.'

The Smiths came on and Morrissey threw a load of gladioli into the crowd. The flat tops picked them up and were throwing them around and doing their slam dancing thing at the front of the gig. As the band started to play 'This Charming Man', somebody threw a pint glass onto the stage and it hit Morrissey. Or it might have been one of the gladioli. He walked off. The band kept playing until halfway through the song and then walked off too. So there were boos and jeers and whistling. Then a roadie came out and said something along the lines of, 'If you don't all fucking calm down then The Smiths are not fucking coming back on, you bunch of fucking idiots', which was again met with glasses and flowers and stuff getting thrown on the stage. Eventually they did come back out and they started playing 'This Charming Man' again. Morrissey said something along the lines of, 'You have a funny way of showing love, Dundee' which we thought was quite funny.

The gig was brilliant. I seem to remember that we met a couple of girls that night, which was an added bonus, we lied about our age and told them we were 18 and studying geography at university. I think they totally saw through us because we never saw them again.

The next time I saw The Smiths was 1985 at the Caird Hall. Del Amitri were supporting them. It's quite interesting to see how spectacularly shit Del Amitri became, because that night they were a Postcard-type jangly band and quite good. I think The Smiths came back again a year later but I kind of went off them by then. When they became more successful, a lot of football casuals in Dundee started wearing Smiths t-shirts. And I thought, 'What can Morrissey possibly say to these guys?' because they were all into fighting and stuff. I was starting to get into things like The Wedding Present and all that C86 stuff. The Smiths were becoming a bit old hat. By the time 'Panic' came out, I just saw them as a chart band. I thought, 'Yeah, I used to like The Smiths but now they've sold out.'

I've seen Morrissey a few times solo but it's never the same as The Smiths. I still listen to them now and again. 'William It Was Really Nothing' is probably my favourite Smiths song. Or possibly 'Handsome Devil', the *Hatful of Hollow* version. It's really raw sounding.

I WAS THERE: GEORGE DUNCAN, AGE 22

I remember seeing Morrissey with the flowers in his back pocket and reading afterwards that this was a gig where they nearly split up after an argument, and in fact the date of the gig was postponed for a few days.

I WAS THERE, JEREMY KIDD, RED GUITARS VOCALIST

The audience chucked beer at Morrissey and he stormed off and refused to return for some considerable time. But when they finally did resume the whole band were clearly hyped-up and played a storm. I can confirm, by the way, that it was not me who took to the stage and harangued the troublemakers on that occasion.

Ticket for the Dundee University show exhorting fans to 'come and see how many necklaces Morrissey's got'.

I WAS THERE: ALASTAIR BRODIE, GROUCHO RECORDS, DUNDEE

I've been in the secondhand record business for 45 years. I started on 1 April 1974 in Cockburn Street Market in Edinburgh and then me and my assistant, who became my partner, decided to set up ourselves. Our bosses didn't want to us to set up in Edinburgh and we had the opportunity of coming up to Dundee. I didn't know Dundee at all but my partner came from Kirriemuir, which wasn't that far away, so we came up with a record collection and £500 and found a shop. Back then you could find an empty shop, find the landlord, get the keys to view it, say 'yes', hand over a cheque for the rent and he'd give you the keys. It would all be done in a day or two.

When we started off it was a smaller version of Cockburn Street Market, which was a hippie market. We were young, 22 year old hippies, and we arrived in Dundee in August 1976 and we enjoyed a lovely hot summer fitting out the shop. Then the Sex Pistols brought out 'Anarchy' in November and everything changed. By our first anniversary we were a full-blown punk shop with all the punk singles and the t-shirts. We got a badge machine and made up badges. People used to make the trek out of town and up the Perth Road just to get the latest stuff.

It went well. We had seven years there and then we got chucked out and so we moved into town, and things were even better because we got a shop at the end of the Overgate Centre, two doors along from the entrance to the Angus Hotel, which was the main city centre hotel. That was quite handy because a lot of the bands that played in Dundee stayed at the Angus and we got various well-known celebs coming in. Probably my favourite one was a hero of mine, Peter Green, and I managed to get a good chat with him.

Roll on to 1984. At that time, the punk scene was still going but the indie scene was really the thing. We never went on to dealing with the major labels. We just kept ourselves indie, doing secondhand stuff and new indie stuff and all the accessories, t-shirts and so on. Being an indie shop we were members of The Cartel. We weren't an HMV so we didn't get all kinds of things thrown at us because we weren't a chart return shop but we did the chart for the *NME* and indie charts and so on. I remember the Cartel rep giving me a copy of the white label of this new band called The Smiths. I would play it quite a bit in the shop. We had a Saturday boy who worked for DC Thomson in the *Beano* offices during the week, a chap called Alan. He did storylines for things like *The Three Bears* and *Little Plum*. But he worked for us on a Saturday and he absolutely loved it. He went from The Jam and such like to The Smiths.

Their debut album came out on 20 February 1984 and two weeks later they played at the university. At that time, I knew the Ents convenor at the university and he used to put us on the guest list for any gigs, which was very handy particularly as I used to live on the next street to the university union. I could say to people, 'Oh, do you fancy going to a gig?' if I had people round and depending what was on, like Hawkwind, people could say, 'Yes, I fancy going to see them' or if it was Mike Oldfield, 'No, I don't think I'll bother!' We saw some really good acts there.

And on Saturday 3rd March The Smiths played there. It was an interesting gig, because the punky type students decided to throw beer at the band and Morrissey wasn't too happy with it. I think he stomped off stage for a while. Anyway, I don't remember too much about it and I'm not even sure I saw the whole gig. But during the day on the Saturday, because the band were staying in the Angus Hotel and Johnny Marr's certainly a record fan, they popped into the shop en masse late on in the afternoon.

I wouldn't have known who they were but Alan the Saturday boy said, 'Oh, that's The Smiths in' so he was the one that was chatting to them most. Unfortunately he passed away some years ago. My memories are of Morrissey in a big long coat and him buying a couple of Dusty Springfield seven inch singles. We had a display cabinet with guitar badges in it by the front door that were one offs. They were made by chap in Fife, an ex-art college student who was making them. He was just the most magnificent miniature painter and he would cut a badge into the shape of a guitar with a fretsaw. They were about two inches long and they sold for next to nothing at that time, five to 10 pounds or something. They were exact in every detail – the wood grain, the lettering on the top, Fender or whatever, and the individual strings. I think he must have used a single hair to get some of those. Johnny Marr was having a look at them and making his choice. I think he bought a Rickenbacker one. He was absolutely delighted with it. One of the other Smiths bought a packet of Rizla kingsize and some hair gel. He didn't bother looking at the records.

I remember I was standing on the shop floor and chatting away with Alan to Johnny Marr and I looked at my watch and realised that on that particular day Scotland were playing Ireland in a rugby international and Scotland were going for the triple crown. We didn't have a TV in the shop but in the Overgate a little bit further up the steps there was a TV rental shop which had various TVs in the window so I excused myself to Johnny Marr and went out up to the TV rental shop and stood looking in the window as Scotland secured the triple crown.

I got Morrissey and Johnny to sign the white label album that I had. It was a plain white sleeve and stapled to the front was an A4 photocopy of the picture from the front of the album with the tracks listed underneath. I wasn't too sure who the other Smiths were so I just got Morrissey and Johnny to sign it. Morrissey wrote, 'Be lucky, Morrissey' in his primary school writing with his name in capitals and underneath Johnny wrote, 'Johnny Marr digs you xxx'. I sold the album umpteen years ago.

When their stuff came out it sold in masses. 'Hand in Glove' sold okay when it came out and then it built up and up. And when 'This Charming Man' came out, that was just pretty mega. Getting the 12 inch of it was pretty good, and we managed to get copies of the 12 inch New York Mix too. They were probably the best-selling act we had. With a lot of bands you'd be ordering ones or twos and with them it was more 30s and 40s.

The next time I saw them was when they played the Caird Hall in September 1985, about 18 months later. By that time they'd exploded. I went along to that. I remember a lot of gladioli. It was one of those concerts, which just put a big smile on your face. They dropped in again; certainly Morrissey and Marr came in. I've got no idea what they purchased that time but it was good to see them in the shop. Now we could officially call them regulars! Since then, any time Johnny Marr's been around the area he's made sure he's dropped in and he was quoted as saying that Groucho's is one of his two favourite record shops in the country, the other one being a place in Manchester.

(Since recording this interview, Alastair Brodie has sadly passed away. Groucho's Record Store can be found at 132 Nethergate, Dundee, DD1 4ED).

FUSION CLUB (AKA RITZY'S)

4 MARCH 1984, ABERDEEN, UK

I WAS THERE: JO BERSTAN, AGE 17

I went with a bus load of my high school chums from Buckie, where we lived, to Aberdeen, which was about just over an hour away. I remember there were gladioli flowers, which Morrissey had in his back pocket. They played songs from the LP out at that time, 'What Difference Does it Make?', 'Hand in Glove' and 'This Charming Man'. It was a fab night.

I WAS THERE: ANDY SMITH

We were wearing NHS-type specs with the lenses poked out and we nicked daffodils from the graveyard and stuck them in our back pockets. After the gig we were singing 'Hand in Glove' on the taxi rank in Back Wind, swirling daffys around our heads, and some guys took offence and a fight broke out. Daffys make a shite weapon.

COASTERS

5 MARCH 1984, EDINBURGH, UK

Vix Vex's ticket for the Edinburgh Coasters gig

Vix Vex on the left remembers a 'squishy night' at Coasters

I WAS THERE: VIX VEX, AGE 15

I don't know if I would ever have classed myself as a fan. I was more into the goth scene - Sisters of Mercy, Bauhaus and that sort of thing. But I had few friends that were into the more independent side of things and what we would have called 'twee bands' back then, such as The Pastels.

I think it was their first big tour. The gig itself was a bit of an oddity. I don't think they expected that surge in popularity. The venue held about 700 people and on the night there were probably about 900 in there so it was absolutely packed. The support band, Red Guitars, was of more interest to me at that particular time, although I don't think I knew who the support were beforehand. Sometimes in those days you didn't know until you turned up.

My biggest memory of that night is just how busy it was. They would definitely have been breaking fire regulations on the night. There were quite a few people flat out on the floor and I don't think it was anything to do with drink. It was the heat and because you were completely squashed in. That again was quite typical. It was a squishy night.

Most of that size of band would play there - bands like Spear of Destiny and Killing Joke. In those days you didn't have barriers at the front - you were right up against the stage. I must have started off there because that would have been where we were headed. But it was a squish. There was almost a sense of, 'This isn't safe'. One of my friends had passed out and she was hauled unceremoniously across the stage and dumped at the side so she watched the whole thing from the side. And at that point there were a few people coming out of the crowd a bit worse for wear.

One girl was propped at the side of the bar and lying down. I asked the bar people, 'Can I have a glass of water? This girl's passed out' and they wanted to charge me, which you're not allowed to do now. But at that time it was like, 'Oh yeah.' At that point I kind of went a bit nuts. For a 15 year old I was a bit feisty. I barged my way into the manager's office and had a real go at him, saying there were far too many people in there and it was a fire hazard. The guy was sitting there looking like a rabbit in the headlights, with this wee goth girl giving it to him!

The Smiths didn't really sound like anybody else. And of course they had that miserable element that appealed to the goth side of things, that 'We're going to reel around the fountain and die somewhere' element. Most of my friends were on the punk side of things rather than the indie side, so there was a real mixture. There was punks, goths, the indie kids with their cardigans on. But possibly for a lot of them it was a curiosity. This was a new band that had been championed by John Peel and any club or anything you were at always had The Smiths playing. Morrissey after that became quite idolised. He always had that swathe of arrogance. I think he always wanted to be worshipped and there was an element of that in the way the crowd reacted.

There wasn't much in the way of interaction and what there was, was a bit poke-proddy. But that wasn't unusual. There was an element of bands being quite scathing towards their audience, much, much more than there is now. His interactions were quite baiting. So I don't know whether he looked out in the crowd and saw this punky element. He almost put the crowd on the back foot. There was a comment about 'playing to spotty teenagers', which didn't go down particularly well. I think Edinburgh crowds are pretty hard to please anyway.

A crowd us of walked up the road afterwards and somehow or other we'd managed to get a gladioli from the stage or his back pocket or somewhere. That was the pickings of the gig.

I WAS THERE: KATIE LLEWELLIN, AGE 17

I had lost a bit of enthusiasm for the flower throwing. Other people I was with thought they were amazing though. I spoke to my ex-boyfriend who said, 'We saw them at Coasters and the band and the audience were pretty annoying so we left before the end. We also saw Carmel and The Clash that weekend - 35 years ago... yikes!'

I WAS THERE: TERRY PATTERSON

This was my first concert since leaving the Army. The venue used to be for roller skating so it was just basically a dance floor. I remember being stripped to the waist and waving my shirt around. The next time I saw them was at the Caley Palais on Lothian Road, a former cinema, which is now a Wetherspoons! The girl I was with had me on her shoulders. Great gigs, great times.

Terry Patterson was at Coasters as was his brother-in-law - in a safari jacket

I WAS THERE: STUART RAE

I was in my first year at Napier College when I saw The Smiths on *Top of the Pops*. Next day at college there was a lot of discussion around the performance of this new band and how 'different' the lead singer was. Then one of the guys in my class said that they were touring and who fancied going? I said 'yes' and the tickets were bought. Coasters was a strange venue because its main function was as a roller disco venue. I remember Morrissey had gladioli in his back pocket when he came on stage, that the crowd were asked to step back from the temporary stage because it had moved and I remember just how brilliant they were live.

I saw them again in September at the Edinburgh Playhouse, a far larger venue, but they were still great live. And then I saw them playing Glasgow Barrowland in July 1986.

I now know it as a great venue where the floor 'bounced' and it certainly did that night.

Even since The Smiths split up, I have continued to listen to their music and have sometimes had to suffer from my friends slagging them off that they were morose. I always retort that these people are not listening to the music properly. Would I go and see them again? Absolutely. They are still one of the best bands I have seen live.

I WAS THERE: ALAN TEMPLETON, AGE 25

I grew up a Velvets and Stooges fan and loved punk and new wave. I hated New Romantic music and The Smiths were a breath of fresh air. I went with my flatmate Alan who got me into The Smiths by buying 'What Difference Does it Make?' 12 inch single. It was a brilliant night and there was a manic atmosphere. A girl was collapsed drunk in a corner at the gig and we pointed her out to the bouncers for her own safety.

For Alan Templeton The Smiths were a breath of fresh air

I WAS THERE: STEVIE WALKER

I saw them twice, at Coasters in Edinburgh and then the next year at the Barrowland. They were fantastic both nights. I managed to get some beads from Morrissey's necklace.

MAYFAIR

7 MARCH 1984, NEWCASTLE-UPON-TYNE, UK

I WAS THERE: MARK SINGLETON

I went with my best friend Ste, also a Smiths fan. We were in our last year at comprehensive school. After saving up our dinner money and paper round wages to get tickets, we got the train from Darlington back in the day when you could get a train to a gig and there would still be a service to bring you home. We were both dressed in our 501s, Ste was wearing a floral design shirt and I had a paisley number on along with denim jackets (I know, double denim - shocking!). Ste was rocking the Mozza hairstyle where I was more Andy Rourke. We had bought the releases so far - again with dinner money - so we had listened to them to death and scoured the sleeve notes so we could memorise the words. Needless to say, we were a tad bit excited about seeing our idols for the first time. We got to the venue, our hearts pounding with excitement. We had not yet discovered beer, or how to get served underage, so coke it was.

When The Smiths came on needless to say the place erupted. The Mayfair had a balcony where on many a subsequent gig I would witness drunk and over exuberant fans dive off hoping to get caught by the crowd below. The crowd were so loud and exuberant that night I thought the balcony would collapse. I don't remember the set list order - I think I was in a dream state - but Morrissey was gyrating away while Marr was just a guitar god who effortlessly made his guitar sing, a sound we had only heard on vinyl prior to the gig. Rourke was less animated but still rocked those renowned basslines, locking in with Joyce on drums. The best back line and songwriting team bar none in my mind. Sod The Beatles, Morrissey and Marr are the best song writing team ever.

I can't recall an encore but what I do remember is the night went far too quickly. We left sweaty and adrenalin-fuelled, with me having had quite possibly the best night of my life so far.

It may have been this Mayfair gig or the one on 17th July 1985 where, near the end, people were spitting, fall out from the punk era, which took a good few years to desist. Mozza did say, 'Stop spitting or we will stop.' People behaved but then later one numpty spat again and Mozza was true to his word and left the stage not to return. The last word was from Marr who said, 'You were warned. What do you expect?' The fans then gave the culprit a good slapping.

TOWN HALL

8 MARCH 1984, MIDDLESBROUGH, UK

I WAS THERE: LESLEY JOHNSON, AGE 14

My first ever gig, I went with my cousin who was two years older and Smiths mad like me. I caught Morrissey's daffodil, which I still have pressed in a photo album. Red Guitars were support and it was a lovely £3.50 a ticket! I also saw the '85 gig supported by James, which was probably my favourite, and the '86 Queen is Dead gig, when they were amazing, very polished and supported by Raymonde. No gigs since have ever beaten them. I could not believe they played our little town three years on the trot.

Lesley Johnson saw The Smiths three times

LANCASTER UNIVERSITY

9 MARCH 1984, LANCASTER, UK

I WAS THERE: PADDY SHENNAN, AGE 19

Less than 10 months later this gig was a world away from that night in Camden Town. I was now studying in Sheffield but couldn't get to their Sheffield University gig in January so waited for the concert nearest my hometown. I remember the massive queue outside the venue and the heat inside the packed hall. Some young women fainted, or at least had to be helped out of the gig, it was just so hot and uncomfortable. My then girlfriend certainly felt uneasy and so we stood towards the back, within easy reach of an exit door just in case she needed to get to the fresh air. What a difference from being able to sit cross-legged on the floor at the Electric Ballroom gig!

The band's debut album had been released in the February, and, as well as 'Hand in

Glove', The Smiths' growing army of devoted fans had fallen in love with floor-filling singles 'This Charming Man' and 'What Difference Does It Make?' This was a band that was already growing out of the university venue circuit. This was a band that everyone was now talking about. This was the band of the moment.

I WAS THERE: RACHEL SOWDEN

My friend Helen was passed along the crowd and lifted off the stage after fainting. I was quite jealous as she reckoned she touched Johnny Marr's hand as she passed him. I pressed my gladioli that Morrissey threw into the crowd.

HAMMERSMITH PALAIS

12 MARCH 1984, LONDON, UK

I WAS THERE: MICHAEL FARRAGHER

I wanted to see them at every opportunity. I didn't have an awful lot of money. But we got to see them the next time they were playing, a month after the Lyceum, at Hammersmith Palais. They played for much longer, about an hour and a half, and Sandie Shaw came on and sang 'I Don't Owe You Anything'. Then we were looking at the music press every week and thinking, 'When are they next playing? We've got to go and see them.'

I'd read in *NME* that Morrissey would go up to the Rough Trade offices in King's Cross fairly regularly. It was coming up to his birthday in May and I thought, 'I'm just going to spend the day up there and wait until I meet him', because they were playing some gigs up in Scotland in June and we really wanted to go but they were sold out. I had a present to give to him for his birthday and I had a letter to give to him, and I was going to be cheeky and say, 'Is there any chance you could get us on the guest list?'

I went into the Rough Trade offices and asked, 'is Morrissey likely to come in?' and they said, 'We don't know. He might turn up today.' Sure enough he did. There weren't any other Smiths with him and I don't remember there being any security. I said, 'I love The Smiths and here's a present' and, 'My sister's really into The Smiths and we'd love to come and see you in Scotland. Is there any chance you could put us on the guest list?' He said, 'Yeah, sure. Give me your names. I'll make sure that you're on the guest lists.'

I'd met Morrissey! Oh my god. It was the most exciting thing that could ever happen. And after that we started following The Smiths on a very regular basis. We started writing to them. We wrote letters to Morrissey and to Johnny through Rough Trade. My sister used to write to Morrissey every week for at least a year. And I wrote to him maybe every two or three weeks. We'd send letters and we'd send presents and we would get replies from Morrissey now and again. We've still got those letters and postcards.

We started going to radio and TV stations, wherever we knew they were going to be on and it was a live appearance. We got to know all of the band at that stage and they knew us. They would sign records for us and they would give us records. Morrissey said we could come to any gig that we wanted to and we would be on all guest lists, so the only gigs that we ever paid for were the Lyceum and Hammersmith Palais shows that we first saw. After that, we were always on Morrissey's guest list or Johnny's.

FREE TRADE HALL

13 MARCH 1984, MANCHESTER, UK

I WAS THERE: STEVE BROWN

The first Smiths song I heard was 'This Charming Man', when a mate played me a video he'd recorded, off *The Tube* on Channel 4. I was struck by how cool Johnny Marr was, with the Sixties hair and shades. I heard the song a few more times on evening shows on Radio 1, probably the *Kid Jensen Show*, and began to adore it.

It was so infectious. I was 18 in 1983, I'd had a fairly shitty childhood and life at home was still pretty unbearable. Music was vital to me, it was all I really cared about in life back then, but I didn't really like anything that was around. It was all a bit forced and I had to kind of make myself like it. 'This Charming Man' was just impossible not to love.

The B-side to 'This Charming Man'

Kev, who showed me the video, and my other mate Lee, were members of the Hacienda, which had been open around 18 months. You had to be, or be with, a member to get in; they used to sign me in and we'd hang around on the balcony upstairs watching the five to 10 proto-yuppies on the dance floor dancing to electro, a music which I didn't understand! The place was freezing and near empty, but we went because it was different and not full of people wanting a fight.

They went to see The Smiths there at the end of '83. I was going to go with them but by this time had watched footage of a college gig that had been shown on BBC2, which I'd recorded, and I inexplicably decided I didn't like the songs! I didn't go and to this day I regret it. They said the gig was fantastic, so I started re-watching the college gig. After about three viewings I'd decided I'd made a big mistake. I loved 'Still Ill' and 'This Night Has Opened My Eyes' especially.

I bought the 12 inch of 'This Charming Man' and played the B-side to death. I still rate 'Accept Yourself' as one of the best songs anyone's ever written. I think the other track was 'Wonderful Woman', one of those beautiful melancholy Smiths ballads.

I bought the debut album as soon as it came out and loved it. It's still in my all-time top ten 35 years later. I did the sensible thing and bought a ticket for the gig at the Free Trade Hall in early '84 with Kev. We were quite near the front and what really struck me was the near-hysteria of the crowd; I went to a lot of gigs but I hadn't seen anything like this - people breathlessly climbing over the seats to get to the front. I sang pretty much every word along with Morrissey, except when they played 'Barbarism Begins at Home'. This must have been a full year before *Meat Is Murder* came out. It's not my favourite song by a long way, but hearing it that first time I was really impressed that they were doing something so different from the first album. It was pretty funky and lithe. The fact that they were progressing so soon after they'd appeared made me respect them even more.

I had the album on rotation all summer, I still get goose bumps when I think of 'I Don't Owe You Anything' playing on those long summer days. Me, Kev and several other mates were on the dole and hearing Morrissey endorsing us being out of work, in those songs, was vindicating in an amusing kind of way. That year was just a succession of better and better moments - 'Heaven Knows I'm Miserable Now', and then 'William, It Was Really Nothing', which I absolutely went mad for. Taping the John Peel sessions and then *Hatful of Hollow* - brilliant.

I couldn't wait for *Meat is Murder* to be released, but when I heard it I was a little underwhelmed. I still think it's one of those 'difficult' second albums. But I loved the humour in the lyrics, 'I'd like to drop my trousers to the Queen…' etc. Morrissey was very Marmite. Everyone I knew either loved or hated him, with no in between. I loved the fact that he was so different, outspoken and pretentious but in a likeable, funny way. He was the only person who had the nerve to slag off the Band Aid single - a very edgy thing to do; I wasn't sure whether I agreed with him but I greatly admired his attitude. We were fascinated by his campness, the way he sang those 'la-di-da-di-dahs' in between the lyrics in the songs.

I WAS THERE, JEREMY KIDD, RED GUITARS VOCALIST

Highlights for me include the Sandie Shaw shows, particularly the Manchester Free Trade Hall one which, if I remember correctly, was The Smiths' first home town gig since their debut on *Top of the Pops*. The band were on great form and all the kids in the stalls went wild and then Sandie Shaw came on and the older folks in the balcony seats, many of whom were chaperoning sons and daughters who were considered too young to go on their own, went wild. It was brilliant, especially because Johnny Marr moved from his usual position stage left to stand next to Andy Rourke stage right. It was a simple gesture that demonstrated a grasp of rock choreography worthy of The Shadows.

I WAS THERE: STEVE MARLAND

I was walking along Underbank in Stockport when I saw a small poster in the Crazy Face clothes shop for a new single by The Smiths, 'This Charming Man'. The shop and brand were owned by Joe Moss who also managed the band. Days later I read a gushing review of the single in the *NME* written by local Reddish lad Paul Morley. I bought the seven inch and later the 12 inch remix from the Virgin shop in Merseyway. The drive of the guitar and rhythm section along with Morrisey's unlikely yelp and yaw seemed quite remarkable . In my modest way I became a fan, buying subsequent singles in their evocative picture sleeves - chucking at the wilfully sly and diverse cultural references.

Rough Trade publicity photo of Johnny Marr by Eric Watson

I was eager to see them live and bought tickets for the Free Trade Hall show. I turned up and sat in the side balcony to the band's right. We all had a clear elevated view - Nia Jones, my gal, and art school pals Josephine Drazek and Steve Jordan. First up were Sheffield's Red Guitars – I still love their tune 'Steeltown'.

The Smiths took the stage to a walk on tune of 'Johnny Remember Me' (my pal). A hometown crowd were well up for a good night and The Smiths sound and presence met all expectations, I was entranced by Marr's guitar and that hi-life, McGuinn, Jansch jangle that made the night come alive. Two thirds in and they were joined by Sandie Shaw for a divine rendition of 'I Don't Owe You Anything', much to Nia's delight as she had bought a copy of Sandie's 'Hand In Glove'. The ticket cost £3.50. I later sold it on eBay for £75!

I now own none of their recordings. I sold all the records for a pound a pop during one of many cash poor life experiences. And I never listen to the tunes, although Mr Marr is a benefactor of The Manchester Modernists, for whom I work.

I WAS THERE: KARREN ABLAZE, FANZINE EDITOR

There are many differing opinions on The Smiths gig at the Free Trade Hall. I had some very enthusiastic reviews of the event.

I watched the beginning of the set, but after a while I wandered over to a distressed Smiths fan who told me, in the comparative peace of the foyer, tales of fans passing out and new chairs being destroyed in the hysteria. Apparently messages had been sent to the group after the second song, asking them to stop playing for a while so that the people who were injured, squashed or passing out could be helped.

Between us we scrawled a note to Morrissey, mentioning the possibility of an interview next time he is in Manchester ('remember Manchester?') and also suggesting that he might have been able to prevent some of the damage at the gig. He handed the letter to a girl selling t-shirts and a few days later I received a reply:

Dear Karen,

I was obviously annoyed by your letter.

It seems that whenever things go wrong at concerts people always blame the group. Nobody told me about your fanzine at the ORS (Oxford Road Show), so exactly what am I supposed to do?

Please don't give me the 'remember Manchester' nonsense; not one living soul in Manchester ever helped The Smiths in our early days – our glorious radio stations, local press, music/media people, people from local record companies. Anything we have achieved we have absolutely earned, and we quite literally do not owe anyone anything.

I will always speak to fanzines whenever they care to speak to me. But you are obviously entirely unaware of our true natures and ideals otherwise you would clearly realise that I would have halted any crowd unpleasantness had I been aware of it. We have sensitive people whose job it is to help people out of the crowd should they need it. Frankly, I do not care about the chairs at the Free Trade hall. Being criminally non-sighted, I can see no further than 10 inches in front of me. I do not ever recognise individuals in an audience.

I do not want an interview with your fanzine because you obviously don't seriously care about me or The Smiths. I don't enjoy being cross-examined; there are OTHER people to condemn, Karen… aren't there? Haven't we done any GOOD things??

Sadly – Morrissey.

I WAS THERE: THOMAS JONES

The Smiths were in full swing by now. The album had been released, and this had the air of a triumphant home town return. The flowers were mostly gone now - although four daffodil-toting boys from Crewe hadn't got that particular memo - but the Free Trade Hall was about to have the night of its life in which the seats would be literally ripped out of the wooden floor. (We stood on top of a mangled wreck of row K at the end of the gig). The Red Guitars put in a blistering set too, one of the best support band slots I've ever seen.

Johnny had moved on from the Rickenbacker and was sporting the Cherry Red Gibson ES-355 with its squashy, fat tones, which starred on the new songs, most memorably 'Girl Afraid' which seemed to be an instrumental until Morrissey finally chimed in and - track of the night – 'Barbarism', complete with Morrissey and

Johnny dancing in a duet masterclass of the 'not-quite-falling-over-dance' that was espoused and copied by a million gawky Eighties teenagers.

Sandie Shaw guested on a delicious 'I Don't Owe You Anything'. The new stuff wasn't to everyone's taste though; some frustrated old fans heckled, 'Play something off the album' when they tried out the prototype *Meat Is Murder* songs. But yes. We ripped the seats out of the floor. I remember thinking that it should be headline news. Sod the Pistols. I was there when The Smiths played.

FREE TRADE HALL
Peter Street, Manchester
Tuesday 13 March 1984 7:30 pm
OUTLAW presents
THE SMITHS
plus Supporting Attraction
SIDE CIRCLE
£3.50 (inc. VAT) C33
No ticket exchanged nor money refunded

Kev Jones copied a colleague's ticket to gain entry to the Free Trade Hall

I WAS THERE: KEV JONES

I saw them on *Top of the Pops* doing 'This Charming Man' and Morrissey swinging the gladioli over his head. *Top of the Pops* was a religious thing on a Thursday night. Sometimes it was the only chance you got to see pop stars apart from in photographs. My dad was sat there saying, 'What the bloody hell is this?' but I thought, 'These are something special. These are great.' It was when 'What Differences Does it Make?' came out that I thought, 'Crikey, these are really good', and I went out and bought that and 'This Charming Man' and 'Hand in Glove' and anything I could get my hands on.

I found out they were playing at the Free Trade Hall but it was sold out - I was gutted. I was living in Failsworth in Manchester at the time. I'd started working for an advertising agency and a guy at work had tickets for the gig. As an advertising agency we had one of the very first laser photocopiers. I was so desperate to go I thought, 'I could try copying this ticket.' We went to the print production department where they had loads of different sorts of paper samples, found a paper almost identical to the paper that the ticket was printed on and copied the ticket. You could tell it was different but it looked pretty good. I thought, 'I'm going to have to chance this.' So we cut it out and put the perfs in it.

I went with a school friend. It was all seated and we were thinking, 'What are we going to do when we get in there?' because we had my work colleague's ticket so we obviously couldn't use his seat. We thought, 'We can't do this. Let's go and see if we can buy a ticket off a tout.' So I went and asked a tout and they said, 'Oh, I can sell you two tickets for £15.' £15 was a lot of money in those days - face value was only £3.50. In the end we thought, 'We'll just chance it.'

In those days, gigs were different. There was a mass of people there just trying to get in at the door and all that was on the door were these two old boys in dinner suits and dickie bows, trying to stem the tide of people coming in and ripping tickets. I remember there being a bit scrum of people trying to get through the door. I handed my ticket over and this old boy took the ticket, ripped it and we were straight in. And I thought, 'Oh wow, we've done it.' And then the second problem that I was thinking about was, 'Where am I going to sit?'

This was the first proper gig that I'd actually been to, if you don't count going to see Gene Pitney with my mum a couple of years earlier. And of course that wasn't a problem at all, because once we were actually in there it was absolute chaos. Nobody sat on the seats. People were stood on the seats and everybody ran down to the front. The ushers inside were trying to keep control but they couldn't. It was just absolutely wild.

There was something special about the connection between the band and that audience. I can vividly remember being stood on a seat and thinking, 'This is amazing.' The atmosphere was incredible. I remember Morrissey coming dancing on with the biggest bunch of gladioli in his back pocket.

UNIVERSITY OF HULL

15 MARCH 1984, HULL, UK

I WAS THERE: SEAN BRYANT

Sean Bryant saw The Smiths at Hull Uni

The Smiths had been scheduled to play at Dingwalls in Hull the previous August but the gig was actually cancelled for some reason so didn't go ahead, and then a couple of weeks later Dingwalls burnt down. I first saw them performing 'This Charming Man' on *Top of the Pops* in 1983. I didn't really like the song but was taken aback by the look of the band, in particular Morrissey who was wearing glasses and a hearing aid. I had been floundering on the tail end of the punk scene, having been a punk since 1978. But punk had become a 'fashion', something it was never supposed to be, and I must have been looking for another scene but with the same ideas. Then The Smiths were back on *Top of the Pops* with ' What Difference Does it Make?' I was hooked. I loved that song and still do.

I *had* to see them live; this song sounded fantastic and the band looked great. I was unemployed so didn't have the money to travel to other cities to see them. However, around December '83 they announced they would be playing at Hull University - wow, fantastic! My then girlfriend said she'd buy me tickets for my birthday. My younger brother had also been impressed when he'd seen them live on *The Tube*, so off my girlfriend and I went on our bikes to Hull Uni and bought four tickets.

I can't remember how we got to the gig on the night as none of us drove and Uni wasn't on a bus route from where we lived; we didn't want to be uncool and arrive on bikes! We had to be signed in as we weren't students and this seemed to take an age, as we didn't know anyone. When we finally got in, I vaguely remember two guys in the Refectory performing an acoustic set. It turned out it was Paul Heaton and Stan Cullimore of The Housemartins.

The venue mainly consisted of students, of which there must have been around 400-500, and we felt a little out of place still having spiky hair. The support band, a local group called The Red Guitars, were quite good but then The Smiths came on and - wow, what a performance! I'd bought the first album a month prior to the gig so knew a lot of the songs and chanted along with the students. Morrissey was throwing out gladioli and was still wearing his hearing aid and glasses. They said everything to me; I was unemployed, didn't want a job, was type-1 diabetic, so always ill, and oh so depressed!

It became very trendy to like The Smiths. A bit like punk, the scene was spoiled. I never bought any more Smiths albums and couldn't even watch them on *Top of the Pops*. However, in recent times my son has become a big fan and so I have now embraced the later albums, particularly *The Queen Is Dead*, which some people think is their best album. But still, for me, the first album will always be their best, for 'Reel A round the Fountain' alone. I have seen Morrissey solo a few times, and Johnny Marr, but nothing compares to the excitement of seeing The Smiths on their first tour.

I WAS THERE: NICK SPENCE

Back in my hometown of Hull, I vaguely knew Tracey Thorn and Ben Watt, better known as Everything But The Girl, named after a local shop sign. Both studied at the University of Hull and lived nearby. One morning I bumped into Ben in the basement of Sydney Scarborough, one of the few record shops in Hull. He was raving about The Smiths, just the best thing he had heard in ages. I was sold. The Smiths came to Hull and Ben and Tracey got me tickets. They shared a very Morrissey-esque bedsit in The Avenues area of Hull so I went round to collect them. My then girlfriend was on a school trip that day so missed out but I took her younger sister, as you do.

It's one of the few gigs from the Eighties I still vividly recall as being so close to the stage I could literally reach out and touch Morrissey. I did. It has to be said that a fair few of the 'fans' present seemed intent on causing trouble. Earlier in the night two student types were throwing beer glasses towards the stage, landing in the crowd at the front. It was scary. What I remember best though is The Smiths, mostly minus Morrissey, dancing around during an extended funky version of 'Barbarism Begins at Home.' Such a great night, such great memories.

I WAS THERE: MALCOLM GREENLEY

I lived through punk - fantastic days - but it fizzled out. It seemed to last longer back in the day and it meant so much. After that, I was into The Jam and all those other bands and then waiting around for something to get passionate about. It was the Peel Sessions - about 20 songs, a lot of them comprised of B-sides, a couple of the singles - just before the first album came out that got me hooked.

It was 1983 and I was 21 or 22 when a friend brought round a cassette of the first John Peel session, which he had recorded off the radio. They did four sessions for Peel and a lot ended up on *Hatful of Hollow*. That cassette, and my friend discovering them for me, kicked it off and changed my life. The melodies were what got me first of all. Johnny Marr's guitar was just like a breath of fresh air, and then you got to dig around with the lyrics and thinking, 'These are pretty strange', so I was drawn in.

And then I was just dying to see them live, and I consider myself to be very lucky. The first time I saw them was at Hull University (I'm from Hull). The first album had just come out about a month or so before and this was the first nationwide headlining tour, to promote the first album. They were just so tight and Johnny Marr's guitar live was just a machine of melody. That's the cheesiest way I can think to describe it. And I think it's always best to see a band just as it's about to break really big, which they were at that time.

Hull Uni was about 500, 600 capacity and it was one of those basement rooms so there wasn't an awful lot of air conditioning. It was absolutely boiling considering it was March. By the end of the night, all the windows were open to let some air in. It was jam packed. There were just beginning to get a real cult audience so it was a passionate atmosphere. I've read online that there were a few hecklers there but I don't remember that. The audience were pretty much my sort of age and in their early 20s, and - strangely – mainly male. There were a lot of women there but generally all of the five Smiths gigs I went to had a predominantly male audience.

I WAS THERE: CAT WEATHERILL

I was in my second year at Hull University. Morrissey threw daffodils into the audience. I say this because I caught one and photographed it lying on top of the poster.

CITY HALL

19 MARCH 1984, SHEFFIELD, UK

I WAS THERE: JONATHAN JORDAN

My group of pals were an odd mix of goths, rockers, punks and New Romantics. We watched every band that came through South Yorkshire. That week we had seen Spear of Destiny, the guitar player that had just left Whitesnake and The Pogues. The Smiths had a good buzz, had been on *Top of the Pops* and were playing our favourite venue, Sheffield City Hall - usual venue of choice for Thin Lizzy, AC/DC and the Halle Orchestra. We bought tickets on the door for less than £5 and found ourselves in the balcony, empty but for us. The venue was half full and totally the wrong place for The Smiths. We tried to dance and 'get into it', but it wasn't happening for us. Even the fans in our group concluded it wasn't a great night, and we ended up in the pub next door before the encores. Young people are amazed and impressed that I have seen The Smiths, but frankly it was a really forgettable gig!

Jonathan Jordan (centre) left before the end of a 'forgettable' gig

TOWER BALLROOM

20 MARCH 1984, EDGBASTON, BIRMINGHAM, UK

I WAS THERE: KEVIN INMAN, AGE 25

This was not your usual venue but it was very interesting. I went with my girlfriend Heather, now my wife. The Smiths came on stage at 9pm. They did stuff from the first album. There were many stage invasions which I thought was irritating but most of the gig was played with people jumping on the stage. I was old for a Smiths fan at 25. We have seen Morrissey many times over the years but sadly only got to see The Smiths the once.

I WAS THERE: SIMON WELLS

Memory is, of course, a liar. But here goes.

The first time I saw The Smiths was at the Tower Ballroom in Birmingham. The first album had just been released and both me and my sixth form friend, Ian Tonks, were passionately in love with the whole group, but Morrissey especially. It was an obsession. They were our band in a way that you lose

Simon Wells saw The Smiths at Birmingham's Tower Ballroom

later in life but is - or was - a defining part of being a teenager. We probably outfitted ourselves in an approximation of how they dressed although I am little hazy on that point. Putting together a look was not one of our talents.

The Tower didn't host many gigs but was a pretty good venue with lots of space and big plastic palm trees, which we loved. It seemed kind of fitting, as gladioli-throwing was still a part of The Smiths live experience and I certainly took a bunch along. The band were fantastic, living in a moment of realisation where they knew they were going to be not just good and popular but important. Maybe even very important.

It's not a feeling I've had at gigs often but there was a sensation of riding a wave. Not just that this was great music but that it was sweeping away some of the horrible machismo that seemed part of becoming an adult in the early Eighties. Thatcherism was in full flow and it was easy to feel as though you were living in claustrophobic, deadening times. Here, the boundaries and the possibilities of everyone there seemed to open up. It felt like a blossoming.

I WAS THERE: BRYAN FARLEY

When they released 'What Difference Does It Make?' the year after we'd booked them at the Fighting Cocks they were big news. They were going on a nationwide tour which was primarily university student unions and because I'd maintained a reasonable relationship with the booking guy contact I had made at Rough Trade, he phoned me up and said, 'They're looking to do a gig in Birmingham. Would you be interested in doing it?' I said, 'Yes, of course,' because I'd liked them from the get-go and now they were becoming the band of the moment.

So we searched around for a venue and found one called the Tower Ballroom in Edgbaston, an old fashioned dancing venue situated on the edge of this inner city reservoir. It was used for things like tea dances and bingo but we just saw it as a glorious place to put a band on because nobody had done it there before. It had a capacity somewhere in excess of 1,000, and we thought, 'We can do well here.'

At the time 'What Difference Does It Make?' was right up there in the charts, which helped enormously because it all fitted together timing-wise. Morrissey was doing that falsetto and it had a really good guitar riff, with Johnny Marr excelling himself. It was right up there at the top when we put them on, so we got lucky.

We did it all ourselves. We printed the posters ourselves. We advertised it ourselves. We even silkscreen printed the tickets - which I think were £4. And we sold them all. We could have sold them five times over such was the demand. And then something happened. There was an illness and they had to postpone it, so the original poster shows a date of February the something or other but they actually played about two or three weeks later because of the postponement.

We did all right out of it financially. We'd been losing money here and there over the previous two or three years, putting on these no-hopers in the Fighting Cocks, so it had been a real labour of love. But at the Tower Ballroom we had The Red Guitars supporting them and we had a fantastic night. It was absolutely packed out. We had people trying to get in. The promoter was happy – he sold shitloads of booze – everyone was happy. We packed it in then. We both had proper jobs. Clive was a senior teacher and I was a retail manager and I had a young family.

After the UK tour, the band took a short break from the road before embarking on a selection of European and Irish dates.

DEMEERVAART VINYL PARTY

21 APRIL 1984, AMSTERDAM, THE NETHERLANDS

I WAS THERE: ANNE DE BRETAGNE, AGE 16

I saw a Smiths concert in Amsterdam. My brother lived there. I was a fan of The Cure amongst others. My brother was 22. He introduced me to The Clash. And to The Smiths!

BREEKEND FESTIVAL

22 APRIL 1984, BREE, BELGIUM

I WAS THERE: WALTER SMEETS, AGE 18

The Smiths played at the Breekend Festival in Bree, Belgium. I didn't know them very well as I was more into garage rock and punk bands. But some of my friends told me they were the next big thing. From the moment they came on stage and started the gig, I knew this was an awesome band. Good songs, a solid guitar sound from Marr and a weird guy with a bunch of flowers in his back pocket and a pair of glasses but with an extremely good voice and loads of charisma. From the first minute the crowd was totally into it.

I started buying the Smiths albums, played them always in my time as a deejay and I'm sure that this unique live performance had changed my way of looking at music in general. It changed my life. It probably made me a better person too.

ULSTER HALL

17 MAY 1984, BELFAST, UK

I WAS THERE: BROMLEY BOW, AGE 18

I was a bit of a diehard so got there early and secured a stage front position. They didn't disappoint live, tight as, not a lot of interaction but just brilliant! And, yeah, he had the gladioli! I went with a friend, Anthony, who played guitar in a band I was in. I played drums. We never made it but we had a blast and got the girls! There was a deejay on RTÉ 2, Dave Fanning, who started playing The Smiths along with all the other cool Eighties bands - James, New Order, etc. - on a Sunday night. The first love of my life bought me their first album and I still treasure it.

I WAS THERE: DAMIEN MAGUIRE

I saw The Smiths twice in Belfast, at the Ulster Hall and then at Whitla Hall in 1986. I don't remember much about Whitla Hall but remember very clearly the Ulster Hall gig. They opened with 'Please, Please, Please…' before going into 'William, It Was Really Nothing'. My cousin got in on the sound check, spoke to the band and got his photograph taken with all of them. He still brags about it.

I WAS THERE: DAMEON PRIESTLY, AGE 18

Dameon Priestley saw The Smiths at the Ulster Hall

A girl I knew called Anne taped her copy of the album for me. I still have that cassette. They instantly struck a chord with me. Their angst and sound, their stories and imagery, resonated with my 17 year old state of mind. The bleak pictures painted of Manchester life and seaside towns, along with darkly humorous lyrics, were perfect for those teens in Belfast who were of a similar mindset. I was also a huge James Dean fan. When I found out Morrissey was too and had written a book, *James Dean Is Not Dead*, I went out and bought a copy. I still have it. It prompted me, five years later, to write my degree thesis on Dean.

Growing up during the Troubles in Belfast meant that we were starved of bands playing for years. So when they came they always received the most enthusiastic of reactions. The 'melancholy fan' label normally associated with The Smiths was not in evidence at that concert. That's for sure.

I went to the gig with a girl called Julie Mills. We met at her house first and filled up on cans of Fosters (hey, it was the Eighties!) We got to the Ulster Hall early enough to see the instantly forgettable Frank Chickens, an odd Japanese pop band. Our tickets were for the balcony but we stayed downstairs and pushed our way to the front.

I bought a bunch of white lilies from the florist at the City Hall to show my allegiance. They lasted about 30 seconds into the first song. I danced, pogoed and sang all the way through. His voice was our voice. My mates were all 23 to 25 years of age. They'd had their time in the sun with the Pistols, The Clash and the rest. I loved all of those bands but this was our time. I remember leaving the concert and getting a lift home from Julie's mum, (we'd missed the last bus). When The Smiths returned in November of the same year I was at the front of the queue. Reel around the fountain.

SFX CENTRE

18 MAY 1984, DUBLIN, IRELAND

I WAS THERE: NIAMH BARRETT, AGE 13

My first gig ever - whopper, right? Gladioli and dancing or, rather, writhing on the ground. Pure Morrissey magic. At 13, I was in heaven.

I WAS THERE: PAUL LITTLE

I saw The Smiths a few times in Dublin in the Eighties. They were absolutely brilliant live and Johnny Marr and Morrissey were amazing onstage. The first time, I went with my mate Giuseppe Roe. We were 14 or 15 and big into the sounds of the day - U2, Simple Minds, Big Country, etc. I have great memories of Morrissey jumping around the stage in the SFX Hall. It's the same venue and stage Bono jumped off in the 'Pride (In the Name of Love)' video.

I WAS THERE: JOE KELLY, AGE 16

Joe Kelly does his best Morrissey impression

I first heard about The Smiths in the summer of 1983 when my friend and neighbour Rob told me about a great new band his older brother had heard on the radio. It was The Smiths first session for *The John Peel Show* on BBC Radio 1 which he'd recorded on a cassette tape. The house I grew up in in Dublin was filled with music. An English uncle brought us Beatles and Elvis records and my three older sisters were buying classic albums from the Sixties and Seventies. Music radio and the weekly *Top of the Pops* show were staples. Aged 15, I was changing from a bowl-haircut chart fan into an angsty adolescent with a jar of hair-gel, and my musical tastes were changing from Top 40 pop to something with more of an edge. The Lotus Eaters' 'The First Picture of You' single released that year was probably a kick-starter for me, and hearing The Smiths' session that same summer cemented my love for this alternative type of music. When the summer ended, another Smiths John Peel session was broadcast and recorded by Rob's brother. I worked out how to connect a ghetto blaster to our hi-fi system at home to make a tape-to-tape copy of the sessions for myself and super-indulge in listening to it.

Other bands that caught my ear soon after that were The Cure, Echo and The Bunnymen, Joy Division, New Order and Cocteau Twins. Of course they were well established bands with a back catalogue to explore, whereas The Smiths were new and now and an immediate bond was established. Their record releases were just starting, so there was very little material available yet.

Sometime later one of The Smiths' concerts - from Derby - was broadcast on television by the BBC and I was enthralled watching it. When it was subsequently re-broadcast I watched it in Rob's house because they had a black and white portable TV with a headphone socket and I was able to connect a cassette-recorder to the TV to record the sound.

My mother was originally from Southend-on-Sea in England. In February 1984 she was going there for her nephew's wedding so I asked her to get me the just-released *The Smiths* album and the 12 inch singles of 'This Charming Man' and 'What Difference Does It Make?' I was sufficiently unseasoned at that stage to go into Dublin city centre to look for them myself. To my endless delight, my mother returned from Britain with all three records. However, the 'This Charming Man' one was the Francois Kevorkian remix version and the 'What Difference...' 12 inch was the alternate one with Morrissey on the sleeve in place of Terence Stamp. I'd inadvertently stepped into the world of rarities at a tender age. I devoured all three records, and those formative months began my tendency to avidly read the covers and inner sleeves front-to-back while the record was playing, and getting to know every aspect of the record - personnel, lyrics, recording studio and so on.

Joe Kelly's complete set of Smiths autographs

Those records and several subsequent Smiths records were bought in The Golden Disc record shop in Southend, which several years later would be featured in the video for Morrissey's 'Everyday is Like Sunday' single.

In early 1984, I didn't know how or where to buy a Smiths t-shirt, so I decided to create my own. I bought a plain red t-shirt in a Dublin shop and went straight to a place in the ILAC Centre that would iron letters onto garments. I got 'THE SMITHS' pressed onto the t-shirt with a bubbly font in a curved formation. It doesn't look very rock 'n' roll now, but I knew no better back then. How proudly I wore the shirt that bore the name of my favourite band.

Around that time it was announced that The Smiths would be playing a concert in Dublin. The venue was to be the Saint Francis Xavier Centre, a local community hall in the north inner city which was regularly used for rock concerts, and known by gig promoters as the SFX Concert Hall. I was so excited and astonished that my favourite band was going to be playing in my city. I'd never been to a concert before and my parents agreed to let me go. Rob was going too. My eldest sister must have got the tickets. She was a university student and had been to some concerts already. She was a trail-blazer in my world. Being a community hall there was no bar there and no alcohol was sold, so there were no age restrictions, and therefore no issues with the 16 year old me and my 15 year old friend attending the concert.

The day of the concert I was so excited, and after school was counting down the clock. My dad drove myself and Rob the four miles to the city centre and dropped us off on Gardiner Street around the corner from the venue on Sherrard Street. He was to pick us up from there afterwards. The hubbub of the people outside the hall increased my excitement. The guy on the door took our tickets and ripped off the stubs and gave us back the rest to keep, and we walked into what was the foyer. We passed through a set of double doors into the venue proper, taking off our jackets and tying them around our waists, me proudly displaying my red Smiths t-shirt. The long rectangular room was already quite full when we got in and we stayed near the back initially. There was a small balcony above us, the middle bit was covered in and on the left and right sides of the balcony there was just enough room for a small amount of people to stand. I could see a couple of photographers up there. The room had a classic look of a community hall, with the high stage not filling the full width of the room to allow for a door either side at floor level.

Shortly after our arrival a man with a voluminous beard walked onto the stage with an acoustic guitar and proceeded to play some songs. I don't remember his name but the music did nothing for me: I was an indie kid now and this didn't fit the bill. I remember thinking that this was the first band I was watching at my first ever concert and it was a let down. After a break there was a second support: The Frank Chickens. I'd taped some of their stuff off the John Peel show so my mood immediately perked up. They were quirky and fun and their set included the couple of songs I knew. Rob and myself were still towards the back of the room, a little hesitant to move into the thickening throng in front of us.

A half an hour after The Frank Chickens finished, The Smiths walked onto the stage. The place went crazy as they started into 'Hand in Glove'. I was immediately spellbound. Nearly a year of fandom - a lifetime for a 16 year old - was suddenly brought from written word, taped broadcasts and circular vinyl to living, breathing, heaving reality with tumultuous thunder - brought to life before my eyes and ears. The crowd arced into a mosh pit at the front, as if organised, yet it was a beautiful chaos that moved in waves, in and out, towards the stage. We moved closer to the front, to the edge of the melée, to get a closer view of the band, and to attempt to dance ourselves. From the TV appearances and photos I'd seen, Morrissey often had flowers in his back pocket but here he seemed to have a whole branch of a tree coming out of his jeans, Johnny with his head flicks to arrange his fringe, Andy with his hefty bass and the high stage meaning Mike was half-hidden behind the drums. The voice, the words, and the odd dancing, the guitar riffs, the thumbing bass and the driving drum sounds forged into mesmerising music that captivated me for nearly an hour. I got a chance to catch my breath as the band left the stage after the main set, and there was that sense of wonder as to what would happen next. They came back onstage to an uproarious reception for an encore that included a reprise of 'Hand in Glove'. And then it was suddenly over.

As the band walked off the stage the lights came on in the hall and the curtains were drawn across the stage. People started heading to the exits at the back and the room emptied quite quickly. But my dad wasn't due to pick us up for another half hour, so we waited in the hall rather than hang around outside. The few stragglers remaining started to line up at the door to the right of the stage, and when we saw the door open, we joined the queue. Within a couple of minutes we were backstage in a small room. The whole band were right there before our eyes. Morrissey was to the left talking to a guy in a wheelchair, while Johnny, Mike and Andy were standing around a small table in front of us. A shiver of excitement ran through me. We saw them signing people's tickets so we approached and handed them our tickets as I tried to think of something to say. As they signed the tickets Johnny complimented me on my red t-shirt and Mike wrote 'Like the t-shirt' as he signed. There were a load of flyers around the floor for a student end-of-exam night out in a nearby hotel. I hastily reckoned that my ticket would be going into my scrapbook so I'd need a second set of autographs to stick in there too, so I picked up one of the flyers and asked them to sign the blank back of that also. We then approached Morrissey, but he was still engrossed in conversation with the guy in the wheelchair and we didn't want to interrupt - well, not too much! We wouldn't have known what to say anyway, so we held out our autographed bits of paper and he duly reached out and signed them for us.

We walked back into the main hall stunned by what had just happened. The merchandise stall at the back was being put away so I ran down and bought a 'This Charming Man' poster for 50p. We went outside a few minutes later and my dad was waiting there in his trusty Volkswagen Beetle. My passion for The Smiths only increased from then on and I obsessively bought every record as soon as I could, usually on the day of release, cycling into town or getting the bus and negotiating a journey home that wouldn't damage the precious cargo. That first concert experience had a profound effect on my life, cementing my love for music and live performance. I've been an avid gig-goer ever since, though alas, the hair-gel is no longer required.

I WAS THERE: SEAMUS DUGGAN

I first saw The Smiths on *Top of the Pops* performing 'This Charming Man' and the next morning I bought the 12 inch. It immediately felt like one of those seismic events. The cooler (and older) kids might have had 'Hand in Glove', and even seen them play the Freshers' Ball in the JCR in Trinity the year before, but for most of us this was going to be the first chance to see The Smiths.

The crowd was one of the most mixed I had ever seen, with other dark-clad Bunnymen fans like myself, ageing hippies, slightly less ageing punks and other, less defined groups of people. But many, many had flowers in their hair or pockets or hands. Indeed gardens on the routes to the SFX had been stripped of all sorts of plant life. A Smiths crowd were not a gardener's best friend.

It was a celebration. Marr seemed like a member of a Sixties band in shades and Byrds fringe but Morrissey was Morrissey, in maternity shirt and with a bouquet in his back pocket. At one point Morrissey threw his shirt into the audience. My friend caught it but by the time he landed all that was left was a sleeve, which I had for years before it disappeared.

SAVOY

20 MAY 1984, CORK, IRELAND

I WAS THERE: COLM O'CALLAGHAN

It was shortly after midnight, early on Wednesday morning, July 29th, 1987, and it was Mark Cagney, host of *The Night Train* on RTÉ Radio 2FM who, as serenely as ever, broke the news. Home alone, and with the rest of my family off on holidays, I'd been in the habit of keeping the radio on longer and louder than usual - long enough, as it happened, to hear Cagney tell the nation's more urbane taxi drivers, shift workers and anoraks that Johnny Marr had left The Smiths. And he more or less left it at that, light on detail, didn't cite his sources and segued as seamlessly as he always did into his next track, which was more than likely a moderately left field, highly-styled album cut, to which he was forever drawn. And, if I slept at all that night, I slept with my mouth open and my jaw hanging.

Cagney had one up on us. He'd either heard soundings of or had sight of that week's issue of the London-based music magazine, *New Musical Express*, in which one of its senior writers, Danny Kelly, citing reliable sources in Manchester, revealed that Morrissey, The Smiths' singer and Marr, the group's guitarist and co-writer, had fallen out and hadn't spoken in months. But while it was a terrific flyer, the story was vague enough on the future of the band and Kelly later admitted he may have 'augmented' his story with lines pulled from the back of his own head. The gut of the scoop was clear, though - on the cusp of the release of their fourth album, all was not well with The Smiths. And this time it was serious.

Although the influential British music weeklies – *NME, Melody Maker* and *Sounds* – all regularly hit the streets around central London by lunchtime on Tuesdays, it was usually Thursday morning or later before those titles were available on the shelves in Easons, on Patrick Street in Cork, where I routinely picked up mine. And so I had an anxious wait before I finally got my hands on *NME*'s speculative exclusive, headlined 'Smiths to split'.

History – and Johnny Rogan, the band's forensic biographer – now tells us that, although The Smiths weren't formally taken off of life-support by Morrissey until mid-September 1987, Marr confirmed directly to Kelly within days of his initial splash that yes, he'd left the group he founded in Manchester barely five years previously. And so, in its issue dated August 8th, 1987, Kelly had his second back-to-back Smiths scoop, this time flush with quotes from inside the band.

For six weeks that summer, my first as a university student, would-be music writer, part-time laundry worker and full-time dreamer, there was really only one story. One which, under sustained scrutiny, was scarcely believable in the first instance and which was always likely to end badly - few groups have, I think, fallen asunder as carelessly and as needlessly as The Smiths, undone in the end by the lack of clear decision-making and delegation that had, since the group's inception, characterised much of its off-stage activity.

The Smiths were the first band I so obsessively lived through and the first band I ever felt like I had shares in. I certainly spent enough on them and, because I'd invested so heavily in them in other respects as well, I tended to defer to Max Boyce's stock punchline when it came to analysing them - I know because I was there.

And I certainly was there, if not at the very start, then certainly close enough to it, having had my head turned as soon as I heard The Smiths on both Dave Fanning's Rock Show on RTÉ Radio 2, John Peel's BBC equivalent and, bizarrely, having caught sight of them on late night television performing 'This Charming Man' on a one-off European music initiative featuring emerging music from across the continent. Captured alongside a feeble, long-lost British outfit, The Immaculate Fools, and a number of freakish cross-continental acts trying, as can often be the case, just a tad too hard, The Smiths stood out as a distinctive star turn simply because, in the abject normality that defined every single aspect of them, they were clearly anything but normal.

I was there too in the old Savoy on Patrick Street when The Smiths played in Cork twice, on May 20th and November 18th, 1984 and when, within actual touching distance of them, they sealed the deal, almost face-to-face, as the most important and influential band of my generation.

Both of those shows took place as I was gearing up to leave secondary school and, with half an eye and two working ears on what was around the corner, fancied myself as a veteran of the local music circuit, having already been to all of one indoor live show and a couple of random outdoor events. But although I'd been squirreling and collecting for a number of years, back-filling the gaps in my developing ELO library, acquiring and swapping new material as regularly as I could and rowing in squarely behind Sindikat, a band from our school who'd done the unthinkable and formed under our noses, The Smiths were the first group whose releases, always flagged well in advance in the music press, I regarded as genuine events and to which I counted down.

And in this respect, the radio was another vital spoke - Peel, and his long-time producer, John Walters, memorably hosted four separate Smiths radio sessions between 1983 and 1986 and, like Fanning, would play all of the group's releases well in advance of their availability in the shops. For which you'd have a second or third-hand cassette on eternal stand-by in the old three-in-one in case either of them dropped an unexpected pre-issue, without warning.

It was Fanning, of course, who alerted us to those first Smiths shows in Ireland – I still consider this sort of carry-on to define the term 'public service broadcasting' – when he announced that they were on their way to play dates in Belfast, Dublin and Cork in support of their debut album. And yet for all of the urgency that under-pinned the band's recorded material, myself and my friend, Philip, didn't really know what to expect when we fetched up outside The Savoy on a Sunday evening in May, 1984, in our long rain-coats, tickets in hand and mad for road.

But from early - and we were there very, very early – it was clear that The Smiths were much more than a little-known secret shared by a handful of us up on the northside.

One of the more interesting aspects of the band's history was how, throughout its career, it attracted fans from right across the social strata, much of it male-skewing and with a prominent contingent of hard shams in among the more introspective, centrally-cast indie-kids. Among whom was another friend of mine, Marc Buckley, another acolyte who arrived at The Savoy, as did numerous others, clutching a bunch of freshly cut flowers and wearing a considerable quiff.

Philip and myself soon found ourselves chatting to a pair of friendly girls we'd met on the tiled stairs and, for whatever reason, we told them we were supporting The Smiths a little later. And there were, of course, numerous similarities between ourselves and The Frank Chickens the gobby Japanese lesbians who were *actually* due to open proceedings.

The Chickens, as with many of Peel's more random curios over the decades, sounded far better in theory that they did in practice and, with their unsteady backing tracks, loops and high-octane, skittish twin vocals, failed to convince the locals, who'd started to assemble in numbers by the time they'd finished a quite bizarre set. They left the stage to the usual heckles and, responding to a not unreasonable suggestion from half-way back that they were, perhaps, not up to championship standard, replied – 'We think you're shit too' – before beating a hasty retreat under a hail of gob, never to be seen in Cork again. A scene we'd witness again, in the same venue and in much the same circumstances, before the year was out.

But once The Smiths took the stage to the jagged, slash-cut opening bars of 'Still Ill', and Morrissey emerged from the shadows, his outsized shirt already opened to the navel, The Frank Chickens had been consigned to the footnotes of what was to become a spectacular history. Over the course of a sharp, frenetic and powerful 16 song set, The Smiths just burned the house down. In the long and diverse history of live shows in Cork, it is easily among one of the most lethal.

Because while that show has remained vivid in the memories of most of those who attended it, many of them left there that night intent on starting their own bands immediately afterwards, boldly going for it and just taking their chances. And those among the audience that were already involved in fledging groups around the city, and there were many, left with plenty of food for thought. If this was where the bar was now set, then what, really, was the point?

But although Morrissey so physically dominated that Cork show - and I couldn't believe how imposing he was, and how he so used his body for emphasis - neither could I get my head around how small and slight Johnny Marr was and how his nimble hands made one guitar sound like three. The songs were already well-known to anyone who'd bought the band's unconvincing debut album, *The Smiths*, and who was familiar with the terrific additional content on their singles. But they also introduced one new number, a protracted, funked-up, bass-prominent beauty called 'Barbarism Begins at Home', during which Morrissey baited the audience with flowers throughout the long instrumental passages and Andy Rourke stepped into the spotlight to reveal just how important his industry and frame of reference was to the band's sound. And we were just learning all of the time.

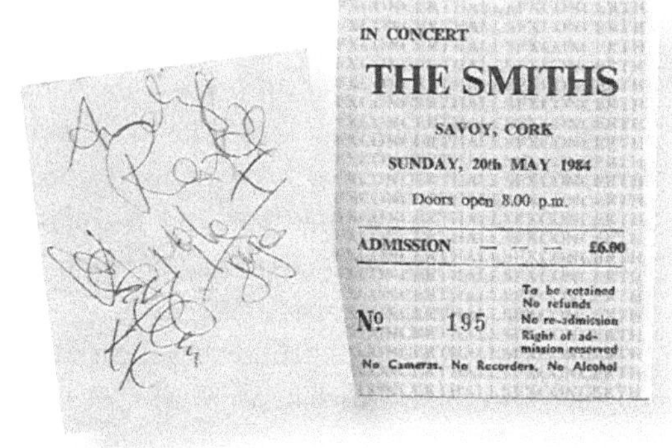

Bernard O'Flynn's ticket for the Savoy and the autographs he got

I WAS THERE: BERNARD O'FLYNN

The Frank Chickens were two oriental girls who were truly dreadful. The Smiths played a stormer, mostly stuff from *The Smiths* album. 'Hand in Glove' is my standout memory. Morrissey wasn't content with a bunch of flowers in his back pocket and came on stage with a large tree branch. He did throw a bouquet to the crowd. A mate of mine caught one flower but was promptly bitten on the wrist by a girl who wanted it.

My mate suggested we go to their hotel, Jurys, after the gig. Personally I thought this was a bit suspect but went along. Morrissey had gone to bed but Mike Joyce and Andy Rourke were chatting to fans. I wound up having a long conversation with Johnny Marr about guitars. He left me with the fact that he would be using a green Telecaster on *Top of the Pops* the following week. He did.

'HEAVEN KNOWS I'M MISERABLE NOW'

RELEASED 21 MAY 1984

One of only two Smiths 45s to reach the UK Top 10, at number 10. 'Heaven Knows I'm Miserable Now' featured famed 1960s football pools winner Viv Nicholson on the picture sleeve. The song seared its way into the public consciousness, forever branding Smiths fans 'miserable'.

GLC JOBS FOR A CHANGE FESTIVAL, JUBILEE GARDENS

10 JUNE 1984, LONDON, UK

I WAS THERE: MARTIN RODDY

The Greater London Council (GLC) Leader Ken Livingstone put on a free gig around the back of the GLC buildings. The same people I walked back with from the Essex Uni gig in February went down to see them. Billy Bragg was the support act and unbelievably The Smiths were the support act to Mari Wilson and The Wilsations! 1984 was one of those 'Which side are you on?' years politically, and living down south I was surrounded by bloody awful Tories (and still am). Ken displayed the unemployment figures (over 3 million) on the roof of the GLC building facing Parliament as a poke in the eye to Thatcher. Attending this gig felt important. The Smiths were an outsider's band but when you were in the crowd it felt like a movement, or a scene that I preferred others not to understand. We left after Mari Wilson's second song. Why wouldn't you?

I WAS THERE: LANCE GILLETT

Someone did a striptease after climbing up the side of a building, stealing Mozzer's limelight.

I WAS THERE: PETER GALE, AGE 19

There was a naked man dancing on a ledge and a lot of the crowd were watching him instead of the band. I also went to see Altered Images before then at Hammersmith Palais and apparently they supported, along with Roman Holiday, but I can't remember them.

I WAS THERE: KAREN KELLY AGE 19

It was a day of celebration in Jubilee Gardens and they played in the evening on the same bill as Mari Wilson and Captain Sensible although he played in another area in the grounds. It was a brilliant day. The Smiths were really good and the crowd loved them. I can't remember the playlist but I knew the tracks at the time and they stole the show.

Karen Kelly saw the free GLC gig

I was more of a UB40 and Style Council fan and didn't realise until many years later how much Morrissey and The Smiths would come to mean to me. After losing my husband 15 years ago, 'You're the One for Me, Fatty' and 'Bigmouth Strikes Again' made me laugh and brought me out of my grief. A few years back I saw the Stone Roses (another grief breaker) and Johnny Marr at Finsbury Park. It was like living my teenage years again, hearing The Smiths' tunes.

I WAS THERE: CHRIS MADDEN

The Smiths were playing in a beautiful setting staged in this courtyard at County Hall. The Redskins were on there as well. I hitched down to see that. I was having a chat with my dad a few years ago and he said, 'You used to just disappear. I knew you were going off to see bands but I didn't realise you were hitchhiking. Otherwise we would have given you the train fare.'

It was guitar music. It was euphoric. The music was perfect for the lyrics and to this day 'The Boy with the Thorn in his Side' is still a record that I go back to. They looked so cool. They were like a mixture of the Beatles and the Stones for our generation. Who else was there who was as culturally significant at that time? They were really, really out there. They looked and sounded unique and stylistically good.

My perception of them is that they were coming from the left field, the ambiguous sexuality. They said it's all right for a young man to be fey and in touch with his feminine side, to be in touch with literature and poetry and art and looking good and using really cultural signifiers. Morrissey's gone from there to now making proclamations about organisations and people who come from those organisations which seem to be diametrically opposed to what he once was. But I'm looking at Morrissey through the prism of what I believe he used to represent. Do we have a right to change our minds? Back in those days, he was carrying a flag for the notion of a type of Britishness, which was very, very nostalgic, very parochial, and perhaps that's where he's stuck at.

I WAS THERE: EVE WENTWORTH

The festival was free. The bill also featured Billy Bragg, The Redskins, Mari Wilson, Misty in Roots and Hank Wangford, who got beaten up by some skinheads that day, as did The Redskins - there were a couple of fairly alarming fights. The sound was surprisingly good for an outdoor gig and the crowd was insane. I remember thinking some guy dancing up on a high ledge was going to fall off and either crack his head on the pavement or get trampled by skinheads.

There were flowers everywhere - flying around, crushed underfoot, tossed overhead. I remember the band and Morrissey especially getting absolutely pelted by them at some points and wondered if they were second-guessing that whole flower gimmick. He had daffodils in his back pocket that time, but they didn't last the whole show.

I'm just five foot three so I didn't have a completely unobstructed view of everything - I've spent a lot of concert time over the years staring at the back of some taller guy's jacket - but I had a pretty good view for most of it and could hear just fine. The set list was mostly familiar. I don't know if we knew 'Nowhere Fast' yet but the rest were the hits and album cuts. 'Girl Afraid', 'This Charming Man', 'Heaven Knows I'm Miserable Now', 'Hand in Glove' - pretty much all of 'em (at the time). The crowd was loving it.

This was the first outdoor festival-type concert I'd ever attended in the UK. It was a bit chaotic but I chalked that up to the fact that it was free, not heavily policed and involved political stuff as well as music. A lot of us in the crowd had been to gigs and events involving the Miners' Strike over the previous months, and some of the bands had been doing shows in support of the miners as well, so there was a bit of overlap there and a protest vibe at the show as a result.

The Smiths did more than one encore, and Morrissey himself might have been involved in the encore chanting at some point, which surprised me. He wasn't very chatty otherwise, unlike Bragg whose stage patter was - then as now - copious and legendary.

After it was over, I remember picking my way through what seemed like a mile of mangled flowers in the gutters and on the sidewalks as I left the South Bank and headed for the Tube. I didn't have a camera with me that day but in retrospect that part might have been the most 'Instagram-worthy' part of the whole experience. I can still see flower petals scattered everywhere and I was picking bits of greenery out of my boot chains for days after. It was definitely one of the more memorable shows of my college years. I still think of it anytime I see flowers tossed around stage or into a crowd at a concert.

MARKET HALL

12 JUNE 1984, CARLISLE, UK

I WAS THERE: PETER MARTIN

Where to begin? The beginning, maybe? I'd heard the name, probably heard them on Peel, etc. but the first time I really took notice was when 'This Charming Man' burst onto our screens on *The Tube* one Friday in October 1983. I went to Volume in Newcastle the very next day to purchase it on seven inch and 12 inch and 'Hand in Glove' on seven inch. I was smitten. Later that month we went to London on a sixth form trip and I bought the New York mixes on 12 inch and the original gladioli t-shirt in yellow. From then on I bought everything, collected everything. Although it seems like no time now, it seemed like forever then, as I waited over six months to see them live. I bought four tickets at Virgin in Eldon Square - for me, Belly, Dixon and my sister's boyfriend Paul, who agreed to drive if we paid for petrol and bought his ticket. A great deal. The Market Hall had sky lights and, as it was the height of summer, it was light when they came on. Most bands you see in the dark but seeing The Smiths in the light made perfect sense. The whole thing was a blur. I would class it as one of my favourite ever gigs but in reality I cannot recall much about it.

Darren Wilkinson and his girlfriend (now wife of 31 years) Bev were and remain Smiths fans

I WAS THERE: DARREN WILKINSON, AGE 18

The Smiths' two previous releases has passed me by but I was instantly grabbed by that repeating guitar riff that runs all the way through 'What Difference Does It Make?' I loved it then and I still do. To my absolute delight the band announced a gig in my hometown of Carlisle at the iconic Market Hall, which described it exactly as it was! Glass-roofed so it never went dark if the gig was in the summer months, it had a high cast iron roof more likely to be found in a railway station, making acoustics a nightmare. The people of Carlisle loved it and reminisce about it still.

It was two days after my 18th birthday when The Smiths arrived to a rapturous welcome. I was there with my girlfriend Bev, aged 16. They opened with 'Nowhere Fast' and the crowd went nuts. I remember Morrissey leaving the stage and the band doing an acoustic version of 'William, It Was Really Nothing' before Johnny appealed to the crowd to behave or Morrissey wouldn't continue, followed by starting the song again. After three encores which included 'What Difference Does It Make?' the gig was over.

Everyone spilled out of the side doors into Market Street. The Smiths headed off to Scotland. I was hooked.

BARROWLANDS BALLROOM

13 JUNE 1984, GLASGOW, UK

I WAS THERE: ANNE MCGLASHAN, AGE 17

I was with my mate Christine. I had been to Barrowlands a few times before but this is the first time there was a queue, all the way around the corner. We must have been early but we stopped to have a wee roll up on the way there. There were people in the queue holding bunches of gladioli. Everyone was buzzing - the atmosphere was electric. It was so packed in the hall - really busy, tight and sweaty. We got a bit excited as we were sure we spotted Elizabeth Fraser from the Cocteau Twins a wee bit in front of us, although this was never confirmed. During the gig we could not believe how Morrissey's jeans stayed on. There were so many hands tugging on his jeans it seemed impossible for them not to have been pulled right off!

While waiting for The Smiths, the girl next to Christine was asking her if she had any liquids in her bag as the girl's leg was soaking wet. 'Nah,' says Christine, 'No liquids.' It wasn't until later, when we managed to squeeze back to the Ladies and Christine pulled her industrial size tin of hairspray from her bag only to find it empty, did we realise the cause of the cold wetness spreading down the girl's leg.

I WAS THERE: STEPHEN MATHISON

Stephen Mathison remembers Morrissey getting a traditional Barras 'welcome' for The Smiths turning up late

I was introduced to The Smiths' music by a school friend at a party. Their music was totally different to any other band around at that time. I wasn't sure if I liked them at first but there was something about the contrast between the upbeat, jingling guitars and the mournful but poetic lyrics. I missed their first gig in Glasgow but was there when they returned to play the iconic Barrowlands Ballroom.

It was a warm June evening and myself and my pal joined the queue to get in, where there were mumblings about the gig starting late. Sure enough, I went up to the door and saw a notice advising that, 'The Smiths are in London recording for *Top of the Pops*, they'll be here ASAP.'

The doors eventually opened and everyone piled in. The mood was not a happy one. Back in '84 there were still a lot of punks knocking around. But the drink was flowing and the mood lifted slighted. After a delay that seemed like hours the support band, The Telephone Boxes, entered stage left. They went into their first song and the punks in the mosh pit and beyond 'welcomed' them to the Barrowlands with a hail of lager, plastic bottles and spit. It didn't get any better. They were pretty awful and I'm sure they were just as glad to finish as the audience were.

There was another break while the roadies got everything ready for The Smiths. When they eventually came on stage it was late and the audience were pretty drunk and extremely pissed off. The opening number didn't last long as Morrissey was soon covered in the same 'welcome' the support act got. He stormed off and it was left to one of the roadies to try and calm the crowd. He too was covered! The crowd demanded a show, they had waited hours for it and they weren't going anywhere.

The Smiths returned and what a show it was. Morrissey was magic, he sang and danced around the stage whipping the crowd up with fabulous renditions of 'Reel Around the Fountain', 'Suffer Little Children', 'Hand in Glove' and 'What Difference Does It Make?' It was a cracking gig, despite starting hours late.

I WAS THERE: STEVIE WALKER

My second time of seeing them and I have never experienced the like of the Barrowland gig before or since. It was more like a cult or spiritual gathering. Typical Glasgow, they sang en masse to every tune. 'William, It Was Really Nothing' was being debuted that night and went down immensely. Morrissey copped an eyeful of spit and rightly threw a wobbly. The roadie came out to warn us. In all reality, it was a moment out of step to be truthful as the gig was rocking. I remember Marr looking at Rourke and his face was a picture - a bit like a kid in a sweetie shop. I don't think they had experienced such love before. Bodies were getting pulled out all over the place with exhaustion.

CAIRD HALL

15 JUNE 1984, DUNDEE, UK

I WAS THERE: JAN BURNETT

Seeing The Smiths twice, in hindsight, was rather an honour. I missed them at Dundee University - if I was going to go to that I would have been more interested in The Red Guitars. 'Good Technology' was so, erm, good. My then girlfriend went to that gig with her dad.

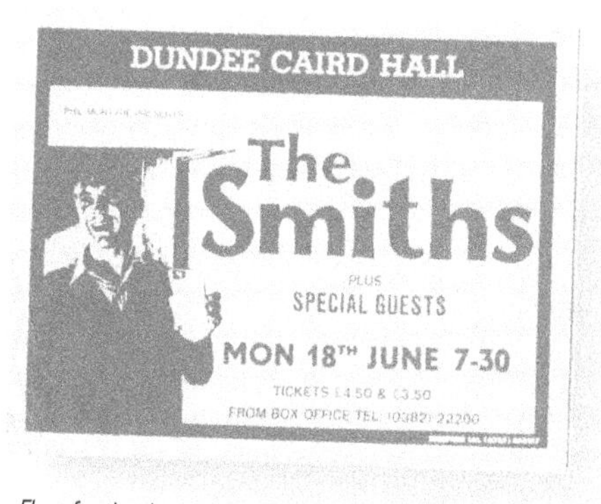

Flyer for the June 1984 Dundee show (with incorrect date). Photo thanks to Jan Burnett

The first and second time for me was at the Caird Hall, Dundee, my hometown and apparently one of the band's favourite venues. This is possibly confirmed by Morrissey playing a few solo shows there. The second show was good but unremarkable to my ears and they stayed at the posher Swallow Hotel just past Invergowrie. We had no chance of meeting them, unlike the first time.

The show was great, manic and hot. The band stayed at the Angus Hotel, now knocked down. That's where all the 'stars' stayed - Duran Duran, Kim Wilde, Howard Jones. We hung out after the show outside the Angus, hoping for a glimpse of the band. Way up high we could see curtains twitch and suddenly a string of various beads were launched down on us by the band, necklaces thrown to them earlier in the night. They were up to high jinx.

Friendly shouting and jaunting continued and in the wee small hours the band appeared to the remaining five or six of us hanging out outside. They were chatty, funny and rather aghast that we had hung about this long. All night I had held under my arm the US 12 inch remix of 'This Charming Man', just recently released. Johnny told me they didn't want it to come out, 'But I'll sign it anyway'. In fact all four of them signed it (I don't think Morrissey signs Smiths records anymore). We all got our autographs - getting pictures wasn't really a thing then - and they eventually headed back in, and we went home and stayed up all night chatting.

Of course 'Everyday Is Like Sunday' is about Dundee, but then everyone says it's about their town.

I WAS THERE: DEREK MOIR

The Smiths did a small tour of Scotland and we went to see them in Dundee. I had been drinking a bottle of red wine, very unusual for a working class youth but inspired by Moz's choice of tipple in Ormskirk. At the end of the gig, we hung round. Johnny Marr remembered us from Ormskirk. He invited me to join him in smoking a massive Camberwell carrot but I declined, as I don't even smoke cigarettes. He then said we could be on the guest list for the rest of the Scottish dates. I was that excited - and pissed/stoned - that I put forward an entourage of the grooviest 25 people I knew. They weren't impressed when we turned up to Aberdeen next day. Soundman Grant Showbiz and the band stood on the steps of the gig and read the riot act to those that had misplaced guest list intentions and refused any further communication with such people - us! I was so embarrassed - it was really only the original four of us that were there on a Monday night after work. Nevertheless, we sneaked in. Next night, we travelled up to Inverness and met them as they arrived to apologise. It was sold out but they let us watch the gig from the side stage. It's a great venue and wow, how gracious.

CAPITOL THEATRE

16 JUNE 1984, ABERDEEN, UK

I WAS THERE: JEFF BRUCE, AGE 13

I had discovered them watching live footage of their gig at the Derby Assembly Rooms which aired on the BBC. This was my first major concert. My mum bought two tickets from the box office at the venue. I remember the intro music of 'Romeo and Juliet' and then the band blasting into 'Nowhere Fast'. The gig flew by but I remember the stage being invaded a few times.

OPERA HOUSE

20 JUNE 1984, BLACKPOOL, UK

I WAS THERE: STEPHANIE HAUBER, AGE 15 OR 16

I don't have a ticket stub, just memories which I will never forget. My older sister's friend rang and asked if I wanted a ticket. She had a spare and knew I liked Morrissey. I had been to one gig before that with the same older crowd. The hardest part was getting past my dad. I was dressed head to foot in my sister's clothes to look older. With girls my age it was probably more the teen crush as he was uber-cool and I thought he looked like a modern James Dean. The atmosphere was amazing and I remember I thought the gig had finished and was about to start leaving. When they did an encore I ran screaming down to the front, or as near as I could get. My husband was a 'proper fan' who knows all the lyrics and everything about The Smiths. He is so jealous I got to see them.

Stephanie Hauber (right) ran to the front for the encore

I WAS THERE: DEBBIE PARKINSON, AGE 16

I only really went because this bloke called David Smith was going on the minibus from Preston and I fancied him. So I got on this minibus to go and see The Smiths and watched a bit of the gig and it was great. Then I went off to the toilets for a wee. In there I bumped into Su Pollard off the telly, she of *Hi-de-Hi!* fame. She admired my outfit.

I had on a pair of brown paisley pyjamas in brushed cotton, like your grandad would wear, that I'd taken in and made into a skintight pair of leggings. I really can't remember if I enjoyed the gig. I do remember that it didn't happen with David Smith. He already had a girlfriend.

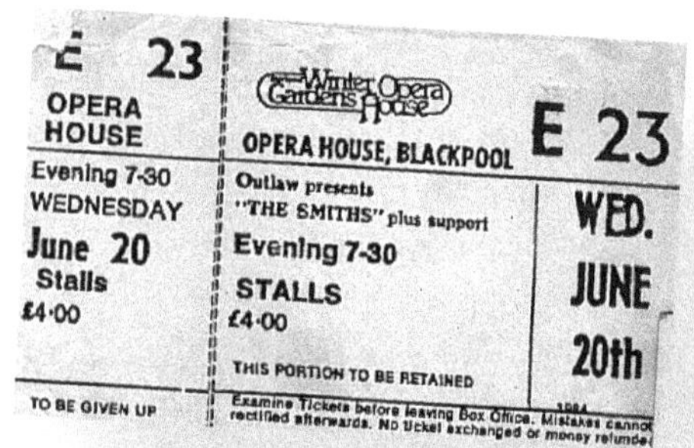

Stephen Christian's ticket for seat E23. There were several tickets for this seat

I WAS THERE: STEPHEN CHRISTIAN

When Smiths tickets went on sale, myself and a friend went into town to buy our tickets from the Opera House box office. It was probably my idea to take our tickets to the local library and use their photocopying machine to make duplicates. The original tickets were poorly printed and on basic white paper so our duplicates looked pretty much identical to the originals. We ended up with five or six sheets of A4 full of 'tickets'. We took them home and I had the genius idea of using a pin to perforate them so the stubs were easy to pull apart from the main ticket.

We never set out to be counterfeiters and I don't remember making lots of, if any, money from selling the tickets, but I do remember avoiding sitting in seats E23 and E24 on the night of the concert. We had given away most of the tickets, all for the same two seats, to a grateful bunch of mates and saw many of them at the concert so the tickets were obviously good enough to fool the door staff and get them into the show. The concert was definitely a sell out. In fact it was filled beyond capacity that night!

CORNWALL COLISEUM

22 JUNE 1984, ST AUSTELL, UK

I WAS THERE: GEORGE E HARRIS

I finished school listening to and was part of the Two Tone tribe, very much into bands like The Beat, The Specials and The Selecter, the more political end of the music. I was a young socialist with ideals. Then I switched to being a goth and a fan of things like Echo and The Bunnymen, Teardrop Explodes and earlier Bauhaus. It was during this period that The Smiths emerged. The Smiths were a bright hope in a field of drudge.

I bought the first album and the singles and became obsessed with the music and imagery - I got fed up with the goth look. The indie thing had taken me. It was bright and it was speaking about us in our bedrooms, the loneliness and all that. Then I became vegetarian because of The Smiths – well, Morrissey. Looking back on it, I think one of the reasons I got into The Smiths was the search for working class heroes and how they wrote songs about that as well as the imagery from the kitchen sink films of the past. It reflected lives in a way which could be seen as political. When Morrissey was pushing the '*Meat Is Murder*' thing, it appealed to my idealism. I still have that, except I do eat some meat these days on health grounds. Unfortunately Morrissey has lost it these days and his views make me vomit. Morrissey is now dead to me.

I WAS THERE: NIGEL PENGELLY

I actually got Morrissey's shirt when he threw it into the crowd and I met Andy Rourke after the gig at the disco around the corner.

CND FESTIVAL

23 JUNE 1984, GLASTONBURY FESTIVAL, UK

I WAS THERE: NICK FOSTER, AGE 16

I originally got into The Smiths via the John Peel show on Radio 1. The release of 'This Charming Man' really got me hooked. It was like nothing I had heard before. I was a big Bunnymen fan but this was completely different. I went out and bought the single, then stayed up to watch a live gig on BBC2. I found out that they were playing Glastonbury and persuaded my parents to let me go with my best mate Jer. We had a fantastic time but The Smiths were the crowning point. Luckily we were of an age where we stayed at the front of the stage regardless of who was on. The Smiths came on early due to a swap with Amazulu. The set was very short - 30 minutes - but the reaction was incredible, with thousands of young fans attempting to climb up the pyramid stage to reach their heroes. Opening with 'William, It Was Really Nothing' it was a hit-packed set, which included B-side 'Jeane'. It was over far too quick, leaving us elated but slightly deflated after all the excitement. The festival still had a day or so to go but it felt like it had already peaked.

Nick Foster (left) begged his parents to let him go to Glastonbury

I WAS THERE: GREG ARCHER

I was eagerly awaiting The Smiths' performance at Glastonbury but their performance was cut short due to a problem with Amazulu (remember them?) turning up late. I also saw them at Cardiff Uni in 1984. That was a fantastic gig and to be feet away from Morrissey and Marr was spine-tingling.

PEEL SESSION, MAIDA VALE STUDIOS

1 AUGUST 1984, LONDON, UK

The band's third Peel Session saw them record 'William, It Was Really Nothing', 'Nowhere Fast', 'Rusholme Ruffians' and 'How Soon Is Now?' for broadcast on 9 August 1984.

Morrissey: Those sessions almost caught the very heart of what we did - there was something messy about them, which was very positive. People are so nervous and desperate when they do those sessions, so it seems to bring the best out of them.

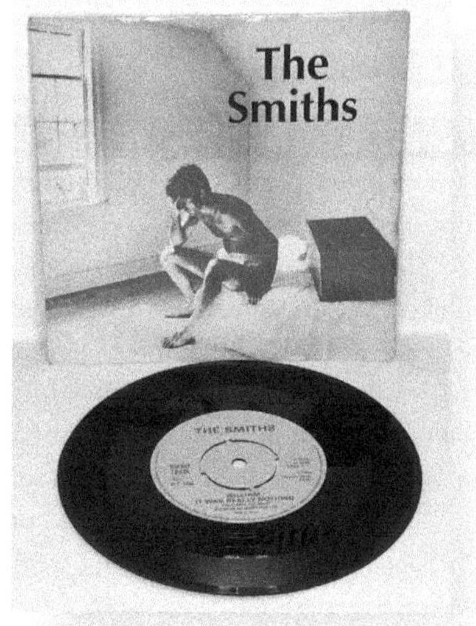

William, It Was Really Nothing

'WILLIAM, IT WAS REALLY NOTHING'

RELEASED 20 AUGUST 1984

Reaching number 17 in the UK, 'William, It Was Really Nothing' had already been part of the band's live set over the preceding months.

GLOUCESTER LEISURE CENTRE

24 SEPTEMBER 1984, GLOUCESTER, UK

Nick Foster doing his best Johnny Marr

I WAS THERE: NICK FOSTER

This was an incredible moment for us young music fans. The leisure centre was not on many bands' touring schedule, so apart from the likes of Howard Jones or Musical Youth, a trip to the Colston Hall in Bristol was generally on the cards. To top things off not only were The Smiths playing, but Echo and The Bunnymen were appearing a few days later. It was to be the best week in our young lives! The attendance process was to get to the venue as early as possible to secure a good place in the queue and then race to the front of the stage as soon as the doors were open. This position was held for the entirety of the gig, regardless of whether you needed a toilet break or not. It was a case of 'holding it in' until the finish,

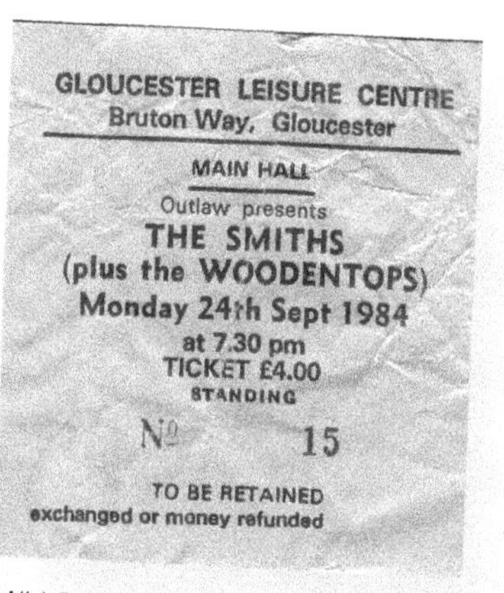

Nick Foster's ticket for the Gloucester gig

and it was also a little while before I really got into the pleasure of having a few pints during a concert. This meant that I was able to witness The Woodentops set in its entirety, another Peel favourite who set the scene admirably before the main band.

Before long the lights dimmed and the opening strains of Prokofiev's 'Romeo and Juliet' filled the auditorium. Where I had previously enough room to stand and watch comfortably, now I felt the air being pushed out of my lungs, my body lifted and propelled nearer to the stage as the crush ensued. The excitement was palpable and you feel the tense expectation for what could be the most important thing to happen to our young lives (up to that point) about to materialise. Then with the entrance of the band, it all kicked off. Launching into 'William', the crowd went wild as Morrissey gyrated, teasing the front stage participants to push in further, like a musical guru bringing his clan to him. The sound was perfect and here were a band at the top of their game, Johnny's chiming guitar equally matched by the tight rhythm section of Rourke and Joyce.

The set flowed, peppered with tracks from the upcoming LP *Meat Is Murder* as well as now familiar tracks from the self-titled first LP but unfortunately, as with all good things, it seemed to be over as quickly as it began. Starting off their first encore with a live debut of 'Please, Please, Please, Let Me Get What I Want' and finishing their second with a rousing rendition of 'Miserable Lie', I finally made my way out to the chilled September evening, with my sweat soaked t-shirt clinging to my body. However I was still warm with the feeling that I had just witnessed the best gig of my young life.

Jo Sayer made a pilgrimage to Salford Lads Club more than 30 years after seeing The Smiths in Gloucester

I WAS THERE: JO SAYERS, AGE 13 OR 14

My first ever gig. Me and a mate, Natalie Easton, went. They were brilliant. They were my favourite band as a teenager. People said they were depressing but I was in love and never got the whole depression thing. The guitar work is just amazing and I suppose with Morrissey being a bit odd it appealed to the alternative youth of the day! I still listen to their music loads now. We did a pilgrimage to the Salford Lads Club a couple of years ago. I want 'There is a Light That Never Goes Out' played at my funeral.

I WAS THERE: ANDY WHITE

My next chance to see the band was at Gloucester Leisure Centre. Support was from The Woodentops, who were pretty good but never really made it. The first album had been out a few months and the band had clearly gained confidence - except maybe Morrissey who was born extremely confident. The rhythm section was tighter than I recall from Leicester and the fan base had grown.

The songs were mostly well known, but included a few from the not yet released *Meat Is Murder*. I believe this was also the first live appearance for 'How Soon Is Now?' I was going through a difficult phase in my love life and this song gave me great comfort.

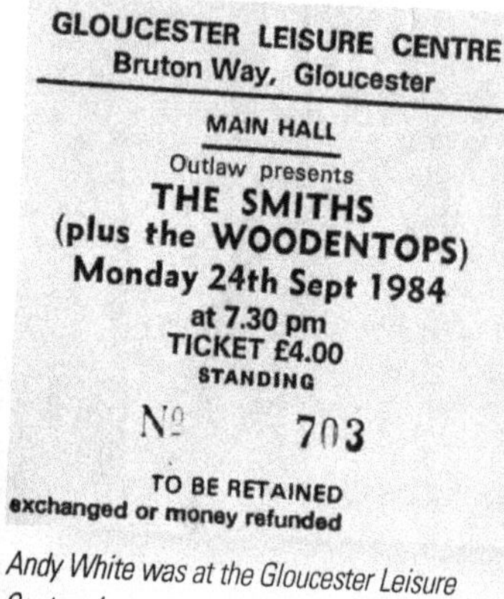

Andy White was at the Gloucester Leisure Centre gig

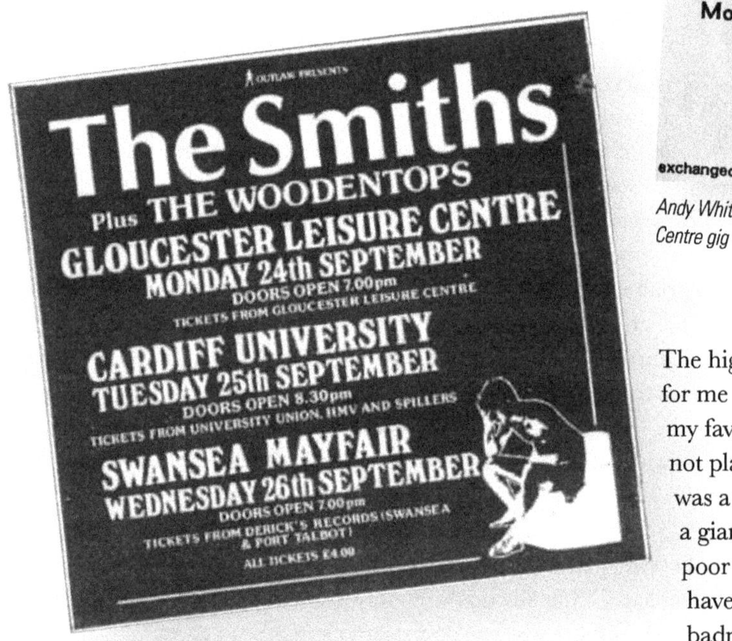

The highlight of the concert for me was 'Jeane', one of my favourite songs and not played in Leicester. It was a poor venue actually, a giant sports hall with poor acoustics. You could have had a game of badminton at the back.

UNIVERSITY OF CARDIFF

25 SEPTEMBER 1984, CARDIFF, UK

I WAS THERE: SIMON DAWES

Morrissey came on swinging a fir tree in the air. He chucked it into the crowd and I remember seeing people holding bits of twig at the end!

I WAS THERE: MICHAEL JONES, AGE 18

As a bored 17 year old motor spare shop assistant I became aware of The Smiths by hearing the singles on the radio and seeing them on *Top of the Pops*. I was struck by the music, lyrics and image. I bought second hand Levis, a few paisley shirts and DM buckled shoes, my hair styled into a quiff emulating the band's look. I don't think the first album left my turntable for six months. They filled the gap that was left by The Jam.

I saw the tour announcement in the *NME*. As I had Fridays off I was delegated by my friends to get the tickets from Spillers Records in Cardiff, taking the early one hour train journey from my hometown in Merthyr. I was first in the queue buying the four pieces

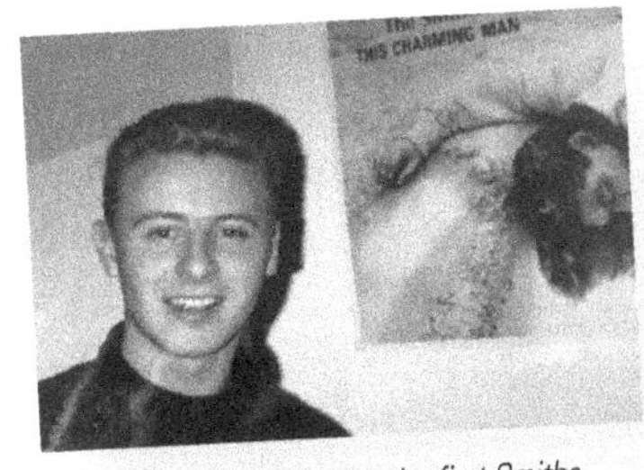

Michael Jones listened to the first Smiths album non-stop for six months

of gold, and was then having to pinch myself that I was going to see them!

A few swift beers and four be-quiffed 18 year old Merthyr lads are getting to the front of the stage - me, Gegsy, Treeny and Slyver. We don't pay much attention to support band The Woodentops. There is some dry ice, booming

Oscar Wilde intro music and there they are. I'm stood front of the stage to the right, looking directly at Johnny Marr. He's cool even with eyeliner. Morrissey has a tree hanging out of his arse pocket. They go right through their album. The crowd are going mental. I'm crushed at the front, soaked with sweat and beer but I don't care. It's just sheer excitement. 'Hand in Glove' hits a nerve and is probably my best memory of the evening. Seeing a band in their prime was something to behold and I don't think I ever experienced that sort of gig again - and I've been to hundreds since. Thanks for the memories.

I WAS THERE: ALLAN PETRIE

I left school in 1982 having gone through punk, heavy rock and ska and also liking bands like Classic Nouveaux, Visage, Soft Cell, etc. So I was always into alternative stuff. We used to drink in a small football club bar even though we were under age – Barry Town FC. One day at the football club Chris McCarthy, my best mate since the age of 6, said he loved a new single by a band called The Smiths. I think it was 'Hand in Glove'. I went away and listened to them and fell in love with them. I used to drive my mum and dad mad as they said Morrissey was a miserable bastard but as a depressed type of teenager, the lyrics felt real to me. I liked the way they used to sing about real issues instead of making lines up which rhymed.

It was a sunny evening as I walked the three miles from my house to Chris's house for the gig. I was wearing my dad's shirt and my sister's beads and had flowers in the arse pocket of my jeans. I got some weird looks walking through Barry! We caught the train to Cardiff and must have looked odd. I remember Morrissey hurling gladioli around and us getting quite close to the front. There weren't loads there but enough to make a great atmosphere. They did two encores and I remember going mad to 'Miserable Lie' at the very end.

I WAS THERE: ROLO MCGINTY, THE WOODENTOPS

The Smiths had come to see The Woodentops at Dingwalls, to see about inviting us to support them on the tour they were about to do. We were a very new band, improved from doing our first tour support with Julian Cope on his comeback. We were majorly excited and off we went. The halls were big and echoey, a sports centre especially. The Smiths themselves were friendly and easy to hang around with. Morrissey was not usually visible, doing press or whatever. So it was more a nod here and there and I had thanked him for putting us on the tour. Only…. we were going down really well and the flowers were all thrown way before The Smiths came on. I don't know if that's normal or not. Indeed Johnny Marr was taunting Morrissey with our new single, 'Move Me', that was just about to go public. Johnny had an advance copy. So just maybe some bad blood was flowing. Then it happened.

It may have been Cardiff. As we drove to the venue we spotted the car driven by our good friend Dave Harper, a vintage Mercedes. In the passenger seats were The Smiths, all asleep. We drove alongside, not too close, to give Dave a quick wave and then whizz off because we were late. Johnny woke up, raised his head and saw us and grinned and waved. As did I think. Morrissey was in the front passenger seat and he turned to look at me. For a split second, as his head was turning, an undulation in the road brought the two cars a tiny bit closer to each other. In the other broken piece of second. Morrissey got a shock and thought, 'Crash!' just as our eyes met. He thought he was going to die and he made the face.

Images drawn by Lee Thacker

We passed and I thought first thing on arrival, apologise. I mean I wasn't driving or anything but still anyway. So I did. It did not go down well. I had mentioned the bump in the road. We were waving at Dave and said the bump was 'a bad coincidence'.

Morrissey repeated that back to me sarcastically. We played a blistering set that night. I've heard from people, for example Rob from Alabama 3, who it turns out was there, who tells me we blew The Smiths off. Old time expression that. I don't see how we could have, 'How Soon Is Now?' was such a hit, you can't beat that.

I remember seeing a guy dancing, exactly mimicking Morrissey. The guy was up on a balcony with a spotlight up there making his shadow enormous as he did the perfect Morrissey. You can't beat that. In the morning we got the news. We were off the tour. I think we had done three of the five and as you could imagine we were absolutely gutted. The next thing was the interview question 'Why did you not finish the Smiths tour?' The question kept coming up. One day I think Alice or me perhaps answered with, 'Oh, it was a silly thing, it wasn't as if we had put a cigarette bomb under the stage or anything, tried to blow them up and they found out.' This quip made its way to print as, 'We tried to blow them up'. How it goes. I personally enjoyed seeing them every night. As a result of that Smiths tour, Everything But The Girl, Tracey and Ben, took us out on a much longer tour that was not only the damn best time, it was our last support tour. They came to see us at Dingwalls too, which we were now headlining. So all three support tours we did, we were checked out firstly at Dingwalls by the artists that took us out.

In November 1984, The Smiths embarked on a tour of Ireland, playing seven shows in the Republic and two in the north, at the University of Coleraine and Belfast. James were support.

SAVOY

11 NOVEMBER 1984, WATERFORD, IRELAND

I WAS THERE: MICHAEL FARRAGHER

When we went to see them in Ireland, we were hitchhiking and had places to stay. We were coming out of Dublin on what is essentially the motorway, hitchhiking to Waterford when a little minibus passed us by and I said, 'That was James!' We'd seen them the night before in Dublin. Nobody really knew James at that point but they noticed us and they reversed back on the motorway and said, 'Are you going to see The Smiths in Waterford?' We said, 'We are!' and they said, 'Jump in and we'll give you a lift!'

During that tour, we didn't get to meet The Smiths all the time. We would always go up to the venues for the sound checks. We'd go up there, spend the day at the venue and wait for them for them to arrive. We'd see them going in and take some photos. We weren't pushy, so we didn't ever force ourselves on them. If they were up for a chat and if they had enough time, sometimes they would hang around outside the venue before they went in, which was great and a lot more relaxed.

And as they got to know us more they let us in to sound checks. They would say, 'Are you coming in?' The band would be doing their drum checks and going through all the songs instrumentally, and Morrissey would be sitting there watching them and singing in the row in front. Then he would get up and sing a few songs and do a few vocal checks.

SFX

12 & 13 NOVEMBER 1984, DUBLIN, IRELAND

I WAS THERE: JAMES ROBERTS

I saw them just the once, in Dublin. *Top of the Pops* was a weekly ritual and their first performance on the show was it for me. I went to the gig on my own because no one I knew would go and so I stood at the back. The two members of Everything But The Girl were a few feet away from me as they were big fans also. Great gig!

I WAS THERE: LISA COLLINS, AGE 16

My 'hipper' school friend, Julie, first heard of The Smiths during one of her summers in London. Julie was really cool and she even listened to Radio Luxembourg before the rest of us knew it existed. Before MTV or SKY TV reached Ireland, we were very limited in our capability to have any exposure to different types of music. My other friend, Denise, was also a big fan of The Smiths. I was very new to the goth scene, having been a mod up until then. The night of the concert, Julie, Denise and myself, all dressed in black, wearing our ghostly white make-up with our hair all back combed, set off with great anticipation to see The Smiths.

Lisa Collins was going through her goth phase when she saw The Smiths

I was just 16 and I knew this was one of the first gigs The Smiths had ever played in Dublin. As an angst-ridden teenager in the early Eighties, Ireland felt the complete opposite to the multicultural thriving cosmopolitan nation it is today. Teenagers were desperately searching for something different from the oppressive culture that we lived in then. The Catholic Church had a chokehold on what was deemed acceptable in all aspects of Irish society. So The Smiths' lyrics and music spoke to us as teenagers feeling trapped by what we felt as an oppressive society.

The SFX was a small, plain, simple, dark dusty old hall with wooden floorboards and a door at one end and a stage at the other and it was just perfect for seeing bands.

Not many people had heard of The Smiths and so the SFX was not very full that night. Because it was such an intimate concert, it felt like all of us in the audience were in on something special together. I was even right up at the front of the stage, something as a true claustrophobe I would normally never do.

At one point during the night, someone threw flowers onto the stage and Morrissey put them in his jeans back pocket, adding to the ones he already had there. I remember a lot of flowers being tossed around that night as Morrissey seemed to glide over the stage singing our favourites such as 'This Charming Man' and 'Please, Please, Please, Let Me Get What I Want'.

Towards the end of the set, Morrissey leaned over to us girls crowded together at the front of the stage and kissed Denise on her cheek! She was in seventh heaven, and the whole bus journey home she vowed never to wash that side of her face again. It didn't matter that we pointed out the impracticality of that. She was determined. I think she waited a few days before she had to eventually wash her face!

Almost a quarter of a century later, in my thirties, I went to see Morrissey at a solo gig in the Bob Hope Theatre in Stockton, California in April 2007. I had been living in the Bay Area for a decade and had not seen Morrissey in concert since the SFX gig.

At the SFX gig he was a more mysterious brooding creature. The 2007 Morrissey seemed to exude a lot more warmth and even engaged in banter between the numbers. A number of his family members were in the audience that particular night and he introduced them to the fans, which was very sweet. He also shared that he had spent many summers in Stockton, when he was younger. This also cleared up, for a lot of the fans there, as to why he was performing during Stockton's Asparagus Festival as he made a lot of jokes gently poking fun at the 'metropolis' of downtown Stockton. I remember thinking how times have changed and how we all soften, as we age. There was even an array of brightly coloured merchandise for sale in the theatre, so different to the smoky dark atmosphere of the SFX gig. I bought a white tank top emblazoned with the word Morrissey in pink for my same friend, Denise, whose cheek he had kissed all those years ago, as a gift for her on my next visit home to Dublin. She wore it proudly.

I WAS THERE: GRAHAM MONTGOMERY, AGE 13

I was about to turn 14. I was probably too young to be going to gigs in town - but if you're good enough, you're old enough! I remember the second song was 'William, It was Really Nothing' and the place went mental. The crowd was swaying from side to side and someone stood on my shoe and I lost it for a while. I found it during 'How Soon Is Now?', with which the crowd sang along with gusto. I don't think this set lasted longer than an hour. I believe they were sick that night and that the next night was much better for the band.

I WAS THERE: DAMIAN READE

It was my first ever gig, James supported them and they too were excellent. On the way to the gig we met Johnny Marr outside the Gresham Hotel and chatted with him for a bit. I still have my signed ticket and I also have the bootleg from that night.

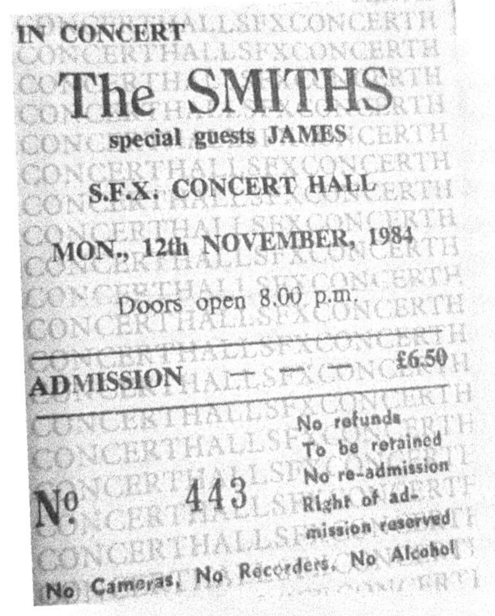

Damian Reade's 1984 Dublin ticket

I WAS THERE: DES FOLEY, AGE 18

I went with my best friend from school, Brian Whelan. We were up near the front. I remember the screams of the audience when The Smiths came on. Everyone sang along with pretty much every song. The atmosphere was great and I remember just being amazed to actually see the band in person for the first time. I was on such a high after the gig that when I got home I blasted out 'This Charming Man' on my bedroom record player. Much to my dad's annoyance, as he was in bed at the time!

I WAS THERE: JOHN FOYLE, AGE 19

I was a year at work, on staff for a department store, anything but return to education. Living at home, I look back and wonder at the tolerance of my parents. I've no memory of pressure to move out etc. I was in a comfortable, cosseted environment. I was and am a big fan of live music. I'd hear all the latest bands on 2FM, RTE Radio 2, particularly the evening shows hosted by Gerry Ryan and Dave Fanning. I wasn't and am not a viewer of much TV. So it was all about the sounds. The weekly music magazine I'd mainly read was *Record Mirror*.

The Smiths were the band to see, as would REM be at the same venue a few weeks later. My memories of both shows are constantly mixed up in my head. Both shows were hysterically received. The venue, on the other end of O'Connell Street, north of O'Connell Bridge, was the north side of Dublin, significant to me as a southsider, then a significant factor. Basically, northsiders were poor, southsiders were rich. My dad may have dropped me at the venue. I'd seen my first show there, on an altarboys outing in the Seventies, seeing Danny Doyle topping the bill of a charity show.

That's when the place was called St Francis Xavier Hall, very much associated with the church. It's rebranding as SFX was considered rather daring, though us teenagers would still have been very much aware of its previous associations. Seeing a rock show there was still slightly daring, a bit bold really, a delight to us as we shook off the stranglehold the clergy still had on Irish society.

I was enthusiastic about keeping up with the new acts. All of that informed my reaction to Morrissey & Co. As the mostly male crowd swayed away under a fog of cigarette smoke and body odour, Moz appeared waving a branch of a tree, getting a roar - part delight, part mocking. His penchant for vegetation was well known - coming on with a branch seemed both appropriate and a kind of knowing irony, that he knew he was already playing up to an image.

They started with 'Please, Please, Please, Let Me Get What I Want'. It was a B-side at that point, only appearing on *Hatful of Hollow* around the time of the show. Whatever, it was well known, with lots of radio play by 2FM. The tracks from the first album were roared along with and ones from what would be *Meat Is Murder* - 'Rusholme Ruffians', 'Barbarism Begins at Home' - less so, but seeming intriguing. The inclusion, towards the end, of 'Jeane' was especially welcome. It was already considered delightfully obscure, a B-side only the hardcore fans could possibly know. It was a fitting ending to a show that was going full blast all the time. People staggered out of the venue drenched in sweat, every bit of clothing damp, stinking of booze and tobacco.

My abiding memory is of a band in complete control of the stage and the audience. Reading later that Maher (Marr) was sick for most of the tour after a rough crossing on the ferry, it's hard to think how much better they could have been if they had been 100 per cent.

I WAS THERE: COLIN KERR

I saw a lot of bands there, but my stand out memory was seeing The Smiths. The first time they played Dublin was at Trinity College, Dublin. Word spread that this was a band that had to be seen and heard.

What set The Smiths apart in the SFX was Morrissey, a frontman like no frontman before him, and Johnny Marr, a guitarist who played guitar like no other guitarist of his generation. And then there were the songs – 'This Charming Man', 'Hand in Glove', 'What Difference Does It Make?', 'Still Ill' and other early classics. I didn't see The Smiths live again but did get to see both Morrissey and Johnny Marr play solo gigs in Dublin. Morrissey was good and Johnny Marr was great, but nothing could recreate the magic of that SFX gig.

I WAS THERE: PAUL ROY, AGE 17

Having siblings made *Top of the Pops* a viewing staple. There was something about The Smiths that immediately stood out. I suppose there is always the teenage musical epiphany of hearing music that resonates and perhaps speaks to you in a new way. I was 17 and went with my friend Alan and his younger sister, so we couldn't go to the pub before or after. I always remember the intensity of 'How Soon Is Now?' That tremulous guitar intro is a favourite of mine, and a track I still listen to. There was a thread of energy through the show; it all seemed more intense and atmospheric. The stage lighting was also something that transfixed me. I had just begun working in my first job and soon after I started my mother turned to me smiling in the kitchen one evening and sang, 'I was looking for a job and then I found a job, and heaven knows I'm miserable now....'

LEISURELAND

17 NOVEMBER 1984, GALWAY, IRELAND

I WAS THERE: MICHAEL FARRAGHER

When Rita and I saw them in Ireland, we got a song dedicated to us. Morrissey had written to us on one occasion and had said, 'Dear kittens, brothers and sisters must always share' and sent us a little something. And at one of the Dublin gigs he said, 'This is for the kittens' and we were saying, 'I wonder if that's us? Do you think he means us?' It could have been anybody. But when we went to see them in Galway on that tour, we'd gone out to the venue and met Morrissey during the day.

Galway Leisureland was a sports venue. Our parents are from Galway so we were going to go and see our cousins and our aunts and uncles and weren't going to follow the rest of the tour. The band were going on to the north of Ireland and we didn't fancy hitchhiking around the north of Ireland because, at that time, to have an English accent around the north of Ireland wasn't completely safe. We met Morrissey and we said, 'Sadly this is our last night. Good luck for the rest of the tour.' And that night he said, 'This is for Michael and Rita. Hope you get home safe.' That was so brilliant.

I was desperate to get a recording of that gig, not as easy as it is now. Now you can go on YouTube and a lot of these recordings are there. Back then it wasn't easy. I advertised in *NME* and *Melody Maker* to ask if anybody had a recording but no one came through. But we were living at home with our parents in Streatham in south London, and Grant Showbiz was living on the same road as us. He produced The Fall, and he did the sound at every Smiths gig. It was just a normal road but the house he lived in had a studio called Cathouse Studios where bands came to record demos. We would meet Grant walking up or down the road and he knew us from all of the gigs that we went to. We never stopped and had a chat with him. We'd never say, 'Any news? Have you got any gossip?' We'd just meet Grant and say 'hi' and 'see you next time'.

After the Galway gig I did stop him on the road and said, 'If there's any chance, Grant, that you've got a recording of the Galway gig, I'd just really like to get a copy of it.' He said, 'I'll have a look. I've got a soundboard recording of practically every gig.' So I said, 'Well, if I pop a blank tape through your letterbox would you be able to give me a copy of it?' He said, 'Sure.' And he did.

I WAS THERE: RITA FARRAGHER

I was still grieving the break up of The Jam at the end of 1982. I completely believed I would never like any band as much as I had liked The Jam so I had to be persuaded by my brother Michael, who was my music guru, to come and listen to The Smiths on the John Peel show. Fairly soon after that, they were playing at London's Lyceum and we went along. It was one of the most electric gigs I have ever been to, and after that gig I was well and truly over The Jam.

Rita and Michael Farragher hitchhiked around Ireland following The Smiths

We then saw them at Hammersmith Palais in March 1984, where Sandie Shaw came on for the encore. Morrissey was in fine form, with plenty of one-liners. The next time I saw The Smiths was at the GLC gig in London, in June '84. Festivals weren't as big a thing then and to see a band you like playing outdoors in the day time was amazing. Michael and I got right up the front for it and was such an exciting time. Being a festival type event, not all the audience were there to see The Smiths but they got a really great reception and I think that's the first time I saw Morrissey throwing glads around.

I can't remember the series of events that followed after that but basically we went to every radio appearance, TV show appearance and gig that we could. Michael went up and met them at Rough Trade offices very early on and Morrissey asked if we were coming to the next gig but we hadn't been able to get tickets so Morrissey said he would put us on the guest list - something he very kindly did many many times during our Smiths days. I started writing to Morrissey early on and he wrote back a few times, which always caused great excitement in the house. Even my mum would recognise his childlike handwriting and know to get it to me as soon as possible. Morrissey was always very kind to us - I think he liked that we were from an Irish family and that we were brother and sister - he once sent us two white label seven inch singles and wrote 'brothers and sisters must always share' on a postcard. He also once sent me a packet of flower seeds and said 'each bud must blossom and grow'.

Johnny was also very generous. When *Meat Is Murder* was due out he was doing an interview at Broadcasting House in London. It had snowed really badly and there were no buses running along Streatham High Road so we decided to walk the three miles to Brixton - in completely unsuitable footwear of course because, after all, we were potentially going to meet a Smith! We got there late so didn't see him going in but waited around and met him after. Unusually, we were the only fans there - others were far too sensible to hang around in the freezing snow. He was so lovely to us and he gave us each a copy of the album - we were buying it anyway but to get a copy from Johnny was special. I remember getting home and just playing it over and over.

The Irish tour they did in 1984 was probably the absolute best time for me. We must have been mad. We had so little money and we were 18, 19 years old, hitchhiking around in November. But Morrissey had sent a letter saying, 'You will be on all guest lists everywhere', so how could we not go?

The band were on the same ferry as us going over. They seemed like superstars to us and we assumed they would be flying over. We had a great chat with Johnny on the ferry. I think Morrissey was in his cabin unwell. It was a terrible crossing and everyone felt ill before the night was out. In Dublin they started with 'Please, Please, Please' which seemed like a bold and brilliant move and it was just magical. Morrissey also dedicated a song to 'the kittens' and we liked to think that was us, as he had called us that in a letter shortly before.

Our first task was to get from Dublin to Waterford in time for the next gig. We'd stayed in a hostel in Dublin and trekked out to the dual carriageway to thumb a lift. After about half an hour we spotted the support band, James, going past in their camper van and we waved. They recognised us as Smiths fans and, unbelievably, turned round and came back to get us. We had a little detour because Tim Booth wanted to find a waterfall to chant at. Michael and I were vegetarian but they introduced us to veganism. They fed us and looked after us and got us to Waterford in time for the sound check - they even took us into the venue with them where we had a chat with Johnny.

That whole little tour was great. We left it after the Galway gig as they were going up north then and we weren't sure about that, with all the trouble there at the time, and we have family near Galway so we went to visit them before heading home. I gave Morrissey a claddagh ring by way of thanks for all the guest lists. When I got home I had a letter from him, on hotel letter headed paper, simply saying, 'I will always wear the ring' and I believe he did until it got taken off his finger by a fan at a gig - in America I think. He dedicated 'Reel Around the Fountain' to us by name at Galway, and wished us a safe trip home, which sent us home floating on air.

SAVOY

18 NOVEMBER 1984, CORK, IRELAND

I WAS THERE: COLM O'CALLAGHAN

The Smiths returned to The Savoy six months after their first appearance there, during which time they'd been sucked slowly in from the margins. But although the group would go on to regularly feature at the business end of the album charts, they never really enjoyed the consistent successes they craved with the shorter form, which was one of Morrissey and Marr's primary ambitions for their group from the get-go.

Even so, the singer had already been rumbled by the tabloids who, picking up on the platinum-plated copy he routinely provided in interviews, had become as regular a freak feature in *The Sun* as he was on the hit parade, portrayed variously as a dangerous, anti-royal traitor, a sexual deviant and a macabre, terrorist-loving, tree-hugging weirdo. Or, if you like, the Jeremy Corbyn of his time.

The Denis Desmond/MCD-promoted, nine-date, eight-town tour of Ireland during November 1984 took place less than one month after the IRA bombing of the Grand Hotel in Brighton, where the British Conservative Party was holding its annual conference, and during a particularly dark period in modern Irish history when loyalist and republican terrorism across the island routinely dominated the news agenda. And at a time too when many formidable contemporary bands just simply wouldn't - or were advised not to - play in the north of Ireland.

With The Smiths on the road in support of their stop-gap compilation album, *Hatful of Hollow*, Morrissey gave the London press a series of typically headline-grabbing quotes during the media campaign to promote it, one of the most notable of which referred to Margaret Thatcher, then Britain's Prime Minister, and who had survived the Brighton bombing, which killed three people and injured 30 more.

'The sorrow of the Brighton bombing', Morrissey claimed, 'is that Thatcher escaped unscathed. I think that, for once, the IRA were accurate in selecting their targets'. And it was against this backdrop, six weeks after U2 released *The Unforgettable Fire* and five months after Bob Dylan's show at Slane Castle was marred by riots around the County Meath town, that The Smiths returned to Ireland. During which they played shows in Letterkenny, Belfast and Coleraine, as well as the usual stop-offs, fetching up in Cork for the second and last time on Sunday, November 18th, 1984, one week before Midge Ure and Bob Geldof recorded the Band Aid single, 'Do They Know It's Christmas'.

The mood inside The Savoy, second time around, was just as frenzied and excitable as it had been earlier that year, and maybe overly-so. The crowd itself was far bigger, as you'd expect, and the promoters had put an extra 50p on the price of the tickets. Once again, myself and Philip were there, close enough to see the magicians work the stage, far enough away to avoid the on-going bash-ball inside the moshing zone. The support this time was provided by James, yet another fledgling and already highly regarded Manchester band (is there ever any other kind?) who'd released a fine first record, the 'Jimone' EP, on the Factory label and who, during their formative years, enjoyed Morrissey's very public patronage. For better and, possibly, for worse.

The Smiths' set had changed quite drastically in the interim. Although they were ostensibly promoting *Hatful of Hollow*, the band was also road-testing several of the tracks that would buttress its second studio album, *Meat Is Murder*. They opened bravely with one of their more introspective cuts, 'Please, Please, Please, Let Me Get What I Want', which had featured as a quality B-side on their 'William, It Was Really Nothing' single earlier that summer, and into which they quickly segued.

Foremost among the clatter of new material was a frantic take on 'What She Said' and, close to the end, a bionic, souped-up 'I Want The One I Can't Have', by which time the atmosphere inside the hall had turned sharply. Marr had become the unwitting target of a hail of spit half-way through, an unfortunate knuckle-walker's pastime that many of us suspected, wrongly, had died after the Sex Pistols signed to a major label.

And after two audible warnings - at one point he arched his callow body back and looked like he was going to lash out - he eventually walked off just shy of the hour mark, taking the rest of the band with him. The Smiths returned, reluctantly enough it seemed to me, to do a two song encore, finishing on a high with 'What Difference Does It Make?', but Marr had the last word; he leaned into a vocal mic on the way off and told the crowd, not incongruously, how he'd 'come to play and not to be spat at', before leaving again, this time for good.

As the house lights came up around The Savoy, a section of the crowd, some checking their watches, began to vent, booing initially - more, I suspect, in the direction of those who'd caused the walk-off than at the band itself - and then, once it was obvious that the show was over and that The Smiths weren't returning, broke into a ridiculous chorus of 'We want James'.

So while the Cork crowd was given an early flavour of some of the more sinewy cuts from *Meat Is Murder*, it also experienced the shortest Smiths set, by at least three songs, of that leg of the tour. But not before Morrissey, as the

band set up for its encore, returned to the stage with a small sapling, which he wielded like a bicycle chain during 'Hand in Glove', and then deposited with gusto into the audience.

The Smiths certainly knew how to make an exit like they knew how to make an entrance. And they never returned to Cork again. As regards the spitting, several shows in Cork were disrupted during this time by the same core of eejits, and in much the same manner. Most of them have, no doubt, gone on to be pillars of Cork society. Why Marr? Quite probably because he was a) close and b) tended to stand his ground, unlike Morrissey who was a moving target.

From where I was, I'm not sure if Morrissey was as keen to abandon ship, but abandon ship they did and, although they returned for a two song encore, that was the last Cork saw of The Smiths.

ULSTER HALL

22 NOVEMBER 1984, BELFAST, UK

I WAS THERE: ROYCE HARPER

Royce Harper saw The Smiths three times

They were and still are a big part of my life. I got into them like a 17 year old would if it was their first band even though I was in my twenties. That's the sort of effect that Morrissey and the boys had on me. I was a punk, but I was listening to music from the age of 13, 14 and I remember my father taking me into the old Smithfield Market in Belfast and buying second hand albums because they were so cheap. And it would have been everything – a Pink Floyd album, a Simon and Garfunkel album, a Roy Harper album. There was even a Billy Connolly album! Even when I was a hardcore punk I was still buying other stuff. I had no hang ups about what was cool and what was not.

After the punk thing, I really liked what people did when they progressed. I was a massive Magazine fan. I hate boxes but they seemed to marry punk with prog. And before The Smiths I was listening to Echo and The Bunnymen, The Cure, Siousxie and The Banshees - all the best of the indie stuff. I was living in Angesley in North Wales when I first came across The Smiths. I'd met some local musicians and I was singing in a band. And a friend of a friend, who was from Liverpool, was talking about the music that he was really into and he lent me The Smiths debut album. He said, 'You've got to listen to this.'

The first time I heard it, I thought the production was a bit muddy but that there was something there. And by the third listen I was hooked – hook, line and sinker! Even through the muddy production Morrissey's lyrics got me. I just thought his lyrics were genius. The first time I saw them would have been when they made their debut on *Top of the Pops*, which knocked me off my seat. The band were so talented and tight. They were like The Beatles and yet this loose, Wildean figure at the front, being able to jump about with his gladioli because they were so tight behind him, was just amazing. There was nothing else on the show that week, or the week before or the week after, that could touch that performance.

There was no work in Anglesey so I got a job back in Belfast and they played Queens University very early in '86 and I went to that gig. It was a brilliant concert. They played a lot of *Meat Is Murder*. I saw them at G-Mex as well, for the Festival of the Tenth

Summer, which was just a must because everybody who was anybody played that. And as far as I was concerned the best bands in the world came from Manchester and Liverpool. They played in the afternoon. I was always a festival goer so I was used to seeing bands playing in the afternoon, at Glastonbury and at those Irish festivals I went to. I was happy as Larry to see so many of my favourite top bands in the one afternoon. It was tremendous.

I read Oscar Wilde in my early teens and Morrissey was coming out and saying, 'This is one of my great inspirations' at a time when Wilde was probably seen by other people as an incredibly uncool and one of yesterday's things. He reinvented Oscar. He reinvented James Dean. He reinvented a lot of people that had been left behind in that decade because he said, 'They mean so much to me.' He was so much of today but also this intelligent sharp lyrical wit in a pop song where other people are singing, 'I want to hold your hand.' His lyrics were sometimes like knives in the back - but done with a smile!

1985

'HOW SOON IS NOW?'

RELEASED 28 JANUARY 1985

'How Soon Is Now?' fared relatively badly in the charts, only reaching number 24. It had featured on *Hatful of Hollow* and was originally the B-side of 'William, It Was Really Nothing'. The re-released single was edited down to four minutes from its original seven.

Johnny Marr: 'It's most people's favourite, I think.'

The Smiths embarked on a UK tour to promote *Meat Is Murder*, playing 23 shows in 39 days. The album had gone to number 1 in the British charts. Most dates were quickly sold out.

GOLDDIGGERS

27 FEBRUARY 1985, CHIPPENHAM, UK

I WAS THERE: RICHARD SHIPMAN, AGE 18

It was the first date of the *Meat Is Murder* tour. It was my local venue and being a huge Smiths fan I could not believe they were playing on my doorstep. I managed to get onstage during a couple of the songs as was the done thing back then and got myself chucked out. But I knew the bouncers, so was straight back in again!

CIVIC HALL

28 FEBRUARY 1985, GUILDFORD, UK

I WAS THERE: ANDREW BLACKHURST

It was a very good concert. The only down side was that most of the numbers were from the new album, *Meat Is Murder*. We were disappointed they didn't play much from their back catalogue and I am sure neither 'What Difference Does It Make?' nor 'This Charming Man' were in the set. But top class all the same. Good concerts were coming thick and fast at the time at the Civic. You didn't need to go to London to find the best acts. They were coming to us in Guildford!

I WAS THERE: NICK DEAVES

I had moved to Guildford, again with work. I had a bedsit for my first year right opposite the Civic Hall. A group of us went including my girlfriend Jenny, now my wife, and some of her friends. I felt a bit protective and apprehensive of the band, as this was my first real gig with Jenny and they had a lot to live up to. But I had nothing to fear as it was a very raucous crowd and lifting one of her friends on to my shoulders broke the ice. Her friend still goes on about it now! In what was a short-lived career, the band were a brilliant moment in time for me and just hit such a chord. I still have all my vinyl and all the reissues. As the lyrics of 'Paint a Vulgar Picture' say, 'Re-issue! Re-package! Re-package! Re-evaluate the songs, Double-pack with a photograph, Extra track (and a tacky badge).'

I WAS THERE: DEL BOXALL, AGE 20

I might have heard them on something like the Peter Powell Radio 1 show and I thought, 'this is different.' I liked a lot of the New Romantic stuff at the time. I'd liked ska. And then in '82 I started liking Simple Minds a bit before they went a bit too big, and then The Smiths came along.

Guildford Civic Hall was a two to three minute walk from where I lived, and I used to go up there when various bands were on. The staff there got to know me

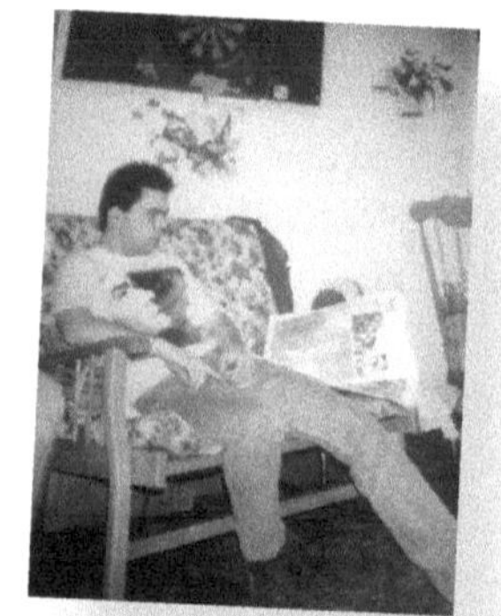

Del Boxall thought The Smiths were different

and they used to give me the posters. You could buy big posters for the whole tour, but they'd have specific ones for that venue and they'd usually get about 10 of them. But I went up there to see if I could get one for The Smiths and they said, 'Well, we've only got three. We can't let you have one this time because we have to put them all outside.'

On the day of the concert the posters were all pasted to the boards outside and two of them got ripped to pieces where people had tried to take them down. But I managed to get the other one. I started peeling at one corner and peeled it off, complete and still wet with paste. I walked home and put it straight on my bedroom wall. That is quite possibly the only one of those posters in existence. It was easier than I thought it would be, back when I moved many years ago, to get it off again because I had some laminate running down one wall and I had managed to put it on there so it came off. It's not in a great condition now. It's all rolled up and I'm worried to touch it in case it all crumbles to pieces.

I loved the way The Smiths came on with Prokofiev at the start. That was the only time I ever saw them. I had a ticket to see Morrissey for the first time last year, in Brighton. But we had loads of snow and we couldn't even get out of the end of my road. I finally got the ticket and I never bloody made it. Maybe one day.

I WAS THERE: GLENN CORPES

I was only vaguely into them. I'd bought 'This Charming Man' on 12 inch and had a cassette copy of the first album but I was into much more obscure stuff. I went to see the support band, The Sid Presley Experience, named after three acts that had died of drug overdoses and with songs mostly about heroin addiction. The people I was with made a point of getting pissed at the bar rather than watching the band. At some point someone mentioned it was their last tour so I walked into the hall and watched them from the back for about 20 minutes. I actually got much more into The Smiths several years later and again about six years ago when my then 18 year old son got more into them than I ever had been.

I WAS THERE: LISA VINE, AGE 17

I discovered their music from the charts. I bought their *Hatful of Hollow* album, which I've still got and still play, and their songs were played very regularly on the juke box in the King's Head pub in Guildford, which attracted the town's rockabilly/alternative crowd. I remember Morrissey coming out on stage and them opening with 'William, It Was Really Nothing'. The Civic just erupted. It was bloody brilliant.

I WAS THERE: TIM NAYLOR

'How would you react if I said that I'm not from Guildford at all?'

It was fair to say that The Smiths gig at Guildford Civic Hall was approached with some trepidation. I had seen the band just over a year earlier at the notorious Reading University gig where fractious elements in the crowd had upset the singer by spitting, throwing water and generally not behaving in the approved manner.

Flyer for the Guildford Civic gig

Morrissey at Reading Uni was disengaged and bored with a crowd that was by no means hanging on his every word and, as he got more distracted, the audience sensed their quarry was weakening and taunted him further. The band performed manfully despite their singer's obvious displeasure at how the gig was unfolding, although Johnny Marr played much of the set with his back to the audience after getting a soaking early on.

Rumours that Morrissey was indeed 'still ill' following a bout of alleged man flu circulated among the onlookers prompting further heckling and, of course, the inevitable happened and he flounced during the encore of 'You've Got Everything Now'. The encore was a bad idea in the first place and, with just ten songs played in full but with little passion, many in the audience left feeling severely short-changed.

This made the Guildford Civic gig the equivalent of a make-or-break date. The night itself was notable for dense fog over the Hampshire-Surrey borders, making the journey over the A31 Hogs Back exceedingly treacherous. With visibility down to a few dozen yards we crawled along the dual carriageway at 20 miles an hour, bringing out the inevitable quips of going 'Nowhere Fast'.

Guildford Civic was a premier circuit venue back in the day with a decent capacity of around 1,400 people and attracted some of the biggest names including Eric Clapton, King Crimson, Bowie's Ziggy tour, Dire Straits and, of course, local boys The Stranglers. Numerous punk-era acts had played the venue and notably the Civic had hosted the first night of the White Riot Tour and The Buzzcocks' Tension Tour, with Joy Division supporting.

Because of the poor driving conditions we'd left for the venue quite early, so got to see James' support slot. And what a belter it was. This wasn't the chart-storming (and frankly much duller) seven piece band of the late Eighties/early Nineties, but the intriguing four piece version that dabbled in edgy indie tunes with a folky twist. Tim Booth was mesmeric at this point in his career, dancing bastardised versions of the hucklebuck or the mashed potato as the band thrashed out their skinny beat tunes. James were already the stars the press said they would become, it was just that no-one else knew it at that stage.

If James were aiming for the stars, then The Smiths had already sealed their place in the firmament. This was a confident, assured band fully in control of their destiny, with a stunning sophomore album under their belts and discovering their groove in more ways than one. The crowd was rammed into the venue by this stage, with a good smattering of Mozzer-alikes, down to NHS specs and even a few hearing aids no doubt purloined from elderly relatives just for the evening ('Nan… can I borrow your hearing aid?' 'Whaaat?').

This was effectively a coming out for the Smiths tribe of Surrey and Hampshire who had grown in number as the band's stature had similarly grown with a run of hit singles. Interestingly, the girl superfan who many of us believed to be muse for 'Sheila Take a Bow' was at this gig. I couldn't possibly tell who she was, but she was definitely named Sheila…

Thankfully, the band of a year earlier were unrecognisable. Much of the previous short set had focussed heavily on the debut LP and this had been replaced with some choice cuts from *Meat Is Murder* and its attendant singles. Only four songs survived from Reading – 'Hand in Glove', 'Heaven Knows I'm Miserable Now', 'Still Ill' and 'Barbarism Begins at Home'.

A spritely 'William, It was Really Nothing' kicked off proceedings and it was a heady rush through the early part of the set, so much so that Morrissey didn't address the audience ('Good evening trendsetters…') until the end of 'Handsome Devil', the fourth song they played. And they were loud, very loud… proper rock band loud, in fact.

The first real show stopper followed immediately, as 'How Soon Is Now?' rang out, with Johnny Marr's vibrato guitar drawing cheers from the crowd. The swooping chords and Morrissey's sonorous vocals prompted a sing-along from some parts of the crowd, now supremely familiar with the song from the flipside of 'William' or from the Peel session from earlier in the year.

Forthcoming single 'Shakespeare's Sister' was introduced as a 'kind little single' followed by a headlong rush through 'Heaven Knows I'm Miserable Now', 'That Joke Isn't Funny Anymore', 'Rusholme Ruffians' and 'Hand in Glove'.

The main set drew to a close with a double whammy of 'Still Ill' and a creepy and affecting '*Meat Is Murder*', the buzzsaw ringing out even more ominously in the opening passage than on the LP version. The band exited stage left but were soon back as the fervent crowd yelled and screamed for more.

The encore of 'Miserable Lie'/'Barbarism Begins at Home' was the icing on the cake for the by now supplicant masses, with dancing on the venue floor. It has been said many times, but the boys in the rhythm section really earned their corn on the latter track, which was simply huge in every respect.

Then they were gone. The crowd filtered out towards the car parks, bus station and railway platforms, peering through the by now near freezing fog. We hung around for a bit while the crowd dispersed, hoping to see the band but gave up as the temperature dropped. The drive home to Fleet was almost surreal as four of us crammed into my Toyota Celica, sliding through the dense murk in silence along the deserted road. We probably wouldn't have heard anyone talking anyway – as I said earlier the band were loud and the ears were still ringing the next day.

It was, in many ways, the near perfect gig. A fabulous and arguably surprising support slot from James, followed by an all-conquering performance from the headliners. I even got a poster for the gig, which I still own 34 years later. I would see The Smiths several times again, including the Royal Albert Hall gig, but they were never as good for me as they were on that night at Guildford Civic. But it's not quite my favourite gig at that venue... a few years later I trod the same boards myself with my band Handsome Bastards and, sorry Mozzer, nothing would ever beat that!

I WAS THERE: MALCOLM WYATT, AGE 17

1985 was an important one for a lad not long turned 17. So many personal landmarks with live music at the forefront. I was a lower sixth-former, wondering now how I fitted in my studies amid such a busy diary. Things took a major turn in the second half of the year, dating for the first time while Saturday and holiday work at my hometown branch of Boots helped pay for a growing vinyl obsession. If my diaries are right, the visit of The Smiths to Guildford Civic Hall was my 19th gig, just three days after the thrill of catching The Ramones up the A3 at the Lyceum in London.

The Smiths also turned out to be my first proper date... of sorts. I'm not convinced my college friend Karen saw it like that mind. She was hardly hanging off my arm. Way too good for the likes of me with self-esteem low on my list of attributes. I can't recall how we ended up going along together or how this fairly-shy lad (painfully, probably) asked her. I'm pretty sure she bought her own ticket, so maybe it was just a case of meeting nearby.

I wasn't obsessive about The Smiths, but I'd been a fan since first hearing John Peel and David 'Kid' Jensen play them, and for me the *Hatful of Hollow* compilation album collecting those BBC Radio One sessions resonated far more than the eponymous debut.

I even cited Mozzer in a General Studies O-level exam that summer, my discourse on vegetarianism ending with the line, 'In the words of Steven Patrick Morrissey, 'Who hears when animals cry?' I like to think the examiner raised his eyebrows, impressed, wondering how this obscure poet had eluded him.

I was learning bass guitar too, a left-hander spending far too much time copying intricate Andy Rourke lines in my bedroom, 'Barbarism Begins at Home' and 'This Charming Man' particular favourites. Not as if it ever came to much more than garage band status for this plodder.

Like The Clash before them, Rourke, Mike Joyce and Johnny Marr looked the part, the latter always the genius for these ears. Ah, those melodies and that delivery. As a backing band they were similarly impressive, and who could resist Sandie Shaw out front.

I never quite knew what to make of Morrissey, but he was engaging and funny in the (mainly) *NME* interviews I read, and those lyrics were often sublime. The gladioli and hearing aid stunts left me cold, only serving to fuel non-believers' arguments in countless pub, workplace and common room arguments in the following months and years as to the band's merits. But there was no doubting the artistry. I guess I saw him the same way I saw many more aloof, camp great poets down the years, such as John Betjeman. A genius wordsmith, so to speak. So many great lines.

A gay workmate later questioned Mozza's tongue-in-cheek celibacy claims from his own memories of nights out in Manchester, but it didn't really matter. He had a turn of phrase which, worked so well, so many of those songs standing up today, 1985's *The Queen is Dead* a masterpiece.

I hadn't warmed to *Meat Is Murder* so much, but it had its highpoints, with the Guildford show impressive from the moment the searchlights swirled around the dancefloor to the accompaniment of Prokoviev's *Romeo and Juliet*, a perfect curtain-raiser. Little more can I recall about that night, something that embarrassed me when interviewing James' Saul Davies and Jim Glennie in later years. Had I even see them? I think so, but have little to base that on.

Nothing came of my date with Karen. Not so much as a stolen kiss under the iron bridge, or even outside nearby music venue the Wooden Bridge. Nature hadn't made a man of me ... yet. Youth, eh – wasted on the young. We're still in touch though, both impressed at having been there.

I WASN'T THERE: JULIA DODD

I had tickets for this but sold them on the door, my friend and I making the monumentally stupid decision to go and see our friends rehearse their band in Cranleigh Scout Hall. I'm still bitterly regretting the decision.

I WAS THERE: ANDY COLES

I was at art college in Farnham in Surrey. I saw them three times. The first time was at Hammersmith Palais. This was the gig where Sandie Shaw came on and sang 'I Don't Owe You Anything'. Before the gig, Johnny Marr walked past us and I was surprised how slight he was. He was wearing a yellow roll neck sweater and black beads.

I then saw them at the GLC Jobs For A Change Festival. This was a beautiful day. I got to see Billy Bragg twice, The Redskins and Mari Wilson before The Smiths came on. There'd been quite a bit of trouble during The Redskins set and I seem to recall a punch up down the front. One of the guys who tagged along with my college friends and myself was on a photography course and managed to get right down the front during The Smiths' set. One of his photos subsequently appeared on the back of *ZigZag* magazine. The band were amazingly tight and played a few fairly new numbers. My prominent memory of the day is getting the sleeve torn on my old suit jacket in the melee so that it was almost hanging off. A puce-faced middle aged man was trying to get to the back of the crowd after initially being trapped down the front and we were laughing at his angry face as he passed by. That'd be me these days!

Guildford Civic was probably the favourite of my Smiths' gigs. The band were on top form. James went down a storm, possibly as Morrissey had raved about them and had chosen their 'What's The World?' song as one of his favourites on Janice Long's Radio One evening show. The Smiths went on to cover and record their own live version later on. James at that point looked like folk group The Spinners, dressed in fisherman's jumpers.

During The Smiths' set I managed to get right down the front and held Morrissey's thumb at some point. The journey home was memorable as we decided, possibly fuelled by excessive quantities of cider, that we would walk the 11 miles back to Farnham. The evening was dreadful, really misty and spooky, and as we walked along the Hog's Back, passing cars silhouetted the trees making it look like a Spielberg movie. We thought our hitchhiking attempt was successful as a car pulled up and we ran to accept his 'offer of a lift'. We reached the car and peered inside at the driver sorting out his seat belt. Three black-clothed figures stood expecting the bloke to open the door and as one of us tapped on the passenger window, he looked up in total fear and sped away as if the ghostly ship's crew from Jon Carpenter's *The Fog* had come for him. Perhaps he'd not seen us and had just stopped to adjust his seatbelt? He probably still tells the tale of how he saw three ghosts on the Hog's Back.

I bought a couple of the posters for the gig for £1 each at the merchandising stand. It's amazing that they survived the journey home. I advertised one on eBay a few years back and it went within half an hour for £300, so that wasn't a bad investment. I still have one framed on my landing.

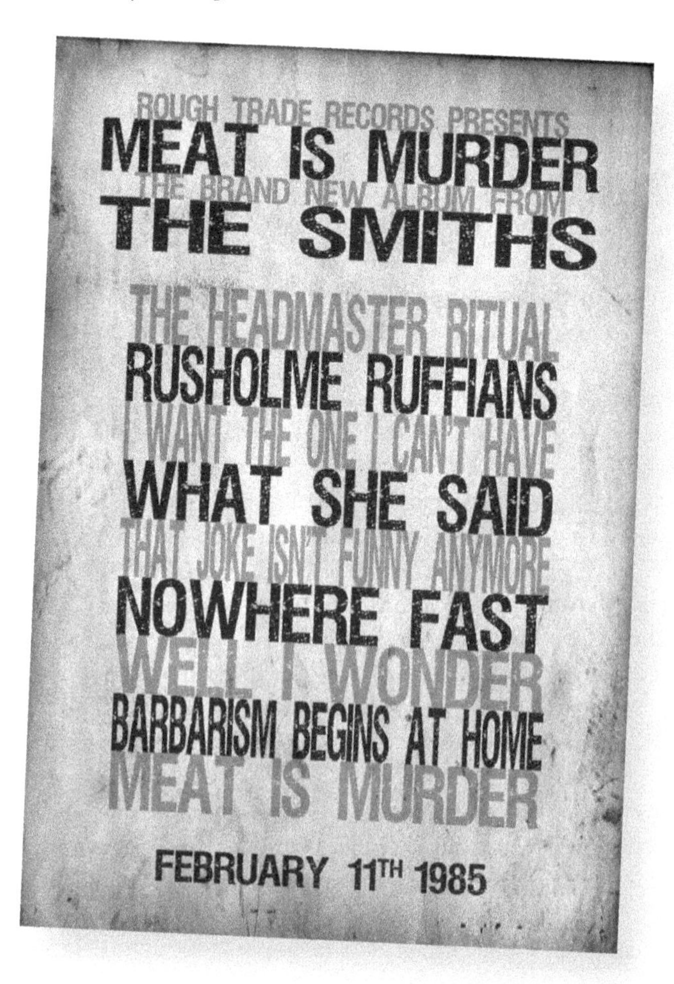

BRIXTON ACADEMY

1 MARCH 1985, LONDON, UK

I WAS THERE: KEITH BRADBURY, AGE 24

A neighbour who worked in radio had heard 'This Charming Man' on John Peel and when he put it on the turntable it just blew me away. I must have played it hundreds of thousands of times since. It's my 'go to' song to put me in a good mood or before I go out. I remember seeing them on *Top of the Pops* and I just fell in love. The fact that Morrissey was from my home city and that he sang about places I knew, and about things that I was going through, made it even more special. I didn't get to see them until 1985 but - wow - what a concert. I had never experienced anything like it. I'd seen mass hysteria before - my first gig was T.Rex at Manchester Free Trade Hall in 1971 - but not on this scale! It began quietly enough as the crowd gathered, and with so many Morrissey clones it was wonderful.

I went with a close friend and we stood about half way up the sloping floor. After a while I noticed people turning and pointing at us, but then realised it was not me they were pointing at but the guy and his girlfriend standing next to us – Pete Burns, eye patch and all, of Dead or Alive. I remember swaying back and forth with the surge of the crowd and Moz asking people to invade the stage. People said there was some fighting but I didn't see any. I couldn't take my eyes off him so there could have been a free for all right in front of me and I doubt I would have noticed. It was the *Meat Is Murder* tour and I remember some people who clearly didn't share Moz's sentiments and, when they started 'Barbarism Begins at Home', booed over the first sounds. But they were soon drowned out – hey, I didn't care - I just sang along. I was spell bound, and have been to this day. My wife is still convinced that if Moz knocked on my door and asked me to run away with him I would. Well, maybe!

I found out when Moz's autobiography came out that he had worked in the same office as me when he was 15 and I was 17. So near and yet so far! I bought every single including 12 inch ones, and every album, and still have them all. I've seen Morrissey solo many times; he is still amazing but the electricity of that night could never really be repeated for me.

I WAS THERE: KRISTIN COLLINS, AGE 17

I was in England from the US for several months on a long holiday before starting college. A few months earlier I was having drinks with a sound engineer friend - no one asked for ID back then - who knew Morrissey and Marr. So when they walked into the pub we were in, they sat down with us for a few rounds. I knew who they were and liked the band, but they weren't huge stars in America, so to me the whole thing seemed quite casual. Various musicians frequented the pubs in the area, so them showing up was not a big deal. I remember chatting with Morrissey about different things including music, and specifically recall both of us saying we liked The Go-Betweens.

That same friend was able to get us into the venue early the night of the show so I could be up front. But things quickly got crazy so I didn't stay up there long. After a few songs I moved back where I was less likely to get bruised and could actually breathe. Honestly, the band sounded pretty rough, but Morrissey was quite happy, exuberantly dancing and interacting with the crowd. He was obviously having fun and was fascinating to watch.

The highlights were 'That Joke Isn't Funny Anymore' and 'How Soon Is Now?' while the 'Barbarism Begins at Home' encore was great. The energy of the whole night was pretty intense, and I left with the feeling that I had just seen something special.

I will always remember my first time seeing Morrissey live. I couldn't know then that a life long obsession had been ignited. Three decades on I've been to well over 50 shows, including shows at this same venue, and I have tickets for more. That first Smiths show opened with 'William, It Was Really Nothing'. And when I last saw Morrissey live, he also opened with this song. What a nice way to bookend 34 years of absolute and unwavering love for The Smiths and Morrissey.

GUILDHALL

3 MARCH 1985, PORTSMOUTH, UK

I WAS THERE: DEBBIE CALLAWAY, AGE 23

They were amazing. I remember Morrissey walking off the stage because fans were spitting at him and him saying, 'It's not 1976!' I was so relieved when he came back on stage. I still have my programme from that concert. I was devastated when they split up. I think I just heard it on the radio. I have three sons aged 35, 29 and 23 who all love them too as they grew up listening to them.

HEXAGON THEATRE

4 MARCH 1985, READING, UK

I WAS THERE: MARC BEATTIE, AGE 15

I remember Tim Booth's horrendous fluffy blue jumper more than anything the main band played, apart from they said they were playing a tune for the first time. I can't remember which one. I really remember nothing about it other than being underwhelmed.

I WAS THERE: ROBERT PARKIN, AGE 15

It was my first gig and I lied to my parents to say a friend's dad was taking us so I could go on my own. I remember trying to emulate Morrissey's quiff with loads of Mum's hairspray, an over-sized collarless grandad shirt and a bunch of daffodils in the back pocket of my 501s. People were selling knock off t-shirts and posters outside the venue. James supported and Tim Booth was dancing like an epileptic. All I can really remember from The Smiths is Morrissey whirling his gladioli around and Johnny Marr just looking so cool. I think the backdrop was the cover photo from the 'That Joke Isn't Funny Anymore' single.

I WAS THERE: MICK ROWLEY, AGE 17

I became an instant fan. Morrissey's lyrics and the music touched me like nothing had before. I had just left school, Thatcher was in power and everything felt directionless and very dull. The Smiths changed everything from then on. I, and so many others, clung on to Morrissey's every word. He made me feel accepted for being an outsider and definitely less alone.

I lived just outside of Reading, so it was great to be able to see them so close to home. I took my 13 year old sister. She wasn't a huge fan but she wanted to see them. I still tell her how lucky she was to have seen one of the most exciting live bands of all time, especially at such a young age. I danced all night, trying my best to imitate Morrissey's every move.

The second time I saw The Smiths was on 24 October 1986 on the *Queen Is Dead* tour, at Brixton Academy. The Railway Children supported and, like James at the Hexagon in Reading, they were brilliant too.

A few months later I bought the *NME* as usual. I was more than heartbroken when I saw the news they'd split. It was the end of an era for me and something that still upsets me today. But at least I got to see them twice, which, is more than most people I know. I'm still a huge fan of Morrissey and have seen him 20 plus times, once in Rome. He'll always be a huge part of my life. I don't ever want The Smiths to reform, as I want my wonderful memories to remain intact. There's no way they'd ever get back together anyway. So many bands mean a lot to me, but The Smiths, and especially Morrissey, changed my life forever.

Photo: Andy Catlin

I WAS THERE: ANDY WHITE

I saw The Smiths twice on the *Meat Is Murder* tour. Reading was notable due to me losing my car. I parked up on a side street near the venue. My intention was to get drunk and sleep in the car, something I did a few times in this era. Trouble was I bumped into Julie, a girl I knew from Basingstoke. She persuaded me to go back to her place with her on the last train - she took advantage of my good nature actually. I awoke in her bed the next morning with a massive hangover and had to get to work in Overton, about 10 miles in the opposite direction from Reading. I got a bus to work, spent most of the day throwing up into the River Test, which ran through the site where I worked, and then persuaded a mate to give me a lift to Reading to collect my car. But when we got to Reading I couldn't find it and we drove round for about two hours before eventually I did.

Back to the gig. I got in the hall early to make sure I saw them and there was a sparse crowd for their short set. I hadn't seen Tim Booth doing his crazy dancing before and drummer Gavan Whelan was out of this world, the best I've ever seen by a distance. I then became something of a James obsessive and saw them about 10 times in 1985-86.

By now The Smiths had massive support. The venue was heaving and I got to the front of the stage during the first song. I got quite a few bruises from the crush - you've not really been to a concert unless you get a few cuts and bruises. Their set was mostly from *Meat Is Murder* plus a few old favourites. I always loved it during 'Still Ill' when Morrissey used to collapse on stage during the chorus. I remember him introducing 'Shakespeare's Sister' as their new single - it was released about two weeks later.

I rate Mike Joyce and Andy Rourke as a functional rhythm section but they are relatively weak compared to Hook and Morris in New Order, Whelan and Glennie in James, Reni and Mani in The Stone Roses. Just think - The Smiths could have been even better. They made it really on the strength of Morrissey with his ego and lyrics - he's not a great singer - and of course Marr's guitar and tunes. Joyce and Rourke were really just filling the gaps, and not contributing that much, relatively speaking. Hence all the later anguish in the courtroom over the royalties.

POOLE ARTS CENTRE

6 MARCH 1985, POOLE, UK

I WAS THERE: STEVE CATTERALL

Down to Poole. By this time, as well as Paul and me, we'd picked up three other regular passengers - Jo, who was a big fan of Johnny's and who we'd initially met at Chippenham, and two Japanese girls, whose names I can't remember anymore. Jo had a history of following The Smiths around and had been to quite a few of the 1984 English dates, so she was a bit of a veteran. The Japanese girls used to turn up at the start of each tour and then disappear afterwards. Those three were with us pretty much right through until late 1986. As well as them, we were starting to recognise a number of regular fans that would turn up at every venue. By the Scottish tour later in the year there would be a band of regulars, which made the travelling and hanging around waiting much more bearable.

The venue at Poole was down by the sea. I remember hearing the sound check sitting in the car park round the back, although with the combination of being outside and the wind off the sea, it was quite hard to make out what songs they were playing. I think it was here that I first heard them playing 'Bigmouth'. Even with the muffled sound it sounded quite different to all the other songs.

Going to many of the shows, you got to hear the songs grow, which was interesting. Actually our experience was probably the opposite of most people's, as we got used to the live versions of songs before we heard the recorded version a lot of the time. I remember being distinctly unimpressed with the recorded version of 'Ask' when it came out, having loved the version they were playing live, which was much more jangly and urgent.

I WAS THERE: CHARLIE PINDER

1985 was one of the best years of my life. I had just started a new job and only a few days later I was about to see the best band that the world has ever seen and will ever see. However, at this stage nobody I knew was of the same opinion! Like many early Smiths fans (I assumed), I travelled to the gig alone, a half an hour bus trip from the Dorset market town of Wimborne Minster to the bright lights of Poole.

Can you guess which band Charlie likes?

I wish I had a phone back then, to look back at a selfie of me in my flowery shirt. I sure I looked a lot less cool than I remember it today. The bus stop was just over the road from the Arts Centre. I had no idea what to expect from the new 'love-hate' band from Manchester. My only other gigs at the Arts Centre had been Black Sabbath with my sister, which was frightening and exciting and obviously deafening, and Madness with school mates, which was great as I actually knew the songs.

I can't remember if there had been a support, but I can remember the thrill of The Smiths walking out to Prokofiev and the loud cheer when the music stopped. The rest is a blur. I stood in awe, first staring at Morrissey and singing every single word of the songs I knew, and then glancing over to Johnny Marr and starring once again, this time in wonderment of his guitar skills and craft.

As the night went on, they did a song that was unknown to me, it was hauntingly beautiful. Months later, I bought a bootleg cassette recording of the following night's gig in Brighton and the song was titled 'Take Me Out'. On the day of the release of *The Queen is Dead*, I picked up my pre-order copy from Square Records in Wimborne and played it to death that evening. To my absolute joy, the song came on and it was actually called 'There is a Light That Never Goes Out' and it confirmed that my love for The Smiths would live for eternity!

I probably remember the gig more because of my Brighton bootleg cassette, which I still have. I know I got home safely and I know that no one at school the next day was particularly impressed that I went to the gig. But I didn't really think that I'd be playing

Smiths songs as much as I do today. I do have a pretty impressive collection on vinyl and it is one of my most prized possessions. For the record, my favourite songs now the dust has settled on The Smiths, are 'Still Ill' and 'Ask'.

The best feeling was taking my daughter to see Morrissey at Bournemouth a few years back. She wanted to go and bought the tickets as a birthday present to me. We stood together and Morrissey was at his brilliant best.

I WAS THERE: RACHEL WALDEN, AGE 17

I went with my boyfriend. Morrissey (I think) had 'Meat is murder' written across his chest or back. The end of the concert was very shocking - it was the sound of the abattoir, the animals screaming and the sound of saws! The *Meat Is Murder* album in my opinion was one of their best. I'm now 50 years old and my ringtone on my phone is 'There is a Light That Never Goes Out'.

THE DOME

7 MARCH 1985, BRIGHTON, UK

I WAS THERE: WAYNE LUNDQVIST FORD, AGE 16

I first remember hearing The Smiths with the release of 'Hand In Glove' when it hit the indie charts. But it wasn't until the release of 'This Charming Man' that I started to sit up and listen. I had just turned 16 and the lyrics spoke to me. I wasn't really sure I was getting the full meaning of them but I didn't really care. It was the bright, chiming guitar of Johnny Marr that really grabbed me.

I bought a copy of The Smiths self-titled album on cassette so I could listen to it on my Sony Walkman. The image of Morrissey waving his gladioli about on *Top of the Pops* kind of stuck with me and made me giggle when I listened to the singles and album, but Marr's guitar was brilliant and that, along with the rhythm section blew me away musically, the first time this had happened to me since The Jam.

A few months after 'This Charming Man', the *Meat Is Murder* album came out. I bought it the same day, again on cassette so I could listen to it through headphones on my motorbike. The abbatoir sound at the beginning of the album was haunting, although not so much that I jumped on board with being a vegetarian. 'Rusholme Ruffians' was my favourite track and I loved the way it sounded like '(Marie's The Name) His Latest Flame' by Elvis. I wasn't an Elvis fan but I had liked that track as a kid and thought it was cool nod to the past, taking something and making it part of our own culture.

My mother was working for a publishing company in Haywards Heath, Sussex and said she worked closely with the promoter Phil McIntyre. So when I saw that Outlaw and Phil McIntyre were promoting the *Meat Is Murder* tour, I asked if she could get me a ticket for the gig at Brighton Dome. A few days before the gig my mother came home with two tickets with 'guest ticket' stamped across the front. I felt really special and went out that night to tell my mates all about it. A friend I rode motorcycles with me then was interested in the gig so I said he could have the other ticket. I can't recall his name now and I think I probably sold it to him a bit cheaper in order to get some petrol money for my bike.

We took the train from Burgess Hill to Brighton so we could have a couple of (under age) beers on the way there or even at the venue. Brighton Dome is a seated venue, an old fashioned concert hall, which seemed an odd setting for The Smiths to play. Most people remained seated through James and I was impressed at how the band swapped and played different instruments through their set.

Finally the lights dipped and 'Dance of the Knights' started playing, probably the first piece of classical music that caught my attention. I spent ages hunting down who it was and what it was called. There was no internet then and going into a record shop and humming the bit you could remember to a fellow spotty youth in HMV was completely out of the question. But I found it a few years later and I still associate it with seeing The Smiths.

As soon as the band hit the stage, people were up and out of the seats. Me and my mate opted, like many others, to stand up on the back of the old wooden seats. Many seats and people were seen collapsing through the opening number 'William, It Was Really Nothing', much to the despair of the middle-aged female stewards who were probably only a little younger than my nan at the time. As much as they pleaded, nobody was sitting back down to watch The Smiths. Morrissey and the band were also showered with gladioli, which was actually quite hilarious.

I can't remember too much about Morrissey as I was pretty much transfixed by Marr and his black Rickenbacker 330, a guitar that I decided I would one day own. (I do now own one but it is the Sunburst version and I still can't play like Johnny!). Apart from studying Marr, I didn't really pay much attention to the rest of the band. I thought Andy Rourke's hair was cool and I had a similar cut a few weeks later but it didn't look as good on me and I grew it out.

They played my favourite songs - 'Rusholme Ruffians', 'Nowhere Fast' and 'That Joke Isn't Funny Anymore'. Everyone left with a smile on their face. My mate wandered around to the back door of the Dome to see if we could catch the band coming out. There weren't many people there and we were about to leave when the band exited the stage door.

Morrissey was the first one out. I said 'hi' and was about to offer up my ticket to be signed but he just rushed past. I thought he was quite aloof but what did I know really? I turned around and Marr was there. He took my ticket and scribbled across the back of it. I told him I enjoyed the gig, I think he said 'great' and then he was gone too.

I stuck with the band and their records right until the end although I never saw them live again. As a radio deejay, I still get a kick and a laugh out of playing 'Hang the DJ' ('Panic') and I think I always will. I still love Marr's guitar and as I got older I started to understand Morrissey's lyrics more and actually got the humour in them that others missed. I was so glad I did see them live at least once.

I WAS THERE: PAUL THOMAS SCOTT FULKER, AGE 18

To this day, the best gig I ever saw. It was incredible. I went with three close mates and a few girls. I was in a band and we were mad on The Smiths, The Icicle Works, The Church, Echo and The Bunnymen and Lloyd Cole. I hadn't been to many gigs so I guess I was in awe. I remember the seats had vegetarian and antivivisection flyers on them. We were all veggies and into animal welfare.

We all ended up on the backs of the chairs on the front few rows. I was stuck behind a guy with a massive spliff. It was a crush waiting to happen. At some point the seats snapped and everyone was on the deck on top of each other. I remember scrambling about trying to get up. Somehow I managed to get close to the front and stayed there for the whole gig.

It went dark and the classical piece by Prokofiev played. Then the lights came on and 'William' started. They looked larger than life. Marr was smiling his head off and I remember him playing his Rickenbacker 360 Jetglo. Rourke was statuesque. He reminded me of a Thunderbird puppet. Weird, I know, but they all did - they must have had make up on or maybe the lights were over-exposing their faces as they looked exactly like popstars!

At the end, Morrissey stripped off his shirt and threw it into the crowd. It was like a pack of dogs ripping at flesh. One of my mates, a girl called Tina, had hold of the whole sleeve and was hanging on to it for dear life! She was smiling and determined not to let go of it. It was a gold base shirt with loads of coloured diamonds all over it. I had Morrissey's glass mineral water bottle off the stage. I kept it for years. I'm not sure if I've still got the shirt remnant.

I WAS THERE: NICK LINAZASORO

There was the hearing aid and flowers thrown from the back pockets. Nothing out of the ordinary!

Nick Linazasoro's ticket for the Brighton show

I WAS THERE: KAREN PARKER

I nearly didn't go and thank god I did. I have loved Morrissey ever since.

I WAS THERE: NICK MYALL

The Smiths had released *Hatful of Hollow* and *Meat Is Murder* since I had seen them in early 1984 and had amassed an amazing catalogue of classic tunes. *Meat Is Murder* is my favourite Smiths album. Most people go for *The Queen Is Dead*, but I always thought *Meat Is Murder* was when they added some extra colour to the tunes with Johnny's intricate guitar patterns lighting up Morrissey's lyrics. I had been playing it to death since it came out, so tickets for the Dome gig were snapped up from Virgin Records in Brighton as soon as the date was announced.

When the day arrived Matt, James and I left Haywards Heath Sixth Form extra early and headed on down to Brighton for the gig. James from Manchester's Factory Records were an inspired choice as the support band on the tour. Morrissey had been banging on about them for weeks in the *NME* and *Melody Maker* (both essential weekly reading at the time) and 'Hymn from a Village' and their other early tunes went down well with the crowd, but the main event was about to happen....

'William, It was Really Nothing', 'What Difference Does It Make?', 'This Charming Man', as well as 'Nowhere Fast', 'What She Said', 'I Want The One I Can't Have' and 'Headmaster Ritual' from the new LP all had the Dome jumping. A strobe light lit up a plain white backdrop as the eerie vibrato intro to 'How Soon Is Now?' signalled another heartfelt sing-along from the audience. Blood red lighting underlined the message of 'Meat Is Murder' while 'That Joke isn't Funny Anymore' hit home with heart breaking impact. Some of the first album also got a run out and 'Miserable Lie' built up to its impressive climax with as much force as ever.

We were also treated to a new song and the rush of 'Shakespeare's Sister' was a high point, the latest single and a bonus for the fans as a standalone track. We were right up the front as usual, bashing Jonny Marr's desert boots in time to the tunes. It was fairly messy but luckily I managed to hang onto my watch and shoes - unlike at the Echo and the Bunnymen gig in Crawley!

As the gig came to a triumphant finale, Morrissey threw his patterned psychedelic shirt into the audience. I can still picture the hilarious sight of a mob of teenage Smiths fans ripping it to shreds. I still have a piece of it somewhere.

I WAS THERE: KAREN WALDON-SAUNDERS, AGE 16

I was really into Duran Duran to begin with, and Depeche Mode, Nik Kershaw and Kajagoogoo. Then I got into The Smiths as an adolescent. I loved the lyrics and Johnny's guitar playing, the jangly guitars. Their music is very funny and witty and downbeat and sarcastic. It's not depressing. It's sardonic and witty. I can remember dancing around my room to *Hatful of Hollow*. My best friend John was also a fan. We went to secondary school together. We went to all the gigs together.

I remember the red seats and it being an all seated venue. Tickets were £5. My memory is that James were booed off but I don't know if that's correct. I remember it being really dark when The Smiths came on and them playing against a black background. There were lots of flashing strobe lights and lots of cow noises for 'Meat Is Murder' and that line, 'heifer whines could be human cries', made a real impression on me.

There was a huge bundle down at the front and I was desperate to go down the front but we didn't. My mum and dad used to drop us off and collect us and we always had to sit. I wasn't allowed to stand at gigs. But if you were close enough you could lean on the stage with your elbows. The bouncers were just keeping people back. I feel really, really lucky that I saw The Smiths live because they didn't last very long. I felt like Morrissey was singing directly to me.

WINTER GARDENS

8 MARCH 1985, MARGATE, UK

I WAS THERE: DAN WELLER

Margate had received more than its fair share of battle scars during the two world wars, so I never considered it 'the seaside town that they forgot to bomb' which Morrissey would sing about so scathingly in 'Everyday is Like Sunday'. Though in 1985 you could have been forgiven for thinking our little resort might be a candidate for dystopian fiction as we continued to struggle on in an era of cheap holidays abroad, our hotels gradually replaced by B&B accommodation for the ill-fated. So when The Smiths added the Winter Gardens to the *Meat Is Murder* tour that year, my initial euphoria was replaced by thoughts of, 'Who the hell is going to attend?'

My fears worsened when I noticed that the ticket I'd paid a fiver for at the box office bore the number 001. Sadly, having given this blue slip of paper the reverence I might have reserved for a winning Wonka bar wrapper, it was turned to confetti at the door on the night of the concert, although I did manage to secure a promotional poster.

Dan Weller's poster for the Margate gig

So what would Moz make of a Margate audience not known for its exuberance at shows? The Smiths stepped out of the wings to pockets of rapturous applause but it was clear that some oafish louts had gone along to heckle the rising star. Wearing gladioli in his back pocket while twirling around like a drunken ballerina, they believed, mocked traditional values of masculinity. A few beers were thrown.

In Thatcher's Britain, Boy George was too obvious a target. With Morrissey, the lines were blurred. A challenge if you like. There wasn't a lot of banter. It was hot in the mosh pit and I had half a mind on keeping my tour programme free from creases. Andy Rourke's thundering bass riff rode tandem with Mike Joyce's workmanlike drums. My ribcage vibrated like a road drill as I studied Johnny Marr effecting his best Keith Richards impression, the chiming notes picked on his Les Paul Gibson ricocheting off the hall's neo-Grecian interior.

And the joy of a new song! 'Shakespeare's Sister' was premiered, which I instantly loved as it surely paid homage to the Buzzcocks. Neutrals may have gone along hoping to hear 'Heaven Knows I'm Miserable Now', but they'd have been disappointed. I personally would have loved the beautiful 'Well I Wonder'. It was a night for the devotee, so an understaffed chant for an encore at the end of the set was rewarded with a sarcastic, 'Well if you're sure? I mean, we wouldn't want to twist your arm or anything.'

Ah, Morrissey. You may have thought you were misunderstood, but did you ever really get us?

I WAS THERE: STEVE WILLIAMS

When I got into The Smiths I was about 14 years old. I was quite an awkward 13, 14 year old and it was like they were singing directly to me. The songs spoke about how I felt and my life. I'm from East London but grew up in Kent. At the time I was living in a small village called Borden, just near Sittingbourne. There were quite a few kids about the same age as myself, and virtually all of us got into The Smiths at the same time. My brother was a couple of years younger than me and he was very into The Smiths too. I bought the first album on the day of release from Woolworths in Sittingbourne. I couldn't wait to get home and play it. It was never off the turntable for weeks after it came out.

We only ever saw them the once. I went with my brother and my best mate at the time, an older lad called Tim Melia. He had seen them previously at the University of Kent at Canterbury. Part of the attraction of seeing The Smiths was because James were supporting them and we had all got into James' first album at the time. *Hymns from the Village* had just come out. So it was a double whammy for us.

My parents got the tickets as a 16th birthday present for me. It was a school day. My brother and I rushed home from school, very excited to be going. It was only a few weeks before I was due to start doing my O levels and CSEs and I remember my parents saying, 'Whatever you do, don't be late.' Tim drove us to the gig. It was about a 40 minute drive from Sittingbourne to Margate so to have them playing so close to home was fantastic. It was the first time I'd ever been to the Winter Gardens – I've seen loads of bands there since – and it's a very atmospheric venue.

It's a very old fashioned venue, over 100 years old, but the way it was decorated was perfect for The Smiths. I don't believe it was sold out because it never felt packed in there. We got there as the doors opened. They played quite a strange, eclectic bunch of songs, lots of album tracks and obscure tracks. They came on and barrelled straight into 'Nowhere Fast'. There was no 'hello'. The crowd were more taken aback watching, whereas I think Morrissey wanted everyone jumping and bouncing and it wasn't like that in there at all. I don't think Morrissey was in the right frame of mind. At the end of the first song, he was moaning at the audience, telling them to get more into it and get more involved. It was quite a subdued atmosphere. I don't think he liked that. He also had lots of problems with feedback on his microphone. Every time he crossed paths with Marr he seemed to get massive feedback. At one point he threw his microphone down mid song. I was thinking, 'Does he actually want to be here?' It was almost like he was fulfilling an appointment. It didn't take anything away from it for us, though, because we were so overjoyed to be seeing The Smiths. At one stage something got thrown on the stage, which Morrissey didn't like. 'Turn the light up. Who threw that?'

To this day, my all time favourite song is 'What Difference Does It Make?' and they didn't play it on the night. So I went home disappointed. Their two biggest songs were that and 'This Charming Man', which they didn't play either. They made a big thing about their next single when they played 'Shakespeare's Sister'. The crowd got excited for that song because it was new and we hadn't heard it before, so that went down very well.

At the end of the main set, they ended one instrument at a time. Morrissey went off and then Andy Rourke and it was just Mike Joyce left on drums and Johnny Marr. And then Mike Joyce stopped and that left Johnny front of stage, just playing the outro to whatever song it was for probably two minutes before just quietly fading away and playing as he walked off the stage.

I WAS THERE: GLEN WILLIAMS

Me, my brother and a really good friend throughout the Eighties just went to gigs all the time. We were brought up in a rural part of Kent where there was nothing to do so the three of us just went gigging whenever there was a gig we could get to. We were very into indie and alternative music. I had a particular affinity with The Smiths because of the political messages and the outspokenness of Morrissey's lyrics. They probably meant a lot more to me and had a lot greater influence over me than a lot of people I know. I became vegetarian almost immediately on the strength of 'Meat Is Murder' and I still am to this day, which is an example of how passionately I felt about the messages Morrissey was writing.

It was an incredible experience - an absolutely outstanding gig and they played all of the songs I wanted to hear. I vividly remember the end of the main set as they finished on 'Meat Is Murder'. All of the band left the stage at different times. Morrissey left first and then either Joyce or Rourke but the very last person left on stage was Johnny Marr. He played a few more bars towards the end of the song just on his own under the spotlight.

Morrissey gets an extremely negative press now. Half of me thinks, 'Oh Morrissey, what are you talking about now?' But half of me thinks it's a freedom of speech issue. 'Well, if that's your opinion, Morrissey, then good for you.' Back in the day, The Smiths seemed quite different from other people, and quite isolated intellectually. They were hopeful, courageous, different and outsiders. Those words stay with me because of Morrissey's lyrics and the political message, the anti-Thatcherism and the vegetarianism. They weren't really things that were written about and sung about in mainstream pop. It's an emotive subject. He's always been outspoken. He's always been courageous. Perhaps back in the days of The Smiths he wasn't as controversial as he is now.

GAUMONT THEATRE

11 MARCH 1985, IPSWICH, UK

I WAS THERE: MARK COWLING

I saw them three times. Ipswich in March '85 was the first. It was an official school trip from Samuel Ward Upper in Haverhill, Suffolk. Our English teacher Mr Lund - a double first from Cambridge - told us, 'Sort the tickets out and get me 40 Marlboro and I'll get the school mini bus sorted.'

I WAS THERE: CHRIS SHARY, AGE 14

In the summer of 1984 my family moved from McGuire Air Force base in New Jersey to Bentwaters Air Force base in Suffolk, England. I was to be entering high school in the fall and my parents wisely decided to rent a home in the tiny English village of Charsfield. While our village was indeed a very small pig farming community, we did have a lot of teens in the neighbourhood. My brother and I quickly became fast friends with the village kids, and they introduced us yanks to all sorts of music we had no idea even existed. At the time Billy Idol and Duran Duran were about all I wanted to listen to.

Chris Shary's ticket and badges for the Ipswich Gaumont gig

That changed rather drastically once I discovered *Top of the Pops*, *Sounds* and the *NME* and started borrowing records and tapes from the kids in my village. I was taking in new music at an alarming rate. When some of the older kids who could drive mentioned that they were planning on seeing The Smiths at the Ipswich Gaumont that following winter I was all in. At the time I was just 14 and my parents were a bit sceptical about me being driven around by other kids. Along with me and my brother, they had seen The Smiths on *Top of the Pops* and I suppose they figured, 'How much trouble could that be? I mean, the singer wears a hearing aid and what appears to be his granddad's old jumpers, for crying out loud.'

If I recall correctly The Smiths set began with siren sounds and flashing police type lights scanning the audience. It went on for what seemed like an eternity, clearly building tension, and then it all cut to Morrissey's fragile voice saying, 'Hello'. They then kicked into 'William, It Was Really Nothing'. The place erupted with dancing, flowers being tossed and the jangliest guitars I have ever heard sweeping over the heads of a few hundred spotty-faced teens. While a lot of the set was unfamiliar to me, I immediately felt like I was in on a massive secret, one I didn't necessarily want to share with the other kids. I recall 'How Soon Is Now?' being haunting and beautiful at the same time, like it was putting us all in some kind of weird trance. That night we all belonged to The Smiths, and they could do what they wanted with us.

Things really got intense with 'Meat Is Murder'. The stage became bathed in red light, and I want to say there were films of slaughterhouses projected over the band but maybe my mind was producing those images. While I was not a vegetarian, I couldn't help but think that song was the best reason I could think of to abandon meat from my diet. I simply couldn't believe anyone was singing about such topics. It didn't seem like you could and not get in trouble - remember I was 14 at the time. 'Meat Is Murder' was dark, cathartic and powerful, completely unlike anything I had ever heard before - or maybe since?

At the end of the evening I had no idea how to even describe it to my parents or friends. It was musical bliss and all I knew was I wanted to keep going to shows and being exposed to music. 34 years later, I am still going to shows on a very regular basis and have devoted my artist life to working with punk bands. The Smiths ignited my love of going to see live music.

I WAS THERE: SHELLEY LINE, AGE 14

I'm a rather lumpy 48 year old woman that lives in Norfolk. For my sins I enjoy watching *The Apprentice* on TV. However, the best part of the whole show is the opening music. 'Oh gosh, she's a prick!' you may be thinking. Can a Smiths fan really enjoy such banality? Well, yea I do, but it's that piece of music, Prokofiev's 'Romeo and Juliet - Dance of the Knights' that I love most about the show. The reason? *You* should already know! It was the band's entrance music for the *Meat Is Murder* tour in 1985 and, no matter where I am or what I'm doing, that piece of music takes my thoughts back to one of the most exciting times of my life. At the sweet and tender age of 14, I had booked myself a coach ticket to travel from Norwich to Ipswich to see my favourite band live. Actually live in the flesh. I was frenzied.

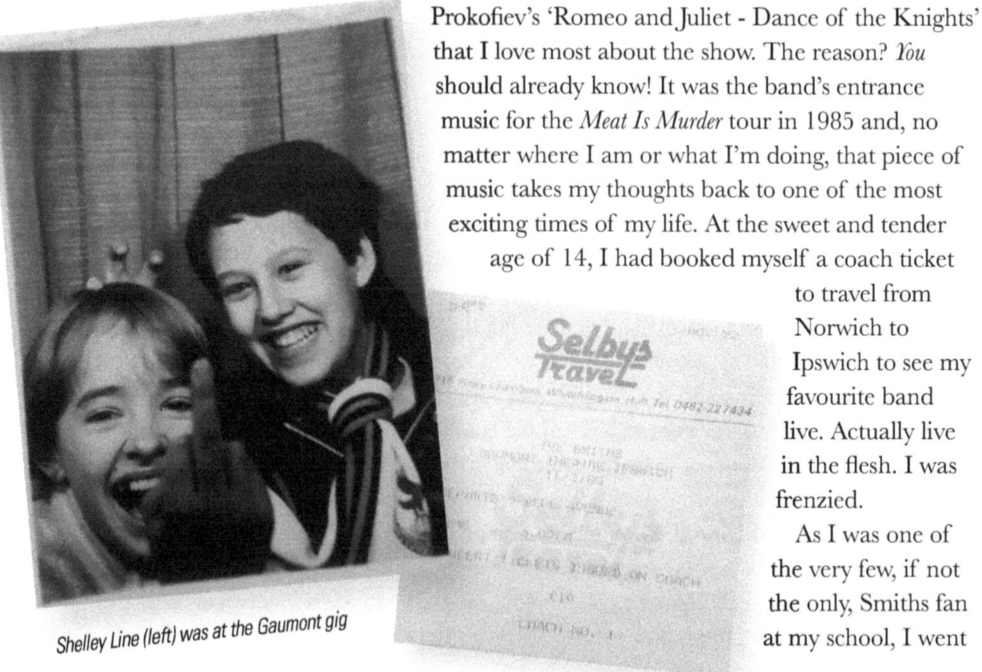

Shelley Line (left) was at the Gaumont gig

As I was one of the very few, if not the only, Smiths fan at my school, I went alone but I figured I would be amongst friends. (Naivety will either be the end or the making of you). I am not criminally shy nor a social butterfly but I knew I had to go. I was terrified of being alone but desperate to see them in equal measures, having missed the opportunity of seeing them in Norwich in February 1984 when, at 13, a chance of a snog at the local disco was too potent a lure. I was a titchy, tiny four feet eight and looked like a boy, so snogs weren't regularly on the radar. But having bought the debut album I was hooked.

I boarded the coach and sat alone with my Walkman and a cassette of *The Smiths* blaring into my ears and probably staring into my own reflection in the window. What a narcissist! I had booked a seated ticket, C4, but as a 14 year old kid from Norwich, how was I to know about the joys of the mosh pit? Inside what I thought was the wonderous Ipswich Gaumont I found my seat and waited.

Morrissey uttered one word, 'Hullo', and the crowd erupted. The set kicked off with 'William…' but to me it was the furthest thing from nothing. It was utter glory. I was watching my god. I sang myself hoarse through each and every song, having bought and played the album relentlessly in the months preceding the gig. I was completely mesmerised by the band. Morrissey said very little throughout the set but sent the audience on a tempestuous journey. There was mayhem for 'How Soon Is Now?' and veneration and complete affinity for 'Meat Is Murder'. The set ended with 'Miserable Lie'. I made no forever friends on that night. Except The Smiths.

ROYAL CONCERT HALL

12 MARCH 1985, NOTTINGHAM, UK

I WAS THERE: DAVID CRAMPTON, AGE 19

David Crampton went to Nottingham's RCH with his wife Julie

They were booked into the wrong venue as the RCH is all seated and they should really have played at Rock City. Moz said something along those lines from the stage. Great gig though. I went with my girlfriend, now my wife, and a couple of friends. The whole gig had a celebratory atmosphere. The Smiths were our group and seemed to speak to us on a personal level.

I WAS THERE: LYNNE DICKENS

They were fantastic and it was a completely different atmosphere from the Assembly Rooms in Derby in 1983. They were really well known and successful by this stage. The crowd knew the songs and Morrissey knew how to play to an audience. I heard they were originally going to play at Rock City in Nottingham but it wouldn't have been big enough.

I WAS THERE: LIZ NETHERWAY

We were all about 17 and lived in Grantham. Not very much happened there, to be honest, so getting tickets for Nottingham Royal Centre was a dream. The *Meat Is Murder* album had only just come out and we all had it, or a tape of it, and had studiously learnt all the lyrics.

Six of us crammed into a Renault 5 which had no working tape player so we had to sing all the way from Grantham to Nottingham, constantly repeating our favourite new line, 'He killed a policeman when he was 13 and somehow that really impressed me' which wasn't nice, as one of the blokes was the son of a local policeman.

We were there easily in time for the support group, James, who were superb with amazing dancing from Tim Booth (who looked about 12) plus all his crazy earwig stuff. Sadly only about 100 people watched them; all the Smiths fans were there but hanging out in the bar or foyer. Their loss. We were in the middle of the stalls - about the tenth row - but when The Smiths came on hundreds of people clambered over the chairs and squeezed into the front rows. I don't remember any security at all.

What can I remember about the set? Two new songs, 'Shakespeare's Sister', which I didn't really like, and 'Stretch Out and Wait', which I loved immediately. 'That Joke Isn't Funny Anymore' was right at the heart of the set, with a spot-lit Morrissey repeating, 'I've seen this happen in other people's lives and now it's happening in mine'. The audience could hardly breathe; it was really dramatic. I remember 'Meat Is Murder' with the abattoir video screen and Morrissey off stage making horrific screaming noises. It was truly shocking, I'd never seen or heard anything like it. And it ended with 'Miserable Lie' as the last encore, one song that we'd all agreed they most definitely wouldn't play.

I'd been to see The Pretenders at the Royal Centre the previous year and after the gig the queues at the big McDonalds next to the venue were hundreds of people long. After The Smiths there was not one person queuing.

I WAS THERE: SIOBHAN KILGANNON

I went with two friends. It was an absolutely brilliant night. Afterwards we went to a club in Nottingham called The Garage where they played The Smiths all night and where I bumped into my brother. I didn't even know he was going to the show. We never ever went out together and I remember having a great if unexpected night with him.
He died suddenly last Christmas Eve. We played The Smiths at his funeral - 'This Charming Man'.

Jo Riddell's boss at Woolworths didn't appreciate the Saturday girl playing 'Shoplifters'

I WAS THERE: JO RIDDELL, AGE 15

I liked The Cure, The Jesus and Mary Chain and New Model Army so I suppose I was always that little bit alternative. I went with my friend Emma Wilson, who was a friend from school. We were both absolutely crazy about The Smiths. Her boyfriend was called Stephen and he really looked quite like Morrissey.

He had the quiff and everything. And in the Eighties, if you were a little bit different like we were, you were into The Smiths. We went to the Nottingham concert hall and I remember seeing them do 'Meat Is Murder'. The concert hall went really dark and then the *Meat Is Murder* backdrop came up in red. You could hear cows mooing at the slaughterhouse and then you could see the blood dripping down the back and Morrissey came on and he started singing. And at that point it made me think, 'Oh my god, where does meat come from?' You don't put two and two together very often when you're 15. And I thought, 'Oh my god, yes meat is murder.' And I was so influenced by what Morrissey said that I thought, 'Well, if he says it, it must be right.' So I've not eaten meat since that day.

I worked at Woolworths at the time, doing a Saturday job in Eastwood. And I got into real trouble because I was just so obsessed with playing Smiths records. I played 'Shoplifters of the World Unite' and my boss came up to me and said, 'This is totally inappropriate for Woolworths.' So then I put on 'Panic' - 'hang the deejay' - and he wasn't very impressed with that either!

VICTORIA HALL

16 MARCH 1985, STOKE-ON-TRENT, UK

I WAS THERE: NICK BARBER

I saw them on six occasions, including twice at the Victoria Hall in Hanley, Stoke-on-Trent. On the second occasion, Morrissey walked off stage when someone threw a sausage at him.

I WAS THERE: KEV JONES

About a year after the Free Trade Hall show I saw them on the *Meat Is Murder* tour in '85. Me and the friend I worked with, and whose ticket I'd copied, used to religiously buy the *NME* every week and we saw an ad for the tour and got tickets for a few gigs - Hanley, Bradford, Sheffield Manchester. The ones that hold great memories for me are Hanley Victoria Hall and Bradford, both lovely old ornate Victorian town halls. Those are fantastic venues to see bands in. The acoustics are absolutely fantastic. They were both completely standing, on the floor, and then they had a couple of balconies around the side. A lot of those venues have fallen off the gig circuit now with the advent of arenas.

They'd started using the Prokofiev 'March of the Capulets' intro music by then. When that started, it went totally pitch black in the auditorium and they had these big searchlights flashing around the audience whilst the intro music was playing at full volume. It was pretty intense. They'd got a little bit bigger by this stage and it was just as wild, if not wilder, with the fervour in the crowd. It was absolutely crazy.

I WAS THERE: CRAIG HATFIELD

It's interesting to see that between the venue printing the tickets and putting them on sale they appear to have upped the price from £4.50 to £5! This was the *Meat Is Murder* tour; the band's only UK number 1 album. Maybe this increased popularity prompted the small price hike?

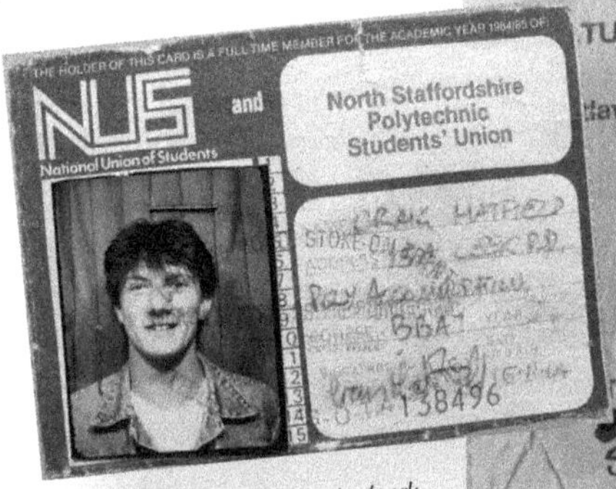

Craig Hatfield remembers the 'pork meteor missile' hitting Moz in the eye

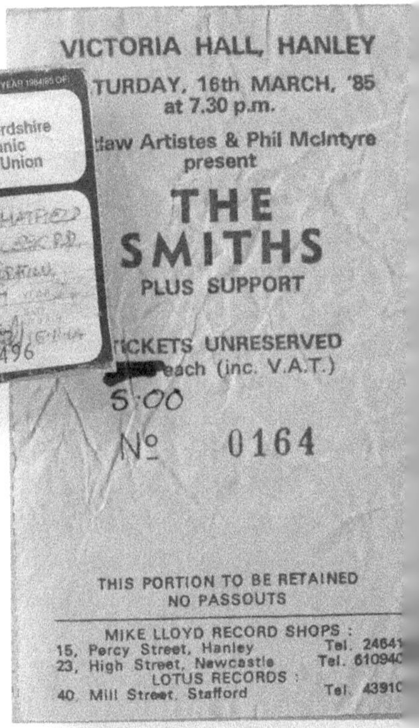

Craig Hatfield's ticket for the Hanley gig

I was in my first year at North Staffs Poly. They were the archetypal student band. I couldn't not go and made sure I got inside the venue early enough to get right down the front; about two back from front and centre of the stage, a good vantage point.

It was a memorable gig for one reason in particular. Part way through a song somebody threw something that hit Morrissey in the face, right between his nose and his eye. He flinched and then stropped off stage for a good few minutes. The band just carried on playing until he returned. I had no idea what it was that had been thrown until later. As I was filing out of the gig with my housemate Steve, we bumped into somebody off his course. He told us that he was stood about halfway back, but was right next to the bloke who threw the object. It was a sausage! And the song that his 'pork Meteor missile' interrupted? ' '! I'm not condoning such loutish behaviour, but I must admit that I was more than a little impressed by the accuracy of the throw, hitting Morrissey square in the face from such a distance. And, even as a vegetarian, I still find this story just a little bit funny.

I WAS THERE: RUSSELL HARPER

I went with a school-mate who always seems to remember a lot more about what we did when we were younger. Someone lobbed a flower at Morrissey and it hit him in the eye during 'Meat Is Murder' and he walked off. The band carried on but walked off eventually. They came back after quite a break and Morrissey said something to the effect of, 'Someone always has to spoil it.'

Russell Harper, third left, in his Duran Duran t-shirt. Moz probably wouldn't approve

I WAS THERE: DARREN APPLEBY

I can't really remember when I first heard about The Smiths but the originality of the music and the connection I had with the lyrics made an instant impact. Soon after, a friend gave me a copy of a bootleg tape with the Hacienda gig on Side A and the Kid Jensen session on Side B. Those words, 'The only thing to be in 1983, is handsome, Handsome Devil!' have stuck with me ever since.

Growing up at a school with few friends due to the fact that I never fitted in made me a prime target for bullying both by fellow pupils and the belligerent ghouls who ran the place. They believed that beating with cane and slipper was an effective way of teaching and it was formative to say the least. To hear Morrissey talk about being an outsider made my day, knowing that this was someone who just knew my life.

My first gigs were tagging along with my brother to Hawkwind, Motorhead, Scorpions, Black Sabbath, etc. but here was a band that was mine. The Smiths were my band, my passion, my life. I had limited funds as a 14 year old, but was able to buy the early singles and avidly listed to Peel and Jensen to hear more. When the chance came to see The Smiths at Stoke Poly I had to be there. My memory is hazy but I remember that the gig was quiet - compared to later tours - and the set list rather short. However the band were as tight as a drum and way ahead of everything else that was around.

Other gigs with other bands came and went, and I sunk all my paper round money into seeing as much live music as I could, but my next Smiths gig was in Hanley at the Victoria Hall. In the pit, the crowd was amazing with passion and singing. This was the *Meat Is Murder* tour and the new material showed a fantastic development of the band as writers and performers. They played a blinding set and to see them develop into such a complete gang was fantastic.

But of course the show went down in Smithdom history as 'The Sausage Incident'. As the evening went on there were several moments of sheer joy and I almost got to the stage barrier to get up and get close to my idols. Then, as the show was getting close to the end, the strains of the factory machines played out as the first bars of 'Meat Is Murder' quietened down the crowd. I didn't see the Phantom Sausage Flinger but I saw them hit Morrissey. I can't say for certain that one actually went into his mouth, but by God it was a good shot! I think the shock was felt by the man himself, but more so by the audience, who couldn't believe what we were seeing.

I WAS THERE - BUT I DIDN'T THROW THE SAUSAGE: GLYN WADE

I saw them three times as I was back at the Victoria Hall for the night of the sausage throwing incident. I know who did the throwing... but I won't tell. And, no, it wasn't me! My mate got on stage and did a backflip to which Morrissey commented, 'What a charming man.' It's such a shame that someone so talented turned into a fascist and it makes it hard to listen to The Smiths now. I know someone who sold all his Morrissey records when he turned. But those gigs were special, intimate and memorable and will remain fond memories.

Glyn Wade was there for Sausagegate

The UK's *Daily Telegraph* later claimed of the sausages that 'each one (was) carefully inscribed with the title of his album, *Meat Is Murder*'.

Morrissey: They hit me in the face and part of them got in my mouth. I had to just run off the stage and heave! I really vomited. Eating meat is the most disgusting thing I can think of. It's like biting into your grandmother.

HIPPODROME

17 MARCH 1985, BIRMINGHAM, UK

I WAS THERE: CLIVE ADAMS

By 1983, it almost seemed like punk had never happened. In terms of English guitar bands that captured the soul of suburban youth The Jam, who disbanded in late '82, had left a void in popular music. The charts were awash with synth pop bands with long winded names such as A Flock of Seagulls and Orchestral Manoeuvres in the Dark. Don't get me wrong, as with all genres of music, there were some gems to be found but much of it left me cold and uninspired.

BIRMINGHAM The big heart of England
BIRMINGHAM HIPPODROME
'THE SMITHS' plus SUPPORT
SUN 17MAR 85 7:30 PM
row seat VISA
FRONT STALLS B 12 £5.00
9-JAN

Clive Adams' ticket for the Hippodrome

Clive Adams obviously liked bands whose name began with

As MTV took off in what had become the age of the music video, it appeared that once again style had become more important than substance. As a young college student I would hang out at the Powerhouse, a medium-sized venue in Birmingham that played host to many of the independent, post-punk and goth bands dominating the pages of the *NME* at the time. I first heard The Smiths when on club nights the doom would be interspersed by 'This Charming Man' and 'What Difference Does it Make?' The surname Smith is ubiquitous and originates from Northern England. The Smiths were a Manchester band, but their music sounded fresh to me, providing a welcome relief from the blandness of corporate pop. With a strong rockabilly rhythm section, poetic lyrics and uplifting jangly guitar, The Smiths were to define Eighties English independent rock.

Mother's Day 1985, and the Smiths were in town playing at the Birmingham Hippodrome. It seemed a strange choice of venue at the time but looking back, playing the Hippodrome enforced for me the idea that The Smiths were apart from their contemporaries. This is a seated venue and we were held back by security from rushing the stage to see the support act, fellow Mancunians James. However security could not hold us back once The Smiths took to the stage. From the opening bars to 'William, It Was Really Nothing' Morrissey owned the stage but at the same time held a sense of vulnerability as he gave in to repeated requests from the crowd to show us a nipple. Though I did not realise it at the time, I now appreciate how lucky I was to see The Smiths play my home town in such an intimate venue.

I WAS THERE: LAWRENCE BRACKSTONE

The Smiths were the only band that I fell in love with on hearing them for the vey first time. The song was 'This Charming Man'. I had pretty well all their releases to date in my collection and was a massive fan of the jangle guitar style of the magical Marr.

Lawrence Brackstone saw The Smiths on Mother's Day 1985

Mother's Day, 17 March 1985. I'd been working in London for the whole week and I caught a National Express coach back to Birmingham where I was met by my mum. I gave her some flowers and then I went home, got some tea and then went out to the gig where I met my two very best friends, Gary Fox and Clive Adams. James were the support act but we weren't interested in them and choose to have a beer in the theatre bar instead, blissfully unaware of how big they were to become. The Smiths were growing in their popularity and getting front row tickets, as we tended to do for other acts, proved difficult. We had seats that were maybe 10 rows back. Interestingly the bouncers were preventing fans getting to their seats in the front stalls with about five minutes to go before the band came out. Suddenly the lights went out and I took a cheeky chance to get a better seat. I literally seat hopped all the rows in the front till I got to the stage and took a place right in front of the microphone stand!

On came the band and the whole place erupted. I couldn't believe my luck at the advantage I'd got with my place. There were two occasions when I had Morrissey's microphone lead in my hand while he was singing and also later on I had his shirt in my grip. There is a bootleg of the gig and a fan in the balcony can be heard shouting out at my actions!

My memory of the night was that it was too short. The remarkable point for me was the final encore of 'Barbarism Begins at Home'. As the song came to a close, one by one each member put down their instrument and departed. It left Mike Joyce as the only one left, tapping away on his drum kit for a couple of minutes. It was for me the best exit I've ever seen.

To this day I am still a massive Smiths fan and my two teenage sons have independently followed the band. I love the classic sound of the Smiths. They were a massively influential part of my growing up and I still hugely remember with great fondness that particular gig.

I WAS THERE: JIM LANE

I don't recall a lot about it, other than they were rather moody and didn't seem to interact with the audience much! I was a long way back too, way too far to see them closely, plus we were all seated, so all in all it's a bit vague and doesn't exactly sit there in my mind in the 'amazing gig I'll never forget' category. Obviously they were in their heyday.

I WAS THERE: SIMON WELLS

It was about a year after I'd seen them at the Tower Ballroom in Edgbaston, maybe even less. The Smiths were getting bigger and I went as part of a crowd. This may sound like some kind of prescient revisionism on my part but Morrissey had already begun to rack up some things in the press that were disappointing. Most notably, in the *NME* that 'reggae is vile'. As someone who grew up in the city in the Seventies, this was somewhere between laughably ill-informed and dumb.

The band were disappointing. The Hip is a fantastic place for theatre and dance but a poor space for gigs - seats only - and everyone on stage oozed a kind of tiredness and tetchiness. Why, I don't know. Perhaps being at the nexus of so many hopes and dreams was difficult to handle over time. At the end, Johnny Marr kicked down the drum kit for no reason that I could see and I remember thinking how that was the kind of tired rock nonsense *my* Smiths were not supposed to be about. It was clear that, for me, they were already over.

As a coda, that was not actually the last time I saw Morrissey live. Some years later, Madness reformed to play in Finsbury Park and he had the name support slot. He sang draped in a Union flag with a skinhead picture for a backdrop. To an integrated audience playing in one of the world's great multicultural cities. It looked - it almost certainly *was* - a pathetic attempt to borrow a boot boy kudos that had long been recognised as often racist. How sad that someone who initially looked like he could help us throw doors wide open was, in the end, actually a lot more interested in closing borders.

I WAS THERE: JULIE SABINE, AGE 22

Julie Sabine was a punk when she saw The Smiths

I was a punk at the time. I used to go to Romeo and Juliets, an alternative club in Birmingham and which was where I first heard The Smiths. 'How Soon Is Now?' is the song that got me hooked on them. The lyrics, the guitar riff and, of course, Morrissey's voice. It's still one of my all time favourite songs. I bought *Hatful of Hollow* and never looked back. The lyrics all seemed to resonate with whatever I was going through emotionally at the time. Also, I found that some of the songs were far from depressing. They were funny. If only people would really listen to the songs and not judge them as depressing surely they would see for themselves? My then boyfriend surprised me with tickets to see them live. We managed to get to the front, right in front of Morrissey. I don't recall there being too many people there but I do recall people staring at us as myself and my then boyfriend looked very different to everyone else, with our Mohican hairstyles. Mine was white blonde all sticking out and we were dressed in black and generally we both stuck out like sore thumbs. But we didn't take any notice.

As soon as I saw Morrissey I screamed my head off with excitement! I sang and danced. They were amazing live and still one of the best bands I've ever seen live. So the gig was ending and my boyfriend said, 'Let's go to the stage door at the back.' There weren't many people there at all - just us and a couple of others inside the door, waiting for the band to come out. Their coach was waiting for them. The band came out, but no Morrissey. Then I saw him! He had a black hat on. Some girls got his autograph but I just stood and couldn't quite believe it was him. He looked over to me and my boyfriend. He was really staring and he waved at us. I was in a state! I was waving like an idiot, saying, 'Oh, he's waving at me – look, look!'

He then got on the coach, pulled back the curtain that was covering the window and waved again and beckoned me to the coach. I was all shy and just shook my head, 'No.' He then smiled at me, I waved one last time and then I turned and went home. Who knows what story I could've told if I'd gone on over to him and got on that coach?

I WAS THERE: PAUL MILES, AGE 14

I was seriously gothic as a young teenager. I had three older sisters and so was going to see bands like Southern Death Cult and The Sisters of Mercy. My sisters were happy because they were going to these alternative clubs. I had long black crimped hair. I was still at school and I remember going in on a Thursday and having to take my black nail varnish off. Then my sister decided to cut my hair. She cut it right up at the top and said,

'Right, you're a Smiths fan now.' I was absolutely livid. But within six months I went to see them at the Hippodrome. From that gig I became quite a big James fan, seeing James 26 times in total.

I got totally into The Smiths and I started buying their vinyl. That was the only thing I would save up for. It was just so different. They didn't seem that mainstream even though they were on *Top of the Pops*. It wasn't the electro-pop thing that was going on. It was the lyrics more than anything. They were so poignant. As a teenager, you were just taking in those lyrics because there wasn't another lyricist like that around at the time. Or ever. I just used to stand in my bedroom singing along, playing their music album after album after album.

They just epitomised cool. Johnny Marr was and still is a legend while Morrissey had this really weird privacy around him as well. You never really knew much about him. He was enigmatic and I really liked that dark, secretive 'fill in the gaps' side to him.

I've never got that 'depressing' thing out of it that people talk about. Their music makes me really happy. I saw Johnny Marr perform with The Killers at Glastonbury in 2019 and when they kicked into 'This Charming Man' it still seemed so relevant. The crowd were going mad. The music is very buoyant and joyful.

'SHAKESPEARE'S SISTER'

RELEASED 18 MARCH 1985

The sleeve art featured Pat Phoenix, Coronation Street actress, in character as Elsie Tanner in Britain's favourite TV soap opera. The single was less of a favourite, only reaching number 26.

CITY HALL

22 MARCH 1985, SHEFFIELD, UK

I WAS THERE: JOHN GOODWIN, AGE 14

I had been into music for some time before I discovered them. I have a sister years older than me who forced me to listen to ska and The Specials. Where I grew up there were lots of influences from The Human League and electronic music so my taste was quite eclectic. But noting gripped me like The Smiths. I first them doing 'What Difference Does it Make?' on *Top of the Pops* when I was 13 in early 1984. I bought two versions of the seven inch single, one with Terence Stamp and the other with Morrissey, at the time not realising the significance. There was something immediately alluring about them that had me transfixed. The music, the lyrics and of course how Morrissey looked. I had talked to some girls I knew who were into music and they said I should get *The Smiths*, their first album. It grew from there. I followed them from then until the day they split and beyond.

I bought every record I could records, cassettes, pictures discs, imports. I bought all my records from Hudsons Records in Chesterfield. Mr Hudson recognised my interest and would save me posters and marketing materials relating to The Smiths, which I have to this day in my loft. I clipped magazines like *Smash Hits* and the *NME* for anything Smiths-related.

I had a great family and was not lonely or locked in my bedroom. But I had been ill and I didn't do things other kids did. I stayed in a lot and remember many holidays where I would make my parents play *Meat Is Murder* on cassette in the car. My mum would say, 'Oh, this is dreary' but I didn't see that at all. The songs were sad, but also funny and uplifting. I would mainly listen alone in the front room of our terraced house. However, I would also listen to them at my friend's house. She was not a girlfriend but a friend who was a girl. She had a letter from Morrissey that we would look at endlessly. I was so jealous - when I wrote to him all I got were some Rough Trade postcards.

The impact of The Smiths was massive. It is a cliché now but The Smiths changed my life. I was not the best at school but Morrissey's lyrics opened up a world of culture - books, film, TV and other music. It seems cringe-worthy now but I started reading Oscar Wilde, Keats and Yeats. This really changed my ideas about books, words and knowledge.

The first time I saw them was at Sheffield City Hall. I had a deal with my friend that I would go with him to see Howard Jones (who was rubbish) and he would come with me to The Smiths. James supported, which was a real bonus. My dad drove us into Sheffield. My dad helped me get tickets every time. He would call up and pay with his giro bank card. Mum and Dad took us to all the gigs. They would go and eat or wait in the car. They were patient and supportive.

The gig was amazing, if not overwhelming, but some things stand out. The ticket I had said 'restricted view' but what this actually meant is that we were right at the front where the seats had been taken out. I have a distinct memory of this bloke calling me over from the seats and asking if we could swap. I did not want to get into trouble so ignored him. I remember looking up at the ceiling of the City Hall, seeing the band's shadows silhouetted against the ceiling by the lights and thinking that I had to be there at that very moment to see that and how it would never be repeated. I also remember being so far forward one could not help but dance. My shirt was sweat-soaked. And the sound the grinding saw made for 'Meat Is Murder' was so powerful, visceral and raw.

I WAS THERE: DAVID GRIFFITHS, AGE 17

I was 17 year old and lost. I'd been a punk from the age of 12 to 15 but fell out of love with music as there wasn't anyone around that blew me away. Then one day a friend called round and said he had a spare ticket to see The Smiths at Sheffield City Hall the following day. I accepted the ticket and went to my first ever gig. I remember the excitement of my 15 year old friend on the day and this rubbed off on me on our way to the gig. Outside the City Hall, the excitement and passion of all The Smiths fans made me inexplicably nervous. The sound in the City Hall was breathtaking and a band I had never heard of entered the stage. From that night James also became a favourite band. I especially relate to their early material and I think it is all to do with them being the first band I ever saw live. Then it happened - The Smiths entered the stage to a barrage of flowers and love. I can remember being blown away by the energy and the stage invasions, the band doing an almost instrumental for one of the encores as Morrissey was mobbed and could not sing, and Morrissey having his shirt ripped from him. The main thing I remember is that I fell in love with music again.

I WAS THERE: MIKE POWELL

I recently scanned five rolls of film I shot of The Smiths at Sheffield City Hall whilst I was at college studying photojournalism. I had heard 'Hand in Glove' and just a couple of others when I knocked on the stage door and asked their manager if I could take some pictures. I was led past the band waiting with guitars to go on, sat at a table full of drinks and flowers, and sat on their PA speakers on the City Hall stage. The crowd barely filled the stalls and the circle and upper circle were virtually empty, all of which would change for the band in just months. A few minutes later they were all squashed at the front reaching out for Morrissey, who was flailing around the stage swinging a bunch of flowers (slowly reduced to mere stalks) and Johnny Marr played a gorgeous cherry 1959 Gibson ES355 with block inlays all night. Fair enough – if I were him I wouldn't let it out of my sight either.

I was amazed at how tight they were. I've been a fan ever since and am now the proud owner of my own cherry 335. Funnily enough I received an email from their drummer, Mike Joyce, some years after telling Mark Radcliffe on Radio 1 the story. I sent him the contact sheets and he was really pleased to see them. I remember crawling around the stage and sitting right by his kit as he belted out some unbelievably solid drumming. Completely brilliant. There is some amateur footage of this gig on YouTube shot by the road crew.

I WAS THERE: JONATHAN JORDAN

My group of pals were an odd mix of goths, rockers, punks and New Romantics. We watched every band that came through South Yorkshire. That week we had seen Spear of Destiny.

The Smiths had a good buzz about them. They had been on *Top of the Pops* and were playing our favourite venue, Sheffield City Hall, the usual venue of choice for Thin Lizzy, AC/DC and the Halle Orchestra. We bought tickets on the door that were less than £5 and found ourselves in the balcony, which was totally empty but for us. The venue was about half full, and was totally the wrong place for The Smiths. We tried to dance and 'get into it' but it wasn't happening for us. Even the fans in our group concluded it wasn't a great night, and we ended up in the pub next door before the encores. Young people are amazed and impressed that I have seen The Smiths but frankly it was a really forgettable gig!

CITY HALL

24 MARCH 1985, NEWCASTLE-UPON-TYNE, UK

I WAS THERE: PETER MARTIN

This time we got the bus as it was our home town gig. I remember the song 'Meat Is Murder' and realising how much I hated it. I wanted the fast ones, the early stuff that they had abandoned to play this dirge. I remember the seats and how it wasn't nearly as good as standing the night before. I also recall 'Shakespeare's Sister', still one of my favourite Smiths songs. I bought the badges of all the singles sleeves and wore Pat Phoenix for about two years solid.

I WAS THERE: ALYSON LAWS, AGE 16

Most girls in my year liked Spandau Ballet and Wham! but I liked the sound of the guitars and Morrisey's quirkiness. My music taste made me different from the other girls and I really liked a lot of different music. I was gutted that I could not get tickets to see them at the Mayfair in Newcastle in 1984. It was a club and you had to be 18 to get in. I really did look 15!

When I saw them at Newcastle City Hall I was forced by my parents to take my 14 year old sister along, so I brainwashed her with the music before the show. I still remember the feeling as the hall was dark, the stage was lit red and booming out of the speakers was Prokofiev's 'Romeo and Juliet'. I was holding my breath. It was totally inspiring to me. Then Johnny Marr's guitar started and I was in awe of this band. I would love to say that the meaning of the lyrics to 'Meat Is Murder' inspired me to become a vegetarian but I may have thought about it for five seconds on the way home.

I WAS THERE: SCOTT P RICHARDSON

The first time I saw them, my sister took me. We were sitting upstairs at the back but the atmosphere was amazing. The next two occasions were part of the same tour - *Meat Is Murder* - and we had to travel to them. They were both amazing shows and I was standing right at the front and got to shake Morrissey's hand on a few occasions. The fourth and last time that I got to see them was at a small local venue where they threatened to walk off the stage as there were a few mindless morons spitting at them, but they did finish the show. I now live in Manchester and have been to Salford Lads Club and had my picture taken there. It was an amazing feeling standing there and knowing that they stood there for that iconic picture.

I WAS THERE: CHRIS TAIT

The Smiths were the band to see on stage at that time and were my generation's shining light. I'd been a fan since their early *Top of the Pops* appearances and some terrific Peel Sessions but I'd missed their previous visits to the city for one reason or another (studying, raising a young family, holding down two jobs, money was too tight to mention, etc.). When *Meat Is Murder* was released, missing the Newcastle City Hall gig to promote the album was not an option. So tickets were purchased, arrangements made and my friend Mark and I took up our positions in the stalls on the big night immediately behind the mixing desk, with a clear view of the engineer's set list and the delights that were to follow. Arch rivals Sunderland had lost the League Cup Final earlier in the day (with an own goal, a penalty miss and relegation to follow - beautiful, what a time to be alive!) so spirits were already high, despite the gig being on a Sunday evening, with the dreaded four letter word - 'work' - in the morning. Tomorrow could stretch out and wait.

For Chris Tait missing the Meat Is Murder show at Newcastle City Hall was not an option

Soon-to-be stadium darlings James provided support showcasing, if memory serves, material from their forthcoming debut album, the stunningly eclectic *Stutter*, a masterpiece in itself. But nothing could have prepared you for the main event and that unique entrance which became The Smiths' trademark.

As the lights dimmed and the opening bars of Prokofiev's 'Romeo and Juliet' drifted out into the crowd, the place erupted. Then, amid strobe lighting and flying beer, The Smiths took to the stage, immediately bursting into the intro to 'William….' Cue further mayhem, a mix of flailing arms, swirling guitar and a classic four-piece English pop group at the very top of their game, delivering songs unlike anything I'd heard before or since.

The set list was remarkable by any standards – melodic, catchy, experimental and in places, dare I say it, there were essences of what I would have described at the time as heavy rock, proof once again that, aside from being the coolest dude on the block, Johnny Marr is undoubtedly the best guitarist this nation has produced, in any genre.

All of the tracks from the new album were given an airing apart from the wistful 'Well I Wonder', alongside some of the early songs which were already gaining cult classic status - 'Hand in Glove', 'Still Ill' and 'Heaven Knows…'. New single 'Shakespeare's Sister' was included too and after two encores, the closing song, 'Barbarism Begins at Home', saw Morrissey leave the stage first to huge acclaim and ended with Rourke and Joyce playing that amazing bass and drum rhythm outro to close the show. It was an undoubted triumph and there was a palpable feeling that this lot were something special.

ROYAL COURT THEATRE

27 MARCH 1985, LIVERPOOL, UK

I WAS THERE: JULIE DANGERFIELD

Memories? Pete Burns in a royal box thingy. James in support. Morrissey opening with, 'We're the other funny Manchester band.' Johnny Marr removing his leather jacket before they did the title track. Me being young young!

I WAS THERE: THOMAS JONES

This was a much more sedate affair. We had only managed to get balcony tickets this time around and had missed out on Manchester tickets altogether such was the explosion in their popularity. James - in their quirky, pre-stadium-friendly incarnation - did a decent set and then our heroes showcased the newly released *Meat Is Murder* LP. The light show had improved dramatically and I remember some laser-like projections accompanying 'That Joke Isn't Funny Anymore', holding the band in a cradle of pink and green light. We also laughed on the way home about how Johnny had listed 'humping' as his main hobby in the souvenir programme.

Royal Court Theatre, Liverpool
Outlaw & Phil McIntyre present—
THE SMITHS plus Support
Wednesday, 27th March 1985
Evening 7.30
SUPPORTED BY JAMES
STALLS STANDING
£4.50
No 260
No Tickets Exchanged nor Money Refunded
No Cameras or Recording Equipment
Official Programmes sold only in the Theatre
A. B. Cooper (Printers) Ltd., Manchester
Retain this portion

ST GEORGE'S HALL

28 MARCH 1985, BRADFORD, UK

I WAS THERE: GRAHAM CLARK

James were the support act and Tim Booth wore a multi-coloured jumper. I still have the (unofficial) t-shirt I bought outside the venue.

I WAS THERE: ANDY WHITE

The fourth and final time I saw them was at St Georges Hall. I met some mates who were going in a city centre pub and told them we had to go early to see James but no-one was persuaded so I ended up going in on my own. Again, a great set from James.

I was at the front again. In those days you had your hands on stage if you were at the front, no sterile zone for the bouncers to parade in or folk giving water out. You could get on stage easily if you fancied it and plenty did, but not me at a Smiths concert. The crush was too much for some people, so these folk - usually girls - were normally hauled out onto the stage and then reappeared at the back of the hall, only to try to get back to the front. I remember Morrissey having a moan about the poor chart position for 'Shakespeare's Sister', which had now been released. Truth be told it was a poor choice for a single - they had plenty of better songs. There was a bit of trouble from some yobbos in the crowd who were spitting at Morrissey. He left the stage at one point, and I thought he wasn't coming back, but after about five minutes he did. The band jammed while he was gone.

I WAS THERE: ANDY WALSH, AGE 17

I'll never forget it. I was a young 17 year old watching my football team home and away when one of lads I knocked about with said he'd got two tickets to see a band in Bradford and did I fancy it? I never expected to be almost bloody hypnotised by this young odd-looking band but they just blew me away and gave me one of the biggest pleasures in life. They are the only band that makes my heart pump like mad when one of their songs comes on.

I think the reason The Smiths really impacted on me was that I went through many music phases such as reggae, Mod/ska, punk, etc. like any normal young lad but never really stuck with any in particular. When I saw The Smiths, I stood there in such awe at four Northern lads like myself who just looked normal but had something that grabbed me instantly. The music was brilliant but the look of the band, and I suppose Morrissey in particular, made me want to be different. I loved the fact that they weren't really mainstream and weren't on TV or radio every two minutes. They felt like they were mine. People would mock and take the piss about The Smiths being miserable and morbid but I'd just think, 'You don't get it, poor you.' And I still do!

I still probably can't explain it and it can be embarrassing trying to tell people I thought these four lads were gods. I got the whole Morrissey thing where lads would try to get to him as if he were some messiah. You just had that feeling in your gut. If I tried to explain this to mates they'd just take the piss and call me a homosexual or whatever. No other band has ever touched me like The Smiths.

DERNGATE THEATRE

29 MARCH 1985, NORTHAMPTON, UK

I WAS THERE: JAMIE CRAMP

The gig had that buzz about it that a band has when it's at the top of its game and the height of its popularity.

I WAS THERE: ANDREW FARMER

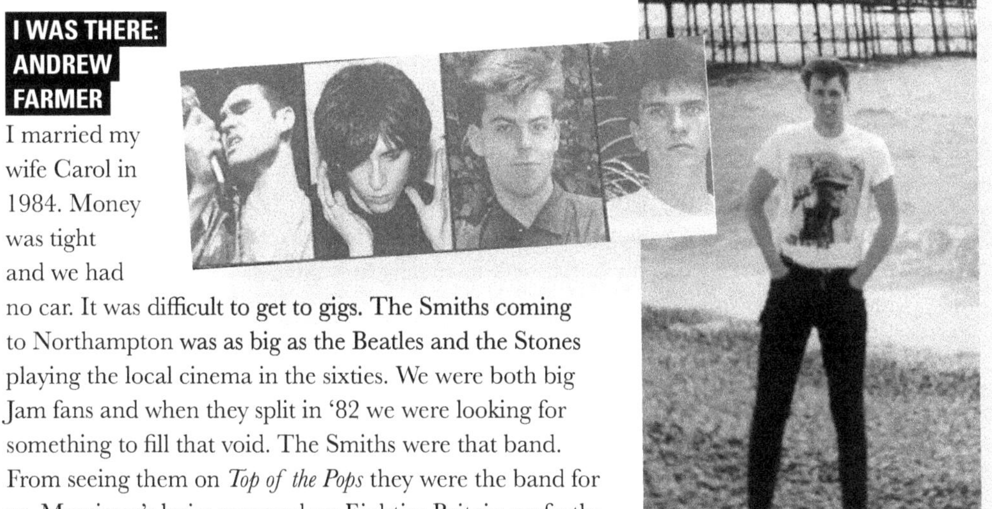

Andrew Farmer saw The Smiths at Northampton's Derngate Theatre

I married my wife Carol in 1984. Money was tight and we had no car. It was difficult to get to gigs. The Smiths coming to Northampton was as big as the Beatles and the Stones playing the local cinema in the sixties. We were both big Jam fans and when they split in '82 we were looking for something to fill that void. The Smiths were that band. From seeing them on *Top of the Pops* they were the band for us. Morrissey's lyrics summed up Eighties Britain perfectly while Marr's tunes took us to places we never been before.

The Derngate had just opened and we were faced with a choice - a friend's wedding or Smiths tickets? On the day the booking office opened, we queued for our tickets and duly got them. The only problem was that it was all seating. How can you sit for The Smiths? Tickets cost the princely sum of £5 each and we were about seven rows from the front. The day of the gig arrived and hair was teased into the best quiff possible.

The venue was very busy, with animal rights activists handing out flyers. These had a dramatic effect on both of us, so much so we both gave up meat. The gig opened with the band James, Tim Booth doing his best to get the crowd going, but mostly everyone stayed seated. They went off.

There was a brief interlude, the lights dimmed and then pandemonium as the band took the stage. Even if you wanted to remain in your chair you weren't going to be allowed to. The atmosphere was electric as everyone rushed towards the stage. The music kicked in and everyone was dancing and singing, with the band whipping the crowd into a frenzy. My personal favourite songs were 'Hand in Glove' and 'How Soon

Is Now?' I think they played 16 or 17 songs including two encores and then they were gone. If they had played for six hours it would have been over too soon. Our bills money was spent on tour programmes, t-shirts and a massive tour poster, which still hangs in our hall.

I kept the review from our local paper, the *Chronicle and Echo*. It opened with the words, 'a messiah arrived in Northampton at the weekend and the result was ecstatic bedlam.' The reviewer went on to say, 'Morrissey has said that his ambition in life is to achieve immortality. He can rest assured that his Derngate performance has made him a legend - something that will not be forgotten for a very long time.'

The Smiths were and still are our Beatles, and we still follow Morrissey and Johnny Marr whenever they tour. Theirs is a light that never goes out.

PALACE THEATRE

31 MARCH 1984, MANCHESTER, UK

I WAS THERE: GILLIAN ANDRIA, AGE 23

Me and my friend Julie went together. It was the first time we'd seen Morrissey and also Tim Booth. We related to the music, with us coming from Manchester, and identified with the same life experiences. The most vivid memory I have of that night is the way both of them danced! You couldn't really hear the music that much. I was 23, Julie was 20. We are still best friends and still go together to watch Morrissey and James. Our kids loved both bands, having grown up with the music. My daughter has a Morrissey tattoo and coincidentally my grandson, her son, shares a birthday with Morrissey.

I WAS THERE: PAUL GREENWOOD

I had just started in a new relationship and I was besotted. It was our first proper date. The Smiths played 'The Headmaster Ritual' and I swear the hairs on the back of my neck stood on end. It was musical euphoria with gladioli all over the stage. I think they did three encores - it was a great set. My girl loved the show so it was a great date. For one night I was in heaven. Sadly, the girl didn't last but I still love The Smiths.

Paul Greenwood was in heaven with The Smiths and a new date

I WAS THERE: JOHANNA ROBERTS, AGE 17

I can't remember when I first heard 'This Charming Man' by The Smiths. It was when Radio 1 played good music and deejays didn't sound like guys who run fairground rides. All I know is that I heard it and it changed my life. After punk and new wave in the late seventies, there had been a move to synthesisers, with bands like OMD, Visage, Duran Duran and Spandau Ballet topping the charts. Suddenly, here were four lads - drums, two guitars and a vocalist - and it spoke to me. I was 15. I was already an avid record buyer. I would go the Play Inn in Eccles on a Saturday and come home with a variety of singles or albums. This was no different. Off I went to purchase the single, in a picture sleeve, with 'Jeane' on the B-side. This was new and this was mine. My first week's wages from my Saturday job went on The Smiths' eponymous album and a pair of jeans. The album was never off the turntable, and as singles and albums were released, they got bought.

I had to be at the Palace. I was too young to go to clubs but this venue was accessible. I rang up the morning they went on sale. Aged 17, I didn't have a credit card. I appealed to the guy on the phone that I needed - needed! - two tickets. He told me he would hold two. I jumped on the bus on a wintry morning and went to the Palace to get them. I had never been so grateful.

Cut to Sunday 31 March, I had on a paisley pyjama top and some sixties beige chinos of my dad's. Outside the Palace were kids with daffodils (FFS, he had gladioli). I bought a programme and 10 button badges, which I still have. I was on the second row, aisle seats. I was so close to the stage. James were on first and, boy, did they wow me. I got into them from that moment too - the freaky dancer and the unusual songs - and for a while ended up in a penpal situation with Jenny, one of the then line-up's girlfriends.

When The Smiths came out I was mesmerised. I only had eyes for Morrissey and Johnny, who was stood on my side of the stage. I'd been to other gigs but this band was mine. Every song meant something to me and I was seeing them live. It blew all the other gigs away.

The stage was bathed in red for 'Meat Is Murder' and the 'heifer whines' rang out across the theatre. It was at that point I became a veggie. Reading back on the set list they did 13 songs and three encores. All I know is that it was fantastic.

I WAS THERE: JULIAN DYSON, AGE 14

I saw The Smiths three times in Manchester - at the Palace, at G-Mex and the second Free Trade Hall gig. I grew up in Baguley in Wythenshawe, a few hundred yards from Johnny Marr. I've met him loads of times. I went to school with Ian Maher, Johnny's brother.

I WAS THERE: ALAN NEAL, AGE 17

I was living at home in Baguley and only later became aware that both Andy Rourke and Mike Joyce were from the same area, literally just up the road. Being from Manchester and yet too young for the likes of Slaughter and the Dogs, The Buzzcocks, The Nosebleeds and Joy Division, I listened to the Two-Tone bands of the early. Nothing really changed for me as a young teenager until 1983. Seeing 'Hand in Glove' for the first time on the telly really changed things for me and others I knew, particularly my best mate Deano.

Deano and I had tickets for what would be my favourite gig to this day - The Smiths at the Palace. That night ended in overwhelming enjoyment and disappointment. The Palace Theatre is just that, an old theatre building in the heart of the city. It was the first time that I had been there since watching panto as a kid. I remember the atmosphere of that night, the subdued but expectant anticipation of the audience, the constraints of the seats and the dark empty stage. Suddenly we were blinded by bright flashing lights and deafened by booming instrumental music.

Here we were, standing in the aisles of plush velour seats, surrounded by Victoriana and 1,500 other kids with quiffs, NHS glasses and the odd hearing aid. Despite this obvious physical similarity, I felt disconnected from everyone else there and I suspect most other people around me felt the same. Then the band appeared out of the gloom and I felt nothing but pure joy. This was my band playing my songs. It is hard to put into words how I felt for the next hour and a half but wonderment - the wonderment at pure utter genius. The rest of the gig comprised of Deano and me trying to invade the stage to snatch a few seconds with Morrissey, a mission in which Deano was the victor and I very much the loser, still tethered in the mass of heaving youngsters. It was one of the strangest gigs I had ever been to - this unconventional band in this traditional rarefied theatre setting.

Deano and I had spotted the tour bus behind the venue earlier and had decided to follow the bus after the gig. We lay in wait in Deano's inconspicuous bright yellow Mark 1 Escort, which only had one working headlight. Our hope was that, as this was the band's hometown gig, the bus would take us to one of the band's homes. We tried to keep our distance from the bus but very quickly the driver became aware of a single beam of light following them down the Parkway headed out of Manchester. We overtook the bus and, anticipating that they were going to Hale Barns, stopped a few miles up the road and pulled out behind the bus to follow it again. At this point the bus then pulled over and waited for us to drive past, then pulled out behind us. This cat and mouse happened a few more times and then we decided to lie in wait just outside Hale Barns. The bus passed us yet again and, to avoid detection this time, we waited two minutes before following it. I'm sure that by now you will have guessed that we never saw the bus again, so I can't tell the story of having a cup of Twinings and a choccie digestive at Morrissey's house.

I WAS THERE: KEV JONES

Kev Jones met The Smiths outside Manchester's Palace Theatre

When they played the Palace, me and my mate went down during the afternoon on the off chance of seeing them come in so we could get their autographs. We took all our records down with us. There were loads of people crowded around the front of the theatre, but we stood on the corner of Oxford Road and Whitworth Street. We thought if they turn up they're going to come in a coach and they're going to come in somewhere around the back. This coach started coming down the road and then just pulled in behind the Palace and we thought, 'Crikey, that looks like that could be it!' There was me and my mate and these two girls who were hanging around there. So the four of us just legged it and followed this coach that was pulling into the loading bay at the back. These big corrugated doors opened and this huge

Kev Jones with Morrissey outside Manchester's Palace Theatre

coach vanished. We were just behind it and we thought, 'Oh, they've gone in. They're not going to come out.'

One of the girls peeped through the crack in the doors and she said, 'they're coming out. They're coming back!' They must have seen us legging after them. The doors opened and, lo and behold, there's Morrissey, Johnny, Andy and Mike just stood there with us. I was absolutely lost for words. So we got our records out and said, 'Please could you sign these?' And then we got pictures with them. That was pretty special.

DE MONTFORT HALL

1 APRIL 1986, LEICESTER, UK

I WAS THERE: VAL LOVE

Myself and school friend Kerry rushed to get our tickets after working all day at Richard Roberts hosiery factory. I didn't really know many other Smiths fans at that time and so I remember other people not getting what all the excitement was about. The big day arrived and I couldn't wait to get home from work. We arrived early, as I wanted to get near the front. There were rumours that some skinheads were out to get Morrissey. It was so hot in there, standing right at the front, jammed against the stage. Kerry couldn't hack it and moved further back, but I wasn't going anywhere!

The place was heaving and I was getting lifted with the crowd to the sounds of 'This Charming Man' and 'How Soon Is Now?' - my favourite tracks. They were so much better live than I expected. Morrissey was resplendent, complete with his trademark hearing aid. I actually touched his legs so many times.

I was getting so hot now. A great lanky skinhead's arm was jammed across my chest and everything was becoming unfocused. I vaguely remember some girl stopping me from sinking to the ground and then the bouncers lifting me out of there and placing me down towards the back near my friend. I can recall it as if it was yesterday. It was one of the highlights of my teenage life.

I WAS THERE: LEE THACKER

Meat Is Murder had been released earlier that year. It was the album that finally made me decide to become a vegetarian, 33 years and counting. I'd been heavily into the anarcho-punk band Crass and read their vegetarian manifestos but it

Lee Thacker's ticket for the De Montfort Hall show he attended dressed 'as Morrissey'

was hearing the track 'Meat Is Murder' that hammered the point home to me. This gig was also the first and last time I ever tried to emulate the look of a band. I was at heart a punk, wearing mostly black clothing and button badges and spiking my hair. For this one and only time I made a misguided sartorial decision to attend the gig 'as Morrissey'. I only owned straight leg black denim trousers and a number of home-made t-shirts (no way could I afford to buy 'proper' t-shirts at gigs: I continued to make my own well into the late Eighties) so I'd have to improvise. I procured a pair of blue jeans, the first and only time I've ever worn such apparel, and a white button up shirt from my father. I finished the look with a string of beads from my mother's jewellery box. I gelled my hair into the best quiff I could muster and I must have looked a complete fool. I only just realised the gig was actually on April Fools' Day! At least I avoided the temptation to pull up some flowers from my back garden and stick them in my back pocket. I got to the gig later than planned as I'd arranged to meet up with a few friends at a bar in town beforehand, meaning I ended up missing the first half of James' set. However, I pushed my way to the front again and danced my ass off, my mum's beads swinging with every Morrissey-inspired move I made!

HIPPODROME

4 APRIL 1985, BRISTOL, UK

I WAS THERE: GREG ARCHER

They were so tight as a band it was unbelievable. I count myself so lucky to have been around at this time to witness one of the finest bands this country has produced.

I WAS THERE: JON SMITH

We travelled by coach from Exeter. The next year, for the *Queen is Dead* tour and still at school, a friend and I organised our own coach and ticket travel to St Austell. So it was that I organised the largest school bunk off in history as 54 students got the coach!

ROYAL ALBERT HALL

6 APRIL 1985, LONDON, UK

I WAS THERE: ALAN HAMMETT

'This Charming Man' on the radio was a breath of fresh air. There was nothing else like The Smiths around at the time. Unfortunately I only got to see them three times. The first time was at the Royal Albert Hall. I went with three friends who'd seen them before. The big surprise of the night was Dead or Alive's Pete Burns coming on to sing a song which went down well. All too soon it was over.

Alan Hammett saw The Smiths three times

I WAS THERE: MICHAEL EVANS, AGE 17

I've probably been to over 1,000 gigs since my first one in 1981 but it's still what I'd call my best ever live gig. I saw them do 'This Charming Man' on *Top of the Pops* and that was it for me. Rickenbacker guitars always make my eyes pop out and there was this strange man smashing flowers on the floor, so after that moment they were the band for me. Previous to that I'd been into Big Country, Simple Minds, Echo and The

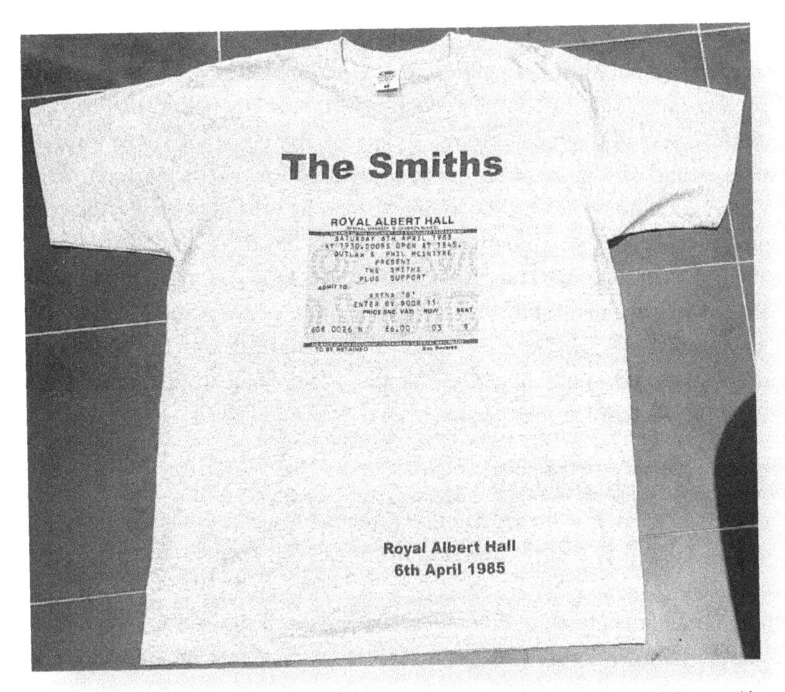

Michael Evans had his ticket made into a t-shirt

Bunnymen. I chucked all those. I'd been to gigs to see Adam and the Ants and Japan, so I was slowly going away from guitar and indie. Then The Smiths came along.

It was a miserable rainy day, which was perfect. I'd been there before for Echo and The Bunnymen. I used to go on my own because I was the only one who liked indie music. Everyone else was into soul music. I still remember it as if it was yesterday. Not that it was a particularly memorable gig. Morrissey said on the night that they'd chosen the wrong venue. Pete Burns came out to do 'Barbarism Begins at Home.' Him and Morrissey were quite good friends so he came out to do an encore with them.

I was at the very front. I got absolutely crushed. Violence is the wrong word but there was an atmosphere there that was more than worship. It was more than passion. It was beyond anything I've ever witnessed. Even to this day I've never witnessed anything like I witnessed at that one Smiths gig. They are my Beatles. I deliberately didn't go to the *Queen Is Dead* tour. And after that they only did the one gig, in Brixton. My parents wouldn't let me go to Brixton. I thought they'd be around forever. Half of me is disappointed that they weren't and half of me is glad.

I WAS THERE: NICK MYALL

To go to two dates on one tour was a bit extravagant in the cash-strapped Eighties of my youth. I did it for The Fall and now of course for The Smiths. The Brighton Dome gig was, and still is, one of the best I've ever been to so Matt, James and me all headed up to London in the week after another dull day at Haywards Heath Sixth Form College for our first ever gig in the capital. I remember talking to Brett Anderson and Matt Osman from Suede who both went to Haywards Heath Sixth Form about the gig that morning. They were both massive Smiths fans and were envious of our trip. The Royal Albert Hall was a brilliant, classically English setting for The Smiths. I don't remember many bands playing there, although I'd seen old film of Cream there in the late Sixties.

The Smiths entered the stage through a cloud of dry ice, smoke and swirling white lights to the sound of 'Dance of the Knights' by Prokoviev. They started with 'How Soon Is Now?' a massive favourite with the fans at the time. Then they turned their attention to the brilliant new album, *Meat Is Murder*. 'Nowhere Fast', 'What She Said' and 'I Want the One I Can't Have' were perfect live rockers and got the fans jumping. They didn't forget the early stuff either, with 'Hand in Glove', 'Still Ill' and 'Handsome Devil' all getting a look in. Two new tracks off the 'Shakespeare's Sister' 12 inch added to the mix and the slow build of 'Miserable Lie' as the finale worked perfectly. Another brilliant gig from a band at their peak.

I WAS THERE: MICHAEL LIKELY

My enduring memories of the gig are that someone threw a string of sausages at Morrissey and that they really screwed up 'How Soon Is Now?'

After three dates in continental Europe in May, in June 1985 The Smiths headed to the United States for their first full North American tour, commencing in Chicago.

ARAGON BALLROOM

7 JUNE 1985, CHICAGO, ILLINOIS

I WAS THERE: GARRETT JENNINGS, AGE 19

They had placed folding chairs out for people to sit in so everyone folded the chairs and threw them in a huge pile in the back of venue and everyone danced/moshed as close as we all could get to the stage. I went with my friends Mike and John. We were all 19 and it was a great show!

I WAS THERE: JIM JOLL

I saw them twice in Chicago. The first time I was with one of my college mates. I had discovered The Smiths by word of mouth at the University of Wisconsin in Madison as a 19 year old freshman. I was fortunate to have some

Jim Joll remembers Morrissey's Oxford dress shirt over his head

very hip dorm mates and they turned me on to many of the singles. I was immediately struck by Moz's voice and Marr's rhythm guitar and hooked from there on in. I combed through the 'zines I could buy at the record stores on campus and was never disappointed by the coverage I found in *Melody Maker* and *NME*. They started playing their videos, or what I always called anti-videos, on MTV's *120 Minutes*. As for the show, what I recall most is Moz dancing and spinning in place with his unbuttoned, white Oxford dress shirt over his head. Quite the striking image at the time and one that's still seared in my mind.

I WAS THERE: THOMAS LENZ, AGE 21

Thomas Lenz's ticket for the Aragon Ballroom

Thomas Lenz with his daughter Hannah

I grew up in Illinois. Not Chicago. About three hours away, nearly Iowa. During my time at university I spent a year abroad, in Spain. On a spring break in April 1984 (age 20) I travelled to various countries including the UK. While in London I visited HMV on Oxford Street and saw lots of posters and promotions for the first Smiths album. I had not heard them but I asked a salesperson about them. On a whim I purchased the cassette. In the remaining months of my year abroad, I listened to the cassette many times on a Sony Walkman and shared this new discovery with my classmates in Spain. Before too long I heard 'This Charming Man' playing around Madrid, in the edgy Rock-Ola club, hang out of La Movida in post-Franco Spain, and in the Rastro flea market where bootleg cassettes abounded.

By the fall of 1984 I was back in the US. On campus some of the students I knew had heard of The Smiths. I found out *Hatful of Hollow* was released during my winter break from university. I walked a mile in the snow to my hometown record store to buy a copy. Spring arrived and I graduated from university.

My sister, a few years younger than me, and two of her friends had also taken an interest in The Smiths. The *Meat Is Murder* LP was out. I found out The Smiths were playing in Chicago and bought tickets. I do not recall how. There was no internet. Perhaps hard copy tickets were sold at a local record store. We bought four and on the day of the concert I drove us in my VW Beetle the three hours to Chicago's Aragon Ballroom.

It seemed all the songs I wanted to hear were played. Morrissey crooned and moved about the stage. Johnny Marr played brilliantly. The band was in top form. When it was over I knew they were a band I'd like to see again if the opportunity presented itself. We had a great time and drove the three hours home.

As the records came out I bought them all. I recorded them all to cassette tapes, memorised the lyrics and probably sang along at far too loud a volume.

In the fall of 1985 I moved to Louisiana for law school. The Smiths were a regular part of the long drive back and forth on Interstate 55, through St. Louis, Missouri, and Memphis, Tennessee and the north to south length of Mississippi over three years. As law school ended, my hope of seeing The Smiths another time also ended. The band broke up. I bought the cassette of Morrissey's solo debut, *Viva Hate*, at a record store in Baton Rouge around the time I graduated from law school. I listened to it on my last voyage north on Interstate 55, returning to Illinois.

Not long after my return to Illinois I moved again. I was looking for a job and then I found a job. In Los Angeles, California. More than 30 years later my sister and friends who attended the concert in Chicago are spread across the US. We still talk about the show we saw in Chicago.

My oldest child is a daughter, 18 years old as I write this. She asked me if I had heard of an English band from the Eighties. She said she likes them a lot and their music speaks to her more than other bands. She asked, 'Are you familiar with The Smiths?' 'Yes,' I said. And I told her this story.

I WAS THERE: THOMAS AUGUSTINE

The opening act was three drag queens lip synching. It was confusing at first, then amusing. I enjoyed both the concerts I saw but the second one was overshadowed by going to see Del Amitri for the first time afterwards. Justin put out so much more energy than Morrissey did on stage. It wasn't that The Smiths put on a bad show. I just stopped being impressed by them or, more specifically, Morrissey.

KINGSWOOD THEATRE

9 JUNE 1985, TORONTO, CANADA

I WAS THERE: CHRISTIAN PATRICK, AGE 12

My parents made my older brother bring me to the show, which was at a theme park outside of Toronto called Kingswood Theatre. It was a very strange setting for a band like The Smiths. It's stranger to think that my brother was into The Smiths at that time, considering that he was a massive metalhead and into bands like Metallica, Judas Priest, Iron Maiden, etc. But over the years I've realised that metalheads love Johnny Marr's guitar playing. When people talk about great guitarists in music history, Johnny Marr's name rarely comes up. But metalheads know what's up. That really stoked the fire in me to want to play guitar when I saw him.

Same with Morrissey, who was at his peak in 1985. He was really embracing himself as an icon and front man. It was ego and arrogance, but was easily forgiven because of his flippancy and sense of humour. That's the thing about The Smiths; they've always been this band that's super dark on the surface, but when you really dive into them you realise that Morrissey - for all his morose and dark undertones - is one of the funniest, most clever lyricists of all time.

I remember them playing 'How Soon Is Now?' and it really changed my life. It seemed like a familiar song, even though I'd only heard it for the first time that night. It is such a haunting, complex ear worm that in reality is a simple, repetitive song, as I realised years later. I found a tape that someone was trading a couple years back and it's from that very show I saw. So, in a weird way, listening to it brings all those memories back even though I should have been too young to remember.

I WAS THERE: PHIL GUERRERO, AGE 14

It was such a long time ago that I don't remember much. It was at Canada's Wonderland at the Kingswood and one of the very few times they played in Canada. I was big into new wave/New Romantic music at the time. I was with my best friend Russ. We were two new wave peas in a pod. I had *Meat Is Murder* on vinyl as well as the 'Barbarism Begins at Home' EP.

I WAS THERE: KEVIN HOLMBERG

The weather that day was great and anticipation for seeing the show was in the air. The Kingswood did a great job of having great UK 'artist of the day' concerts. CFNY was a strong promoter of post punk and New Wave acts. My two favourite Kingswood shows were The Smiths and Siouxsie and The Banshees. My first recollection of them was hearing 'Hand in Glove'. At that time they were *NME* and *Melody Maker* darlings. I remember buying 'This Charming Man', which was the second single I purchased by them, and playing the grooves off the EP. There was such a great, happy feel to that record. I purchased the debut LP as a UK import. It was on Rough Trade and missing 'This Charming Man'. The Sire US release would soon remedy this, as 'This Charming Man' was garnering lots of airplay. The Smiths replicated this when *Meat Is Murder* was released as an import without 'How Soon Is Now?' The concert crowd consisted of fans that knew all of the songs. Morrissey was a rock star frontman that had the crowd's complete attention. Marr quietly displayed mastery of his craft, but it was Morrissey's stage. The show was a little over one and a half hours and had two encores. They left an amazing legacy. This music was so fresh and timely. I have The Smiths poster with my ticket stub mounted in my music room.

I WAS THERE: DAVE KAPLE

The show took place as part of the *Meat Is Murder* tour in Toronto, or more specifically Vaughan, in Ontario, Canada at the Kingswood Music Theatre, an open air theatre with a covered bandshell and exposed lawn seats for the audience. I only had a handful of concerts under my belt at this time. Truthfully, I didn't know what to expect. Billy Bragg opened the gig. We as a crowd were shy but we got louder and then Morrissey encouraged the crowd to come closer. By the end, fans were on the stage hugging him and kissing him and he soaked it all in. Fans even threw the newly laid turf up on stage, throwing the sod like frisbees. It was bizarre.

I WAS THERE: LORRAINE RENNER

I was in high school when I first started listening to them. I was hooked as soon as I heard 'How Soon Is Now?' That song pretty much was on every mix tape I made, as was 'The Queen is Dead', 'Panic', 'This Charming Man' just to name a few. I would crank my stereo, Walkman or whatever I was listening to music on at the time whenever I heard any Smiths song come on. I remember the first time I saw them was at the now defunct Kingswood Music Theatre just North of Toronto in 1985 and then again in 1986. They were amazing! Every song they played, every lyric that Morrissey sang in that oh-so-distinctive Morrissey voice, Johnny Marr's riffs on guitar and of course Mike and Andy... it was awesome. At the end of the first concert, the crowd started cheering and banging on the seat backs in front of them hoping for an encore. It was such a racket but Morrissey loved it. He said, 'I am not sure how you are making that sound but keep on doing it.'

I WAS THERE: DANYA MACDONALD, AGE 18

We bought the tickets for the concert and the amusement park and I remember a few hours before the concert was about to begin we heard the famous guitar riff for 'How Soon Is Now?' echo through the park and my anticipation grew into a frenzy. Of course at that time in my life the Smiths meant everything to me during a high school unrequited love period. Funny enough his name was William (Bill).... It was really nothing, ha! Morrissey to me at the time was gorgeous and our seats were close enough to the stage that I went from noticing only him and then acknowledging the power artists have to instantly connect with millions of people, making them physically feel connected. I adored the seemingly whimsical delivery of poignant political/authority hypocrisies in the lyrics.

BEACON THEATER

17 JUNE 1985, NEW YORK, NEW YORK

I WAS THERE: JOSEPH HUGHES, AGE 16

It was the night before the French Regent's Exam in NYC (a comprehensive subject exam for third year of high school). I went with my girlfriend at the time. Her parents drove us home. It was life-changing. Every song was magic. When they opened with 'Meat Is Murder' the stage backdrop turned blood red. I can still see it. They closed with 'Barbarism Begins at Home' and left the stage one at a time. It was unforgettable. I'm pretty sure I was gape-mouthed the whole time, and I can honestly say that gig looms large in my memory as a milestone event, even 34 years later. My whole concept of bands and live music and art all started forming that night. I went to Tower Records in the next day or two and bought whatever imports or compilations I could find.

I WAS THERE: CHRISTINE LICAUSI, AGE 20

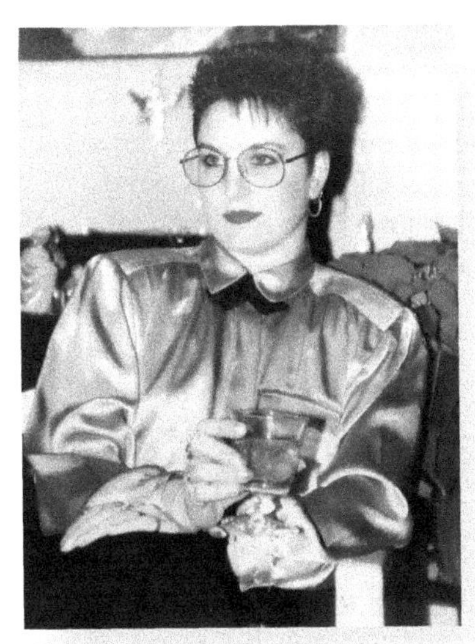

Christine LiCausi remembers the opening song 'William, It Was Really Nothing'

My first concert ever. They opened with 'William, It Was Really Nothing', my favourite Smiths song to this day. I went with my new 17 year old punk rocker boyfriend Larry, who had turned me onto their music soon after we met that month. We were both from Long Island but spent a lot of time in the city that summer. I immediately fell in love. With the music - and the guy.

I will never forget that show since it was my first but also because of the music and their showmanship. To this day it holds a special place in my heart. It was about love, and death, and angst and loss. All emotions I could relate to at the time, and now... I loved that band for speaking to me that way.

Morrissey was in top form, and put on an amazing show. He really whipped us all into a fan frenzy with his stage persona. I'm a huge fan of Johnny Marr too. I'm a sucker for guitar players. (I married one in 1997, and lost him in 2008... I turned him onto their music too.) Larry and I had an amazing time, and hated to see it end. They did three encores.

But the real trip happened after the show! As Larry and I got up to leave, and start walking out of the theatre, we noticed a group of people ahead of us that really stood out. As we got closer we realised it was Andy Warhol and his entourage! They had been sitting just a few rows back from us the entire show and we didn't even know it. I will never forget seeing them in the lobby as we left, and saying hello. They all walked out just a few yards behind us. How could I ever forget that night!

BEACON THEATRE

18 JUNE 1985, NEW YORK, NEW YORK

Morrissey and Marr at the Beacon Theatre. Photo courtesy of John Baxter

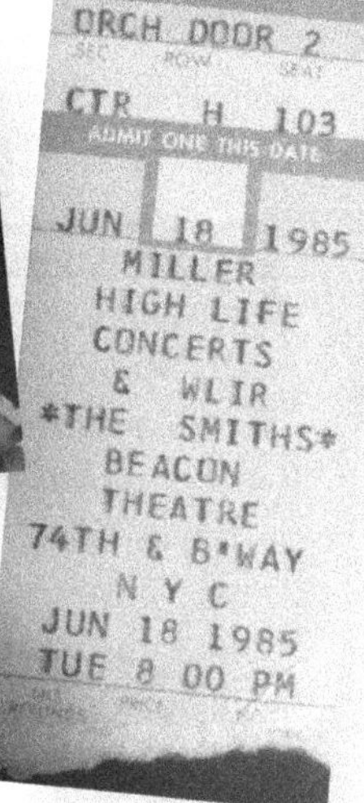

John Baxter's ticket for the Beacon Theater show

I WAS THERE: JOHN BAXTER, AGE 16

My older brother was in the Ron Delsener ticket club and procured tickets for me. Delsener was a concert promoter and club members were guaranteed seats at sold out shows. My brother was mostly attending large stadium shows at this time, but I was interested in all the new music shows that were playing the smaller venues.

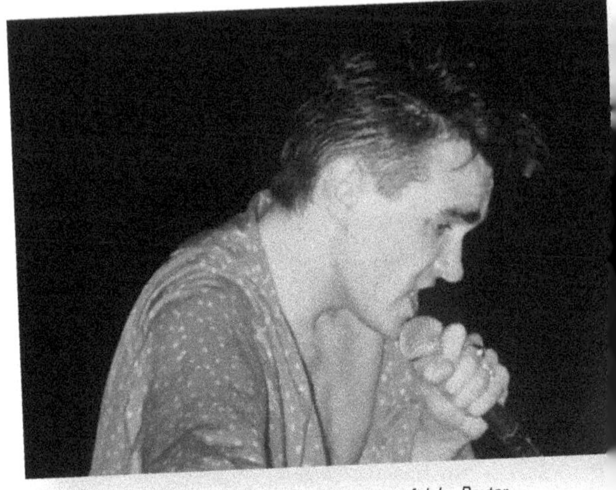

Morrissey at the Beacon Theatre. Photo courtesy of John Baxter

My first Smiths concert was at the Beacon Theatre, one of New York's most beautiful concert venues. I took the train into the city from our home in the suburbs of Long Island, about an hour away. The Beacon is a former movie theatre opened in 1929 with three tiers and just under 3,000 seats. And to my surprise our seats were 12th row centre! I brought three school friends who also loved The Smiths. 1985 in the suburbs could be pretty conservative in style and music taste. If it wasn't top 40, most teens weren't interested. I was happy to find my tribe in school and we were easy to spot with mohawks, thrift shop clothing, combat boots and cardigans. Our classmates dressed like their parents and we wanted none of that!

After Billy Bragg, The Smiths took to the stage and opened with 'Meat Is Murder'. With only two albums at this time, every song was well known and much loved. I remember they closed with 'How Soon Is Now?' before several encores. We had read and seen pictures in the music magazines how Morrissey let fans storm the stage and sure enough my friend Edna made her attempt. One security person decided there was enough teens on stage, but she wriggled past him and bounced around onstage victorious. Ah, if only I hadn't run out of film in my camera and captured that moment for her! No digital in those days and I could barely afford the 24 exposures I had!

The concert ended and I bought a *Meat Is Murder* t-shirt and a tour programme and lingered outside the theatre afterwards. Then Billy Bragg strolled out alone and unnoticed, his guitar slung over one shoulder. I asked him to sign my Smiths programme and he kindly obliged. I rode the train home on that special concert high where your ears are still ringing but you hope it lasts.

I WAS THERE: RACHEL FELDER, AGE 16

I grew up listening to British and American punk rock and I subsequently became close to the Ramones. I was always obsessed with British indie music from early on. For me, British punk rock had a straight line to British indie music. My trajectory ended up with a lot of professional and personal musical connections.

I'm American but did sixth form in England at a very traditional school. I had a little radio on which I would listen to John Peel. Peel and Radio 1 in the evenings was my lifeline and where I heard many artists for the first time, and where I first heard The Smiths. I don't remember which song it was. I remember it sounding earth shattering. You'd hear lots of good things on Peel. I used to listen to Radio Caroline too when that was still going.

The sound of The Smiths that evening was arresting and distracting and so assertive that there was no way you couldn't pay attention. I used to listen to the radio as background music but that was not background music. That pulled you in.

Billy Bragg opened up for them, who I was also super-duper into at the time. Still to this day it's one of the most compelling concerts I've ever seen. I remember how Morrissey moved on stage. Today we live in a world where gender bending and sexual ambiguity is embraced and it's a good thing and it's widely accepted. But that wasn't the world then. The artists that played with gender roles and their sexuality were more in the Bowie direction, much more overt. So it wasn't just what Morrissey would say in interviews. It was the way he moved on stage and even his choice of clothing, these blousy shirts that were clearly feminine although there wasn't make up or long hair or any of that. I found that fascinating. That made him and his band feel unique and relevant and cool and music your parents would hate, which is exactly what you wanted when you were 16.

It was assertive music, jangly but not spiky, sharp but not overly angry. A lot of the English bands I had been into beforehand were bands like The Jam, whose last American show at the old Palladium I remember it vividly. The Jam had a certain anger about them. That wasn't what The Smiths were about. The lyrics had a darkness but the music was so upbeat and it just grabbed you.

So I saw that show and then I saw all the other New York shows, because they would always play New York on their tours. I was always compelled and I loved them to the end. Although I found the direction they went in progressively a little less interesting as they got more mainstream, their records they were always good. The concerts were always that way too.

I'm lucky enough to have seen many influential bands. I started going to gigs very young and saw a lot of seminal English bands play reasonably small places in New York. There's not that many gigs that you remember so vividly so many years later. I still think of The Smiths as the standard that other bands have to meet.

Andy Rourke at the Beacon Theatre. Photo by John Baxter

A few weeks ago I saw a band from Dublin called Fontaines DC and I remember thinking of that early Smiths show. And I had the same thought the first time I saw the Arctic Monkeys in a tiny venue here.

There was a passion and a potency about The Smiths that was and is still huge. It felt like there was a purity to what that band was doing that today is a little bit harder to achieve, in the age of Instagram and hype. We live in a world that is much faster to get 'buzz' happening. In Britain and the world at the time, that wasn't the case. So you could almost sense that excitement of them playing in New York for the first time. I became a journalist that wrote mostly about music for years. I ended up working at a record label doing A&R. I ended up reviewing a Morrissey album for *Rolling Stone*.

It wasn't a small evening, that night at the Beacon, in the big picture of evenings for me. It had a great impact on what I ended up doing professionally and with my life.

I'm not very into seeing reunion shows. I've seen Morrissey solo once. He played a big run of shows here on Broadway in May 2019. I didn't get tickets on purpose. Seeing The Smiths are precious memories to me of young, passionate, naïve - in the most beautiful way - men. I'm not eager to see middle-aged men try to repeat that magic. It doesn't usually happen that way.

PALLADIUM THEATER

27 & 28 JUNE 1985, HOLLYWOOD, CALIFORNIA

I WAS THERE: GREG GABRY, AGE 21

For Greg Gabry witnessing The Smiths l... was his Beatles at Shea Stadium mome...

I really didn't know what to expect as the band was still quite new to me at the time, but my friends were definitely into them and had all the vinyl to prove it. I was only really familiar with the songs that I had heard on KROQ (106.7FM radio in LA) like 'This Charming Man' and 'Heaven Knows I'm Miserable Now', but I had heard everything else at my friends' houses or in their cars and was quickly becoming a fan.

When we got to the Palladium, I felt like I may not be the only one who didn't quite get it yet, as there were almost equal size contingents of punks, surfers, Hollywood glam types and even some hair band looking dudes - it was quite a mix. I will admit we 'partied' rather heavily before getting into Hollywood so recollections of the evening are quite hazy, but I recall the opening act was very bizarre, as it featured an incredibly robust drag queen on stage who serenaded the crowd with operatic selections. The crowd wasn't all that appreciative.

The crowd became a bit unruly with lots of yelling, some booing and minor skirmishes amongst us standing on the floor. Perhaps this was out of boredom or nervousness, and of course drugs and alcohol, but the unruliness continued throughout the show, so much so that it was mentioned from on stage a few times. I recall feeling a bit scolded. I wish I could remember more specific details of the night, and if I could go back and give my 21-year old self some advice it would be that when he spends money on tickets to see potentially iconic bands, he should scale back on the alcohol and hallucinogens so he can remember things more clearly in the future!

When the band finally took the stage and a long, slow melodic introduction started, the tension and excitement in the crowd shot up tremendously. I've been told since then that that opening tune was 'Meat Is Murder'. It was the second song I remember vividly, for when I heard the introduction to 'Hand in Glove' and wishing for harmonica, which was absent, myself and others went a bit nuts. That's when it sunk in that I was actually seeing The Smiths and it felt like a really big deal; you got the sense that this band was capable of big things. Morrissey up on stage held your attention like no other lead singers we were seeing at that time, and the guitar work was mesmerising. Seeing The Smiths for the first time that night felt like our generation's Beatles at Shea Stadium experience; something that could never be duplicated and which we would remember forever.

I WAS THERE: PHILLIP LÓPEZ JIMÉNEZ, AGE 16

In '85 I was becoming more into music, like I was with movies, and started reading *NME* and *Melody Maker* to know what was happening in England and *Flipside* and *MMR* for the States. My musical tastes were punk, post punk and rockabilly. I first heard The Smiths in '84 on KROQ, a radio station out of Los Angeles. The song was 'What Difference Does It Make?' I loved it but I figured it was a new song from The Polecats as it sounded quite like them! When the deejay said it was a band called The Smiths, I made a mental note. The first album I got was *Hatful of Hollow*.

The Smiths were getting a big buzz in the UK and US and they were right up my alley. My tastes leaned toward more guitar-oriented stuff than techno. I liked Depeche Mode but so did 12 year old girls! When I read in *NME* that Morrissey was the president of The Cramps fan club and that he preferred American bands like X, I became more interested, as The Cramps were and still are my favourite band.

By this point in my life I had dropped out of school and was a bit wild. I went to the show with some people I knew but they were a bit square and hung out on the balcony. I was on the floor at the stage. Because there was a buzz about the band and this was their first LA show, the crowd was a mix of punks and bubblegummers. The opening act was a bunch of drag queens, that's when it started raining spit.

I had hooked up with this chick there earlier and I threw my leather jacket over her and said, 'Shit this is like a fuckin' Fear show!' Loogies were flying everywhere. The final drag queen was dressed like a baby with diaper and bottle and singing 'Shortnin' Bread'. (I am not making this shit up). The crowd started getting a bit violent. Then some guy started groping the girl I was with and I popped him in the face. I remember thinking, 'This is the fuckin' Smiths, not some local HC show!' The drag queens left and the lights came on and we waited.

After a while the lights shut off and it was total darkness. Then - boom - a bright spotlight popped on from the back of the stage, pointing up and forming columns of light. Then pre-recorded music turned on and I recognised the tune. A few other people in the crowd recognised it too. This went on for a minute or two and then the band came out and jumped right into 'Meat Is Murder'. I was like, 'Okay, now I get it.' That sure was an attention grabber though!

People were jumping on stage and halfway through their set someone grabbed Johnny Marr's leg and he fell and someone took his wireless and Morrissey stormed off. Marr said that if he didn't get his wireless they were going to leave. Then someone in the crowd screamed that he was gonna kick the shit out of whoever had it. Finally it flew out of the audience and into Marr's hands. Then Marr had to persuade Morrissey to come back out. He came back out and said that we were the most unruly crowd he'd ever seen and lectured us some more and then they finally started playing again.

I wish I could remember the girl's name I hooked with. I'm not a big Morrissey fan and never got his solo stuff, though I like some of the songs. I love The Smiths but don't really listen to them often. Being Latino and liking them has become a bizarre stereotype, to say the least. That show was predominantly Anglo. Now, I'm sure, it would be different.

I WAS THERE: DONNA KLAUSER

I first heard them on KROQ. I remember scrounging for change to get tickets for me and my boyfriend (now my husband) for $15. $15? Those tickets are priceless now! I remember Morrissey swinging his flowers. 'Meat Is Murder' was their first song and I remember hearing a cow mooing and the sound of a butcher's saw in the background. I thought I saw an image of a cow. Many young gay men were crying and hugging themselves. This was the height of the AIDS crisis and I now understand the relevance of having The Smiths performance with a gay lead singer. My little sister kept trying to squirm her way up the front and we kept pulling her back. There was no mosh pit. I just felt that this was an intense musical experience.

I WAS THERE: LARRY WEATHERFORD, AGE 17

The Smiths were a great band for four 17 year old dudes to see. We walked up to the Palladium as a limo pulled in the back and the guys got out. All four of them! Johnny Marr bummed a cigarette from me. I had to hand it to them through a chain-link fence. They were pretty cordial. Morrissey didn't say anything but Mike Joyce was friendly. They were on their way in as we were all saying, 'We really like you!' They humbly thanked us and went inside. When the show started it was very aggressive, more like the punk shows I went to and what I envisioned The Smiths show would be like. We were pretty big guys so we rushed to the front. Had we not been big we would've been crushed against the wooden barrier between us and the stage. We were front and centre - Morrissey's wingtips were in our face. The band sounded amazing and we had a fantastic time.

'THE BOY WITH THE THORN IN HIS SIDE'

RELEASED 16 SEPTEMBER 1985

'The Boy With the Thorn in his Side' had a video that featured The Smiths in the studio, helping it to reach number 23. Truman Capote was the cover star on the picture sleeve, although not all the band were familiar with him.

SINGLE OF THE WEEK

THE SMITHS 'The Boy With The Thorn In His Side' (Rough Trade) Call me predictable, call me boring, call me sentimental – I don't care. The worries of the world float away as the new single from the ever lovable Smiths arrives on my desk. Still on Rough Trade, still adorning the covers with Morrissey's heroes (Truman Capote looking like Ernie Wise this time), and still making the most perfect pop music ever created. A light 'Williamesque' backing has Morrissey trilling and warbling his exquisite way around Johnny Marr's simple melodies. After the slip that 'Shakespeare's Sister' proved to be and the questionable decision to release 'That Joke Isn't Funny Anymore' – probably the only track on 'Meat Is Murder' that *shouldn't* have been a single – the group brush off the dust from a thousand gleeful cries of 'has beens' and resume normal service.

Morrissey: When I put him on the cover of the Smiths single 'The Boy With the Thorn In His Side' a certain member of the Smiths (who unfortunately is still alive) said, 'Is that Ernie Wise?'

After a two month break from touring, The Smiths were back out on the road in September, undertaking a seven date Scottish tour taking in Edinburgh, Glasgow, Dundee and Aberdeen but also less familiar stop offs for rock bands – Irvine, Lerwick and Inverness.

MAGNUM LEISURE CENTRE

22 SEPTEMBER 1985, IRVINE, UK

I WAS THERE: MICHAEL FARRAGHER

All our money went on travelling around to see The Smiths and sometimes on places to stay. A lot of the times when we were travelling to see them in England we would stay in a coach station or a train station or even a public toilet, because we couldn't afford a hotel. The great occasions were when they went further away. That was too far to come back and forth to London from the gig and we stayed in youth hostels. Those were really good.

There was a planned tour of Italy which, I think was in '85 and we were all set to go and Morrissey sent us the dates and said, 'We are playing in Italy and then they cancelled it at the last minute.' There had been a death threat and Morrissey decided that the tour was off. In all, when I counted up how many times we saw them, it was around 50.

I WAS THERE: YVONNE BENNIE

Yvonne (left) and sister Liz weren't allowed to keep their tickets

My sister Liz and I saw them at the Magnum Leisure Centre. It's since been demolished. It's the only gig we went to in the Eighties where they retained our tickets, and my sis and I were not happy. We begged to be able to keep them but to no avail. The Smiths were my favourite band then. I dressed in all black as I was indie then but for the gig I wore one white glove as homage to the song, 'Hand in Glove'. A few years later I was talking to a work colleague who had been at the gig and who said, 'There was a girl there wearing one white glove, we thought that was strange?' I replied, 'That was me' and laughed. We were from Kilmarnock and my sister always says I was the first girl in our town to walk around wearing my shirt outside my jeans like Morrissey. I also once ran into our local butcher's shop on our main street and shouted, 'Meat is murder!'

I WAS THERE: FRANCIS LOPEZ, AGE 21

I was unemployed, skint and playing in my own band, Catch 22. Music was my life. I was always first into Speed Records in Ayr the morning of a Smiths release and the guy that ran the shop always gave me a poster to go along with the records I bought. I still have a couple. My most cherished being the 'Shakespeare's Sister' poster featuring Pat Phoenix as Elsie Tanner.

The only time I'd seen The Smiths live was on BBC – it might have been *The Oxford Road Show* or *Rock Goes To College* or one of those shows. But it was awful and they were awful so when I saw the advert for their gig at Irvine Magnum, I have to be honest I thought, 'On record they are great but live, I might give it a miss.'

No one I knew wanted to go and see them so when the Sunday arrived, I eventually encouraged myself to go. I set off at three o'clock in the afternoon and hitchhiked the 28 miles from New Cumnock to Irvine. It was a dark and dreich night, so everything that was keeping me in the house was being thrown at me: they were shit live, no money for the bus, the cold, damp evening and the thought of hitchhiking it back at night time and not knowing what time in the morning I'd get back home. They all combined to keep me nudging towards just staying in my warm room.

But I got there. I can't remember how many lifts it took! When I got into the hall at the Magnum it was already pretty busy. I decided to position myself roughly in the middle of the crowd. Even though I was hooked on The Smiths I still recall feeling sort of ambivalent and more amused to be seeing them than excited.

Down went the lights, on went 'Dance of the Knights' by Prokofiev and on they came. 'Guess who?' roared Morrissey. How stupid I'd been. Right from the off, it was like a tsunami of being blasted at me. It felt like getting the biggest punch in the stomach. I remember at the time comparing it to what it must have been like to go to a Motorhead gig with them starting the set off with 'Ace Of Spades'. The sheer power just amazed me. The complete opposite to what I'd seen that Saturday afternoon, watching a limp and unenthusiastic performance on BBC2. It was awesome - and I never use that word to describe anything. What made it even more special was that they were using us, us in tiny insignificant Ayrshire - a place that had been devastated by Thatcher's cruel pit closures after the miners were defeated, battered and bruised by her bitter and twisted cruelty on a population she knew nothing about and didn't want to know - to debut three songs. We were the first to hear them live. They could've chosen anywhere to play them live first, but they chose us. That meant so much to us because we had so little to cheer us up at that time.

After three encores, the gig finished, and I was completely knackered. It felt great. I hitchhiked it home alone (see what I did there?) but I can't recall a single thing about the journey or what time I got back. All I remember is that I was in no hurry - I'd just been to the best gig I'd ever go to.

PLAYHOUSE

24 SEPTEMBER 1985, EDINBURGH, UK

I WAS THERE: PETER MARTIN

I remember mooching about Edinburgh all day, throwing stones at Steve Joyce, as we met him for the first time, and kissing Morrissey on the cheek as he came out of the sound check. We missed the train home as we refused to leave before the band had finished. We had to get the next one, which didn't stop at Cramlington meaning a taxi back from the town.

BARROWLAND BALLROOM

25 SEPTEMBER 1985, GLASGOW, UK

I WAS THERE: PETER DORIS

I still have a bit of Morrissey's shirt from that night. The audience tore it to bits.

I WAS THERE: ANNETTE FLYNN

You can hear Morrissey, on a bootleg of this show, saying, 'This song is dedicated to someone who gave me something this afternoon.' Well, that would be me. But I didn't know at that time. I had delivered a parcel to the Barrowland containing a card with a huge black false moustache, a very random gift which I thought would appeal to his sense of humour. The following week, I received a letter to my home address on Rough Trade letterhead, containing album postcards and on the letter was, 'Were you out there? I waited at the Fountain and you didn't come. Do you still care?' I was at work when I got it. My mother called to say, 'That freaky fucker has sent you another letter - what's all this about?'

I WAS THERE: GILLIAN DOUGLAS, AGE 17

I went to both gigs with a school friend who I later found out was also going out with my boyfriend, so we had a serious falling out and haven't spoken since! The 1985 gig was on a school night but just before the Scottish September holiday weekend. I was allowed to go on the proviso that my grandfather dropped me off and picked me up. Thankfully he agreed to do so round the corner in East Campbell Street - we were trying to be cool. In 1986, I was going home on the bus at lunchtime after a morning's shopping in Glasgow city centre when I noticed a queue for the gig forming outside the Barras. I jumped off the bus, called my mum from a payphone and begged her to pick my friend up and bring her and our gig tickets down to the Barras as I was joining the queue.

I WAS THERE: JAMES MACNEIL

I was lucky enough to see The Smiths three times at the Glasgow Barrowlands. The one with the most memories for me was on the *Meat Is Murder* tour, which I attended with my late brother John. The build up to the concert was made even more special because *The Tube* was filming it. You could just feel the crowd were at fever pitch before the group came on. They didn't disappoint from the first note of 'Shakespeare's Sister' to the last song, 'Miserable Lie'. I was holding on for dear life with the crowd swaying. The atmosphere was electric with the group and crowd playing off each other. We walked home that night knowing that we had witnessed something truly special.

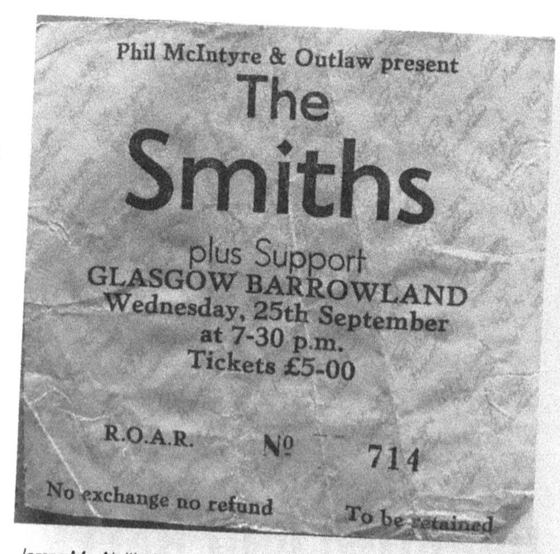
Phil McIntyre & Outlaw present
The Smiths
plus Support
GLASGOW BARROWLAND
Wednesday, 25th September
at 7-30 p.m.
Tickets £5-00
R.O.A.R. Nº 714
No exchange no refund
To be retained

James MacNeil's ticket for the Barrowlands show

I WAS THERE: ALAN MCADAM

A friend from school and college was a big Smiths fan, and so I went along to see them for the first time. I had liked the first few singles but hadn't really got into the debut album. *Meat Is Murder* was very different and I loved it from the off. So the experience of hearing this live was incredible. They came out to demented, wild applause and launched into a great set, with Andy Rourke stock still and Mike Joyce appearing to enjoy the experience, but not really giving much away. Johnny Marr looked cool and floral, with some beads and looking at the crowd going wild. Morrissey was spinning around and encouraging the crowd into delirium. The songs were fantastic live particularly 'Meat Is Murder', which sounded creepy and haunting in the vast space of Barrowlands.

I WAS THERE: SEÁN Ó DONNGHAILE

I saw them twice at Barrowlands. I've seen hundreds of bands since but nothing has ever matched the first time I saw The Smiths. A girl fainted on me. I took her over to First Aid. When the band came off Andy Rourke saw her and came over to see if she was okay. Nice touch. There was only nine months between those gigs but by the second gig it was almost out of control. Lots of people had jumped on the bandwagon who I felt never really got The Smiths.

CAIRD HALL

26 SEPTEMBER 1985, DUNDEE, UK

I WAS THERE: DEREK MOIR

The last time we saw them was the *Meat Is Murder* tour in Dundee. They had become a screaming teenage pop band, kinda 'phoney Beatlemania, bitten and tossed....' I had never experienced that and it was weird as they were still great but some essence had been taken away.

They were beautiful and warm and welcoming and clever and working class and phenomenal. I had been raised on Radio 1 and The Beatles, *Pet Sounds* and Motown as a kid and got punk rock at 11. I spent all my paper round money on back cataloguing The Adverts and Desperate Bicycles. Now the DIY post punk indie Rough Trade scene was ours and we made sure to use it. I started a band, did a Peel session, released two singles, got single of the week in *Melody Maker* and worked in a cooperative that brought bands like McCarthy, GFL, My Bloody Valentine, The Wedding Present and 1000 Violins to Perth and to Scotland. Truly inspirational.

Johnny Marr disallowed David Cameron to like The Smiths (What did Cameron not get about 'The Eton Rifles'?) and I have so much more sympathy and empathy for Johnny Marr. Morrissey has abandoned what we felt was the political, sexual, leftist intellectual revolution of the Eighties.

CAPITAL THEATRE

30 SEPTEMBER 1985, ABERDEEN, UK

I WAS THERE: STEPHEN RAFFERTY, AGE 16

I went along with a couple of mates from Peterhead. The Capital Theatre was an all seated venue with the front four rows taken out. You weren't allowed to stand but as soon as the band came on there was a huge surge that the bouncers couldn't control and the front was full, most of them pretty rowdy Aberdeen soccer casuals. I stayed back in the sixth row where I could see everything. I remember seeing them that day on some morning programme and they played 'The Boy With the Thorn in His Side.' That's probably the song that sticks with me the most. They kicked off with 'Shakespeare's Sister' so it would have been pretty mental. On the bus back to Peterhead a lad who was a couple of years older than me had a piece of Morrissey's shirt. It must have been a square that was all of two inches by two inches. He was chuffed to fuck.

Johnny Marr by Michael Farragher

I WAS THERE: RITA FARRAGHER

The Scottish tour in 1985 was an amazing little tour. Starting in Irvine, somewhere we had never heard of before - I loved it that The Smiths played in out of the way places. That tour took us to Inverness - Eden Court Theatre - we had to kill a couple of days in Inverness and we loved it there. I actually moved there about 15 years later. The gig was also the only time they performed 'Asleep'. We couldn't afford the ferry from Aberdeen to Lerwick so we missed the Shetland show, which we heard was amazing. We just hung around in Aberdeen for a few days feeling miserable and I have hated Aberdeen ever since.

On a few occasions Morrissey invited us into the venue to watch the soundcheck - maybe a half a dozen times. That was always great, they sometimes did songs that weren't part of the set. We saw them do 'Unloveable' at a soundcheck and I don't think they ever did that live.

I WAS THERE: ROY SHARPLES

I first came across The Smiths aged 11 when they performed 'Heaven Knows I'm Miserable Now' on *Top of the Pops* in 1984. My grandma bought it for me from Woolworths on Union Street. The whole package was an art statement and quintessentially northern British. The two up two down - it's grim up north. It was about seeing the beauty in the ugliness, the poetry in redbrick industrial architecture, smoking chimneys and factories. The Smiths were the outsider's outsiders. They influenced people's perceptions, values and how they looked, dressed and sounded whilst fuelling movements such as the 'real' independent music scene, vegetarianism and animal rights. Many of their songs are like a time capsule to me in that they capture a moment in time in my life. My Uncle Stewart took me to see them. An unforgettable experience, they kicked in with 'Shakespeare's Sister', with the highlights being How Soon Is Now?, 'Heaven Knows I'm Miserable Now', 'This Charming Man' and 'William, It Was Really Nothing'.

I WAS THERE: IAIN WELLER

I won the tickets from the local radio station, Northsound, probably from the Bryan Burnett slot. He played all the post punk stuff on a Saturday night. The tickets were for the balcony so I spent the first couple of songs trying to get downstairs past the bouncers. I managed that and went down the front as far as I could go. I remember people asking for 'Barbarism Begins at Home' and Morrissey said, 'We don't play that anymore.'

Iain Weller remembers an amazing gig by The Smiths

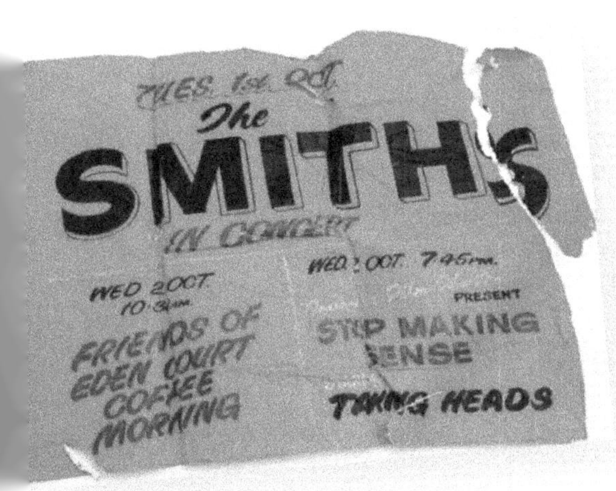

EDENCOURT

1 OCTOBER 1985, INVERNESS, UK

I WAS THERE: MICHAEL MORRISON

I didn't know much about them at the time. I just went along with my mate Graham Maclennan, who was a big fan.

I WAS THERE: GRAHAM MACLENNAN, AGE 18

I was a student at Inverness College. It was a great venue. I was seated and it was my first experience of live music. I also remember buying a yellow *Meat Is Murder* t-shirt with the iconic cover on it and no mention of The Smiths. The support band, Easterhouse, really impressed me but The Smiths blew me away, particularly 'William, It Was Really Nothing'.

In December 1985 the band assembled in Salford for a photo session that was to yield an iconic image.

SALFORD LADS CLUB

13 DECEMBER 1985, SALFORD, UK

I WAS THERE: STEPHEN WRIGHT

I took the photograph of The Smiths outside Salford Lads Club that was used for the sleeve of *The Queen Is Dead*. The shoot really should have gone to a big-name photographer - an Anton Corbijn or a Pennie Smith - but it went to me, a fan using my first Nikon with the 'wrong' lens. I'd sent Rough Trade pictures of the band playing, and Morrissey liked them. The first Smiths live show I shot was in 1984 at the Free Trade Hall. I was so skint I could only afford one reel of film and had to walk a long way home. From this show I caught the shot of dead flowers hanging from Morrissey's jeans. My favourite live shot is of Morrissey waving flowers above his head. I took it from the side of the stage hidden in the lighting rig.

More live shows followed and then Rough Trade asked me to shoot the Salford Lads session. Morrissey wanted an iconic Manchester location. We also tried Victoria Station but it was too dark, so we ended up at Salford Lads Club. It was shot on a cold, dark, winter day - yet somehow it has a darkness that sets the right mood. You can see Johnny Marr shivering in some shots. I like the casual, staggered way they are standing, and they're nicely framed by the arches. But I always say it's the band, not the photo, that is classic. Morrissey has a Mona Lisa expression: it's neither a smile nor a smirk, but he's very much in command. If you look at the body language, you can tell he was king of the pack.

My darkroom was also my bedroom. I kept my processing chemicals in old lemonade bottles. I think the cheap equipment, and the fact there was so little light, gave the photo a grittiness, like a 1950s picture.

Morrissey ultimately chose the picture for the sleeve. He sent me a postcard afterwards to say thank you. It was written in his famous spidery handwriting: 'A sweeter set of pictures were never taken. I smiled for a full minute (phone Roy Castle – that's a record).'

Apparently it's the most famous photo of The Smiths and that makes me smile. Fans come from all over the world to recreate the shot. The round trip from the centre of Manchester is probably £25 by cab, so I've done my bit for taxi-drivers over the years. Years later I've got to go into the Salford Lads club and meet the people there, which has been a real honour. I gave an image to the Salford Lads Club to raise funds and they managed to raise over £60,000 from t-shirt sales using it.

I love it that people enjoy the image years later and that I caught them at their magnificent peak. I count myself as very lucky, as a huge fan, to have got the opportunity to see and shoot them live and then to get to meet them and produce the Salford Lads image. Of all the bands I shot it was The Smiths I loved seeing most and none of the albums really beat the atmosphere of their live shows.

You can see some of my images of The Smiths and other artists at www.smithsphotos.com.

1986

CITY HALL

31 JANUARY 1986, NEWCASTLE-UPON-TYNE, UK

I WAS THERE: ALYSON LAWS, AGE 16

I thought my ticket to Live Aid at Wembley could not be beaten. But in 1986 I was a member of the youth arm of the Labour Party and spent £5 on the best ticket of my life - Red Wedge at Newcastle City Hall. I loved Billy Bragg and his politics and how we were all going to fight against Thatcher together. I thought £5 to see Paul Weller and The Style Council, The Communards, Prefab Sprout and Billy Bragg amongst others and all in my home town was an opportunity not to be missed. My sister again came along together with my good friend. We had tickets in the stalls, fourth row from the front, and we thought we had made it that night. The gig was inspiring and I can't remember who was on stage when they announced the next artist, 'Smith….' We stopped and thought, 'No, it can't be....' It wasn't. Wendy Smith from Prefab Sprout came on stage. She was fantastic and we enjoyed it but we had been taken to the edge and although we did not expect what was coming, we got a hint and thought, 'They are winding us up!'

Then the announcement, 'The Smiths!' and in front of me were – The Smiths! The excitement of the crowd was immense. I have not felt that feeling since, just a sense of overwhelming amazement that this band were in front of us. In front of me! Four songs later it was over but to this day I still remember that as one of the best gigs of my life.

I WAS THERE: PETER MARTIN

Only Johnny Marr was billed to perform. This was also the only night of the tour that The Smiths turned up to. How lucky was that? Four songs of absolute brilliance. I went with lads who were more interested in The Style Council than The Smiths but all agreed that The Smiths stole the show.

I WAS THERE: PETER SMITH

One of the most memorable gigs I have been to. Red Wedge was a collective of musicians, fronted by Billy Bragg, who set out to engage young people with politics, and the Labour Party in particular, during the period leading up to the 1987 general election, in the hope of ousting the Conservative government of Margaret Thatcher. Billy Bragg was joined in Red Wedge by Paul Weller and The Communards lead singer Jimmy Somerville. Red Wedge organised a number of major tours and concert. The first and most memorable, took place in January and February 1986, and featured Bragg, Paul Weller's band The Style Council, The Communards, Junior Giscombe and Lorna Gee. The core touring acts were joined by other guest bands throughout the tour.

All of the bands performed short sets; a few songs each. The Communards were impressive, Jimmy Somerville's soaring vocals were amazing, and The Style Council were also good. DC Lee guested with them and sang 'See the Day'. Local heroes Prefab Sprout also went down well.

But The Smiths stole the show. There were whispers around the hall that something special was going to happen. Without any real warning, they were announced and stormed straight into 'Shakespeare's Sister', followed by 'I Want the One I Can't Have', 'The Boy With the Thorn in His Side' and 'Bigmouth Strikes Again' - 'our new single'. There is something about a short set; it allows a band to focus and to maintain a high level of energy and passion throughout. The Smiths were simply phenomenal that night; there was a buzz about them at the time, and everyone was delighted to see them perform. But it was more than that. It was as if they had decided to put everything into those four songs; the power, the intensity, and Morrissey and Marr's performance were a step above anything I had seen them deliver before (or since) that night. It was as if they knew that they were simply the best band on the planet at the time, and they came out with the confidence and ability to deliver a word class, stunning performance. We sat there, feeling that we were witnessing something special. It was that good. It was the best time I saw The Smiths, and a performance that will stay with me for ever. Perfect rock 'n' roll in four songs and 20 or so short minutes.

Johnny Marr: The Red Wedge gig at Newcastle City Hall was one of the best things we ever did. Andy and I had done a couple of gigs already with Billy Bragg in Manchester and Birmingham the week before... I was telling Morrissey about it and he was fairly up for just doing an impromptu show. So we drove up to Newcastle, without telling anyone. I walked into the sound check...the other bands were a little bit perplexed as to what we were doing there. We had no instruments, so we borrowed The Style Council's equipment and just tore the roof off the place. In the middle of the set we just walked on to this announcement and the place went bananas.

Morrissey: When we took to the stage the audience reeled back in horror. They took their Walkmans off and threw down their cardigans. Suddenly the place was alight, aflame with passion!

In February 1986, The Smiths appeared at a benefit gig for beleaguered Liverpool City Council under the banner 'With Love From Manchester'.

Originally scheduled to play Liverpool on 8 February 1984 but postponed until 14 March of that year, The Smiths returned to the city two years later

ROYAL COURT

8 FEBRUARY 1986, LIVERPOOL, UK

I WAS THERE: STUART EDWARDS

1986 was a politicised time in Liverpool. I was in my second term at Liverpool Polytechnic and the city was in a mess. The Militant Tendency factions in the city's council were in a stand-off with Margaret Thatcher. The deputy leader of the Council, Derek Hatton, had led the setting of an illegal budget with the Council spending £30m more than they had available. Hatton was an ex-fireman but frankly he looked and dressed like an ex-footballer. He claimed that the £30m excess had effectively been 'stolen' by Conservative central Government. All manner of civic services were grinding to a halt. I remember not being able to attend lectures on a number of occasions because the buildings weren't being opened. This was the least of the impact of the Liverpool actions - bins weren't being emptied, the city was shutting down and council employees were being given their redundancy notices.

The issue had gone all the way to the top of the Labour Party, which was tearing itself apart to establish its own identity and values. Matters had come to a head at the party conference in October of 1985. The leader, Neil Kinnock, had given one of the most impassioned and potentially divisive speeches in living memory. Senior Labour party members walked out in disgust and Kinnock was heckled by Hatton in particular.

Things descended even more deeply as the winter drew in. Whilst the majority of the council were traditional Labour, the Trotskyite 'Loony Left' (as the British press had dubbed them) element had a stranglehold on the city. Sympathy also existed due to the collective governmental neglect that had existed since Liverpool's grand days as one of the world's foremost ports which precipitated terminal decline.

So in February 1986, one flamboyant North West socialist, Tony Wilson reached out to another in Hatton. Wilson booked the Royal Court Theatre in Liverpool and under the catalogue reference of FAC 152 organised *With Love From Manchester* with corresponding t- shirt.

The bands played for expenses and tickets were £6 each. The object of the exercise was to support the 58 Liverpool councillors who by that point had been sacked and faced significant legal bills. Wilson started as a reporter in Liverpool in the early Seventies before ending up as the mainstay of Granada TV's early evening news coverage. He had previously worked closely with Roger Eagle who ran the legendary Eric's club in Liverpool. They shared bands between the Liverpool club and Wilson's Factory night in Manchester before the eventual opening of the Hacienda. Wilson and Eagle eventually had a falling out over the roster for Factory which was initially intended as a North West music label rather than solely Mancunian. The straw which broke the camel's back was Orchestral Manoeuvres in the Dark, who Wilson wanted and Eagle and his colleague Pete Fulwell didn't. The pair split but Wilson still felt a residual fondness and responsibility for Liverpool, hence the concert.

So I queued up for my ticket and arrived early to enjoy an evening of stellar Manchester music, featuring three bands that were all in their prime – New Order, The Fall and The Smiths. New Order opened proceedings on the basis that they had the most gear and it would be easier to clear the stage after they had finished rather than set up. Each band were allocated a 45 minute set so the roadies went to work and The Fall entered the arena. The feeling in the Royal Court at the time was that The Fall were the lesser of the three bands but their set was possibly the highlight of the evening.

The Smiths followed. This was just as *The Queen Is Dead* was being finished and the set drew mostly from the forthcoming album and *Meat Is Murder*. 'Vicar in a Tutu', 'Cemetry Gates' and 'Frankly, Mr Shankly' were all debuted that evening.

After walking on to 'Montagues and Capulets' (before we were sick of it due to *The Apprentice*!), they opened with 'Shakespeare's Sister'. The set ignored the early material with Johnny teasing with the intros to 'This Charming Man' and 'What Difference Does It Make?'. Highlights for me were 'Rusholme Ruffians', which had the full '(Marie's The Name) His Latest Flame' intro, and the earliest track, 'William, It Was Really Nothing'.

After encores of 'Meat Is Murder' and 'Stretch Out and Wait', members of the bands joined John Cooper Clarke, The Farm and The Redskins on stage for a ramshackle version of 'Maggie's Farm'. I seem to remember a few Newcastle Brown bottles being chucked but can't recall what prompted it. The evening ended and I headed back to Garston reflecting on seeing these three bands at pivotal stages in their careers.

The councillors lost their court battle and the Militant Tendency contingent were expelled from the Labour Party. Derek Hatton enjoyed a chequered career in media before heading to Cyprus as a property developer at the start of the century. I doubt any of those council workers who received their redundancy notices enjoyed such a fortunate conclusion to their careers.

I WAS THERE: NICK BARBER

The Smiths played a chunk of *The Queen Is Dead*, which had been featuring in their live set for a while. A number of the audience were familiar with the songs as there was a strong trade in bootleg cassettes - I used to get mine from an underground market stall near Manchester's Arndale Centre. The guy who ran the stall had a series of contacts, who would use the Sony Professional Walkman to get good quality recordings of Manchester gigs and you could often pick them up from the stall the day after the shows. On the bootleg of the Liverpool gig, you can hear me shouting, 'Do your Elvis impression!' (such wit) before the 'Marie's the Name'/'Rusholme Ruffians' mini-medley. I remember the gig ended in a somewhat shambolic fashion after the Smiths' set when, instead of an encore, Derek Hatton and Margi Clarke appeared, much to the audience's disgruntlement as we wanted more from The Smiths.

I WAS THERE: JULIE CALLAGHAN, AGE 27

I witnessed some amazing gigs in the late Seventies in a little punk club called Eric's in Liverpool. The Clash, Siouxsie, Talking Heads, Ramones, The Slits, X-Ray Spex, Joy Division, Buzzcocks… the list goes on.. I was a fervent Smiths fan, had just discovered them and was enthralled. I just can't remember much about the gig. But I have kept my souvenir t-shirt after all these years!

Julie Callaghan still has her souvenir t-shirt from the 'With Love From Manchester' show

I WAS THERE: MARK WILLIAMS

I recall Morrissey introducing 'Frankly Mr. Shankly' by saying something along the lines of, 'This song isn't about who you may think it's about.' Of course, he was referring to the legendary Liverpool FC manager Bill Shankly. A Liverpudlian to the side of me shouted, 'Is he taking the piss?' as the band struck up the song's debut live performance. All in all the short 45 minute set went well, with Morrissey customarily throwing his purple-striped shirt into the audience and with me luckily being close enough to grab it in mid-air. Within a second there must have been half a dozen of us pulling at the tough nylon garb without successfully ripping it until an enterprising youth in the crowd pulled out his flick knife and started to cut strip off it for us all. Unfortunately my portion of the shirt has been sadly lost. I used to have it on my bedroom wall with a review of the concert which included a photo of Morrissey wearing it.

I WAS THERE: KEV JONES

I was right at the front at that gig. I undid Morrissey's shoelace because he was right in front of me. Nowadays there's a barrier and you've got the security in front of the stage. But back then you were right up against the stage and you could just reach over. Morrissey was always making contact with the audience, shaking hands and I remember vividly holding onto his shoelace and undoing it. I was trying to get the shoelace out of the shoe, thinking that would be a good memento to have, but I didn't actually manage it. I also managed to get hold of Andy Rourke's set list. I just shouted at one of the roadies to ask if I could have it.

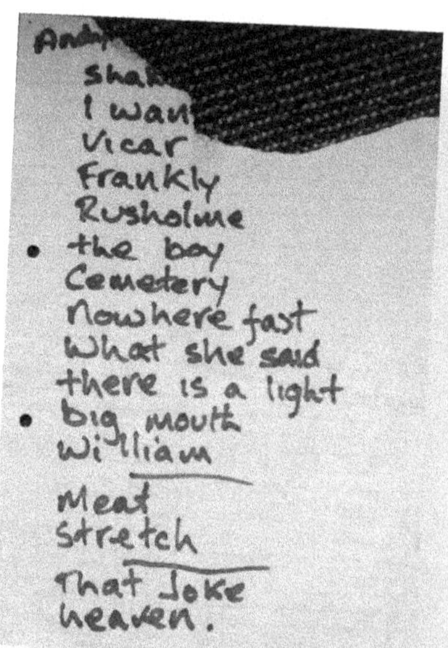

Kev Jones managed to bag Andy Rouke's setlist from the Royal Court show

NATIONAL STADIUM

10 FEBRUARY 1986, DUBLIN, IRELAND

I WAS THERE: DES FOLEY

I went with my girlfriend Sinead. We had seats up in the stalls to the left of the stage, but facing in towards the audience rather than the stage; the upside of this was that we were directly above the entrance and exit that the band would use to come on and off stage. Morrissey wore a green jumper on stage when they first came on. The stadium was packed and I remember people going crazy when the band came on. Fans always seemed to be right at the front of the stage too; I don't remember there being any barriers of gaps between stage and audience like you'd have now. The band played a blistering set. I distinctly remember them starting with '(Marie's the Name) His Latest Flame)' and then going into 'Rusholme Ruffians' and the roar when the audience recognition kicked in. Smiths gigs were always very exciting, high energy gigs and audiences were always highly vocal. Me and Sinead took advantage of our position to shout down to Mike Joyce when they came off stage at the end of the set. We asked him for the vest t-shirt he was wearing and he duly obliged, took it off and threw it up to us. We did the same again, after they'd finished the encores and again he duly obliged, so we got two t-shirts worn by him on stage during that gig. We were beside ourselves as they were fantastic souvenirs to have. Sinead and I eventually split up and she kept the t-shirts!

I WAS THERE: GRAHAM MONTGOMERY

I don't recall much about this apart from possibly seeing a member of U2 in the balcony. My friend's uncle used to get us free and reserved seats in the press box at the Stadium. I think Craig Gannon was playing with them. A lot of what they played was off *Meat Is Murder*, an album I didn't like as much as *Hatful of Hollow*.

I WAS THERE: PAUL PAGE

In all the gigs I have attended, I don't think I have ever witnessed such hysterical adoration for a band. There was this kind of lovely chaos about it - fans desperate to get close to Morrissey were constantly invading the stage, and constantly being intercepted by security and tossed back into the melee. Those that evaded security would throw their arms around their messiah before being forcibly prised away.

The front of the stage was a heaving mass of Morrissey lookalikes, arms outstretched, singing along to every single word. It was really something else. I was in my late teens but had really only started going to gigs the previous year. I had seen bands like Echo and The Bunnymen and New Order but this was a completely different experience. It was like an indie version of Beatlemania in some ways.

While Morrissey was the main focus of attention, I had just started playing guitar, and I was mesmerised by Johnny Marr. He made it look so effortless. The epitome of cool.

They finished the set with 'Meat Is Murder' and left the stage bathed in blood red. They returned for a rapturously received encore and then they were gone. They never played Dublin again. I went on to play with a Dublin band called Whipping Boy and I know those formative live shows I witnessed with bands like The Bunnymen, The Cocteau Twins and The Smiths lit the fuse and inspired not just me but probably a whole generation of musicians in Dublin from that era.

I WAS THERE: TOM LOFTUS, AGE 19

It was an incredible atmosphere before they came on with a real sense of expectation. The Smiths were considered the best British band at the time and so much was going on in the background that us fans were unaware of - Andy's heroin addiction, the delayed release of *The Queen Is Dead* - but The Smiths pulled off one of the greatest gigs I have ever been to.

'BIGMOUTH STRIKES AGAIN'

RELEASED 22 MAY 1986

The lead single from *The Queen Is Dead*, 'Bigmouth Strikes Again' reached number 26. James Dean, one of Morrissey's heroes, rode a motorbike on the picture sleeve.

THE QUEEN IS DEAD

RELEASED 16 JUNE 1986

The Smiths' third official album was released and reached number 2 on the UK album charts. The *NME* was to rank it as the greatest album of all time in 2013.

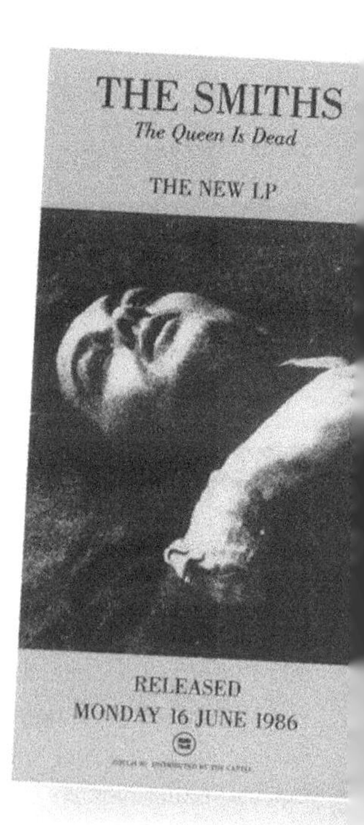

EURO-TUBE, TYNE TEES STUDIO

5 JULY 1986, NEWCASTLE-UPON-TYNE, UK

I WAS THERE: PETER MARTIN

They only played two tracks but this was one of my favourite ever gigs. We had just managed to get tickets for this Euro-Tube special. After a few too many ales in The Barley Mow, we arrived well-oiled and met Craig Gannon in the loos. If you watch the videos of this on YouTube you'll see a group dancing on each other's shoulders. Well, that is us. When we went back to he Barley Mow people came up and shook our hands as they'd all just watched us on the TV. Fame, fame, fatal fame....

BARROWLANDS

16 JULY 1986, GLASGOW, UK

John Canning saw The Smiths at Barrowlands

I WAS THERE: JOHN CANNING, AGE 15

I lived in Livingston, around 30 miles east of Glasgow, and took the bus into Glasgow with my friends Peter 'Doris' Doris and David 'Ramo' Ramsay. The bus got us into Glasgow around 3pm with the gig not scheduled to start till around 8pm.

We went straight to the iconic Barrowlands venue and hung around outside with a few other fans. After an hour or two, what we thought could have been the tour bus pulled up outside the front of the venue. Doris, who was not known for his athletic prowess, took off to reach the front door of the bus before everyone else. The bus took off again with Doris and the other fans in hot pursuit. The bus then went right around the whole block of the venue and after a minute or two arrived back at the front door of the venue with Doris leading the chasing pack. The door opened and Morrissey alone got off the bus with Doris reaching him first, putting his hand on his shoulder, shaking his hand and no doubt telling him how great he thought Morrissey was. Throughout all of this, Ramo and I were far too reserved to move from our spot and just observed the whole thing. Doris touching Morrissey kept us going for the next hour or two until the doors opened and we entered the venue.

We were about tenth in the queue and ran straight upstairs to ensure we got into the first row of the all standing venue. We never moved, for fear of losing our place, not for the toilet or to try and get served at the bar as three spotty 15 year olds.

The support band was The Railway Children. Many of the fans started spitting towards the lead singer of the support, which was quite commonplace at that time in Glasgow as some kind of warped show of affection. After about 10 minutes the lead singer said, 'There's a lot of wankers in here tonight', which as you can imagine did not go down too well. Then after a few minutes more, the band walked off as the spitting increased. For the record, I'd just like to add that Morrissey seemed to take the spitting in the spirit that it was intended!

Eventually The Smiths came on and the place went berserk as they started with 'Bigmouth Strikes Again', followed by 'Panic'. I have absolutely no recollection of what songs followed, as the front of the gig just exploded with such an outpouring of mainly, young, male hero-worship and adulation. Honestly, it was almost a religious experience and I have never experienced anything like it since. I remember feeling like I might cry.

At one point, Morrissey reached into the crowd and was pulled in, inadvertently crowd surfing whilst having his shirt torn off. Ramo and another guy managed to grab an end each and they both pulled and tore the shirt in two. Ramo later cut his part into three bits so that Doris and I also received a bit of the great man's shirt.

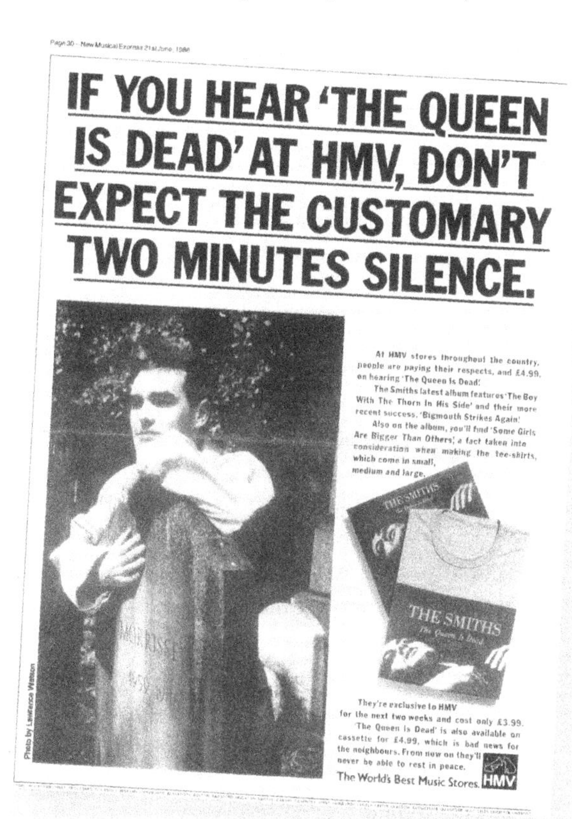

The middle of the gig is a bit of a blur, as we all got split up in the melée and had to drop back a few rows to catch our breath as we genuinely could not keep up that early pace, with the venue's famous spring-loaded floor being put through its paces. I don't know if that is a myth about the floor but it was certainly bouncing that night! It was frantic, with people falling and then being helped back up again by total strangers. Bedlam.

During one of the encores, I remember 'I Know It's Over' and 'Rusholme Ruffians' which merged into 'Marie's The Name' being played. All of the band members came out and each threw a bunch of flowers into the crowd. I leapt like the proverbial salmon and caught a decent amount of Andy Rourke's bunch, which I also shared out with Ramo and Doris. I think I put my share of the flowers into my 1979 *Shoot* annual and that they're still there, in a box somewhere in my mum and dad's loft, along with a section of Morrissey's shirt and Billy Bragg's used plectrum and autograph from a gig the following month.

Only when I walked outside did I realise just how soaked with sweat I was. My t-shirt, jeans, socks and pants were as wet as if I had jumped into a swimming pool and nearly everyone was exactly the same.

I still refer to this gig as my all time favourite. I remember seeing so many lone, young, male fans, keeping themselves to themselves prior to the band coming on, and vividly remember them exploding with passion, love, total adoration for the band, and especially Morrissey. For years afterwards, I'd argue with people who referred to The Smiths as boring, saying, 'I've seen them live, there is nothing boring about The Smiths.' I've also noticed that via Facebook so many of my schoolmates now claim to love the band. But when I was at school, I distinctly remember no more than eight to 10 people in my year and the two years above loving them. I'm just glad I was able to see what was so special about them when I was 14 and first discovered them. I wasn't there at the very beginning, but I was there whilst they were still together and lucky enough to see them live.

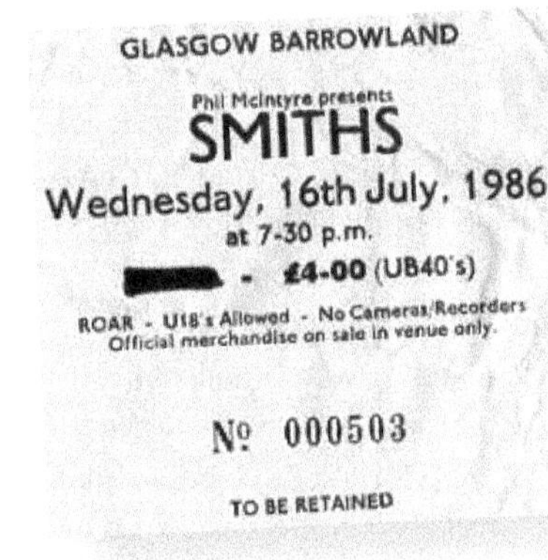
GLASGOW BARROWLAND
Phil McIntyre presents
SMITHS
Wednesday, 16th July, 1986
at 7-30 p.m.
- £4-00 (UB40's)
ROAR - U18's Allowed - No Cameras/Recorders
Official merchandise on sale in venue only.
№ 000503
TO BE RETAINED

Barrowlands '86

I WAS THERE: ANNETTE FLYNN

I started my first 'real' relationship with a Rockabilly and collector of all things Fifties. He was not a fan of indie music or any music outwith this genre. I bought him a ticket for this gig. He reluctantly accepted as the new relationship meant (in hindsight, sadly) that we didn't go anywhere apart. Just before they played 'I Know It's Over', Morrissey said, 'Annette, Annette, we'll get you yet…' The Rockabilly turned to me and said, 'WTF, is that you?' Some girls behind me shouted, 'Fuck her - who the hell's Annette?' In shock, I just kept me eyes glued to Morrissey and my mouth shut. The Rockabilly was staring at me to look at him but I kept my eyes front not wanting to draw attention to myself.

The dedication was surreal. The next day, as many of us did, we visited the Barrowland's Market. There was a stall there, which produced cassette tapes of the previous night's gigs. So I bought it and legged it home to listen to it. I must have worn out that dedication, listening to it daily. The Rockabilly quizzed me about it for days in a slightly controlling and possessive style. The relationship didn't last. 28 years after this I saw the light. All the letters, decorated envelopes and personal memorabilia like tickets, the Barrowland cassettes, record factory postcards the Rockabilly would not return to me when I left him. In the weeks leading up to the end of our 24 year marriage, all these items inexplicably disappeared.

I WAS THERE: DOMINIC JOHN

I had missed the *Meat Is Murder* tour as I lost my sight at the time and underwent numerous eye operations, in and out of hospital for about a year. Consequently I had to give my ticket to a pal, who managed to bring a section of a huge bush that Morrissey threw into the audience. I still have it inside the cover of my *Queen Is Dead* album. The following year, even though I was still quite ill, I went to see them. My brother pulled a few strings and I was smuggled in through a back stair in a pub down stairs and watched the show from the wings. I was almost on the stage the whole time. I had also been promised that the band would come and say 'hello' at the end, but they went off the other side and my chance was gone. I found out later that the guy who arranged it all was Arthur Thomson Jr, the notorious East End gangster. Good times.

I WAS THERE: STEPHEN MATHISON

I moved from Glasgow to East Lothian with my work - which I absolutely hated - in July '86. I was desperate for a decent night out in Glasgow. It just so happened that the boys were playing at the Barrowlands again. The rumours of a split in the band were rife so I had to go and see them before it was too late. I gave my pal a shout, tickets were bought and I was heading back through to the land of the living for what would be their final hurrah at The Barrowlands. The concert was going to be a classic.

We headed to the Barras and went into the bar next door for a pre concert pint or two. This place, sadly now shut, was sight to behold, a Celtic fan's mecca and also a go-go bar. I'm not sure what the dancers thought when The Smiths were playing over the jukebox though!

The Barras was packed that night and it was brilliant. Channel 4 were there filming. The cameramen were getting in the way of the stage divers so the bouncers had their hands full trying to eject them and pull the fainters out of the front. At the encore Morrissey came on stage with a massive 'The Queen Is Dead' placard just to whip the crowd up - as if they needed it. I can remember watching the show on Channel 4 and actually managing to spot myself in the crowd.

I still love The Smiths' music. I play it all the time in my shop - I'm a barber. I liked Mozzer's early solo stuff and bought the albums but I wasn't keen on Your Arsenal and didn't come back until You are the Quarry which, I thought was excellent.

I went to see Mozzer's gig at the Usher Hall in Edinburgh in the Nineties. It was terrible. He played for one hour, didn't say a word to the crowd and the atmosphere was awful. I took my now wife to a Morrissey gig at the SECC in Glasgow in (I think) 2007. Terrible venue but fantastic gig! And I went to see him a couple of years ago at the Hydro in Glasgow and yet again he was bloody brilliant. I didn't get to see him there the last time he played but he was getting a bit controversial by then and said a few dodgy comments about Scottish politics. However, I did have tickets for his gig in Edinburgh this year which was unfortunately cancelled due to 'logistical problems'. Perhaps he'll return but it would be amazing if it was with The Smiths! I'd get tickets for the Manchester gig if that ever happened!

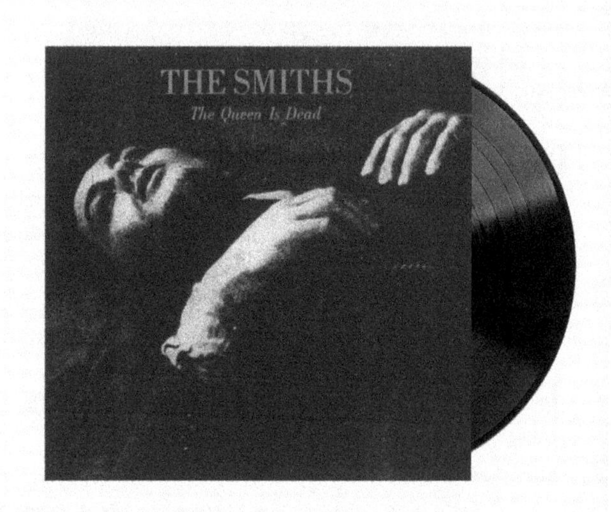

I WAS THERE: ALAN MCADAM

They came onto a darkened Barrowlands to 'Dance of the Knights' by Prokofiev, the most dramatic entrance I had seen, with the tension building and building until they launched into their set. Craig Gannon was also on guitar and subsequently the sound was huge and the crowd went crazy. I'm sure stage invaders kept grabbing at Morrissey, but I can't remember. I just know that it was incredibly hot and crazy in that venue that night. My ticket was too damp to keep and it subsequently disintegrated. This band and this relatively recently reopened venue were made for one another.

I WAS THERE: STEPHEN RAFFERTY

I arrived at 2.30pm to try and get a place down the front. The queue was already the length of the Barrowlands. I stood in the queue with one of my friends for a couple of hours but then wanted to get a drink so I nipped across the road to the corner shop. I had a spare ticket due to one of my friends letting me down. In those days, touting was illegal so I didn't shout out that I had a spare. When I came out of the shop a lad that had been following The Smiths on most of the tour asked me if I had a spare ticket so I sold it to him. I was chuffed that I was able to off load it.

When I got back in the queue I told my friend that I had sold the ticket. The lad in front of us turned round and said, 'Did you have spare tickets?' to which I replied, 'Yes.' He then told me that the queue we were in was for tickets that were handed back and that were going on general sale. I could have made a fortune selling mine to the highest bidder. But I was happier that the lad following The Smiths around got in to see them.

That gig was absolutely mental. If you've ever been in the Barras you'll know what I'm talking about. I managed to get down right in front of the centre stage and then afterwards went to the backstage door to wait for them leaving. I got my reward, shaking both Morrissey and Johnny Marr's hands as they left to board the tour bus.

MAYFAIR

17 JULY 1986, NEWCASTLE-UPON-TYNE, UK

I WAS THERE: PETER MARTIN

Afterwards we went to Cramlington train station and painted 'The Queen Is Dead' on the newly whitewashed walls. This was in 'honour' of an appearance from her at the station the next day. Sadly, someone painted over it before she arrived. I'm sure she would have appreciated our gesture.

I WAS THERE: COLIN BOOTH

Half way through the set some idiots started throwing empty bottles at them on stage. The band asked them to stop but another bottle was thrown and the band walked off. It was the only time I got to see them. They split up not long after.

I WAS THERE: LESLEY FEARON, AGE 16

The Mayfair is sadly no longer in existence. My lasting memory, apart from the strong smell of cannabis, was the lights going out and the band's entrance music blasting out before the band came on. The feeling I had has never been replicated and I'm now aged 50! Morrissey ended up walking off stage as some idiots at the front had been spitting at the stage.

I had seen them at Newcastle City Hall during the Red Wedge concert. There were rumours milling around that night that The Smiths were due to play but we didn't believe it. How wrong we were! They only did a short stint of about four or five songs but they made an already brilliant night even better. That was another superb time seeing the best band in the world. In my opinion they still are.

I WAS THERE: CHRIS TAIT

I would see The Smiths live again just once more, when they returned to the city to promote their seminal third album (or their fourth, if you count *Hatful of Hollow*). By then however, problems with their relationship with Rough Trade and the money issues which would come to define the band's aftermath were already simmering in the background. For me though, this show, and the venue in particular, had added significance as The Smiths were booked to play The Mayfair in Newcastle, home of 'raaark'. This was the indie kids storming the citadel of the city's long-haired, leather-trousered rockers, the metal-heads we'd spent years verbally battling at school, although 'storming' may be something of an exaggeration. We were literate, sensitive soft indie kids after all.

As it turned out, the evening was something of a disaster for me. I recall standing half-crushed on one of the Mayfair's famous spiral staircases as the band, now a five-piece with the addition of Craig Gannon (once of Aztec Camera, so of course I approved), were subject to a torrent of abuse from sections of the audience. An element of what one assumes were Mayfair regulars in the crowd taunted the band throughout, hurling bodily fluids and verbal insults in Morrissey's direction, forcing him to eventually leave the stage during the closer, 'Hand in Glove'. Johnny then famously delivered the line, '...If the people spit, then the people spit....' and, after a couple of false dawns when we thought our hero might return, that was pretty much that. A sad end to a wonderful period in our musical history.

I WAS THERE: DARREN WILKINSON

It was a further year before I saw The Smiths for the third time, this time on the *Queen Is Dead* tour. I still think this is the finest album the band produced. Every track is a banger and the title track is possibly my favourite Smiths song. It was the same old rigmarole to get tickets and off we went again across the Pennines to the North East. We arrived in good time. The Mayfair was an old ballroom and we staked our place on the low balcony overlooking the stage and waited. When The Smiths took to the stage the floor went mad - too mad - and I was pleased to be on that balcony. Pints were thrown and general chaos ensued. There were scuffles and spitting and these things were becoming the norm and Morrissey didn't like it. My fading memory told me he walked off mid gig not to return. I have since read reviews of the gig that say it was during the encore. I just remember being gutted. I bought the tour t-shirt and headed home. I wore that t-shirt to death until one day many years later I couldn't find it and my wife admitted that she had thrown it out as it was looking tatty. She threw several others away too - a heinous crime. I have only recently forgiven her.

I WAS THERE: PAUL JEFFREY

I discovered them in January 1984 when they were on *Top of the Pops* doing 'What Differences Does It Make?' I thought, 'This is a bit different is this.' I was 10 or 11. They stood out a mile and of course there was a total lack of interest from the *Top of the Pops* crowd.

Then I saw them on *The Tube* doing 'Hand in Glove' and 'Still Ill'. I'd go and buy seven inch singles for 50p with my pocket money from Woolworths. I was too young to see them on the *Meat Is Murder* tour But they came back to the Mayfair in July 1986. I didn't have any clue about it being an over 18s venue. I managed to convince a friend of mine to come with me. We told our parents we were going to the cinema and so there I was with my quiff, my button down shirt, my burgundy tie, my DMs and my suit jacket.

I went up to the venue with a group of Smiths fans who were milling around central Newcastle when I got off the Metro. I got to the door of the venue and it was very apparent I wasn't 18. And the security guy looked at me and looked at my friend and went, 'You're not coming in.' There was no way I could say, 'I'm 18.' I wasn't an old looking 13 year old. And, to quote Morrissey, I went home and cried and wanted to die.

Organised by Factory Records to 'celebrate Manchester' and specifically the first performance by The Sex Pistols at the Lesser Free Trade Hall in Manchester on 4 June 1976, the Festival of the Tenth Summer culminated in an all day music festival at the Greater Manchester Exhibition Centre (or G-Mex).

FESTIVAL OF THE TENTH SUMMER, G-MEX

19 JULY 1986, MANCHESTER, UK

I WAS THERE: CLIVE ADAMS

I took a sickie from work and accompanied a mate up in his Ford Escort as we had tickets for the Festival of the Tenth Summer, a whole day featuring many of Manchester's most iconic artists and bands. For many of the 12,000 or so in the crowd, The Smiths were the band to bring the house down. From the opening 'Bigmouth Strikes Again', I quickly realised that just like the Pistols gig at the Manchester Lesser Free Trade Hall ten years previously, this gig would also be one for the history books of the future. At times, Morrissey's voice was drowned out as the crowd sang along in joyous celebration. To this day, I never understood why so many dismissed The Smiths as doom merchants. I remember John Peel stating that lyrics by The Smiths made him 'laugh out loud', which very little else did for him back in the Eighties. That's the point. The Smiths were - and still are - unique in their ability to make you laugh, cry, hope, and wonder. 30 years on they are still as relevant as they have ever been.

I WAS THERE: MARK WILLIAMS

I arrived at the Piccadilly bus terminal in Manchester with no ticket for the event and no viable way to get back home to North Shropshire at the end of the evening. But I strolled down to the event and luckily bagged myself the last ticket at face value off a tout outside the newly opened G-Mex Centre. I was in! The huge venue was nowhere near full and it was quite easy to mill around whilst the lower order bands played. It was around this point in the afternoon that I met some other folk from my home town of Oswestry and happily secured a lift home with them. Eventually The Smiths appeared on the stage after performances from Pete Shelley of The Buzzcocks, The Fall, John Cooper Clarke and the Virgin Prunes. I remember the evening sunlight shone through the pane glass roof of the hall as Prokofiev's 'Romeo and Juliet' intro music heralded their arrival and they burst into a resounding rendition of 'Big Mouth Strikes Again'. From then on it was sheer pandemonium in the front rows, with Morrissey egging us on while holding a placard with 'The Queen Is Dead' on it. I also recall him introducing their forthcoming single 'Ask'. Morrissey changed his shirt for the last song, which he subsequently threw into the crowd. I was once again fortunate enough to be able to grasp at the white cotton polka dot shirt, which thankfully ripped apart easily this time. You can see the photographic evidence of this in the middle of the gate fold live album *Rank* where I can be seen at the centre of the image pulling the shirt apart. I still have the piece of shirt in my sock drawer to this day.

On the way home, the minivan we were travelling in broke down near Warrington which is where we spent the remainder of the night, but not before the bizarre occurrence of a 1950s-style American Cadillac type car that drove slowly past us with two women sitting on its wide flat bonnet waving to us as the car's stereo blasted out music. I still scratch my head about this incident to this day. In the early morning, we finally got the van started and I got to my bed for a few more hours sleep before I prepared myself for my second Smiths gig of the weekend at Salford University. This time I was on a scheduled bus trip from Wrexham and, after a game of footy with my mates, I embarked on the bus that was going to take me to what Johnny Marr described as his favourite Smiths gig of all time.

I WAS THERE: DAVID ALLEN

The first of the two times I saw them was at the opening of G-Mex with a great line-up. But me and my mates were there for The Smiths. I had the feeling that Morrissey couldn't cut it live, but I was so wrong. His vocals were brilliant, the band was brilliant and the crowd was the most enthusiastic I've ever seen at a gig. It was one of those gigs that would make the generations who got into them later envious. Even now, if I happen to mention I've seen The Smiths live, it's met with respect and envy in equal measure.

I WAS THERE: JAMES DONNELLY, AGE 19

I went to college with a lad whose brother worked in the recording studio for the first album. He brought the demo in. It was amazing and I was hooked. That was about October 1983. I saw them at G-Mex celebrating 10 years of punk. It was an all day event with other artists performing. The crowd were only interested in The Smiths and that's all I was there for - nothing else but The Smiths! They did *The Queen Is Dead* set. I'm from Rusholme in Manchester and I knew exactly what they were singing about in the first line of 'Rusholme Ruffians' and the last night of the fair. It was a yearly event and I was there on the night, in Platt Fields in Rusholme. Morrissey's songs just said it all. I always thought he was singing about my school in 'the Headmaster Ritual'.

I WAS THERE: JOHN GOODWIN

The image in the centrefold of *Rank* shows fans tearing at the shirt Morrissey threw into the crowd at the end of the set. My blond curly hair can be seen in the centre of that photo. I grabbed a huge chunk of cuff and sleeve of the spotty shirt. Despite the sweat, it smelt amazing and I had the shirt pinned to my bedroom wall until I went to uni two years later.

I WAS THERE: MALCOLM GREENLEY

They were on about six o'clock. It was around 10 years since The Sex Pistols played that famous gig at the Lesser Free Trade Hall where about 40 people turned up, Morrissey being one along with members of what would become Joy Division and also Mark E Smith. So it was a really important gig that spawned the Manchester music scene. As an old railway station it was hard to get a good sound in G-Mex

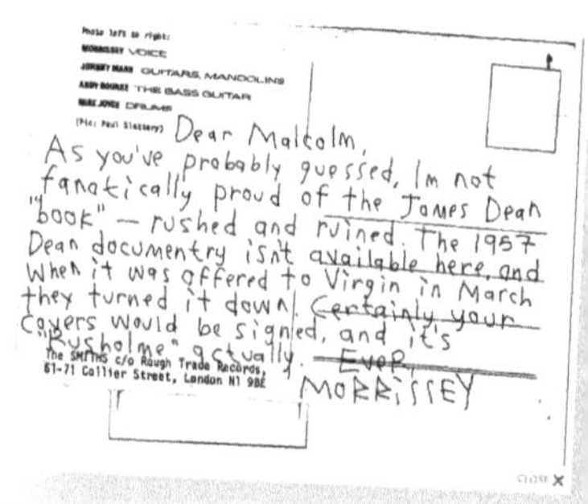

Dear Malcolm,
As you've probably guessed, I'm not fanatically proud of the James Dean "book" – rushed and ruined. The 1957 Dean documentry isn't available here, and when it was offered to Virgin in March they turned it down. ~~Certainly your~~ Covers would be signed, and it's "Rusholme" actually. ~~Ever,~~
MORRISSEY

The SMITHS c/o Rough Trade Records,
61-71 Collier Street, London N1 9BE

Malcolm Greenley got several postcards from Morrissey

Hello Malcolm,
"This Night Has Opened My Eyes" will be on an LP comprised of radio sessions to be released in September.
A new single is ~~rea~~ released on August 24th
I'm glad you mentioned "Girl Afraid", it seemed to have been overlooked by most people.
Not happy/not sad,
MORRISSEY

October 19th
Dear Malcolm, Im sorry I couldnt get all the group to sign the sleeves, but they were away for four days, and when things are left at RT they tend to get lost. I played the tape on a train to Manchester, it was truely romantic. The Bill Bast book is impossible to find, but Ive read it and its really boring. Im sure you could get the jacket somewhere in London. My birthdate is May 22nd! The LP is out Nov 2nd! Be well — M.

because it's so cavernous. The sound tends to bounce around the walls and the high ceiling. It was still good to see them there.

I wrote to Morrissey and he wrote back to me. I was just amazed when I got a response. I wrote because of my obsession with the band. When I get into certain bands it's full on. I tried the lucky option and just stuck a letter in the post c/o Rough Trade Records. I was lucky enough that they got to him. He was relatively famous then. I doubt you would get through to him now. The correspondence lasted for a couple of months. He got too famous, too busy I presume, but it was nice while it lasted. I sent all my Smiths covers there to get signed and he was the only one available to sign them. I'm hoping to one day meet the rest of the band and get them to sign them as well. I've still got the postcards and the letter back. And I've still got the envelopes in green crayon. I remember my mum saying, 'Who the hell is writing to you in green crayon?'

He was seriously into James Dean - I think he still is - and I sent him a cassette of this radio documentary about James Dean. He mentions that in one of the letters as well. It was great when I met him. It was really, really, really weird meeting him. He spoke so quietly. You could hardly hear him. You had to lean in and get right next to him. I said, 'I'm Malcolm, I wrote to you a couple of years ago.' He paused for a second and said, 'James Dean,' and I thought, 'I can't believe he's remembered me'. I was amazed at that. He's a strange person, there's no doubt about it. He's an odd guy, but all the better for it.

I WAS THERE: PETER MARTIN

We got a coach on a pre-paid package trip from Newcastle. We didn't come back on the bus as we stayed over for the next night in Salford. We tracked Johnny Marr down to a big hotel in the city centre as he'd promised us tickets. To our surprise he was as good as his word and we duly left with spare tickets for the next two gigs. The gig itself was great. Loads of bands celebrating the ten years since punk broke in Manchester. The Smiths were on early, New Order were headliners. I really don't think we realised how great these gigs were at the time.

I WAS THERE: STEVEN WRIGLEY

I'm from Saddleworth originally. The annoying thing is, being from Manchester, I could have seen them a million times over. But it was that time when you started going out and not going to as many gigs, and then I went to college in mid-Wales and of course they never came anywhere near. And it was impossible then to get back, it was hours to get back to see them anywhere. The G-Mex gig just tied in with one of the summer holidays and me and a few of my mates from school all got tickets and went down for that day.

At the end of '82 all my favourite bands seemed to be splitting up. The Jam, the real Clash had finished, Stiff Little Fingers. Those punky new wavy bands that people my age were all into, and there was suddenly this void. It was so funny. I was only 16 and I remember thinking, 'Oh no, this is the end of proper music.' And then of course The Smiths suddenly arrived, which was kind of perfect. I became aware of them through John Peel. He was playing them right from the get-go.

My brother was into them, and we'd hear them when we went out, but it was a slow one with me. I didn't immediately go, 'Oh, these are suddenly the best band ever.' I thought the first album was great but the production was so bad. 'This Charming Man' was obviously brilliant, but I was already getting a bit too cynical and I was thinking, 'Ah well, this could be a one hit wonder.' In real time then, it was 'What Difference Does it Make?' We were going out in Oldham and Manchester and that was huge. It was everywhere. And we thought, 'Oh, this is going to be good.' But then *Hatful of Hollow* came out and I was going, 'Yeah well, load of Peel sessions.' They weren't brilliant. I'd rather have something well done in the studio than new takes on other tunes.

It took me until about *Meat Is Murder*, to be honest. Me and my mates were already vegetarian so it was great to hear that and hear what they were saying. It was such a good day. We were buzzing and looking forward to The Smiths. By then, they and New Order were by far my favourite bands. We were drinking. The Fall were on and they were brilliant. The Smiths were coming on about six o'clock and it wasn't like they were the big headliners because Tony Wilson organised it so that New Order were going to be the headliners. It seemed weird because it was still light in this massive arena. You never really went to big arena gigs in those days. They didn't really exist unless you wanted to see the Rolling Stones or whatever.

It was just a brilliant time. *The Queen Is Dead* had been released and I was thinking, 'This is the best album ever'. I remember 'Ask' was just about to be released as their new single, which I'd never heard, and they did that live. And of course, never having seen Morrissey before, he was just brilliant. He had his 'Queen Is dead' sign, waving that around, and his 'Two light ales' placard.

I remember Paul Morley being there. I remember him being funny, whatever he said. We had all these people coming on and off. I did have a cassette of the concert. I think it was broadcast. Sandie Shaw was on directly before The Smiths, and she did 'Hand in Glove' and 'Jeanne'. It was this build up of anticipation and going, 'Ooh, Sandie Shaw,' and not really knowing who she was other than that she was the 'Puppet on a String' woman Morrissey was obsessed with.

The Smiths were just unbelievable. They knocked everybody out of the water, including New Order, who were pretty average that night to be honest. They were still in that 'We're not very good live' kind of phase. The Smiths were just head and shoulders above the rest. That made me think, 'The Smiths are just the best band ever,' which I still now believe.

I WAS THERE: ALAN BUTTERWORTH, AGE 19

I had already seen two amazing gigs by The Smiths, at the Palace Theatre and the following year at the Free Trade Hall. But the two that still resonate happened over the same weekend in July 1986. The Smiths were set to play a Factory Records-organised event called The Festival of the Tenth Summer and then a much smaller gig at Salford University the next day.

I remember going into G-Mex early in the day and A Certain Ratio already being on stage. Myself and my gig-going pal Mike made our way down to the front - after a quick trip to the bar to get a beer in - to watch the rest of ACR's set. To be honest the next couple of hours went by in a blur. I can remember enjoying The Fall, people throwing plastic pint pots at Derek Hatton, who was compering, and a particular highlight was someone managing to get on stage and trying to hit Andy McCluskey of OMD with a plastic tray from the bar! Andy soldiered on doing his geography teacher dance whilst simultaneously ducking out of the way of the beer tray until the bouncers were able to drag the guy off stage!

As early evening approached I can recall getting right to the front and a buzz of excitement in the venue as we waited for The Smiths to come on. The area where we were got fuller and fuller as people rushed to the front. Moz strolled on stage holding his 'Queen Is Dead' placard and looked immaculate in white Levis and a white shirt, opened half way down. 'The Queen Is Dead' kicked in and all hell broke loose down the front. In the crush I lost a shoe but I was having such a good time I didn't care. A bit later in the set I saw it being thrown on stage by someone. When it was all over 40 or so sweaty fantastic minutes later, the roadies were clearing the stage and I shouted for one of them to throw my shoe back. Thankfully he did!

Lots of drinks of water were needed and once myself and Mike had recovered we both thought, 'Bloody hell, that was fantastic. And we still have New Order to come on yet!' Later on we took the short walk to Devilles nightclub so we could carry on partying. We couldn't believe we would be seeing The Smiths again at a much smaller venue the next night.

I WAS THERE: ANDY MCCLUSKEY, OMD

I suffer from stage fright. I'm much calmer than I was, because it finally dawned on me that if people have bought a ticket to see us they probably already like the music so we're onto a winner. I think the most terrified I've ever been was playing the Festival of the Tenth Summer. We thought we'd do it as a 'thank you' to Factory, and because we wanted to remember that we'd started 10 years previously, just me and Paul Humphreys and a tape recorder. What we hadn't factored in was that we'd be playing in front of 8,000 Smiths fans. I was more and more frightened as the day went on. I was so nervous I threw up before I went on. Matters were made worse by Paul Morley introducing us on stage as, 'And now, two rich bastards from Los Angeles.'

I WAS THERE: CAROLINE ALLEN, AGE 16

I got to know who The Smiths were when I was about 13, when 'This Charming Man' came out and my older sister bought the single. We shared a bedroom so I used to have to listen to it all the time and got quite fond of it. From then on I just carried on listening to whatever they brought out. My two best friends at the time, Nicky and Jenny, liked them as well so we listened to them together.

G-Mex was the first time I saw them live, with Nicky and Jenny. We got up at three o'clock in the morning, got the first bus into Manchester from Macclesfield and got there really, really early - about 7am. We wanted to be on the front row.

We sat outside and got chatting to other Smiths fans. We got on the front row. I can't really remember much about anyone else who was on. All I was bothered about was seeing The Smiths because seeing them for the first time was so exciting.

It started at about midday. They were on at about six. We stood at the front for hours and hours, not eating anything and not going to the toilet - nothing. Kevin Cummins' book, *Manchester: Looking for the Light Through the Pouring Rain* has a picture of the whole front row, but there's a particular picture of me and Nicky stood looking really miserable. We weren't miserable. We were just like, 'Come on, when are The Smiths going to come on, for crying out loud?' The Smiths were just brilliant and when they'd gone off we had to get out because we were just desperate for the toilet, basically! So we pushed our way out. All my memories of that show are overtaken by the next day, because we went to Salford University the next day for the gig there at Maxwell Hall.

MAXWELL HALL, SALFORD UNIVERSITY

20 JULY 1986, SALFORD, UK

I WAS THERE: CAROLINE ALLEN

The best gig I've ever been to in my life. And Johnny Marr says it was the best gig The Smiths ever played. Everything about it was just insane. If people went they were lucky to be there. I feel really, really lucky that I was part of that gig. Whatever other really brilliant gigs I've been to in my life, that was just something else.

There was a bit of a stage invasion. We were on the front row again, because we'd queued up at the crack of dawn again, so we got pulled onto the stage. We were part of that stage invasion when the stage collapsed a little bit.

What made it such a special gig was the whole atmosphere. It was loud, it was hot, sweaty. The crowd was just bouncing. It was intense but a little bit intimidating as well. A lot of lads, Smiths fans, were quite rowdy. You'd see the same lads as you'd seen the day before, rowdy and shouting. The banter between Morrissey and the crowd was really good as well. I had a bootleg tape of the concert. I listened to it so much I could mouth all the things that Morrissey said between every song. He was really, really on form.

Loads of people were stage invading. I think it was 'Still Ill', the second-to-last song, when people started getting on stage. I thought I was going to die if I didn't get pulled on the stage because it was that squashed and horrible and really quite scary.

It was mental, but really brilliant, just brilliant. I was covered in bruises the next day. But everybody was really lovely as well. Everybody was helping you get on stage. Nobody was pushing you out of the way or anything. Everybody was in it together and they all wanted everybody to get on stage. If the whole crowd could have got on stage it would just have been perfect.

And the bouncers just gave up trying in the end because there were loads of people on stage. You can see the whole gig on YouTube. Just by watching that you can see how intense it was. I love watching it back now and thinking, 'My god, I can't believe I was there.'

I WAS THERE: KHALID AHMED

It was the day after G-Mex and a small venue, less than 1,000 people. I just remember the intensity of the gig – it was hot and sweaty. This was the tour when Morrissey paraded 'The Queen Is Dead' placard during that song. Watching The Smiths was an event, a chance to share the love we all had for them. They were a funny conundrum; Morrissey's lyrics were sensitive and intelligent but the music when played live brought out manic responses from the crowd, who were mainly manly blokes. They were just a great combination with Morrissey the poet and Marr in effect a would-be rock guitarist. Ordinarily that combination wouldn't work, but it certainly did!

I WAS THERE: ANDY DAWSON

I was listening to Piccadilly Radio in my bedroom in 1984 when this song came on, 'How Soon Is Now?'. I was blown away and hooked on Morrissey and The Smiths from then on. I bought every 12 inch vinyl single. This was my life. The songs said everything about my life in the North West England. I scanned the *Manchester Evening News* every Friday night for Smiths concerts. I bought my ticket for Salford University at Piccadilly Records: £4 standing. I can recall a Smiths poster on the stairs being torn down. The box office was on the side of the Free Trade Hall in Manchester. I got centre circle £6.50 and took my girlfriend at the time. All I can remember is Morrissey holding up a

'The Queen Is Dead' placard. The concert was packed. They finished with 'Still Ill'.

Afterwards I bought a 'Queen Is Dead' t-shirt from a street seller along with six by four foot tour posters of *Meat Is Murder* and *The Queen Is Dead* tour. These were on my bedroom wall for years. I also bought postcards from the underground market in Manchester and with my saved newspaper cuttings and tickets did a framed picture, which again was put up in my bedroom. I still have it.

I lived near Altrincham in Cheshire. Mike Joyce was often seen pushing a pram down George Street. One day Morrissey came into Altrincham Post Office with a dog, and said to a girl working on the counter, 'You look sad' and went out, returning with a big bunch of flowers for her. Kevin Cummins did a photo shoot at Dunham Massey. There used to be a car park on Charcoal Lane, on the right near the stile to Dunham Park. My friend went for a midweek walk and saw Morrissey, parked up on his own. The car was crammed full of flowers.

I WAS THERE: DARREN APPLEBY

By this time, girls had started to feature in my life and I got tickets for both me and my girlfriend to go to Salford University on a coach organised by our local record shop. Knowing what the gigs were like, I was asked if we could sit in the balcony and, frankly, I was going to do everything the girl wanted in return for a cheeky snog on the bus home. So whilst the gig was mental, we had a good vantage point to see the sheer joy of my fellow fans. Apart from 'Money Changes Everything', which I still think is one of their weakest songs, it couldn't have been a better gig musically. But the fact that it was almost a homecoming gig meant that the cries of 'Salford, Salford!' rang around the venue. It was the most pleasurably violent gig I have ever been to. It was quite literally like a war zone. The stage invaders, the noise of the crowd, Morrissey swinging his placards around, Johnny Marr's cymbal ride leading into 'The Queen Is Dead', Craig Gannon being a shy new boy, and the fact that the band were on such good form, meant that this is still my number one gig ever. I've seen loads of bands since, both the big boys like the Stones, Stone Roses and Iron Maiden in stadiums as well as tiny unsigned bands in tiny venues, and nothing has ever come close. Reading that Johnny Marr also said it was the best gig he had played in The Smiths makes me feel honoured that I was there to witness it.

Seeing Morrissey solo at Hanley a final time in 2011 was like reliving my youth once more. I actually bunked off work to queue for tickets. Now with my wife, we witnessed more than one 40-something grown man moved to tears. It was almost like a Holy Communion.

Morrissey might have fallen out of favour with the mainstream media recently due to his opinions, and Johnny Marr has gone on to be the 'Johnny Fucking Marr' of legend, but along with Andy Rourke's sublime bass lines and Mike Joyce's pounding beat, The Smiths are and were the best band ever and made me the man I am today. And even though Johnny inspired me to pick up the guitar at 15, I still can't play 'This Charming Man' at 50!

I WAS THERE: NICK BARBER

I saw the back-to-back shows at G-Mex and Salford University. The atmosphere at G-Mex was a bit subdued apart from at the front of the crowd, as the size of the venue and the Neanderthal security kept a lid on things. Salford was one of the wildest gigs I've been to in 40-odd years of gig-going in several countries. I have photos from the Salford gig and a couple from the Liverpool Royal Court show I took on a Kodak Instamatic. The Salford ones were featured in a *Mojo* article a few years back and uncredited, which I wasn't too happy about.

I WAS THERE: STEVE BROWN

I saw the Smiths twice in 1986, and had two very brief encounters with Morrissey. I was getting into other stuff, jangly Sixties bands like The Byrds - probably a Smiths influence there - and we were listening to a lot of reggae. We didn't share Morrissey's views on it! And I discovered hip-hop, a big moment for me. I left home in April 1986 – the best thing I ever did - and was now sharing a house with my friend Kev, who bought a copy of *The Queen Is Dead.*

To be honest I was barely interested in hearing it. I had moved on, but my ears pricked up at the first notes of the title track. Some of the songs were beautiful, the obvious ones like 'There Is a Light…' but also 'Some Girls are Bigger than Others'. I had a disagreement with my son recently about that song; he thought it was meaningless and naff, but to me it was perfect Smiths: funny, quirky lyrics that no-one else could have written, with a sort of fatalism about them even though they didn't seem to be about anything, and so catchy - a lovely melody and that genius guitar playing. Morrissey's lyrics were better and funnier than ever, kind of self-referential and world-weary and soaked in black humour. The music was quite varied; it had moved on a long way from the simplicity of the first album.

One of the best things about The Smiths were the B-sides; way back from 'Accept Yourself' to later stuff like 'Half a Person' and 'You Just Haven't Earned It Yet Baby', all hidden gold; and the Peel Sessions! I recorded a Peel Session that included 'London' which sounded amazing, better than the released version. I think it was in '86 that 'Rubber Ring' and 'Asleep' appeared on the B-side of one of the singles. 'Asleep' was stunning. The darker side of Morrissey's lyrics seemed to be getting even darker, yet more beautiful. I was a Smiths fan again!

When they played Salford University, loads of us went. It was a relatively small venue for a band as big as they now were and it was heaving. The atmosphere was buzzing and quite laddish; whether it was just a Manchester thing I don't know, but the band now seemed to have a lot of everyday teenage jack-the-lads amongst its fans, lads who you would normally expect to see on the football terraces. To me it showed how the realness of The Smiths' songs could reach parts that other music couldn't. I thought this was great; the fans were boisterous but good natured and there was no hint of aggro. This was how Manchester came to be throughout the late Eighties; the kids who you would have previously crossed the road to avoid were now mixing with students and young professionals and everyone got on great. Gigs and clubs were amazing at that time. Although the type of people in the crowd had changed, it was still a typical Smiths gig in that it was made up evenly of girls and lads, as it had been at previous gigs in '84 and '85.

I was determined to get on the stage. Smiths' gigs had traditionally ended with the crowd dancing on the stage with the band although I had never got up there myself. We were stood near the back and towards the end of the gig I started to work my way to the front, which wasn't easy as it was so rammed. By the time they came back on for the encore I was right at the front and felt like I had no choice now but to get on the stage; I was being squashed by the crowd and the heat was intense.

As far as I remember it wasn't easy to climb onstage, but eventually I managed it. I had made it! I was the only fan up there. There was Morrissey, stood right there.... I put my arm on his shoulder, the stage lights in my eyes, and was immediately grabbed by a security guy or roadie. I'd been onstage for about a second and now I was being shoved backwards very quickly towards the back of the stage and out through a door.

I went down the stairs and out of a fire door, walked round to the front and back in - it was near the end of the night so there was no one on the door - up the stairs and back into the hall where The Smiths were still playing. My mates were still stood where I'd left them. I said, 'All right lads?' They were laughing, 'Where did you come from?' 'Was that you on the stage?' I was a bit dismayed to see the stage was now full of people; no-one had kicked them off! I guess I was unfortunate because I was the first one up there.

I WAS THERE: MARK WILLIAMS

It was yet another hot sticky night as we climbed off the bus but this time into the darkened hall of the university. I wouldn't say it was the favourite of my five Smiths gigs but it was most certainly the most manic. The security fence collapsed halfway through the concert. I also helped pull a few girls out of the crowd who were being seriously crushed. You can see me quite clearly at the start of 'His Latest Flame'/'Rusholme Ruffians' in the footage on You Tube.

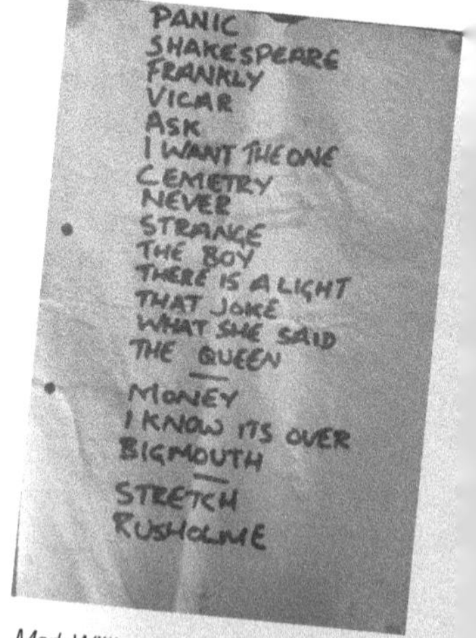

Mark Williams' setlist from Salford Uni

I WAS THERE: AL BUTTERWORTH

We got the bus into Manchester city centre and then walked the mile and a half out to the university. I recall it was a lovely summer's evening and as we approached the venue I recognised a few faces from the previous day's gig at G-Mex. We could not get tickets for downstairs standing so had to make do with the balcony. Mike and I made our way upstairs and tried to get as close to the front as possible. It was heaving upstairs but looking down onto the standing area we could see how full it was and it looked scarily overcrowded. It was only years later I found out how lax the security was and that lots of people were able to get in without tickets. The place felt hot and sweaty and everybody seemed to be tingling with anticipation.

The lights go down, Prokofiev comes on and once again the place erupts! The set was very similar to the previous day but we didn't care. We just danced and sang along to every word with sweat dripping from the ceiling. After each song a cry of 'Salford, Salford' was chanted by a lot of the audience. After five or six times it got a bit annoying. Even Morrissey got fed up with it and mock growled, 'Stretford, Stretford' back at the crowd a few times. The balcony was bouncing up and down with the weight of people dancing, and looking downstairs I could see roadies struggling to hold the speakers to try and stop them bouncing into the crowd. The concert ended and we made our way outside. Myself and Mike crashed down with exhaustion onto a grass verge outside the venue along with quite a few others. And that was it, all over. I was only 19 years old and my passion for music has stayed with me into my Fifties. I still get out to gigs a couple of times a month but nothing has come close to that wonderful weekend in July 1986. The best gigging weekend of my life.

I WAS THERE: CHRIS GREEN, AGE 18

I lived in Lower Broughton. Where Peel Park is, there's a little bridge that crosses over to an estate called Spike Island. I lived just across the bridge, 200 yards on the right hand side, half a mile from Salford Uni.

The Jam had split up and we needed a focus and The Smiths were it for us. I found Morrissey amazing to look at. He was so different to what we'd been used to. Because I'd been into The Jam, who were clean cut and I was a mod. And there was this political stuff going on. There was nothing for us.

We were all into music. My mate Jimmy McManus was into The Human League. My mate Stuart was a year older and he got me into The Jam and when they folded, he got me into The Smiths and Echo and The Bunnymen. Stuart's a Mod. Stuart had a paper round and wore a two-tone suit on his paper round. With his money he could afford to buy decent stuff. I wasn't as blessed financially. When my mates all had proper Mod parkas, I had one with a red lining like little kids have.

I distinctly remember where Stuart lived on Earl Street, facing The Croft where they dropped the houses. We were stood round the fire one night and Stuart started talking about The Smiths' 'Hand in Glove' single that he'd just bought. He said, 'Come round and listen to it.' So we walked the 50 yards to his house and as soon as I heard 'Hand in Glove' I was absolutely smitten and went out and bought it. From that point on, every single that came out, we were there on the day - at HMV or wherever - buying it.

Apart from Stuart, we were all into football around the age of 15, 16. My dad died suddenly of a heart attack when I was 15 so my head was all over the pace. For a little while I lost my way. I wouldn't say I was a football thug but we went to football and got into trouble. About 15 or 16 of us used to have a Mitchells self-drive hire van and we used to go all over the country. When City were in the old First Division, we used to have a fight with anyone we could bump into, but nothing vicious.

The gig meant so much because it was on our doorstep. I'd been listening to The Smiths for two or three years by then. If my memory serves me right, everyone knocked on for me on the way. None of us had tickets. We all had bottles of cider. We walked through the park, sat on the steps leading up to Maxwell Hall, finished our drinks and then we all went round and sat on the grass. There was a group of girls from our estate there. They all dressed the same. They all used to wear black Doc Marten shoes, socks up to the knees and little frilly skirts. They were younger even than me. 20 of us walked up the stairs looking like Salford scallies, not a ticket between us.

There were a lot of flat tops there, Morrissettes, but we just looked like we were going to a match. I remember it being really warm, beers, sat outside, just chatting. Someone discovered that the window to the girls toilets was open a little bit so we forced it a little bit more, we all got through and managed to sneak into the gig.

So we all bowled in there and straight away, and because we were all drunk, we were chanting 'Salford, Salford' all the time. It must have been fucking totally annoying for everyone else, this mob of drunken youths. And then when the gig started we realised that downstairs was where the action was. When Prokofiev's 'Romeo and Juliet' started the hairs went up on the back of my neck. When Morrissey came dancing onto the stage everyone was screaming, the first thing he said was, 'Who needs G-Mex?' and of course it all went off.

Every time a song finished the crowd cheered. And we were just annoying. We were singing 'Sal-ford. Sal-ford.' But it went on and on while they were changing guitars and tuning up. And at one point Morrissey started singing, 'Stret-ford, Stret-ford', and of course that wound everyone up.

I've since found on YouTube some clips. My mate Denis Hughes, bless him, had a big head and you can clearly see him perched half on the stage. Morrissey's there and Denis is looking round for everyone else and you can see heads bobbing about and that would have been us, but it's really blurred. Our mate Steve Bradshaw, who was a city fan and a postman, just comes dancing on from the side of the stage, grabs Morrissey around the neck and everyone goes mental and then he gets ejected.

We pushed onto the stage, and as we pitched forward, the stage collapsed. I vividly remember going head first towards Mike Joyce's drums. There were dozens on the stage. I remember Morrissey coming on for the encore and laughing and saying something about, 'If you don't leave now, you'll miss the last bus.'

I never saw any trouble at any of the Smiths gigs I went to. I know that Johnny Marr has said somewhere that it's one of his favourite gigs and to say you were at Salford, and it was a little gig, you got a little bit of a buzz about it because I can say I was there.

I bumped into Mike Joyce going down to London on the train seven or eight years ago. We were both in first class. Mike was sat in his seat with his wife and he looked up. I had a proper Weller haircut at the time - before my hair started going, I had the full on sideboards. He looked at me and I looked at him and I went, 'Hiya Mike.' He went, 'Where do I know you from?' And I said, 'The last time you saw me I was going arse over tit over your drum kit at Maxwell Hall in 1986.' And he said, 'Ah, that's where I recognise you from!'

I WAS THERE: DEREK HAZELL

The Smiths had been an important part of my teenage years after listening and dancing to them on the dancefloor of the State nightclub in Liverpool. 18 years old and living in Liverpool, and being an avid Liverpool supporter going to all the home games and away and there being a nasty rivalry between Liverpool FC and Manchester United, going to Manchester with a Scouse accent was like running the gauntlet.

I remember seeing an advert in the *Liverpool Echo*. Tickets for The Smiths were going on sale on Friday for Salford Uni. This was the warm up gig for the *Queen is Dead* tour. In the run up to the gig I was taken very ill with the flu and was bedridden. On the morning of the gig I could hardly stand, never mind go to a concert. But there was no way I was going to miss this. Somehow, I got out of bed, phoned my friend Haze and we were going!

We had arranged for a friend to drive us there so we got picked up. We went down the East Lancs to Manchester but on the way the car broke down. Luckily it was just the fan belt which was soon fixed and so we were on our way again. Next stop - Salford Uni. Of course, the first port of call was the bar and a few double whiskies, washed down with a pint of lager. From the uni bar, we could hear cheers from inside the hall and in a rush to get there I kicked about four full pints all over the floor - but who cared? The most important band of my life were going on stage.

They opened with in my opinion their finest moment, 'The Queen Is Dead', and then flew through the whole album. The whole crowd was one in movement, with people diving on stage. This was a true rock and roll event and it will never be forgotten. The gig was over in a second but I will remember it for a lifetime.

I WAS THERE: JOHANNA ROBERTS

I had posters and t-shirts (oh, where did they go?) and their name scrawled on my army bag that I used for college. I tuned in to Radio 1 when they played them live at Kilburn Hall (later the recording for *Rank*) introduced by Andy Peebles. I taped a Morrissey interview on Piccadilly Radio with Mike Sweeney, which I still have. I watched Moz with Margi Clarke on *The Tube*. I loved *The Old Grey Whistle Test* that followed them in the studio as they recorded *The Queen Is Dead*. RIP *Whistle Test*, it was bloody marvellous.

I had done my A-levels and was getting ready for university. I was looking in the window of Piccadilly Records and there, the last item on the gig list, it was - The Smiths to play Salford University. I mustered all the change in my purse and went down to the box office to get two tickets. I couldn't afford to wait.

It was a balmy summer's evening outside Maxwell Hall. I saw The Smiths come out from their soundcheck to get in a limo; unlike now, when I would have bowled over, I stood back and just looked at them. As the door opening time got close the crowds were vast. There were eight glass doors of which they only opened two. I am little and literally got carried in by a wave of people.

We stood close to the stage. James Maker's band Raymond was on first and I remember them smashing a guitar and fucking the stage up. That had to be sorted before the gig could go on. The place erupted when The Smiths came on. I was getting crushed at the front and escaped upstairs. We found seats, which isn't very rock and roll, but I could see and I wasn't dying.

The bouncers were holding on to the speakers for fear they would topple over as the over-filled room bounced. It turns out there was extra stage set out for the speakers which was rather weak, hence Raymonde's ability to wreck it.

Everyone fell out of that gig sweating. I remember Chapel Street swarming with Smiths fans. The wonderful thing about the internet is that videos from that evening surfaced, so to be able to watch back some of the night, regardless of how grainy, is so special.

By 1987, *Strangeways* was released and the band announced their split. I was devastated. When the (very few) other fans I knew at Uni claimed adoration for The Smiths, I 'knew' they could never feel like I did about them. And then Morrissey emerged as a solo artist, and I have followed him religiously ever since. At 51, my love for that band has never waned. I was known - am known - as a Smiths fan. I have a Morrissey tattoo, my house is a shrine to the Smiths and Morrissey and we married in the Smiths room at Salford Lads Club.

I have met all five of them, including Craig. Johnny is a humble, wonderful individual. To hear him do Smiths tracks is so special, given his guitar skills. I am honoured to have been alive when they were at their height and to have seen them perform. So many people, including my husband, tell me they wish they had, so I feel blessed that I did. I know every word to every song, and I still play The Smiths daily. Their music got me through the trickiest years of adolescence and it has never aged.

I WAS THERE: JOHN MARSHALL, AGE 19

I was a young up-and-coming drummer and a keen fan of the local music scene. I was born in Hyde, Greater Manchester and became aware of The Smiths in late 1984. The music was just so different to anything that was around and appealed to me almost right away. Johnny Marr had to be the coolest-dressed man on the planet

I'd been into Piccadilly Records to buy a ticket for G-Mex and they had none left but said, 'We have some for Salford.' I was unaware of this gig and bought three tickets there and then. I think I paid £6 each for them. I took my older sister, who was a keen fan, and my mate's girlfriend as he was on military service in Germany and asked me to look after her (We were just friends, may I add).

The venue was absolutely packed out. I heard later that because the door staff were not taking tickets on the door, people were just going to the loos and passing the tickets through the windows so all their mates could come in as well. The gig started and you couldn't breathe. It was summer and red hot. I remember going out afterwards looking like I'd just swam across the local boating lake.

As they went through the set list the crowd seemed to get bigger and bigger, with people jumping on stage. The venue staff had to lash ropes around the speakers to stop them falling into the crowd as the floor bounced with the fans.

I've seen hundreds of live bands over the years. I was a drummer for many years and played countless gigs and became a sound engineer and managed bands until retiring from music in my thirties. I can honestly say this was the most manic gig I ever went to.

I WAS THERE: BILLIE MCGRAIL

I was at the Salford Uni and Free Trade Hall gigs in 1986. I fell madly in love with the band and Morrissey when I saw and heard 'This Charming Man'. It was unlike anything I'd heard before and I felt I'd found my lyrical soul mate. There were cameras at the Salford Uni gig for *The South Bank Show* and I summoned up the courage and strength to be part of the stage invasion. It was almost the end of the gig and emotions and adoration were running high. I was helped over the barrier where I clambered onto the stage and knelt on the left hand side of Morrissey - and was awe struck. I even worshipped him like a god and was applauded by the crowd! I stayed until the end of the gig where the bouncers removed us gently off stage.

I WAS THERE: JOHN PARKES

I managed to get in and get to the side of the stage. They were doing the sound check - 'Ask'. I wanted to speak to Morrissey. I don't know what I was going to say to him. But I was apprehended by, I believe, the manager and two other people who very roughly threw me out.

Salford University was a fantastic gig. It was just mental, it really was. I could see water running down the walls. The stage didn't look very secure either. I came out of there and because there were no trains back to Warrington where I lived and worked I was going to hitch. The very first people I spoke to I said, 'Is anybody going to Warrington or thereabouts?' and this guy said to me, 'Yeah, we're going to Warrington.' I said, 'Great. Can I have a lift if there's space?' And he said, 'Yeah. But we're waiting for our mate.' It was ages. The crowd had all disappeared and this lad turned up. 'We're going to Wallington.' I said, 'Well, I want to go to Warrington.' 'No, we're going to Wallington', which is a place in Surrey. So I'm there in the middle of Salford, young lad, no money. It was very late at night and I ended up walking down the hard shoulder of the M62, all the way back. I was thumbing a lift but nobody was stopping. It took me all night. Fortunately I worked at Winwick Hospital, which is just off the junction of the M62, and I lived in the nurses' residence there. So after walking 12 miles at least I was on the junction of the motorway. That was quite epic really. It's a wonder the police didn't pick me up. In fact it might have been a blessing if the police had picked me up.

I WAS THERE: RITA FARRAGHER

A standout gig was Salford. So many great moments and songs they hadn't done for ages. I would not want to have missed that one. They played for longer than usual and we had to run like mad to catch our coach home or face sleeping in the bus station again. I got a postcard from Morrissey afterwards saying, 'We saw you running away from Salford.' We did make the coach by the way!

Johnny Marr: Even though we had played G-Mex the night before, the Salford show felt like a homecoming. The hall was packed to insanity that night and it turned out to be one of the best shows we ever played; we rocked the plaster off the walls and shook the foundations. At one point the PA had to be tied down with rope because it was about to

tumble down and the ceiling of the room below later had to be rebuilt because it was at breaking point. It was an unforgettable night in an unforgettable town.

'PANIC'

RELEASED 21 JULY 1986

During the band's lifetime, only two singles ('Heaven Knows I'm Miserable Now' and 'Sheila Take a Bow') did better than the number 11 position that 'Panic' achieved in the UK charts. It managed national radio airplay despite the chorus of 'hang the deejay' as Morrissey reflected that 'the music that they constantly play... says nothing to me about my life.'

From Salford, The Smiths travelled to North America for their second and what would prove to be their final tour there.

KINGSWOOD MUSIC THEATRE

31 JULY 1986, TORONTO, CANADA

I WAS THERE: STEWART ALI

The first time I ever heard them was at a dance in Hamilton, Ontario, very near Toronto. I was 15. The deejay was a bit older than all the patrons and introduced the crowd to some of the more obscure Eighties music. 'Love Like Blood' by Killing Joke, which I loved, had just finished playing so I was up on the dance floor. As that song finished, this beautiful distorted-sounding guitar filled my ears and struck me like no other music I've ever known. 'How Soon Is Now?' I moved closer to the speakers and just listened in awe. It was the most amazing song I had heard so far in my life. I asked the deejay who it was.

The next day, Saturday, I bussed downtown Hamilton to a fantastic record store called Cheapies. There was always a line up of people for tickets and 12 inch releases. I'd forgotten the name of the song but remembered The Smiths. I asked for the new Smiths song. They told me they only carried the full album. 'How Soon Is Now?' had been released on *Hatful of Hollow*. From that moment on I have never loved a material thing more than this record. I played it over and over again. I listened to 'How Soon Is Now?' 10 times before being patient enough to listen to the whole album all the way through. Song by song they all became my favourites. Everyone has that one staple album in their lives from an impressionable age. This was clearly mine.

I have since bought it again, lost it and my son, 24, bought it me on vinyl for my 45th birthday. It's still my very favourite all time ever album and I know it better than my own face in the mirror. Soon after buying the vinyl from Cheapies, I acquired a Walkman so bought it on tape as well. When *The Queen Is Dead* came out I purchased it on cassette. I loved this album too, so much.

The kids in my high school had great taste in music because of our local radio station, Toronto's CFNY, with Alan Cross. We were exposed to an array of very eclectic, recent and obscure Eighties music. I heard 'How Soon Is Now?' often on CFNY within days of hearing it at the dance. Then CFNY announced a tour was to follow the release of *The Queen Is Dead*. The Smiths were coming to Toronto. I called my friend in hysterics right away: 'We have to wait in line all night.' We were young and not allowed to do it but knew a few boys who wanted to go and were willing to camp out and buy us tickets.

My very best friend, Michelle, also liked The Smiths. We prepared for the concert by listening to the albums over and over. The boys that got us the tickets ended up driving (thanks, guys!) to the concert. We went early and split with the boys in order that Michelle and I could go our own way on the rides. We rode the most daring and had a blast all day.

The Smiths were due on stage at 7pm. This day was one of the best of my life, the rush from the rides and the rush from seeing your ultimate favourite band.

I WAS THERE: DEREK RUBINOFF, AGE 15

I went with Susan Horton. We were both working at the theme park at the time. We were 15 or so. At the back it was open-air and there was a lawn. Morrissey seemed plastered and was spinning around on stage wearing a cardigan; he was twirling a protest sign that said 'The Queen Is Dead'. He had to leave the stage once or twice because he seemed to be so drunk. The band would play an instrumental during his breaks. The crowd got nuts; people were banging on the plastic seats. Rows of attached seats started to fail and got knocked over. People started to rush the stage. The girl I was with grabbed me and we started to rush down the aisle to the stage; security guards were grabbing us and stopped us but others broke through. People jumped on stage and the band fled. I remember some Mods dancing on stage after the band left. At some point security got the kids off the stage and the band came out and played more. It was the craziest show I ever saw. It was exhilarating. It felt a little like *Quadrophenia*.

I WAS THERE: SUSAN THORNTON

At one point Morrissey wasn't looking too well. He left the stage while the band played an instrumental for quite some time. Then he came back in a different outfit and looked much refreshed!

I WAS THERE: STEVE SINGH

The only thing I remember is Morrissey letting everyone on stage at the end. He had a daisy in his pocket. It was just another show at the time. No one knew that record and band would become such classics!

UNIVERSITÉ DE MONTRÉAL CEPSUM

3 AUGUST 1986, MONTREAL, CANADA

I WAS THERE: MARC PELLETIER

Back in 1985 I heard the song 'What Difference does it Make?' by The Smiths and thought it was great. Then I took a chance with *Meat Is Murder*. Suddenly I was hooked, both by the lyrics and the music. Then I bought *The Queen Is Dead*, definitely one of the best LPs of all time, so when I heard that they would be playing live at the CEPSUM at Montreal University I rushed to get a ticket. A small place with a few hundred people, maybe less, and no seat reserve, the stage was low and we even could go on stage at anytime and shake hands with Morrissey. It was very special. The picture I took with my old Kodak was when I was about 20 feet from him. It was a very friendly ambience, the set list was of course great with all the hits and more and it was the first time I'd heard the song 'Panic'. I was so pleased I was there because they never came back. Even Morrissey never came back solo in Montreal – until 2019!

Moz by Marc, on stage in Montreal

GREAT WOODS PERFORMING ARTS CENTER

5 AUGUST 1986, MANSFIELD, MASSACHUSETTS

I WAS THERE: MARK NEEDHAM

I became an avid Smiths fan in 1984. My sister and my girlfriend of six months became adamant fans as well. I remember the loud roar and excitement from the crowd when the lights went off and the intro music came on. The band opened with 'How Soon Is Now?' and when I looked to my left, I saw a classmate climbing up on the stage. He actually made it to Morrissey and hugged him and was then taken off the stage. About four songs in and after drinking several beers, I had to use the restroom but I said to myself, 'I've waited so long to see The Smiths and I'm not missing a second' so I grabbed a cup and discreetly peed in it so I wouldn't miss a second of the show! The show was amazing and it was a very long set list. It was close to a two hour concert but it literally felt like 20 minutes.

The favourite song of my girlfriend of one and a half years was 'Asleep', from the first moment she heard it. Flash forward nine months later and she shockingly passed away in her sleep from an undiagnosed heart condition.

I WAS THERE: PETER APPEL

I was living in London in the fall of 1983 and stayed for about six months in Paddington, doing a semester abroad with my school and majoring in Theater Arts. We saw about 108 shows in a three month period. It was insane and brilliant. I loved Camden Palace and Camden, the Kings Road, Speaker's Corner and everything. I was out and about one day and a bloke selling cassette tapes told me to listen to this new band - 'They're pretty good.' Well I wish I had listened to that tape while I was still in London. But whoever gave me that tape launched me into a lifelong obsession with a band named The Smiths.

Peter Appel saw The Smiths in Mansfield MA

I got to see them at Great Woods Amphitheater - Morrissey holding 'The Queen Is Dead' sign and then the brilliant show taking off. It is one of the greatest nights of my life. They recently released that show with the deluxe reissue of *The Queen Is Dead*. Remastered of course. I have seen and met both Morrissey and Marr in their post-Smiths careers and was given a pick from Johnny that I've carried in my wallet since that night. Morrissey I have followed forever including Manchester, Blackburn, Glasgow and London in the UK. This great and ultra important band have literally saved me over and over and over. There is a light that never goes out.

PIER 84

6 AUGUST 1986, NEW YORK, NEW YORK

I WAS THERE: FREDERICK GUBITOSI

The Pier was on the water and a lot of big bands played there. I didn't know much about them. A friend had played some tracks for me and I thought their sound was different from everything else. I scalped a ticket because it was sold out but got it at face value. They did songs from *The Queen Is Dead* and *Meat Is Murder*. A few people rushed the stage.

Moz in action on The Queen Is Dead tour

I WAS THERE: ANDY SCHWARTZ

I saw The Smiths live in NYC at an open air show on a Hudson River pier on the west side of Manhattan. The American folk singer/songwriter Phranc supported and was not well received, which I guess made Morrissey quite miffed and thus delayed the Smiths' entrance for an additional 30 to 45 minutes. I don't recall much about their set - I mean it was good, maybe very good, I just can't remember the tunes, the high points, etc. I do remember running into a couple of friends and innocently asking what this new drug was called crack!

I WAS THERE: JOSEPH HUGHES, AGE 17

This was a concert venue just south of the Intrepid aircraft carrier museum, jutting out into the Hudson River. I was about to start college. I went with my best friend Steve and my girlfriend. It was general admission and we waited outside all night to get in. We ended up getting about 20 people back. I remember talking to some 'old' couple (probably aged 25 or so), who had seen their infamous New Year's Eve gig at Danceteria. Even in 1986, that was the stuff of legend. They were amazing. Craig Gannon played, and they sounded great. I remember some overheads for the backdrop, including tombstones for 'Cemetry Gates' It was an exhausting, sweaty, dramatic, unforgettable time.

I WAS THERE: PIOTR ORLOV, AGE 17

Sadly the band really did not make too much of an impression on me. Being a Smiths fan going in - I liked 'How Soon Is Now?' but had also just started listening to the then-new *The Queen Is Dead* - it's fair to say I was a little disappointed. They were very straightforward. The *New York Times* reviewed the show and said, 'The sell out audience… sang along on most verses and choruses' and that, 'Onstage, Morrissey moved in a kind of ecstatic slow-motion – wind-milling his arms, wrestling with his shirt, twirling as if entranced. In songs that could teeter into self-pity, he maintained an intelligent, if troubled, dignity.'

I WAS THERE: QUINN JOHNSON, AGE 17

I'm Afro American and originally from Philadelphia. As a teenager I went away to a boarding school in Connecticut from 1980 to 1983 and was exposed to a lot of Seventies music – The Doors, Jimi Hendrix, Led Zeppelin, The Beatles. Around 1981, a friend came back from England and brought back UB40, The Specials and The Clash and I started going in that direction. That music just resonated with me, so when I graduated and went back home to a town outside of New Haven, there was a radio station that played quote, unquote the new wave music. But the only thing New Haven is known for is Yale University and the first hamburger. Other than that there's really nothing there.

Going into high school in 1984 to 1986, I had that musical pedigree and I went to a lot of shows. It wasn't difficult to get to New York to see shows. I went to Live Aid as well. Because when I saw the groups that were billed to play I thought that some of the groups that were in London were actually going to be in Philadelphia!

By '85, '86, I was in a clique, some of whom really liked David Bowie and The Clash and The Violent Femmes. The offshoot, the year behind me, were into Depeche Mode, The Smiths, The Cure and New Order. When *The Queen Is Dead* came out, we got it and listened to it. 'Some Girls Are Bigger Than Others' and the way it starts out and then fades down and then comes back in is pure genius.

When I found out they were playing Pier 84 I got the tickets and two or three of us went. From the opening moment to the last, the fans knew every verse and they sang. I'd never seen any performer get as many things from the audience - flowers, books, anything - than what Morrissey got. He got so much love and so much gratitude. I was just totally floored by that. It was a total singalong from the first song to the end. I'm so glad I went, because they broke up after that.

MUSIC HALL

11 AUGUST 1986, CLEVELAND, OHIO

I WAS THERE: ROB LOGSDON

I remember spilling a pitcher of Guinness on my buddy at the pub before the show. I also correctly predicted the opening song, 'There is a Light That Never Goes Out'. The entire show was surreal in that we had listened to The Smiths while in college so much during the previous two years that we were in tune with everything they were performing. Morrissey had a Jim Morrison-like presence over the crowd. He sometimes didn't look at the crowd and sang whilst lying on his back. Johnny Marr seemed to be in a zone. I don't recall ever seeing a guitarist that was so smooth. His style, with his incredible breaks and timing, mesmerized us. His sound is unmistakable and unduplicated.

FULTON THEATER

12 AUGUST 1986, PITTSBURGH, PENNSYLVANIA

I WAS THERE: LISA ANN BONOMO, AGE 18

I went with my best friend Beth and we had a blast. I knew about The Smiths from alternative/college radio and from reading *Smash Hits* and other UK magazines. We had an independent record shop called Eide's that carried a lot of UK imports and I bought all of my imported vinyl there.

Lisa Ann Bonomo with Johnny Marr and Janice

I have seen Morrissey twice solo and Johnny Marr once - I actually met him after the gig and he was lovely! I was in the first row in a small venue for the 2009 Morrissey show - he touched my hand and my friend Janice, who I didn't know was there just two rows behind me, got a piece of his shirt which she had framed. That was a great gig.

For the Johnny Marr gig we got there super early and it was all just standing room only, so we were right up against the stage. He is just so talented, it was just incredible to see him and then meet him. His son played with him, which is so cool. I attended the Marr concert and the 2012 Morrissey concert with my friend Janice (pictured on the right with Johnny).

I WAS THERE: JOHN QUALLEY

I remember Morrissey being all over the stage. It was a very good performance. 'How Soon Is Now?' was incredible. I felt lucky to have seen it as they kind of collapsed after the tour. I definitely saw them at their pinnacle.

ARAGON BALLROOM

15 AUGUST 1986, CHICAGO, ILLINOIS

I WAS THERE: KERA BOLONIK

I was a rising high school junior when David, one of my oldest friends, called and told me he'd bought us tickets to see The Smiths for their *Queen Is Dead* tour. The Smiths were, for me, like the Prozac that didn't yet exist; I'd been in the grips of a powerful depression - heaven knows I was miserable then - and the misery of which the Moz sang, and with such candour, provided an ideal antidote.

There was only one issue: my parents. They forbade me from seeing concerts. They were overprotective and convinced that music venues were places where bad things happened. Sex and drugs and rock 'n' roll. In part because they had rarely been to concerts, and when they had they'd seen people pass joints, and they'd never smoked pot.

But they'd known David since he was 3, they were friendly with his mother. He anticipated all my parents' issues, so he gamed it out. He bought my ticket so saying no would have been rude. He arranged for our ride to and fro, so they couldn't use the excuse that they wouldn't drive us there. Instead, my parents put me on probation for the three weeks leading up to the concert, scrutinising my every move, waiting for an opportunity to take away the privilege of my attending the concert. I'd never been so prudent, so well behaved in my life. That's how eager I was to see The Smiths.

David and I arrived early so we could stand as close to the stage as possible. A butch-lesbian folk singer named Phranc opened, singing songs about such things as physical education teachers she harboured crushes on. I'd never seen a performer sing, or even speak so openly about same-sex desire. I was red in the face. Even though I physically resembled her not at all - a femme clad in an Oxford shirt buttoned all the way up, clasped at the top by a vintage brooch, harem pants and Chinese slippers, my hair highlighted in bleach - and couldn't imagine pining for a PE teacher, I definitely identified with same-sex love, and was in awe of her courage in articulating it. But I was also not ready. My eyes were fixed on the floor.

The Smiths emerged about 45 minutes later, which felt like an eternity to us but was so welcome as the sounds of Johnny Marr's opening riff to 'How Soon Is Now?' enveloped the Ballroom. A doe-eyed young man rushed the stage with a bouquet of roses to welcome Morrissey as he came to the mic, seguing to 'The Queen Is Dead'. The Moz gave him a brief sly smile, took the flowers and proceeded to smash them against the left amp, then the right. The kid looked around with a mixture of horror and awe, not quite knowing how to react. Nor did David or I. I remember saying something to the effect of, 'Um, nice guy?' The Moz was predictably surly, but then again that was his persona, it felt performative. They delivered an incredible performance, covering songs from the then-new album and many tracks from *Meat Is Murder*, *Hatful of Hollow* and the debut (we call it *Rough Trade* here in the States). They ended with an even more haunting version of 'Meat Is Murder', which resonated deeply with me at the time because I was a vegetarian for about five minutes.

I wish I could still fit into my *Queen Is Dead* t-shirt, then contraband in my parents' household and a reminder of that perfect night - an evening of communal sardonic sulking for me and an evening of anxiety for my parents, convinced it was the end of innocence. That would come years later.

I WAS THERE: VIRGINIA DEVLIN, AGE 18

Seeing The Smiths live is definitely something I brag about from time to time and a true highlight of my punk days. While the band started playing larger venues on that tour, the Aragon is a more intimate space. The concert promoters must not have been big Smiths fans, because the main floor was set up with rows and rows of folding chairs. As soon as the band started playing, and in a rather orderly fashion given the circumstances of a packed, sweaty room, we all started folding up the chairs and passing them to the back over our heads. I don't recall security intervening at all. It was inevitable - we needed to clear the floor to dance and sing our hearts out with Morrissey! At the end of the night, there was a huge pile of chairs in the back of the room.

Virginia Devlin took part in a mass movement – of chairs!

I WAS THERE: JIM JOLL

The '85 show wasn't 100 per cent sold out, but just one year later, The Smiths were much more widely known here in the States and Chicago, being a very progressive town musically, was ready for them. I procured tickets for myself and friends for the show and it was a complete sell-out. The band was equally amazing the second go around for me and I wish that I had other opportunities to see them again. I suppose that is a popular lament among The Smiths faithful. My favourite songs? 'Unhappy Birthday' and 'Vicar in a Tutu'.

Jim Joll caught The Smiths at their pinnacle

I WAS THERE: KEVIN WILLIAMS

The Smiths caught my ear at Metro, a Chicago venue with a smart bar downstairs. They were playing 'How Soon Is Now?'. I went out and bought the cassette. 'Reel Around the Fountain' took some getting used to.

I WAS THERE: MARK MICHICICH, AGE 21

To this day, Morrissey and Marr inspire a hand-on-my-heart loyalty that I will take with me to the grave. They have had the kind of impact on my life that is only rivalled by the likes of Lennon or Bowie. I consider The Smiths to be among the greatest bands of all time, and equals to The Beatles, The Clash… you get the idea.

I've tried really hard to remember the very moment I first heard The Smiths. I'm sure it was one of four songs. I have old memories of hearing 'Hand In Glove', 'This Charming Man', 'What Difference Does It Make?' and 'How Soon Is Now?' on different mix tapes from friends.

Mark Michicich saw The Smiths at the Aragon Ballroom

The first Smiths record I ever bought was *Hatful of Hollow*. I worked backwards from there, picking up the first album afterwards as well as the first two 1983 seven inch singles and then all of the 1984 12 inch singles, including the different mixes of 'This Charming Man' and them backing Sandie Shaw. I searched and bought up as much Smiths material as I could find - videos, magazines, books, you name it. I even sought out live recordings and Morrissey's book on James Dean. From *Hatful of Hollow* on, I bought every Smiths record as it came out.

In 1984, I was a 19 year old college student at the University of Illinois at Urbana-Champaign. I spent a lot of time in a student run concert organization, Star Course, that promoted concerts on the college campus. The Star Course staff were all music fanatics, routinely hitting the local independent record shops like Record Swap to see if Charlie (AKA The Quaker) had put a Smiths single up on the new releases wall. We drove to other cities, especially Chicago (where I was from), to see live shows that we weren't able to bring to the college campus.

My first opportunity to see The Smiths live was June 1985 at Chicago's Aragon Ballroom. I was 20 and with my girlfriend (now wife), Margie, and college friends from Star Course. I was intimately familiar with the set list but was surprised to hear Elvis' '(Marie's the Name) His Latest Flame' being mashed up with 'Rusholme Ruffians'.

The Aragon *Meat Is Murder* show was not sold out. This confused and saddened me. It seemed like a gross miscarriage of justice. How could Chicago not fill this ballroom to see the most important band in the world at this moment in time? I'm not sure the crowd even went much further back than the soundboard. But those who were there were absolutely mad for them. I remember a friend, Gwen, turning to me after 'How

Soon Is Now?' and saying, 'That was the pinnacle of human existence.'

My second (and last) opportunity to see The Smiths live was again in Chicago at the Aragon Ballroom in 1986. I had to lie to my boss to miss work to see them. I told my boss that my dad was finally graduating college having gone to night school for years, and that the whole family had to go to the ceremony. I, of course, went to see The Smiths. Again I was with my future wife, and life-long friends from Star Course.

This time the Aragon completely sold out. Chicago had made me proud and recognised *The Queen Is Dead* for the masterpiece that it was. While I was intimately familiar with the set list, they played 'Panic', which had already been released in the UK but which I heard for the first time that night. I also remember them playing 'What She Said' differently from the previous tour. This time it was mashed up with 'Rubber Ring'.

Mark Michicich's tour programme

I was surprised that there was a fifth member of the band, Craig Gannon, on rhythm guitar. At first I thought, 'One does not simply add a member to The Smiths. John, Paul, George and Ringo never walked out on stage with Larry.' But then I heard Gannon and had to admit to myself that he did do a nice job filling out their sound live. Mostly I remember Morrissey just being Morrissey as only Morrissey can. And frantically waving a giant 'Queen Is Dead' sign. And beautifully singing songs like 'I Know It's Over' and 'There is a Light That Never Goes Out'.

I was pleased to hear the latter again, recorded all those years ago on that very night. Leading up to the re-release of the deluxe version of *The Queen Is Dead*, each week iTunes released a live version of each track in order from a different night of the 1986 tour. 'There is a Light That Never Goes Out' was taken from my Aragon show. I was at that gig. Yes, I was there.

I WAS THERE: RICH SCHUMANN

G.A. GEN ADM A 13.50
GENAL ADMISSION
BUDWEISER/JAM PRESENT
THE SMITHS
AT
ARAGON BALLROOM
LAWRENCE AND BROADWAY
FRI AUG 15 1986 8:00 PM

Rich Schumann's ticket stub after it got soaked through

It started at 8pm and the ticket price was $13.50. Boy that's cheap now! I went with my buddy Tony Schaffer and we pushed our way up to the front. It got so hot in the place that stage security was taking gallon jugs of water and dumping it on people. I got soaked and my ticket stub did too. It looks like it went through a car wash. They had to take a girl out because she passed out and I remember seeing the bouncers carrying her in that area between the stage and the crowd. Morrissey got a bundle of roses thrown on the stage and when they played 'I Want the One I Can't Have' he beat those flowers over the front speakers, annihilating them.

Taking the bus home we were freezing because of how wet we were from all the water that was poured on us due to the intense heat inside the building. My ticket is in such bad shape as a result of the water that I had to use a pen and write all the information back on it because all the ink got washed almost away on it.

I WAS THERE: STEPHANIE SNYDER, AGE 16

I was back from spending 10 months in Ireland, where I had seen The Smiths in February. The Aragon is general admission and the custom for shows back then was to line up early to ensure the best spot at the gig. So I got there at 3am. That was not necessary but that's hindsight - the next people to show up got there at noon on the day of the show. My friends and I had been out there about 12 hours when we saw that there was activity around the back doors to the stage. People lined up along the alley that separated the north side of the building from the public parking garage opposite so we could see people unloading and carrying things in and that is where the band would access the building as well.

Stephanie Snyder saw The Smiths in Dublin and Chicago

The stage was on the second floor of the building. My friend Sara and I decided we wanted to sneak in and try and meet The Smiths, and Morrissey in particular. We were 16 and for the past couple of years we had tremendous success meeting musicians such as U2. We went up the back stairs where the roadies were moving in and out. It was pretty dim in there. The Aragon had tall windows, maybe 10 feet high, with heavy red drapes over them. I never knew there were windows because it was always dark out when I was there previously. No one really paid attention to us at first, as they were busy setting up for the show. We ducked behind a curtain. Johnny Marr was on the stage doing a sound check. Sara and I whispered to each other trying to figure out what to do.

Suddenly there seemed to be security everywhere, though they hadn't seen us. Then Morrissey passed near where we were and we bolted from behind the curtains to talk to him. I think I had some horrible poetry I wrote to give him. As we got near him a guy stopped us and was already saying we had to go and Morrissey said, 'Let them go,' and the guy did. We hugged Morrissey and he graciously hugged us back. He smelled really good. I feel bad for him because we had been hanging out in an alley for 12 hours. I gave him some horrible poetry I had written and that's all I remember from that. He was lovely and then security had us go out the front doors.

The show was wonderful. I was up front on the barricade and the crowd had me pinned against it, it was so full. Security up front were great and gave us water during the show. And when people passed out from the heat we'd pass them over our heads to the front and help lower them to security so First Aid could help them.

I WAS THERE: PAUL WEISS

I was in high school. My older sister, who turned me on to The Smiths, took me to the show. I didn't have a camera with me, a mistake I would not make again. There was the longest line of fans waiting to get in; indeed, of the untold dozens of show I have seen there, I don't recall a line stretching around the building and block until years later, when Nirvana played there in 1993.

Paul Weiss remembers Morrissey singing from a prone position

I remember standing in the crowd up close to the stage, with all these chairs on the floor that were later hauled off the dance floor and passing them overhead one by one after The Smiths took the stage. I watched intently as a mysterious figure - Johnny Marr - played guitar in the back corner of the stage. He was almost hiding, he was so inconspicuous. It was incredibly tough to see him, and next to impossible to see his guitar fretwork, yet the sounds emanating from his guitar sounded like several guitars playing all at once.

I remember watching intently as Morrissey, who at that point was an almost-iconic figure - even before the internet and cell phones, when we had to get our information from fanzines and rock magazines - was flitting around the stage, with gladioli sticking out of his back pocket. The strangest part of the show was Morrissey spending most of his time singing while lying flat on his back on stage; he sang many songs in that prone position.

From the cavalcade of guitar to Morrissey's *sui generis* stage presence, the first of dozens of Morrissey concerts I have attended, I have never seen anything like The Smiths, before or after.

UNIVERSAL AMPHITHEATER

25 & 26 AUGUST 1986, LOS ANGELES, CALIFORNIA

I WAS THERE: MIKE HEAD

The shows that I saw in '85 at the Hollywood Palladium were just scorchers. They were on fire and these were some of the best concerts I've ever seen in my life. They were still a four piece then. In 1986 I saw them at both the Universal Amphitheater in Universal City, California and at Irvine Meadows down in Irvine, California. Those shows were good but the audiences were on controlled substances like you would not believe. At Universal Amphitheater they were serving liquor to minors and one of them threw up right behind us. He was probably all of 14. At the Irvine show, there was angel dust going around. I do not partake in that stuff but there were a lot of people who did. And they were trying to climb up on the stage. Morrissey was really pissed off.

I WAS THERE: MAGGY LIND, AGE 30

In 1985 I went on my dream vacation to Europe. I had wanted to go since I was a kid, and especially to England as I was a massive Beatles fan. My first stop was London and I went to a Virgin record store, looking at albums. I thought they were a bit bulky to carry around Europe for three weeks, so asked the guy at the register for some 45 single suggestions. He handed me The Smiths' 'The Boy with the Thorn in his Side' and Depeche Mode's 'Shake the Disease'. I bought them both. I wasn't that familiar with The Smiths name but as soon as I played the single I recognised the vocalist's voice and became a total fan!

In 1986 I got tickets for the Universal Amphitheater show from a ticket agency located in a department store. My seats were about halfway up the theatre so I could see the stage pretty well. I took my 28 year old brother. He had not fully embraced the new wave/punk rock sound, as I had back in 1978, but I was trying to get him to listen to new music. He knew I was always looking to hear new bands so he decided to go to the concert with me.

The concert was unlike any I had ever been to. Everyone in the audience stood for the entire show. This venue had excellent sight lines and there really wasn't a bad seat in the whole place, but everybody was on their feet through the entire show. I've seen a lot of concerts there, but usually people stand up during the encore, not for the entire show!

Morrissey was very dramatic, faux fainting and draping himself over the monitors and eventually on the floor of the stage. People were going nuts and I was blown away by his voice, which was so incredible, so original and one of a kind. He was just so unbelievably unique a performer. He was in his prime and he was magic. He had a vulnerability that was very appealing. I remember being very impressed by the band. They were right there with him and Johnny Marr's guitar playing was so memorable, he made his guitar sing! He's just a sonic guitar player. My younger brother was totally impressed and could not believe he witnessed this concert. We used to talk about it often. I personally will never forget it. The crowd was with him and the band were with the crowd. It was a beautiful experience.

IRVINE MEADOWS AMPHITHEATRE

28 AUGUST 1986, LAGUNA, CALIFORNIA

I WAS THERE: KATHERINE RIOS, AGE 13

I went on the second night with my two older sisters. The first night opener, I heard, had trash and bottles thrown at them and constant shouting such that they didn't ever attempt to perform. The night I went, The Smiths went on at 8. The venue was an open air amphitheatre and had a hard concert stop at 11. But they kept playing. The venue shut off the sound. They kept playing. It was incredible. Towards the end of the concert, before the sound was shut off, fans ran to the stage. I can't remember what song they were playing but the stage was full of fans. Morrissey was singing and a large breasted blonde was dancing and decided to pull her top down, exposing her breasts. Morrissey gave her a look of disgust and turned away from her. Johnny Marr just shook his head and kept playing.

I WAS THERE: TYLER W STRINGER

Morrissey actually showed up then at gigs. To be honest, I don't remember if Johnny Marr was there or not by then. I was never really concerned with him. Once the guitar is established, any great player can mimic it, except for maybe The Edge. I was never the biggest Smiths fan. I like them, sure, but it was more for the girlfriend back then. I used to see Morrissey once in awhile in Beverly Hills over the years. I always ran into him at Barneys. He shopped a lot.

STATE UNIVERSITY OPEN AIR THEATER

29 AUGUST 1986, SAN DIEGO, CALIFORNIA

I WAS THERE: MIKE MCGARY, AGE 22

The Smiths got airplay on our local radio station, 91x, from the beginning. I kind of lumped them into the bigger 'new wave' acts of the time. Once I actually heard *Louder Than Bombs*, I realised they were much better than their poppy counterparts.

I was 22 and with my girlfriend at the time. She introduced me to them when *Meat Is Murder* came out and I was an instant convert. She ran on stage, grabbed Morrissey and got a piece of his shirt. In those days it was primarily girls who rushed the stage. Craig Gannon was playing with them too. It was a great show on a beautiful San Diego summer evening. Those were the days. They are still my favourite band.

SDSU OPEN AIR THEATER

29 AUGUST 1986, SAN DIEGO, CALIFORNIA

I WAS THERE: TRENA BELK

I was front row centre at the SDSU Open Air Theater. Morrissey gave me a long stemmed red rose and held my hand for about 30 seconds. It was amazing! He was amazing! I can tell you he is a gentleman. You can see it in his eyes.

CU EVENTS CENTER

3 SEPTEMBER 1986, BOULDER, COLORADO

I WAS THERE: SAM O'DANIEL, AGE 16

1985 was a watershed year for me. There was a lot going on for me emotionally and physically, and perhaps that's why the music from that year is so strongly embedded in my psyche. 1985 might be the best year for music, ever. I didn't discover Meat Is Murder until autumn of the year I started high school. There was a girl in one of my classes - I'm not sure how we met, other than sitting next to each other. She had teased-up dyed black hair and wore goth-style clothes and makeup, for which I'll admit to always having a weakness. In plain terms, I had a complete crush on her, and she seemed so confident and cool and all the things you think about other kids at that age. Some days she would take my spiral notebooks and write in them. Through some investigation, I eventually found that what she was writing were lyrics from *Meat Is Murder*. I was already a Smiths fan, having discovered *Hatful of Hollow* while on a spring break trip with my friend earlier that year in Fallbrook, California. Something in Morrissey's forlorn, pleading, aching lyrics connected directly to my adolescent brain. *Meat Is Murder* with its clear anti-meat and anti-school/bullying/authority stance – both challenged and drew me in further.

I've mentioned that I knew the lyrics to a couple songs before I knew the actual songs themselves, which I think helped me get more out of this album lyrically than I normally would have. Usually I hear the music and then get into the lyrics later. Possibly a vocal melody can draw me in, but lyrics are typically secondary in those early listens. I can maybe think of a few artists that the lyrics as a whole jumped out more immediately - Billy Bragg's *Talking with the Taxman About Poetry*, for example. Then again, when Morrissey starts songs with bits like 'I'd like to drop my trousers to the world,' you listen. I suppose I would have made the effort to find out what he was singing regardless.

I don't recall that much of the show. We were pretty far back. I just remember seeing them on stage and looking for Johnny. They toured with a second guitarist and I couldn't quite make out which was Johnny for a while. I've read that the band weren't very into it and that matches my recollection.

MCALISTER AUDITORIUM

8 SEPTEMBER 1986, NEW ORLEANS, LOUISIANA

I WAS THERE: ROY ANDERSON

In the winter of 1985, I had just started attending Birmingham-Southern College, a small, liberal arts school in Birmingham, Alabama. I had just failed out of another small, liberal arts college, Millsaps, and was new on campus and looking for people with whom I could connect. I had gone to a prestigious day school in my hometown of Mobile, Alabama and knew some students at Birmingham-Southern but most were very button-down types and I wanted to branch out a little. As has always been the case, it's easy to identify the cool kids - the ones who were a little off the beaten path and into better music. For me, in the Eighties, that was primarily bands of the jangle pop variety, and REM specifically, although I had been a fan of the punk scene and bands like Siouxsie and The Banshees, Joy Division and New Order. I was introduced to a group of girls on campus who were obviously into that sort of thing, the Siouxsie eye liner being a dead giveaway. And it was through them I first heard 'Reel Around the Fountain'.

I had also been into a few English bands in high school like Aztec Camera and The Style Council. For people not so focused on the guitar, there may not be much crossover between those bands and The Smiths. But Johnny Marr was definitely channeling some Roddy Frame on that one. It's all about the major sevenths. And it easily drew me in.

This was just prior to *Meat Is Murder* being released Stateside. And when that album finally dropped, a buddy of mine and I went to the local record shop to pick up the vinyl. It was over for me at that point. I had become a die-hard Smiths devotee even though I was singing 'sun and air' rather than 'son and heir'.

In 1986, I had dropped out after a year at Birmingham-Southern to join a band and keep up my ill-conceived pursuit of musical greatness. *The Queen Is Dead* dropped and, pun intended, so did I. My drug of choice back then was LSD and some friends of mine and I spent a good 12 hours tripping our faces off and listening to that album on repeat. By the way, if you're in that frame of mind, 'I Know It's Over', trust me.

But then the big news came. The Smiths were touring the US and would be doing a show in New Orleans, just a couple of hours away. I'm still not sure why but I ended up getting tickets with my best friend's little sister, picked up some acid and made the trip. They played at McAllister Auditorium on the Tulane University campus where I had also recently seen Siouxsie do an epic show on her *Cities in Dust* tour. The Smiths show was completely different. You couldn't get near the stage for the throngs of young gay men in their cardigans and fake horn-rimmed glasses. Similar to current Morrissey shows these days.

And you'll forgive me for not remembering the set list but I was transfixed by Johnny Marr's guitar rig. Marr currently is a Fender guy. He has his own signature Jaguar and is all about Fender tube amps. Though he did use Fender amps in the studio in the Eighties, live he was running through Roland Jazz Chorus 120s, monstrously loud solid state amps. He had two of those, side by side, on stage and was running through a smaller unit as a preamp that I could never identify. Perhaps a Mesa Boogie Mk II as had been favoured by James Honeyman Scott of The Pretenders. And the guitars he was playing back then were Rickenbacker 360s, the weapon of choice for Peter Buck of REM.

I remember being amazed by the backing tracks employed during 'How Soon Is Now?' and the beautiful backdrop projected behind the band during 'Cemetry Gates'. Being a meat eater, I remembered stepping out of the auditorium when the lights all went red and the moaning cow sounds announced 'Meat Is Murder' about to be played. It's not good to feel that guilty while you're tripping.

For the most part I just remember standing there, jaw dropped, watching Johnny Marr's hands and being amazed at how simple it all looked as he was playing it live and knowing how difficult it is to actually do.

The coolest note about that whole Smiths experience back then was that one of the girls who had introduced me to the band is actually the girl in the 'How Soon Is Now?' video. I don't even remember her name, maybe Karen, but she was a model. Birmingham-Southern was on a trimester system where most students studied abroad for the month of January. She was in London for hers and was spotted on the street by a guy with a camera who asked her to dance for him, she in her way-too-big Eighties sweater and Czech army field hat. She never met the band and I don't think she ever even visited Manchester. It was just a random encounter that ended up being what it is.

I'm still a major fan of The Smiths and I've had the chance to see Morrissey live a couple of times as well. I'm still a big fan of the guitarists he recruits - Alain White, Boz Boorer and Jesse Tobias. And I'm also a fan of the recent stuff from Johnny Marr. But that period in life, driving around on rainy days listening to 'William, It was Really Nothing' and trying to make myself be depressed like any good Smiths fan would? Those were the best of times. Mopey yet sweet. And that concert memory, fuzzy at it is, is still a small peak in my 52 years.

Although the band had played to bigger and more enthusiastic crowds, the remaining four dates of the 1986 US tour – in Miami, Atlanta, Nashville and New York – were cancelled.

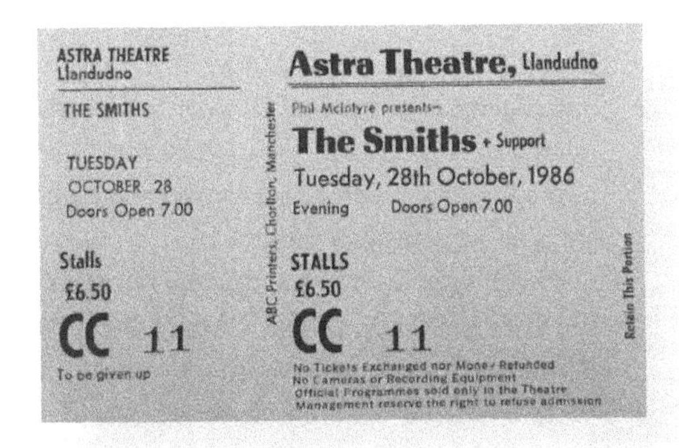

THE QUEEN IS DEAD TOUR

The Queen Is Dead was promoted on the October 1986 UK tour, which comprised 12 dates. A thirteenth show (at Llandudno, on 28 October 1986) was cancelled after the Preston Guildhall show was cut short. Rather than gladioli, Morrissey's stage props now included a placard not unlike The Ramones' infamous 'Gabba Gabba Hey' banner, one announcing 'The Queen Is Dead' and another stating 'Two Light Ales Please'. He also waved a noose when performing 'Panic'. The Kilburn National Ballroom show was to be recorded by the BBC and was later released, in truncated form, as the *Rank* album a year after the band had split.

SANDS CENTRE

13 OCTOBER 1986, CARLISLE, UK

I WAS THERE: DAVE NICHOLSON

I saw them at Carlisle Sands Centre in 1986. I remember watching Johnny Marr. I loved his style and his Brian Jones haircut. I met Johnny in 2019 and told him I saw The Smiths in Carlisle - he couldn't remember playing there. I'll let him off with that one as it was 30 years ago. We were talking for over 15 minutes. I was with a friend and he said, 'How did you two meet?' She said it was years ago when we knocked about on scooters. Johnny asked if I still had mine and what model it was. He said, 'Oh yeah, Mani was into scooters' and in my head I'm thinking, 'Mani, Stone Roses....'

Dave Nicholson met Johnny Marr in 2019

I WAS THERE: LEONARDO MANFREDI, AGE 16

Carlisle does not feature greatly in the wider history of rock and pop. When bands announced their tour dates there wasn't usually much point rushing to see if Cumbria was anywhere on the itinerary. Quite simply, until the Sands Centre opened in 1985 there wasn't really anywhere with a meaningful capacity for them to play. In the Spring of '86 I'd stood on the Sands stage myself as part of my school choir's performance of *Carmina Burana* - not exactly a precursor to dizzying hedonism and rock 'n' roll excess. So it felt like a major coup and a glorious antithesis to this that The Smiths came to town and it generated a palpable buzz among my peers. These days, tickets would probably sell out in seconds online but back then it required the more analogue solution of going to the box office and handing over the cash. It surprises me to this day that I was able to get a ticket with such minimal fuss.

16 years old at the time, I had a burgeoning love of music but hadn't really embraced the live experience. In fact I'd only attended my first gig in August 1986, Prince at Wembley Arena, which was an awe-inspiring show. However, because my ticket placed me what felt like half a mile away from the stage it was hard not to feel a bit detached and it didn't really prepare me for the sound and the fury of a band at its peak and almost within touching distance. Less than two months later came my first truly visceral live music experience.

Certainly there were many more devoted fans among the 1,800 in the room than me at the start of that night, but I felt determined to fight my way to the front, in contrast to my trip to Wembley. It seemed like a good idea at the time. A quick glance at the set list confirms what my often unreliable memory tells me: 'The Queen Is Dead,' 'Panic,' 'I Want the One I Can't Have' offered a thunderous opening, although I was as overwhelmed by the crush behind me as much as the music in front. I lasted three songs, the bruises on my chest a testament to the ferocity of the passion in the room, before retreating to a safer distance halfway back. If there'd ever been panic on the streets of Carlisle it had moved indoors for a couple of hours, fuelled by Morrissey's 'Hang the DJ' placard, Mike Joyce's fierce drumming and Johnny Marr's bewitching, bewildering guitar. The obligatory stage invasions ensued and I watched friends of mine attempt their own incursions, too breathless to join them.

Looking at it now, it seems like a perfect set: if I'd chosen it myself I don't think it would look too different. 'There is a Light…', 'London', 'How Soon Is Now?', it truly felt like an 'I was there' experience. As it turned out, there weren't too many more gigs after this one. A review of that night written by Dave Sexton in *Record Mirror,* which began by pronouncing The Smiths 'probably the best band in Britain' included the prophetic lines, 'It remains the juxtaposition of Morrissey and Marr that makes the band (and undoubtedly will break them too) but now is their moment.' Around nine months later the moment was over.

I WAS THERE: GARY ROBINSON, AGE 16

This was my first ever proper live music gig! My mate who was 15 was doing the lights and gave me his AAA pass. Johnny Marr gave him his strings. Like the little fan boy I was, I brought a gift for Morrissey, a specially made mug that I had asked to be inscribed with 'Hang the Queen' with a silhouette picture of the Queen's head on it. Bit harsh I know! The shop refused but said, 'What if we put 'The Queen - Friend of the People' but cross out the 'r' so it reads 'fiend'?' My mate passed the mug and a note to Morrissey. I hope he appreciated it!

30 years later, I was playing in a Smiths tribute act Girlfriend and a Korma. (Now I'm solo as The Boy With the Thorn in his Side). We were booked to play a spot down the road in Cumbria on the exact night 30 years later to mark the night. Loads in the audience that were there 30 years earlier came to see us. We did the whole album and a classics set as well. Great night!

A few days later I went to Preston Guild Hall and was at the gig where the band were forced to cancel the gig part way into 'The Queen Is Dead' opener as Morrissey was hit by a coin and cut and taken to hospital. Ended up in a near riot! My Smiths gigs were certainly eventful

I WAS THERE: CAROLINGTON BROAD, AGE 16

It was the first 'proper' gig I had been to. I remember seeing people climbing on stage and thinking I could get up there, so I made my way to the front. Carlisle Sands Centre is like a sports hall so the stage wasn't very high. I got up and managed to get to Morrissey's side. It was all a blur really. Years and years later I found the article about the gig and through that I was able to find actual footage of the gig and me dancing with Morrissey.

I WAS THERE: DARREN WILKINSON

I didn't have too long to wait before The Smiths arrived in my hometown of Carlisle for the second time, in October 1986. Now 20, little did I know that this would be the last time I would see the band live and that less than a year later they would have split up. I remember they did 'Panic' and everyone just waited for the nod it makes to Carlisle, Morrissey whirling a noose around above his head.

Carlisle is not known for exuberant crowds. When I saw The Cult a few years later Ian Astbury announced at the end of the gig, 'Thank you Carlisle, you have been shit. We won't be back', but The Smiths were in town and this was different. The stage invasion during the encore was huge and thankfully didn't result in Morrissey taking the huff and walking off. And that was it: I never saw The Smiths again.

I have seen Morrissey a few times since but it's just not the same, maybe I'm just older. I still get my fix by going to see The Smyths, a tremendous tribute to the real thing, several times a year. Each time is like a time machine where my mind is younger than my body. During a recent gig at The Ritz in Manchester I made the rash decision to enter the mosh at the front. It didn't end too well. One lyric sprang to mind, 'Does the mind rule the body, or does the body rule the mind, I dunno?' I have never tired of listening to The Smiths, probably never will.

TOWN HALL

14 OCTOBER 1986, MIDDLESBROUGH, UK

MIDDLESBROUGH TOWN HALL
Phil McIntyre Promotions
presents
The Smiths
plus Support
Thursday, 8th March 1984
at 7.30 p.m. Doors Open 7.00 p.m.
No Refunds or Exchanges
Tickets £3.50 Nº 602 MAIN HALL

I WAS THERE: ANGELA LAMBERT

We queued around the old town hall ready for the crypt gig. I remember a lot of aggro at first in the mosh pit, although it settled down. Moz was as flamboyant as ever and whipped us all into a frenzy. I think he enjoyed taunting us. That night opened my eyes… to live indie music and I've never deviated since. Morrissey is a modern day poet and his lyrical genius transcends generations since.

I WAS THERE: DEREK FARRELL, AGE 14

I discovered them whilst at school in in mid Eighties. I remember seeing them on the *Old Grey Whistle Test.* When I saw them, I actually ended up at the front of the stage despite having a ticket for the stalls. I did my paper round the next day in my tour t-shirt.

I WAS THERE: MALCOLM GREENLEY

The Middlesbrough gig was the best I ever saw them. That was when Craig Gannon was the fifth Smith for a short time. I thought they were at their absolute peak then live. They really were a strong unit. By then the notoriety and the controversy was well established. I think *The Queen Is Dead* went straight in the charts at number 2 and it must have been a couple of weeks after that so it was a charged atmosphere. It was a wild night, a really electrifying atmosphere.

I WAS THERE: JENNY GAUNT

I fell under the spell of The Smiths from the beginning. I heard 'Hand In Glove' played on the radio and I was mesmerised. I fell in love with Morrissey's voice straight away. His lyrics took the mundane and made it glamorous. I would pore over all the music weekly's for releases, news and tour dates. I dutifully recorded all their TV appearances, which I still have on VHS.

I saw them on three occasions, all at Middlesbrough Town Hall. There was an unspoken bond between the fans, which is just as well because I was 16, clumsy and shy - too shy speak to anyone! Everyone came together on many levels and the other chart acts were irrelevant to me. Morrissey was also a fellow vegetarian, which gave me a meaningful connection.

At the last gig I attended, I remember a fan clambering down the velvet curtains from one of the boxes, pulling the curtain down with him. Devotional chaos reigned! Then, whilst ascending the stairs, Johnny Marr and Angie were coming down but I didn't actually meet him. I just grinned and he grinned back. One day I might be lucky enough to meet him or Morrissey.

I am happy and proud to say I'm still under the influence of The Smiths and Morrissey to this day. I am still going to Morrissey, Johnny Marr and Mike Joyce gigs. I have a large collection of vinyl, ephemera, t-shirts, posters and collectibles from over the years. Each piece tells a tale and 'it's time the tale were told'!

CIVIC HALL

15 OCTOBER 1986, WOLVERHAMPTON, UK

I WAS THERE: HELEN HULSTON, AGE 21

There was quite a big group of us. I went with my brother, his two mates and my sister, all of whom would have been 18 at the time, and my partner at the time and his friend from school, who were 21. I bought us all tickets and remember going to the telephone box to find out who wanted me to get them. I still have my ticket. It cost £6.50!

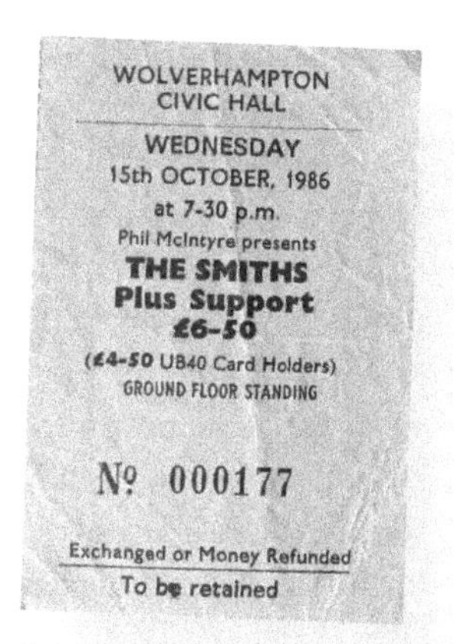

Helen Hulston's ticket for Wolverhampton Civic

I WAS THERE: NICK BARBER

I spent most of that gig near to the sound desk - I later picked up a video bootleg of the show, which seemed to have been recorded from the balcony. I was back at the Civic Hall for Morrissey's first solo gig but failed to get in - the venue was deemed full when I was about 30 people away from getting in. I did see Morrissey arrive and he appeared at a side window to wave to those outside.

I WAS THERE: CHRIS BUCKLEY

In the early Eighties I was a die hard fan of Paul Weller and The Jam. However, after they'd split up in 1982 he disappeared up himself - I soon became disenchanted with The Style Council! Gone were the guitars and great lyrics, which were replaced by keyboards and lyrics about long hot summers and being the best thing. I first heard of The Smiths from the John Peel radio show about 1983 and when I saw them on *Top of the Pops* with 'This Charming Man' I was hooked. I subsequently bought their LPs and played them to death. The media claimed Morrissey to be miserable and gloomy but I actually found his lyrics laugh out loud funny, and intelligent at the same time.

I managed to get tickets to the gig at Wolves Civic Hall and positioned myself on the upper balcony awaiting the start of the gig. Suddenly the lights went out and opera music played loudly for what seemed an eternity. Now this was different. The atmosphere was now electric and suddenly they were there on stage launching into 'The Queen Is Dead', complete with Mozzer swirling a noose around on stage and doing that disjointed awkward dance that he does. Song after song was played and I knew every song and lyric, and the crowd did too. Eventually the lights came on and it was time to go home with my ears ringing and my body dripping in sweat. I've seen many bands since this gig and none have ever come close - not even Morrissey solo.

I WAS THERE: MICHAEL BUSHELL

My wife and I saw them twice, on both the *Meat Is Murder* and *Queen Is Dead* tours. We saw the latter at Wolverhampton Civic Hall. We sat in the balcony and watched the writhing mass standing below us. It reminded me of the snake pit in *Raiders of the Lost Ark*! Simply put, this was the greatest night of my life. If I'd been told this was the Second Coming I'd have believed them.

For Michael and Patricia Bushell seeing The Smiths was like they had died and gone to heaven

We both remember the walls steaming as we came out (it was a cold night). They played for just over an hour and quite frankly I'm not sure we could stand any more. The intensity was overwhelming. I've seen hundreds of gigs and some very great artists at the top of their powers but absolutely nothing came anywhere close to this. By the time they got to 'I Know It's Over' I thought I'd actually died and gone to heaven. What amazes me is that when I talk to young music fans about what I've heard and who I've seen the number one thing I can tell them is what it was like to see The Smiths. As time moves on, they seem to rise and rise in the firmament of greatness and legend. That night in Wolverhampton is etched in my soul. At that point The Smiths were way beyond just being a band, they were a reason to live. Seeing The Smiths live has never been surpassed as the highlight of my life. My wife, I know, would say the same.

I WAS THERE: DAVE JONES

My girlfriend at the time was a massive Smiths fan as am I. We both regularly went to psychobilly gigs to see such bands as The Meteors and The Guana Batz. At those gigs the wreckin' (moshing) was violent and fierce, so we were prepared for a lively gig. The crowd was boisterous with fans climbing on to the stage to hug Morrissey. As the gig progressed, I launched Helen into a moshin melee. We sang along to all the hits, danced, moshed, jumped around and finally, as we left, purchased a massive Salford boys club poster from a street vendor. It remains easily the best gig I have attended.

I WAS THERE: JUSTIN WALSALL

I was at that gig. They did two encores. I remember the 'Draize Train' being one of the songs.

I WAS THERE: NICOLA WESTWOOD

The Smiths featured heavily in my teens, from that Friday night episode of *The Tube*, with the likely simpering introduction from the late Paula Yates, through to my doing extra shifts in my job as a cinema usherette to buy the first album. I felt I'd really found something, musically and aesthetically, that I completely got, and soon men's cardigans, shoes, old 501s and an insane quiff-and-plait combo, locked down with Elnette, was my daily garb, with the music of Morrissey and Marr being all I would listen too. I became 'that Smiths fan'.

I spent the summer of 1986 working in a bar in Sorrento in Italy, returned late August to Anita Dobson take on the *Eastenders* theme as number one, the sinking feeling I was back to school for last year of A levels soon and amazingly, to the news that The Smiths – my Smiths - were going to be playing at Wolverhampton Civic Hall, not 14 miles from my house. Now this was a time where buying tickets meant queuing in real time and getting in line early, with no presales or suchlike, and I remember the bus journey, the box office, the four tickets I had. The four tickets that I effortlessly resold to friends, one simply invited because he had a car to get us there and back.

I distinctly remember the night of the gig. I wore a dress from Miss Selfridges, shoes from a shop in Liverpool, big black clumpy brothel creepers, a faded tan and a gold bracelet I'd spent my summer wages on. Inside the venue it was packed, heaving with teenagers. I remember passing comment on how cramped and chaotic it was and someone said, 'Wait 'til they come on'.

I'd like to say I remember the gig minute to minute but I don't. Luckily for me, however, the gaps in set list and faded memories regarding atmosphere are filled with a YouTube video of the whole wonderful thing, from the infamous Profokiev walk on music, to Morrissey's 'Heeeeelllo' to... the end. Hot, sweaty, a lost gold bracelet but an 'I was there' storyline that, even over three decades later – and despite everything, Morrissey! - still results in a 'lucky you' from those that know or knew what The Smiths meant at that time.

I WAS THERE: MARK WILLIAMS

Personally, this was my favourite of the five concerts that I attended by The Smiths. Maybe it was also Morrissey's favoured venue as well, as he made his live solo debut here a couple of years later. The support act of the evening was a band called Raymonde who I was a fan of as well. The singer caught me singing along with a couple of their songs and gave me a nod in the audience. When they went off I necked a few pints as the bar ran along side of the concert hall. I never usually drink at any gigs as a rule, so I got caught out slightly when the Prokofiev intro began and the band struck up 'The Queen Is Dead' and I still had a pint in my hand. The lager was quickly drunk and I was soon in the thick of it at the front of the stage. The set list trundled along nicely with fans clambering on stage just for the slightest grasp of their heroes before they were led away. I was of course one of these folk and at my first attempt at accessing the stage I was unceremoniously pushed back in to the audience; only for me to get straight back up and successfully hug Morrissey before security put a hand on my shoulder to lead me off stage. I walked off friendly enough with him, with us both exchanging brief pleasantries until we got to the side of the stage were he gave me a push in my back as I ascended the narrow staircase down.

I landed at the bottom with no lasting injuries. But with my temper now riled I was determined he wasn't going to have the last laugh. So once again I got to the front of the crowd and urged them to push me up for a third time, just as the introduction to 'Bigmouth Strikes Again' rang out around the venue. The security man moved towards me again, but being a lad of quite a muscular stature, I told him in no uncertain terms what I was going to do to him if he laid his hand on me again. So we came to an amicable agreement and he let me stay on stage throughout the final song of the evening as long as I didn't interfere with their performance. Has any other fan singularly stayed on stage with them for so long apart from me? Thankfully this concert was recorded for posterity by someone in the crowd, so you can witness me on stage to the left of the stage throughout the length of the song. You can even see me asking for Andy Rourke's plectrum at the end, which he graciously gave me. I also got hold of the taped down set list off the stage of the gig, which I still have in my possession along with the Salford University one, which I acquired a few months earlier.

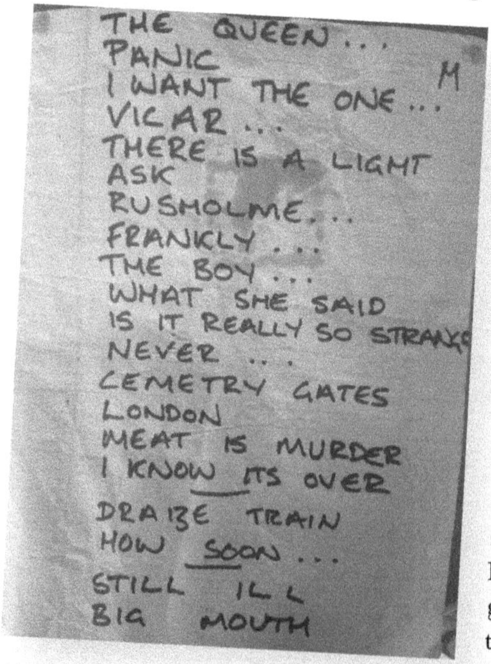

Mark Williams' set list liberated from the stage at the Wolverhampton Civic

CORNWALL COLISEUM

17 OCTOBER 1986,
ST AUSTELL, CORNWALL

I WAS THERE:
LEE TREWHELA, AGE 16

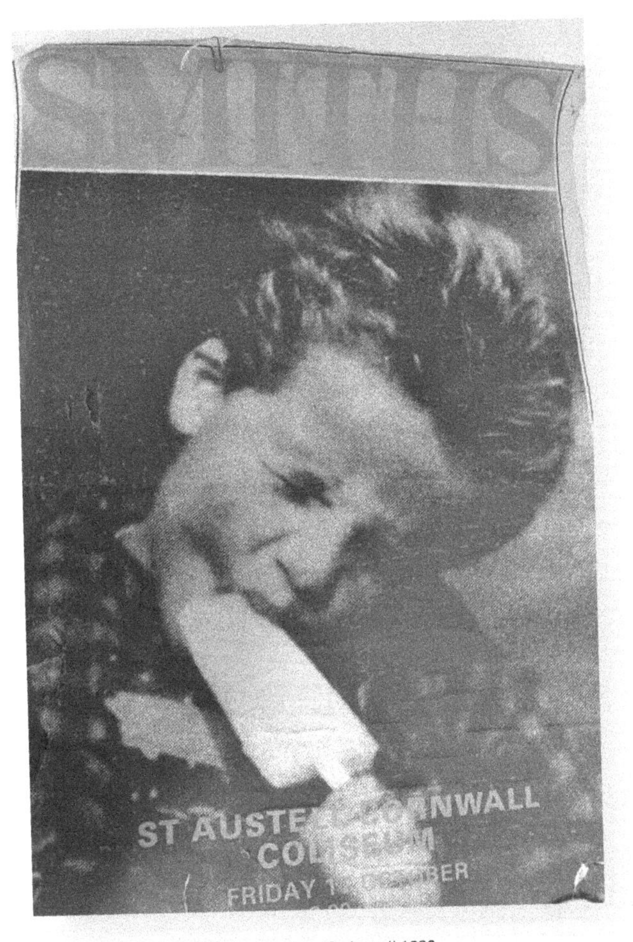

Poster for the Cornwall Coliseum gig in St Austell 1986

In some ways being a teenage Smiths fan in Cornwall was the epitome of what Morrissey was singing about - trapped and lovelorn at the arse of end of nowhere. Cornwall in the 21st century - all hipster restaurants and TV fame - is far from the county of the Eighties where there really was nothing to do.

So thank heavens for the Cornwall Coliseum - a legendary venue, long since scat down (as we say in these parts) which boasted every artist of the time from Adam and the Ants to X-Mal Deutschland.

You can imagine the joy of this flat-topped Smiths fanatic when the band played the cavernous venue at Carlyon Bay beach two weeks shy of my 17th birthday.

This was actually the second Coliseum appearance by The Smiths, them having previously played there in June 1984. No I didn't, and I don't know why now, but I wish I had. Anyway, the 1986 gig is still ingrained on my psyche with added Craig Gannon on guitar and James Maker on stupid dancing.

Morrissey strode on with his 'The Queen Is Dead' flag and there followed one of the most sublime concerts I've ever seen.

Highlights were many, of course, from the double opening whammy of 'The Queen Is Dead' and 'Panic' to the thrill of hearing 'His Latest Flame' meshed with 'Rusholme Ruffians'. Surely any Smiths concert which featured 'There is a Light That Never Goes Out' - tossed away too early as the fifth song - 'The Boy With The Thorn in his Side', 'Meat Is Murder', 'Bigmouth Strikes Again', 'I Know It's Over', 'How Soon Is Now?' and 'Still Ill' has to go down in history? They even played my favourite, the steaming and storming 'London'.

I had to wait another 20 years before anything remotely Smiths-related returned to Kernow - Morrissey played a solo show at the Hall for Cornwall in 2006. By this time I was a reporter so how gleeful was I when he refused to play unless the daytime farmers' market in the venue removed all its meat. In fact, he bought it all and had it sent to a local homeless shelter. It's easy to forget now, but he could be loveable. It gave me a national story and a memorable birthday stay in Cornwall for Moz, who still seemed on a high from his celebrations the night before.

I WAS THERE: PAUL ASPLIN

I caught them twice on the *Queen Is Dead* tour. I was due to go backstage afterwards at St Austell but due to some issue with Raymonde and their dressing room the chance of a lifetime was cancelled. I remember James Maker appearing on stage. It was a chaotic evening. It was my first Smiths gig and I spent it down the front. From what I remember there was a bit of a dressing room 'rearrangement' by Raymonde and the management were trying to sort it out so my visit was called off.

Very annoying. Although not quite as annoying as getting an invite to appear in the 'Stop Me If You Think....' video and for a number of reasons not being able to.

I WAS THERE: NICK BYRNE, AGE 17

Me and my mate Hag were big Smiths fans and we saw them at Cornwall Coliseum in 1986. We were down the front and it was amazing. There was a fantastic atmosphere of togetherness. They were a wonderful band and it was a wonderful night which I will remember for evermore.

I WAS THERE: MIKE CRAIG

Me and a mate drove down in an open top Triumph Spitfire. We didn't have tickets. My mate was in the army and had just got back. We went down and paid on the door. Coming out, the handbrake broke on the steep hill out of the venue and I had to get out and hold the car while he got it back into gear and then jump in as he was moving.

I WAS THERE: ROGER ROWE

Some mates of mine ransacked some poor sod's garden and sold the flowers in the car park because Morrissey had just been on *Top of the Pops* with flowers in the back pocket of his Levi's.

I WAS THERE: RACHEL SARA

I saw them at Cornwall Coliseum in 1986 on the *Queen Is Dead* tour. I was in love with Johnny Marr and I took a photo and he saw the flash and waved at me!

LEISURE CENTRE

18 OCTOBER 1986, GLOUCESTER, UK

Kate Arnold witnessed a post-gig traffic jam

I WAS THERE: KATE ARNOLD

Still my best gig entrance ever. The drum intro to 'The Queen Is Dead' and Morrissey dancing in from stage left brandishing a placard with the title of the song on and - I think, although I might be making this up - a noose around his neck. I still see this every time I hear that intro. Other than that, although I know I enjoyed the actual gig (of course I did, despite the fact that the acoustics in that hall were always – always! - piss poor) the best thing was that as we left the Leisure Centre afterwards, which was never really set up for gigs at the best of times, their tour bus had got blocked in in the car park, so they hadn't been able to make a swift exit before we all poured out. The curtains stayed firmly closed for a while (and I don't blame them to be honest because word got round pretty quick). But then Johnny Marr whipped back his curtain to wave and smile. He was with a lady - I guess it was his wife. Then he whipped back another curtain to show us a cowering - and unimpressed - Morrissey, with his glasses back on. I felt for him, I really did. Luckily for him, cars were moved and they were soon able to get away. He still came back though. I saw him there a few years later, around 1991.

I WAS THERE: JUSTIN BURTON

I saw them a few times. When I saw them in Gloucester it was amazing, and to this day I don't think there's a band lyrically that can beat them. Morrissey was a lyrical genius and Johnny Marr's guitar riffs are just amazing. I was about 14 or 15 the first time I saw them. Me and a great friend of mine, Andy Fox, went to several gigs. Not only did we see The Smiths but we also saw The Cure and The Pogues and U2 on the Joshua Tree tour at Wembley with Chrissie Hynde and The Pretenders as the support act.

Justin Burton saw The Smiths in Gloucester

GLOUCESTER LEISURE CENTRE
Bruton Way, Gloucester
MAIN HALL
Phil McIntyre presents
THE SMITHS
plus support
Saturday 18th October 1986
Doors Open 7.00
TICKET £6.50
(£4.50 on production of UB.40 card)
STANDING
№ 1436
TO BE RETAINED
exchanged or money refunded

Justin Burton's ticket for the Gloucester gig

NEWPORT LEISURE CENTRE

19 OCTOBER 1986, NEWPORT, UK

I WAS THERE: GREG ARCHER

The Newport Centre gig was unfortunately memorable for all the wrong reasons. Sadly some clown in the audience tried to pull Morrissey into the crowd. The band played a couple of instrumentals whilst Morrissey composed himself, but the announcement that he wouldn't be returning to the stage led to a riot inside the venue which ruined what should have been a magical night.

I WAS THERE: DEBORAH PENHALLURICK, AGE 17

I got into The Smiths as an impressionable 16 year old. I remember thinking how cool they looked on *Top Of The Pops* with Morrissey dancing around with bunches of flowers in his back pocket. It was just so different to all the pop that was in the charts at that time.

Deborah Penhallurick saw The Smiths at Newport. But only briefly

I bought the albums on cassette (I didn't get much pocket money). I've still got *Hatful of Hollow*. I don't know what happened to the others. I'd spend hours in my bedroom listening to them. The tunes were so catchy and the lyrics were so meaningful.

I had never been to a concert before and my mum didn't want me to go. My older brother was a music fan and assured my mum that there was never any trouble at concerts so she agreed to let me go and I arranged to go with my friend, Debbie Ascough. Well, that concert turned out to be pretty legendary as Morrissey was pulled off stage after a few songs, refused to come back on and a riot broke out.

I can't remember how far on they got before Morrissey was pulled off but until then I was in awe of it all. The crowd was quite aggressive anyway as I remember, and kind of intense. I fixated on Johnny Marr. He was so cool - and still is!

Halfway through 'The Boy With the Thorn in his Side', Morrissey shook hands with the crowd at the front and they yanked him in. He was down for a fair while it seemed before security got him out. So he went off stage and the band kept playing for a while. The crowd were chanting for Morrissey but after a while it became apparent that he wasn't coming back on. The aggression in the crowd intensified and all hell broke loose. As a sensible 17 year old girl I got myself out of there. I think we went home on the bus.

I can remember being really disappointed that it finished early and didn't think much more of it. When I got home my poor mother was panic-stricken. No mobiles in those days and the news had reported a riot there. I still love The Smiths music and still follow Johnny Marr. The highlight of my Glastonbury in 2019 was The Killers playing 'This Charming Man' on the Pyramid stage with Johnny. And, of course, Johnny's own set!

I WAS THERE: TIM GAMLIN, AGE 21

I remember seeing them in 1983 at the Derby Assembly Rooms on an *Old Grey Whistle Test* special on TV. It was mad because the stage was full of fans. I had never heard of them so I thought I would check them out and after watching it that was it - I was hooked!

I saw them live the following year in the student's union in Cardiff and again in 1986 on the *Queen Is Dead* tour in my hometown of Newport in Wales. After five or six songs Morrissey was dragged off the stage. Then all hell broke loose.

I WAS THERE: PHILIP HOLLEY

I remember attending that gig with my wife. We stood at the back of the concert hall at the top of the stairs. We seemed to be waiting quite some time and then suddenly taped music began to build up and a bank of lights spun around to face the crowd. People started cheering and then on came the band, followed by Morrissey. The band started playing and Morrissey began leaning out into the crowd, handing out flowers. Whether he lost his balance or was pulled he tumbled into the crowd who immediately started crowd surfing him. The next thing I remember seeing was a roadie run across the stage and launch himself into the crowd. Unfortunately he landed on top of Morrissey and they both disappeared into the crowd. Several seconds later Morrissey was thrown from the crowd back onto the stage. All this time the band continued to play. Morrissey was led from the stage by a roadie and the band played on and on and on.

An announcement was then made that Morrissey would not be returning to the stage and the band walked off. The crowd started booing and throwing things at the roadies as they unplugged the equipment, I'm not sure if the roadies retaliated but several of the crowd climbed onto the stage and started fighting with the roadies. Next thing I saw was the side doors open and police pouring in and moving people out of the auditorium. No refund was ever given.

Whatever happened to 'the show must go on' ethos? The big Jessie.

I WAS THERE: DARREN JONES, AGE 20

I was really excited as my mate had seen them in Gloucester the night before and told me 'Meat Is Murder' was awesome. Legend has it that Morrissey was pulled off the stage as they came on and they refused to continue, but that's not true. They got a good few songs in before that happened - maybe 40 minutes – and then he was grabbed, there was a lot of argy bargy and the lights went up and we realised that was it.

I WAS THERE: RHYDDIAN LEWIS, AGE 20

I went with a few of my friends who unfortunately have passed away. The Smiths had not long come on when Morrissey slipped or was pulled off and fell into the crowd. He refused to come back on and a riot then ensued, with speakers and drinks being thrown. That was when we left. The next day *The Sun* said the riot happened due to the name of the tour.

I WAS THERE: ALLAN PETRIE

After Cardiff in 1984, I remember being on the dole for five months, playing darts in my bedroom and listening over and over to *Meat Is Murder* on vinyl on my little record player. Some of the lyrics inspired me to write poetry.

Around 10 songs in, Morrissey was shaking people's hands whilst singing and was dragged to the floor and had to be carried off the stage. The band played an instrumental whilst we waited for Morrissey to return and a guy came on stage to say Morrissey would be back on soon. Another announcement was made a short time after and the gig was abandoned as Morrissey was taken to hospital.

I remember all hell breaking out, people starting throwing stuff and being jostled by the police, who were called as a mini riot broke out.

Later on I met a girl from Gloucester who worked at a local hotel and she got me each of the band's room cards with their names on them from when they stayed and played in Gloucester.

I WAS THERE: MARCUS PONTING

The only time I got to see The Smiths the gig ended with a riot and with Morrissey in hospital. It's the most important gig I've ever been to. It was perfect until over enthusiasm on the front row caused a delay - they played The Fall during the break - and then cancellation. The riot then ensued. I bought a huge *The Queen Is Dead* poster and went home.

I WAS THERE: JONATHAN JONES

He was touching hands with the crowd and someone pulled him in. I think the riot started because of the announcements that were made saying the band would be back on shortly. I remember seeing a report in *The Sun* saying angry royalists had dragged Morrissey off stage and then rioted. They always have talked out of their arse. And it's still one of the best gigs I've been to!

I WAS THERE: MATTHEW WILCE

Riot! Our love for The Smiths was gushing, like many at that time. Still is now, regardless of silly old Moz nowadays. Nice seat. No way am I going down the front for this one. I'm watching everything. Marr... jeez, you don't get this in Newport, Morrissey... the same. Rourke, Joyce? Wow. Take me back to dear ol' blighty.....drums kick in...fuck that, I'm off to the pit. 'Queen Is Dead', 'Frankly, Mr Shankly', 'Panic', etc., etc. Bliss. Some dickhead pulls Morrissey in. Landed close by and looked a little bit shocked. Bouncers jumped in, got him out. Band played on. Three instrumentals, I think? Someone came out to tell us gig was over. Bottles flew, monitors were trashed. Newport was angry. We were done by some dickhead. It was still one of the greatest gigs I've seen and probably due to the notoriety, the most memorable. Long live The Smiths.

I WAS THERE: ANDY WAINWIGHT

I was there with my now wife. The band came on and played a stunning set for 20 to 30 minutes with Morrissey on top form. At the end of one number he dived into the audience. The band seemed nonplussed, as if it was expected, and launched into an instrumental (possibly 'How Soon Is Now?'). Johnny Marr kept the band going with further instrumentals. After what seemed like an age but could have been just a short while, and with no sign of Morrissey, they left the stage. The lights came up and it was announced that Morrissey had been injured and the concert would not be continuing. I seem to recall a general feeling of deflation and there may have been some jeering. Upon leaving, it was noticeable that there was a large police presence outside. I suspect they were expecting some angry punters but I can't recall anything untoward happening.

'ASK'

RELEASED 20 OCTOBER 1986

'Ask' reached number 14. Craig Gannon claimed credit for the chord structure.

ROYAL CONCERT HALL

21 OCTOBER 1986, NOTTINGHAM, UK

I WAS THERE: JOHN GOODWIN

The sound was powerful with the addition of Gannon but he was a supporting player and never a real member of The Smiths. I bought a peachy/pink t-shirt with a boy sucking on an ice-lolly.

I WAS THERE: ADRIAN KEELING

After seeing them in Sheffield in January 1984, I bought everything - record, import, etc. - that I could find and afford. I ended up at Nottingham Trent and they were playing the Royal Concert Hall there in my first week. A mate on the course asked if I wanted to try and get tickets, so we went on the day in the afternoon and got some returns. It was a great gig, which is available on YouTube, filmed from behind the stage so you can see a lot of the audience. I'm not on that video, but there are a couple of girls that danced on stage at the end. We saw them in town the next day and ended spending most of the afternoon with them.

I WAS THERE: JACKIE NUTTY

As for many of my peers, The Smiths were part of my formative years and I was already pretty obsessed with them for about two years by the time I'd purchased tickets. I'd seen a few other bands at the Royal Concert Hall in Nottingham, an all seater venue that you wouldn't normally associate with a band like The Smiths. The atmosphere that night was what can only be described as charged, something I'd not been used to at the previous gigs I'd attended.

Most of my friends were obsessed with Morrissey, but I'd always been more interested in the stylish guitarist Johnny Marr and with my hero just a few feet in front of me I was transfixed in awe at both his musical ability and also his effortlessly cool style.

With the passionate performance from Morrissey and the steady heartbeat and pulse of the percussion of Mike Joyce and Andy Rourke, the melodic, euphoric riffs of Marr were just rapturous.

Towards the end of the gig, during 'The Boy with the Thorn in his Side', some people in the first few rows decide to invade the stage and I decided this was my only chance to share the stage with my heroes. What could possibly go wrong?

With trepidation, I put my foot on the chair in front of me, lost my balance and grabbed the nearest thing to me to break my fall. I looked up in horror as I saw the thing I had grabbed to stop my fall was – Johnny's foot! I swiftly let go and ended up in an ungainly heap on the floor. Not exactly the cool impression I'd intended to make.

It'd be 27 years before I came face to face with Johnny again. When the time came and I met my hero, I quite wisely I kept quiet about my failed attempt at a stage invasion.

NATIONAL BALLROOM

23 OCTOBER 1986, KILBURN, LONDON, UK

Andrew Maltman (rear centre, here with The Black Cillas) was at the Kilburn National Ballroom

I WAS THERE: ANDREW MALTMAN, AGE 31

I was 31 at the time I went to see The Smiths. Suddenly they'd seemed to be all over television. I used to watch an early evening programme called *The Tube*. In 1984 they featured The Smiths performing 'Hand In Glove', 'Still Ill' and 'Barbarism Begins at Home'. On other shows such as *Top of the Pops* and the *Oxford Road Show* they had mimed early singles but on *The Tube* they played live and their true capabilities shone out bright and clear.

My own experience of their influence began in 1985 when I was lured into a London-based band on the promise of a guaranteed gig at the famous Marquee Club. After that we settled for the name Black Cillas and began playing regularly at the Bull and Gate in Kentish Town and got a couple of reviews in *Melody Maker* and *NME*. Our sound was heavily based on what is now termed jangle pop ('the sound of 86') and it was hardly surprising when we were compared with The Smiths, either favourably or unfavourably. I used to go to gigs with our bass player Ben Bartlett. We saw such bands as The Fall, The Cramps, Iggy Pop, etc. There was a bit of a rush for Smiths tickets when they played Kilburn National Ballroom in '86 but we somehow got lucky. My diary records the venue as being 'grossly overcrowded and taking ages to get back out via inadequate stairs/exits'. The reward was seeing the five piece version of The Smiths going full tilt. The second guitar seemed to give them more of a huge wall of sound rather than any extra dimension but that probably had more to do with the acoustics and sound system at the venue. (Ben and I both thought the PA system looked a bit undersized). Morrissey surprised me when he first walked on stage. I'd expected him to politely mutter a few brief greetings but he barked a very deep "ello' at the audience. They launched into a powerhouse set and played all their crowd pleaser numbers toward the end of an exhaustive 90 minutes. No one went home disappointed that night.

I WAS THERE: STEVE BROWN

My aforementioned mates Kev and Lee, the Hacienda members, now had a band together called Soil. Their drummer lived in Stretford and was friendly with a band from around there called Easterhouse, who were apparently friendly with Morrissey and/or Johnny Marr, so Soil ended up getting a gig supporting The Smiths at Kilburn Ballroom in north London. Me and a couple of other mates jumped at the chance to be roadies, so we all went down to London in the archetypal battered Ford Transit. We were in the support band's little dressing room when we heard The Smiths were sound checking, so a couple of us went out to have a look.

It was a typical boring sound check – 'one two, one two' and endless banging on the bass drum. Morrissey was stood in the hall a few yards in front of the stage, watching the rest of the band do their thing. I was in a band myself throughout the Eighties and always carried a demo tape around. This was a chance I couldn't miss! I walked over, legs shaking, and said that we wanted to support The Smiths as well, and gave him the tape. I felt guilty about intruding on him but he didn't seem bothered. He was exactly as he came across in TV interviews, a little bit inscrutable; he said, 'Well I'll certainly give it a listen' in that polite, vaguely arch way, head slightly on one side. I don't think he recognised me from the Salford stage, well if he did he didn't say so!

I was desperate to tell him what a hero he was and all that, but I thought he'd probably have heard that stuff a million times before, and I didn't want to start gushing. When time came for Morrissey to sound check, a roadie politely told us to make ourselves scarce. We never heard anything back about the demo tape. I wonder if he's still got it or whether it went straight into some landfill?

I was privileged to be given the job of operating Soil's slide projector on stage, projecting pictures of completely random things such as parsnips, Kev's cat (Henry), etc., etc. onto the backdrop behind the drums. Before Soil went on I crept onto the side of the stage, stooping and trying not to be noticed. I'd been going to gigs since I was 14 and always stared at the roadies doing whatever technical jobs, a little bit awestruck. Now I glanced around and realised that hundreds of people in this big, elegant theatre were looking up at me on this huge stage under the lights. I was desperate to just stand up and look back at all of them and take all of it in, but I had a job to do and I was supposed to be inconspicuous, so I restrained myself. There were a load of BBC vans outside when we came out after the gig, they'd been recording it, and a few months later it was released as the live album, *Rank*.

We stayed the night at Soil's singers' parents' house in Essex. Driving back there in the early hours, I was in the back, sandwiched between the amps. We were going round a roundabout somewhere east of London when one of the back doors of the old knackered Transit flew open and the snare drum, which Soil had borrowed from another Stretford band called The Valentines, went rolling out into the road. I shouted, 'Whoaah - pull over!' Whoever was driving did a U-turn and as we were going back round the roundabout a car in front of us stopped, the door flew open and an arm reached out and pulled the upended snare drum into the car, and the car shot off! There was no way the Transit was catching up, so all we could do was swear loudly in profuse disbelief. I couldn't help stifling a laugh actually; I didn't have to pay to replace it.

I wasn't too surprised when The Smiths split up a few months later; as far as a fan like me could see they always seemed too honest and true to themselves to be dragging the band on past its peak. I admit to feeling very slightly betrayed when they got a second guitarist in. Nothing against Craig Gannon, I actually became friendly with him a year or two later when Lee and Craig both joined a sort of Manchester super group called The Cradle, and then my band played on the same bill as Craig's next group, The Family Way. He was a really nice guy. But you know how it is when you're young and a band you've grown up with, and feel very close to, changes the magic formula; you take it a little personally. Anyway when *Strangeways* came out, although I thought I'd now left The Smiths behind, I couldn't hold myself back and I bought it out of a burning curiosity. I was glad I did; it's brilliant basically - the tunes, the savagely funny lyrics. I almost want to say it's better than the first album, but that first album occupied a magical moment in my life.

In my reckoning they went out on a high and left a fantastic and important legacy. It must have been '88 when I was in the Hacienda on one of those great Thursday student nights, the place now pretty full and on an upward curve. The mix of funk, hip-hop and indie halted for half an hour while the deejay played back-to-back Smiths. There was a crowd of younger people, the lads with hair shaved at the back and quiffs at the front, and wire-framed glasses, going mental. Apparently it was some sort of organised trip to Manchester for Smiths fans, possibly from somewhere in Europe. I stopped dancing and just soaked up the music. What made me really happy was about 25 years later, when my oldest son got into The Smiths at around the age of 15 and totally unprompted from me. One of my younger sons also started listening to them a couple of years later; they were on their own journeys of discovery just like I had been and I envied them, they were hearing all that stuff for the first time. Discussing the music with the two of them gave me quite a buzz, and made me remember how special that music was to me.

I WAS THERE: STEVE CATTERALL

I had never been to the National Ballroom in Kilburn before, so I had no idea what to expect with security and hall layout. But I wanted to try and film all three of the London dates, so I brought my camera along anyway. I went up to Paul's place in Kentish Town first, and we went across to Kilburn together. The hall was on the High Road with the entrance on a corner. It looked like an old concert hall. We hung around outside on the street, watching as the people filed in to see what security was like. It didn't look good. Everyone was having to show their tickets as they first entered the building and then they were frisked. We waited for quite some time, hoping that somehow things might get a bit more lax as we got closer to show time. Eventually there was no time left, so we made our move. I handed in my ticket and flashed my out-of-date Access All Areas pass - and they waved me through without blinking. I'm starting to believe this pass will always work... I shouldn't worry so much about it.

But now there's not much time before the show starts and I've no idea where I can film from. I go upstairs - the balcony seems the best bet. It's a big D-shaped balcony, with seats all around. Most people are seated, but there are already a number of people loitering at the edge of the balcony. There's an aisle right down the middle and some space down at the front. The lights go down and the 'Romeo and Juliet' intro starts up. We dash down the aisle to the front and squeeze into a space. I'm almost dead centre and in a pretty much perfect position to film, although there's nowhere to easily rest the camera, and there's a fair bit of jostling. But there's no time to worry and out comes the camera and on it goes. I start filming just as the intro to 'The Queen Is Dead' starts up.

It's not a bad film. A bit shaky at the start and there's a lot more of just straight shots of Morrissey. The filming position I had gave me a great view, but wasn't ideal for handling the camera - it wasn't always easy to see the viewfinder without the picture shaking, so I tended to set up a shot and try and keep the camera steady for as long as I could. This meant that the film doesn't follow the action as well as some of the other ones.

The show itself was good. London dates are always a bit funny, as there's an element of 'come on impress us' in the crowd, which you don't tend to get out of the capital. So the crowd tend to hold back a little. But as Johnny said, there hasn't been a bad Smiths gig, and this one has its moments. Morrissey is on good form with his in-between song comments and there's a great version of 'I Know It's Over'.

I WAS THERE: ROBERTO FERDENZI

I saw The Smiths play live three times, all in '86. I saw them at the Kilburn National Ballroom, the following night at the Brixton Academy and finally their last ever live gig at the Brixton Academy. What more can I say other than that they were the best three live gigs I have ever seen - just magical. I couldn't believe I was seeing my musical

Roberto Ferdenzi saw the last three London shows The Smiths ever played

icons and heroes in the flesh. The memory of those three shows will live with me forever, especially the first one, as this was the very first live gig I ever attended. The third one, of course, turned out to be their last ever gig, although, no one knew this at the time.

BRIXTON ACADEMY

24 OCTOBER 1986, LONDON, UK

I WAS THERE: ANDREW FURTEK

There was no support band, just what seemed like an eternity of George Formby. Then the band came on. I've been to many gigs but this gig was - and still is - the best I've ever been to. They were incredible live, with such power, poise and passion. It was mesmerising. I'm so glad I saw them. They split soon after.

I WAS THERE: KELVIN BILLING

I loved every minute, from 'Why Don't Women Like Me?' by George Formby and then the volume was turned up for Prokofiev and then on they came. It was just pure energy, with a writhing mass of bodies almost in one. At times you could take both feet of the floor and still be carried around in the mass. My only disappointment was that they didn't play 'Barbarism', but it is an evening I'll never forget. 1986 seems so long ago.

I WAS THERE: TIM MARTIN

I still have the ticket stub. They came on to 'Take Me Back to Dear Old Blighty'. For 'Hang the DJ' ('Panic'), Morrissey had a noose spinning above his head. There were flowers in the back pocket. I think the album was a big influence over me. It changed my mood. But now I look for more positive, simpler sounding things. But I remember that evening. For those two hours I really thought I was at the centre of the world.

I WAS THERE: DAVID BEARDMORE

I saw them at the National in Kilburn, which was recorded as the *Rank* album, and two or three times at the Brixton Academy, including their last ever gig. I also saw them at the Hammersmith Palais and at the Free Trade Hall in Manchester. I remember seeing 'Hand in Glove' on *Top of the Pops*. It was like seeing David Bowie playing 'Starman' 10 years earlier. That was a major moment. I was 15 then. I think the first single I got was the seven inch 'Hand in Glove'.

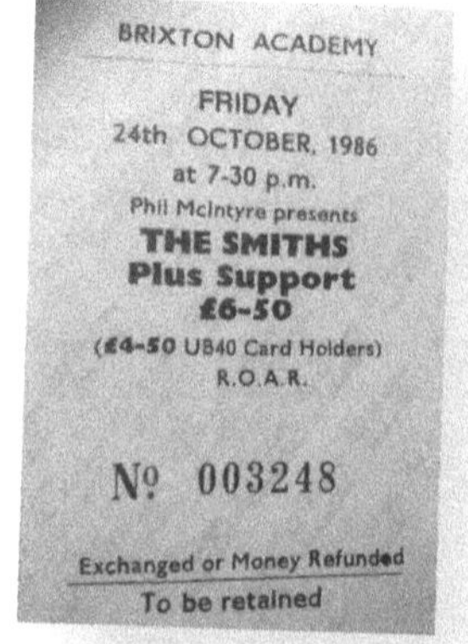

David Beardmore saw the Brixton Queen Is Dead show

I was going to loads of gigs. I probably went to a gig once a week ever since I was at college. I moved to London when I was 18 and spent all my working life in London. In Manchester I used to go to lots of gigs in the early Seventies - some heavy rock stuff like Deep

Purple, Wishbone Ash, Yes, Emerson, Lake and Palmer and all that kind of stuff. I saw David Bowie on the Ziggy Stardust tour at the Hardrock in Manchester before he 'killed himself' at Hammersmith which is one of the most amazing gigs in my life. I saw Lou Reed there. He came on stage about midnight and I had to leave before he finished because I was 16 or 17 and had to get home. I saw the Sensational Alex Harvey Band. And I saw Elton John there when he was good. The Hardrock was a cracking venue. It used to be a ten pin bowling alley. The ceiling was quite low. There was an electronic wall that slowly turned around that turned it into a discotheque, as they were called then.

I don't know what it was about The Smiths that attracted me to them. They just sounded great, you know? Great lyrics. I always found them very funny, and I liked all the artwork with all the northern aspect to it. Two or three of us used to go to gigs. We went to Brixton Academy and when we got inside the auditorium there was a guy selling spliffs quite openly for a quid: 'Do you want to buy a ready-rolled spliff?' They were always very raucous gigs. But never much more than an hour.

We had seats at the Free Trade hall. That was a very bouncy gig. I was sat next to a younger couple and Sandie Shaw came on to do 'Hand in Glove' with them. The girl was saying, 'Who's that? Who's that?' And of course it was obvious to me. It was Sandie Shaw!

LONDON PALLADIUM

26 OCTOBER 1986, LONDON, UK

I WAS THERE: ALAN HAMMETT

The last time I saw them was at the London Palladium although I didn't ever think this would be the last time I saw them live. They were now a five piece with Craig Cannon joining. This seemed to give Johnny Marr even more confidence, as he seemed to be dancing and smoking more on stage. Also Morrissey had his props - the rope for 'Hang the DJ' from 'Panic' and his 'The Queen Is Dead' placard. They both seemed to be having a lot of fun on stage and they were sounding better than ever. But only nine months later they'd split up although they did leave us with another great album in *Strangeways, Here We Come*. It was a shame they didn't get to tour this live!

I WAS THERE: PAUL WHITE

Sadly my ticket has long since disappeared but not the memory of the gig. Nor the excitement of the first day of each single release to see what the cover pic was.

I WAS THERE: PETER MARTIN

The final time I saw The Smiths. Obviously I didn't realise this at the time. We drove down to London and spent most of the day trying to get tickets. We thought Johnny had let us down so managed to get tickets from the people hanging around all day. Then when the Palladium opened we were told that there were four on the door for us. Much to their surprise and joy we gave our tickets to the people we'd met during the day who hadn't managed to get sorted. An all seater venue was never going to be the best but Morrissey was on top form and it was good to actually watch the boys perform rather than spend the whole gig just trying to stand up and breathe, as a lot of the previous ones had been about.

After the curtailed performance at Newport in South Wales, the Preston Guild Hall gig saw the fans getting less than they'd bargained for.

GUILD HALL

27 OCTOBER 1986, PRESTON, UK

I WAS THERE: MARCUS PARNELL, AGE 22

I got a call on the day of the gig at about five o'clock off a friend who's no longer with us, Gary Barton. His mother worked in the box office at the Guild Hall. He said his mum had sorted us out a couple of passes, in return for which we had to watch the fire escapes to make sure people weren't opening the doors to let their mates in. I'm pretty bloody sure it was sold out and that there were a lot of people milling around outside and trying to sneak in. And lo and behold they were on – and they were offand it was all over before it began. I didn't see what had happened. People said it was a two pence coin that had been cut down. I am not 100 per cent whether he got hit by anything. There was a lot of confusion about whether he was going to come back on again. 20 minutes later we got the announcement that they wouldn't be coming back on and that was it. Everybody was up in arms. There was lots of booingand fire extinguishers were let off. But the lights were all up and that was it. Gone. Finished. Done. People went around picking up ticket stubs off the floor to get the money back.I've heard stories since that they'd been at the Guild Hall in the afternoon, then gone back to the Midland Hotel in Manchester and been signed up to do some big American tour, and they didn't want to do the Preston show after that.

I WAS THERE: LEN KENNEDY, AGE 18

I was 18. The Smiths were, quite simply, everything to me. My clothes, my hair, my music, my films, my books - all on prescription from Morrissey. For some reason, Liverpool was omitted from the *Queen Is Dead* tour. This was odd as The Smiths had always had a great relationship with the city. This meant for me and my fellow Smiths acolyte Kenny a trip to North Wales or Preston. Either way we were going to miss the last train home. But who cares? A night sleeping rough would be worth it for the euphoric evening of Smiths that lay ahead...

I WAS THERE: MARK BICKERDIKE

Absolute madness ensued for at least a minute or so when the intro music stopped and the next thing we knew the band had walked off stage, never to return, Morrissey (apparently) being the victim of an item thrown from the crowd. I was absolutely gutted. It was made even more uncomfortable by having to suffer the support band Raymonde.

I WAS THERE: CAROLINE ALLEN

I didn't really see them properly this time because it's when Morrissey went off after the first song. This was a big deal for us because we were only 16. We didn't travel very far and we'd gone to Preston, which seemed like miles away to us at the time.

But we thought, 'We want to see them again', and we'd heard that this other gig had been cancelled so we didn't even know if it was going to go ahead.

We got front row position again, and it would have been just brilliant because, if he hadn't have gone off, it would have been the perfect gig. Because we had a brilliant spot and we weren't too crushed and we had just a brilliant view. I don't know to this day what it was that hit him. But he wasn't coming back on.

People say it was a coin. I don't know. When he went off we thought, 'There's no way he's going to go away for good. He'll come back on.' And he just didn't, and we were absolutely devastated. We were absolutely gutted.

It kicked off a little bit when Morrissey wouldn't come back on. The crowd were really shouting and were getting quite angry. The atmosphere definitely took a turn for the worse when he didn't come back on.

MY SISTER WAS THERE: EMILY KELLY

My friend Jane was at the Preston Smiths gig with my sister Louisa (Whizz), who recalls the gig starting and people throwing items at the stage from the beginning. At some point someone threw a 50p (the press described it after as a sharpened 50p) at Morrissey, which hit him in the face. He then walked off stage and didn't return. Preston Guild Hall, where the event was held, told the audience that if they had their ticket stubs they could get their money back. There was then a scramble on the floor for ticket stubs!

FREE TRADE HALL

30 OCTOBER 1986, MANCHESTER, UK

I WAS THERE: CAROLINE ALLEN

After Preston there were rumours that it might not go ahead so we were absolutely panicking. But it did. We had pretty bad tickets for this one. We

Preston - Whizz (left) and Jane witnessed a mad scramble for discarded tickets at Preston Guild Hall

were in the side circle, so we didn't have the best view of the stage. But we hung around outside the stage door before to see them arriving - we always used to do that - so we saw them all when they came in.

There was a lovely crowd of people outside the Free Trade Hall, at the back door as well, some of whom didn't have tickets. We were all chatting. These girls who were there were gutted that they didn't have tickets themselves but they were saying, 'Have a brilliant time, we really hope you have a good time.' They couldn't get tickets and they'd never seen The Smiths live, but they weren't jealous. We bought Johnny Marr some socks as a birthday present and we managed to give it to him as he was walking in. I don't know what we were thinking.

We met Johnny a few weeks later, because these girls we were talking to at the gig had told us, 'Johnny lives here' and 'Andy lives there'. They basically told us where they all lived. One Saturday a few weeks later, me and Nicky and Jenny decided to go to Altrincham hoping we might bump into one of the Smiths and by chance we bumped into these girls, so they showed us where the band all lived, and the week after we went back to Johnny Marr's house.

We were naughty. We just sat outside, like teenage fans do. Mike Joyce pulled up in his car and went into Johnny's and Johnny came out and we spent ages chatting to Johnny and Mike. Johnny remembered the socks that we bought him and said they were a bit small. Because he's only quite small, we thought he had small feet as well.

The Free Trade Hall gig was absolutely brilliant. Nothing ever touched Salford, but that was a brilliant atmosphere as well. And I didn't realise that was the last time I'd ever see them live.

I WAS THERE: CRAIG MULHERN, AGE 16

I couldn't believe my luck. I was staring at the poster in the shop window of EGS Records in Wakefield, which advertised gig tickets for sale. There it was, The Smiths. From memory, the tickets were £12 each including £5 coach travel from The Spaniard pub in Wakefield. Or were they £12 plus £5 coach travel? I've slept since then. My favourite time of the year, leading up to Bonfire Night - the clear starry skies and the smell. I love that smell, I can't explain it. I had to go in and check to see if they had any tickets still available.

I'd just come out of my many years of shyness, though I still felt a little shy from time to time, no idea why. I had recently discovered girls. Up to that point I'd always been into football, climbing trees, playing conkers and doing other lad-type things that boys did at that age. I nearly wet myself with excitement when the shop assistant told me they had a few tickets left, though I felt shy as hell, but excited in anticipation at the same time asking them. 'I'll be right back,' I said, 'I need to go see how much money I can withdraw from my account. Please save two, I'll be five minutes.'

I had just enough money in my account to buy three. I was shaking when the bank machine gave me my money. I couldn't get back to EGS fast enough. 'Three tickets please,' I said. I cradled them like gold all the way back on the 485 bus to Ackworth.

I was sweet 16, still at school, and had got into The Smiths about a year before. My mum still reminds me to this day that she was so pleased when I left home that she wouldn't have to listen to another Smiths song again, only then to pull her hair out when one of my younger brothers started listening to them when I left.

I guess Morrissey, along with several Leeds United football players, was my idol. I tried to dress like him. He was the coolest person on the planet when I saw a picture of him in a pair of white Levi 501s. I owned a long red woollen cardigan, which my friends had affectionately called 'concert cardie', as I'd worn it to a few gigs. I thought at the time it was the type of thing Morrissey would wear. I just knew that concert cardie would make an appearance on 30 October 1986.

My friend Juls jumped at the chance when I told him I had three tickets. Now, who was going to have the third, as my girlfriend at the time, Andrea, didn't want to go? 'I'd rather stick pins in my eyes', I think her response was. I had a very close-knit group of about half dozen friends. We played football together, did 'lads' things together, but none of the others were really into The Smiths at that point.

Our next-door neighbour had two daughters, one a year older than I (she would later become Juls' girlfriend) and one a year younger than I. The older one was a stuck-up snob and seemed to look down on me, but the younger one - Leah - was lovely. I bumped into her by chance - I guess she really never left the house other than for school - and I couldn't resist telling her I was off to see The Smith's. Leah couldn't believe my luck and told me she was their biggest fan. That wasn't possible, I thought. I was. That was it. Leah was to have the third ticket.

I managed to sneak a pint at The Spaniard before jumping on the coach for Manchester. I guess I looked older than my 16 years back then. I don't remember much of the journey, until I looked out of the window of the coach, and everything in Manchester appeared grey. It reminded me of seeing *Coronation Street* on a small black and white TV when I was younger.

Next thing, there was a crowd. Mainly guys. And every single one looked like Morrissey, much more than I. There were guys with National Health glasses, flowery shirts and gladioli sticking out of their back pockets. I thought I'd gone to a Morrissey fancy dress party.

Juls, Leah and I parked ourselves right behind the mixing desk. I'd read so much bad publicity regarding this tour in the newspapers I delivered before school to earn a few quid. Outrage in some parts of the national press at Morrissey swinging a noose on stage and holding a sign proclaiming 'The Queen Is Dead'.

Before we knew it, the lights dimmed and Prokofiev's 'Romeo and Juliet, No 13 Dance of the Knights' started playing. It still makes the hairs on the back of my neck stand on end whenever I hear it now. And there they were, The Smiths, right in front of my very eyes.

I'd been so excited for weeks knowing I was going to be there in Manchester that night. And yet it was over before I knew it. I knew it was over, before it even began. The most memorable songs that night were 'The Queen Is Dead', 'How Soon Is Now?', 'Rusholme Ruffians' - Juls had to shout to tell me it was '(Marie's the Name) His Latest Flame)' that kickstarted the song, 'What She Said' (with 'Rubber Ring' as the intro) and 'Meat Is Murder' with 'The Headmaster Ritual' intro.

I bought a 'The Queen Is Dead' t-shirt outside from some scally, which I probably still own somewhere in one of the many boxes I've packed away. Likewise, I still own the gig ticket and bus ticket, which I'll never throw away. No doubt my son will when I'm gone.

I've been to so many memorable gigs over the years, which include seeing a disappointing REM in Huddersfield (the acoustics were shite - however they made up for it many years later at Lancashire Cricket Ground when I thought the bass was going to smash right through my chest), Marilyn Manson at Roundhay Park in Leeds, Eminem a few times in the early days, a totally off her face Amy Winehouse in Manchester before The Arctic Monkeys came on, and of course the gig I waited nearly 30 years to see, the one and only Ms Kate Bush. And yet The Smiths, less than two weeks before my 17th birthday, remains without a shadow of a doubt the best gig I've ever been to in my life.

I WAS THERE: THOMAS JONES

This was of course the swansong, though we didn't know it at the time. Again we couldn't get stalls tickets due to their popularity, so we 'gurgled from the circle'. Morrissey took the stage wielding a placard that read 'Two Light Ales Please'. I think there had been some controversy about a 'Queen Is Dead' placard at previous gigs, and I think there had also been a recent incident where he'd been hit by a missile (again) and refused to carry on. It seemed to be in those later Smiths gigs that he was occasionally sacrificing melody for theatricality in the way he messed with the lines, and used a variety of daft voices to emphasise or undermine his own lyrics. This was certainly the least memorable of the four gigs. In retrospect it was easy to see that the magic was fading.

I WAS THERE: JAYNE O'CONNOR

My first proper gig. I took my sister for her 21st. I can still remember as plain as day Morrissey coming on to '(Marie's the Name) His Latest Flame' combined with 'The Last Night of the Fair' ('Rusholme Ruffians'). It was brilliant.

I WAS THERE: JOHN PARKES

I don't think I was that concerned when I heard they were splitting. I didn't like *Strangeways Here We Come*. It's not a record I play a lot. I was already coming out of my love affair with The Smiths. I was reverting back to the other music that I was progressing with - John Coltrane, Miles Davis, Wayne Shorter. I moved to London round about the same time and it was a renaissance of the jazz scene. The Smiths went on the back burner.

I worked at Tooting Bec hospital, which isn't there now, and as much as I'd moved on from The Smiths, I still had a few Smiths t-shirts. One day I came out of Tooting Bec hospital to go on the Tube into London and I got up to Tooting Bec station and this guy walked past me and gave me this really nice smile and it was Mike Joyce. I didn't think anything else of it, but this was '87 and it turns out The Smiths were recording in Streatham, ten minutes away from Tooting Bec.

I WAS THERE: VICKI MARES-PAGE

I lived in Old Trafford as a teenager, literally around the corner from where Morrissey lived on Kings Road. He went to the boys' Catholic school St Marys and I went to the sister school Cardinal Vaughan, albeit 11 years apart. I was the usual angst-ridden teenager so naturally gravitated to the music of The Smiths. My older sister by three years, Carole, was a huge music fan and had been to lots of gigs including quite a few from that particular Smiths tour. We didn't have much money growing up but I really wanted to go to that gig and begged my family for the money for a ticket, which Carole bought for me. It was a very exciting time looking forward to my very first gig.

Carole, as a seasoned gig-goer, said we should go into town early to hang around the Britannia Hotel as that was where the band were staying. After waiting there for a while, Morrissey and Marr arrived and I remember they were very generous with their time and signed autographs and had photos taken. I was too star-struck. I think I stood with my mouth open the whole time.

We got to the Free Trade Hall early and were first in the queue - me, my sister and another four of my sister's friends. We were right at the front of the stage and this was before barriers installed, so we were against the stage.

They came onstage with Morrissey waving a placard which said 'The Queen Is Dead'. It was amazing and I was in my element but very quickly I was separated from my sister and her friends. I think I was the only girl at the front and I was terrified that if I got stuck in the crowd somewhere my sister wouldn't know where I was, so I clung onto the stage monitor for dear life. There was a brilliant moment during 'How Soon Is Now?' where Morrissey knelt on the stage and held my hand. It was probably only a couple of seconds but it felt like an age.

I was only half enjoying this amazing gig as I was getting crushed against the stage. Then I was scared and probably in tears and the guy behind me realised I needed to get out and was shouting to the security but they didn't hear or notice. Then he shouted in my ear, 'Do you want to go on stage?' and I said 'no' but he said to other people to push me up because I was getting squashed. The next thing I knew I was stood on the stage a few feet from Morrissey. In a split second I knew it was a once-in-a-lifetime moment so I put my arm around the front of him and kissed him on the cheek! My sister said the crowd cheered but I didn't notice. Then I walked off the left hand side of the stage and Mike Joyce winked at me. I practically collapsed onto the security man who was very kind and took me for some water (I guess security then was very different to now). He asked me who I was with and I told him my sister and that she was still in the gig. He said I couldn't go back in but that I could stand at the side door to listen to the encore. I then had to wait with him until my sister came out and found me. He was a nice, kind man. The song playing when I got onstage was 'I Know It's Over' and it's still one of my favourites. I never saw the man who pushed me on that stage but I'm eternally grateful to him, even if he was one of the ones crushing me. The front of the stage was a deep red colour. I realised after that I was wearing blue jeans and a blue floral shirt (very Morrissey) which I'd borrowed from a friend. Both were ruined by the red dye which had rubbed off on me and stained them.

Carole had gone to loads of Smiths gigs but never got close to getting on the stage or holding Morrissey's hand. I'd managed both at my first gig. When she finally found me after the gig she gave me such a whack!

I WAS THERE: CHRIS GREEN

We had no tickets and everyone was queuing up and mingling outside - and this was down to me, and I'm not having anyone else claim this - but they were building at the end of the Free Trade Hall and they had big wooden sheets up surrounding the construction site inside. We were looking at how we could get in, going up to the door, how many bouncers are on and that sort of thing.

I went round the end of the building and I got myself through the wood and there was a hole in the wall covered up with a bit of tarpaulin. I pulled the tarp open and there was a human-sized hole but slightly wider. I peered in and right in front of me was a yellow builder's ladder. I looked up and it went up and up and up for about three floors. It was all breeze block, there was all building stuff and cement and everything going on inside. I had a shufty up and it was really high.

Me, Dibs and Stan Bowen went in, had a scoot up and peered over. And, as we peered over, we could see it was just a corridor next to the bar on one of the upper floors. So we went back down and back round to the front, gathered everyone together and said, 'Listen, come and have a look a this' and we went in. Everyone just went up the ladder.

There must have been 25 of us – boom, boom, boom, boom, boom - we all come bowling over the top. Full of shit, full of dust everywhere. We were absolutely hanging. We went straight to the bar. We were proper mucky, proper hanging. People were looking at us.

We were waiting and as the gig started and they said you could go in, we just gathered en masse at the top of the stairs and we just boom, boom, boom, boom, boom again. It was just a case of dodging around the door staff to get in. That was an absolute belter.

I remember finding a little James Dean badge on the floor that this girl had lost and I gave it to her and I thought that would get me in with her but she wasn't interested. Because I was covered in dust and shit. I probably looked like a football thug.

I WAS THERE: MANAMI NANRI, AGE 23

The Smiths never came to Japan but I was extremely lucky to be studying in Wimbledon from September 1986 to July 1987 and so had the chance to see four gigs on the *Queen Is Dead* tour, at Kilburn National Ballroom, twice at Brixton Academy and at the Free Trade Hall in Manchester. I took a National Express from Victoria Coach Station to Manchester, travelling up without a ticket, as I so desperately wanted to see them play on home turf.

Manami Nanri with Morrissey outside Brixton Academy, a few days after the Free Trade Hall show

In 1983 I travelled to the UK for the first time, staying with an old couple for a month to take English lessons. I took a train to London every day and ended up bringing back 20 or 30 records. But Smiths records were not amongst them. A year later, I returned with my college mate for a month, booking a holiday flat in London. We travelled to Brighton - I wanted to go after watching *Quadrophenia* and Dover, Oxford, Leicester where my pen friend lived and Scotland, where I went to see Simple Minds.

Again, I popped into record shops and bought 20 or 30 records, this time including *The Smiths*. When I first played it, I wasn't sure I liked it and didn't play it again for some months. However the next time, I was strangely struck by their sound and was interested in the lyrics. I bought *Hatful of Hollow* from an import record shop, which made me get more into both the lyrical world and the sound - the combination of those were what made The Smiths.

I was 23. Although I graduated from college as a secretary and took all the available English subjects, I wasn't satisfied with my own English skills. So in 1986 I flew to the UK again and worked in an office for two and a half years, staying with a family in Wimbledon. I had no people or friends around me who liked The Smiths and I remember once being asked if I became depressed or gloomy listening to their music. It was really mean to say such a thing but I really didn't care about those people, people who didn't understand the world of The Smiths.

On the day of the Manchester gig, I arrived and hurried to Tourist Information to book somewhere to stay for the night. There were other people there as well and we all were introduced to the same B&B and were recommended to share a taxi. An elderly lady, two teenage boys and me, a Japanese woman, all sat in a black cab. That was probably an odd sight! I sat next to the lady and the two boys were in front of me, face to face. I could see the boys had many Smiths badges on their sacks. Although it was obvious, I asked them if they were going to the gig. They said 'yes!' in astonishment but with smiles. As I said I was going too, and was a complete stranger from Japan, they kindly offered to guide me to the Free Trade Hall.

After we checked in at the B&B, they waited for me and we caught a bus to the city centre. They were a bit shy but kind and friendly and when we arrived at the Free Trade Hall, they introduced me to other friends and said I was from Japan. The other friends all kindly welcomed me and showed me their photographs of The Smiths. When they knew that I didn't have a ticket, they let me know where I could possibly get one and said to rejoin them after. Not long after I was successfully back with the ticket, a car arrived and Morrissey got out of it.

My mind went blank for a few seconds but, instinctively, I got close to Morrissey, holding a memo and a pen. I asked him for his autograph with my name, 'To Manami'. As it was an unfamiliar foreign name, Morrissey asked me to spell it out. As I did, he kindly wrote my name one letter at a time and then his name underneath. In my imagination, Morrissey was rather hard to approach and not snobbish but proud and a little reserved. And he could be moody. It was a lovely surprise that he was gentle, mild-mannered and a tender-hearted person.

Morrissey chatted to some people and then entered the venue via the stage door, after which other fans gathered around me and asked me what I was talking to Morrissey about. They were all happy for me and pleased I had been lucky enough to talk to him.

At the concert, the opening song was 'Ask' followed by 'The Queen Is Dead' and then 'Panic'. Then, Morrissey greeted the audience by saying 'Hello, nice to be back!' I still remember the cheerful, welcoming fans at the venue.

I had another chance to see him at the 12 December gig at Brixton Academy and he agreed to pose for a photograph with me. Standing next to him, I could feel his warmth and geniality and I still have the memory of his pleasant fragrance.

Hearing Johnny had left the band in 1987 meant the end of The Smiths for me. I was devastated but hoped that whatever the problems were they would be solved and they'd reunite. To me, Morrissey's lyrics and vocals, Johnny's song writing and the guitar and Andy's bass and Mike's drum all have to be there. Morrissey sings Smiths songs at his gigs but it's not the sound of The Smiths. Johnny sings and plays The Smiths too and the sound is almost The Smiths but it still isn't the same. Their solo performances of Smiths songs make me think of the days when they were all together and make me slightly sad that those days won't come back anymore.

ROYAL ALBERT HALL

14 NOVEMBER 1986, LONDON, UK

I WASN'T THERE: RICHARD BLANT, AGE 17

Richard Blant had a ticket for the postponed Royal Albert Hall gig

I was beside myself with excitement as I was going along to see The Smiths at the Royal Albert Hall in an anti-apartheid gig with The Fall in support. To say The Smiths had been an obsession of mine would be to underplay it. Everyone who got it was great. Everyone who didn't was beneath contempt. Ever since I bought the first album and the 12 inch of 'Heaven Knows I'm Miserable Now' with my 15th birthday money, there had been only one group.

I still remember where I was sat when I heard the terrible news: on the top floor of Longueville block in an A-level Sociology class. I felt like I had been stabbed. The crushing disappointment that others had heard the gig was cancelled - at first I thought they were winding me up (I was not very reserved about my Smiths obsession) and then to add a touch of teenage hideousness, a few of them were laughing that it was cancelled.

The night before (or possibly more) Johnny Marr had been drinking heavily and crashed his car. He was only slightly injured - it could have been far, far worse - but he was unable to pick up his guitar and play. Postponed.

The thought of a 17 year old me sat in a lesson crying makes the 49 year old me very sad. The thought of a group of them laughing at a 17 year old me makes the 49 year old me very angry.

The gig itself was to be rearranged just before Christmas on 12 December 1986 in Brixton. I chose to cash my ticket in - money being tight and Christmas presents to be bought. I'll go on the next tour, I assured myself. Early in 1987, I saw an interview with Morrissey in - I think *Q* magazine - saying he didn't know whether he wanted The Smiths to tour any more. Alarm bells rang loudly.

For anyone who knows The Smiths mythology, 12 December 1986 was the last gig that The Smiths ever played in the UK. I missed it because of Christmas and I have never regretted anything more. I would never make that choice again.

I am now 49 and my only regret in life was never seeing The Smiths play live. I have seen Morrissey in all his majesty (and some ropier gigs to be fair) and I have seen Johnny Marr in all of his brilliance. In 2018 I saw Morrissey and Marr play 'How Soon Is Now' (albeit nine months apart) but (in my delusional way) I count that as a reunion.

PEEL SESSION, MAIDA VALE STUDIOS

2 DECEMBER 1986, LONDON, UK

The band's fourth and final Peel Session saw them record four tracks – 'Is It Really So Strange?', 'London', 'Half a Person' and 'Sweet and Tender Hooligan'. These were broadcast on 17 December 1986. 'Sweet and Tender Hooligan' and 'Is It Really So Strange?' were later released on the *Louder Than Bombs* album.

BRIXTON ACADEMY

12 DECEMBER 1986, LONDON, UK

I WAS THERE: SALLY WILLIAMS

My first Smiths gig turned out to be their last. My memory is really hazy as it was more than 30 years ago and it was the last day of my first term at uni, so we'd been in the bar all day. It was really exciting though. I went with my house mate who was from Manchester and really into The Smiths. I'm from Liverpool and was into the Bunnymen but I went along for the ride and - it was amazing! I was surprised how energetic Morrissey was and I wasn't prepared for the level of showmanship - him swinging a noose around and holding up signs so I guess 'Panic' must have been on the set list. I made a short film for the BBC about Morrissey fans a few years ago and none of them had seen The Smiths, which made me feel even luckier to have been there.

I WAS THERE: MICHAEL FARRAGHER

That show was stand out. Craig Gannon had done the previous tour with them. Their sound had changed. If you listen to something like *Rank*, they had this huge sound. The two guitars allowed Johnny to do lots of things that he couldn't do when he was on stage by himself. But when they did the Brixton gig they were back to being a four piece again and the set was completely different from what they'd done two months earlier. For so many songs you were thinking, 'That is a first.' They did 'This Night has Opened my Eyes' for the first time in years. They did this fantastic segueway from 'Miserable Lie' into 'London ', which they'd never done before and obviously never got the chance to do again and which was brilliant. They premiered 'Shoplifters'. They did a fantastic version of 'Hand in Glove'. It was incredible that that was the last song that they played, although no one knew it at the time.

There's a lovely moment in the video of that Brixton show where Johnny goes over to Andy and they're playing together and Morrissey comes and joins them and the three of them are on the side of the stage and they look like they're having a fantastic time. They're all smiling and it doesn't look like there's any kind of problem with the band. It's hard to believe that less than a year later they'd split up.

I WAS THERE: JOHN DEOL

John Doel and his sister Sandy saw the last ever Smiths gig

It was the only time I saw The Smiths. I'd just left school. I was about 12 years old in 1982. I've got three older sisters and they're all really music mad. We were all music mad in our house. I'm from Birmingham and I'm Indian. We're British Asians.

My parents were Indian they came over in 1968 and I was born the following year. My parents were educated so they could speak English but we were all learning to embrace the popular culture at the same time and everyone including Mum and Dad loved music. These were my parents' first years in Britain and my earliest years and we all loved *Top of the Pops*.

My sister Sandy, who's three years older than me, was going on about this band who were playing at the Tower Ballroom, this little venue in Edgbaston. She was saying, 'There's a big buzz going around and some of the older kids at school are talking about this band, The Smiths,' and just around that time they appeared on *Top of the Pops*. They looked other worldly. This guy had flowers in his pocket and he just looked so cool. And the guitarist looked hip in his own way, with a really cool guitar.

You don't get much pocket money when you're 11 or 12 but Sandy managed to get the money together to buy the first album and in the weeks after getting that we were all obsessed. We'd tape every *Top of the Pops* appearance on our video recorder. And they were on a programme called *Riverside* on BBC2.

We all became hugely into them but I was very young and so I couldn't get tickets when they played in Birmingham and Wolverhampton in '84 or '85. Then in 1986 Sandy was at the University of Surrey in Guildford. I'd just left school. She was actually in her year out. I was an avid reader of the *NME* and *Melody Maker* and *Sounds* by then and I saw that The Smiths were playing an anti-apartheid gig in Brixton. I think it was a rearranged gig because Johnny Marr had had his car accident.

The next time Sandy phoned home to say 'hello' and see how we were all doing, I told her about this gig that The Smiths were playing in Brixton and she headed down there and got two tickets. I remember her saying that it was nearly sold out.

Of course, no one knew it was going to be their final gig and that they would split up seven or eight months later. I remember how excited I was just getting the coach down. That buzz never quite leaves until you walk into the building. London was all new and exciting to me. I remember walking into Brixton Academy and we opened the doors downstairs. It's a great venue.

It's quite cavernous, and one of the biggest non-seated venues in London with a big dance floor that dips down, but the whole room was absolutely rammed all the way back to the door. We looked at each other and just went, 'We're not going to get in there. Or we're not going to be able to see if we do.' We're both quite short. I'm five foot eight. She's five foot two. But Sandy said, 'I've been here before. There's an upstairs area' so we went upstairs with just a handful of people and a really good view. Pete Shelley was already on. So we saw some of the Buzzcocks' set.

It was just rapturous when The Smiths came on. A lot of people think of The Smiths as having a similar audience to Morrissey, quite fey and a bit camp. It wasn't. It was a normal football crowd type of gig. I remember looking downstairs, seeing how it was absolutely rammed, and thinking - how can people breathe down there?

It was a very joyous gig. It was like a football crowd, it was that rowdy, like when you scored, with your mates. We now know it as The Smiths' final gig but they certainly weren't breaking up at that point. They were all over each other, with loads of hugging, and it was so celebratory. Johnny and Andy, schoolmates, with their arms around each other's shoulders. Morrissey messing around with Johnny Marr.

They played 'Shoplifters of the World Unite' for the first and only time and, when he announced it, we didn't even know the song because it hadn't been released, but everybody cheered at what sounded like such an outrageous statement. There was quite a lot of banter with the crowd. The place went mad when they played 'Hand in Glove'. Then they went off and came back on for an encore. They didn't play for that long, about an hour and 15 minutes, but it was such a tight set.

With The Smiths it always felt like you were in a club. You'd chosen to be in this club called 'The Smiths' that said 'no' to Wham!, Five Star and all that poppy stuff. You were in this clique.

I was 15 when *Meat Is Murder* came out. I'd see in the *Melody Maker* and the *NME* when they announced the album release dates, so I'd be ready. I was at HMV in Birmingham New Street that morning. I can't remember what excuse I used to go in late to school but I got away with it. So I was there as it opened, got the first copy and when I took that record home and heard that final track, it was excruciating. You hear a cow dying. Like many fans I'd never connected the food on my plate to the animal. A few days before the release The Smiths had been on *Whistle Test* with an album report. They'd been in the studio with them and Morrissey explained why eating meat is wrong. At that point, like many of us, I'd have done anything The Smiths told us to do. But that really just made sense. It was really tough. My mother didn't think I'd last a week as a vegetarian. And here we are 30 odd years on. I haven't touched meat since that day.

After university, I ended up working for MTV for nine years. I've never met Morrissey but I've met the other three Smiths. When I told Andy Rourke that I'd been a vegetarian since 1985, I remember him saying, 'Oh no mate, after a few months I was back on the meat because I missed it too much.' I was a bit downhearted at that. But then I met Mike Joyce, and Johnny Marr when he was doing Electronic, and I remember Johnny saying to me, 'I'm really proud that my music can have that effect. I'm really proud of you.' If my hero says that about me I'll stick with it for the rest of my life.

Michael Rose saw the final show

I WAS THERE: MICHAEL ROSE

I became a full-on fan of The Smiths in between the *Meat Is Murder* and *The Queen Is Dead* albums. So 1986 was the first time I bought a Smiths album as a new release and *The Queen Is Dead* was played to death. I was relatively new to gig-going at the time but knew I wanted to see The Smiths live when tour dates were announced. Three London dates were scheduled for October, all at different venues, and I was gutted at not being able to get tickets for any of them.

Fast forward to December 1986 and The Smiths are playing a one off show at the Brixton Academy as a benefit for Artists Against Apartheid. Once again, with no ticket, I could only dream of seeing them at this stage. As luck would have it, on hearing of this, a friend was gifted some money so that we could go and buy a ticket from a tout, something we'd never done before! On 12th December we arrived at Brixton tube station, buying tickets from the first seller we encountered on the platform.

Inside, excitement levels were off the scale and we tried to get as far forward as possible. As the lights went down and the band came onto the stage, we fully expected to hear 'The Queen Is Dead', the opener for the album tour, but instead the band launched into recent single 'Ask'. The pace was not to let up, with 'Bigmouth Strikes Again' and 'London' following. I'd only been to a handful of gigs ever at this point, but don't remember anywhere where the audience felt as wild. This was something different. We were treated to 'Some Girls are Bigger than Others' which hadn't been played on the recent tour, so it was now clear the band had mixed things up a bit for this gig. We also got to hear upcoming single 'Shoplifters of the World Unite' as a new addition to the set list.

What happened next is my most overriding memory of the concert. When the familiar intro to 'There Is a Light That Never Goes Out' rang out, there was another massive surge forward from the crowd. I was now so wrapped up in the whole experience I decided to go with it and get nearer the stage. Back then, Brixton Academy had a bottle neck created by raised sections either side of the floor and I was squeezed through it and in doing so fell to the ground. I was trampled, with people walking over me as they were forced forward with the momentum of the crowd. I panicked, feeling pain and claustrophobia, but with the help of the adrenalin rush that followed, managed to right myself and get back up. The adulation from the crowd singing back at Morrissey was amazing: 'To die by your side' indeed! I remember thinking, 'What a way to have nearly gone!'

I was relieved when things calmed down at some point, and the band played a track I really never expected to hear, 'This Night Has Opened My Eyes'. The main set was wrapped up with 'Panic' and Morrissey swinging a noose around, and I recall feeling disappointed that they'd only played for about 45 minutes. When they came back on, I finally got to hear 'The Queen Is Dead'. The gig ended with 'Hand in Glove', and

I pointed out to my friend on the way home that it was kind of amazing that they'd opened with their most current single and ended with their first.

What is obviously amazing about this gig now, and which no one knew at the time, is that it was to be their last ever. How poignant that the closing song ended with, 'And I'll probably never see you again.' This also means it was the one and only time the band performed 'Some Girls Are Bigger Than Others' and 'Shoplifters of the World Unite', adding to how unique it was. I have since always felt privileged and incredibly lucky that I got to see The Smiths live. Although I've gone on to see Morrissey over 20 times, it's not the same, is it?

I WAS THERE: MARK WATERS, AGE 16

I'd had a rough few years in my teens and The Smiths were always there for me. My mum surprised me with a ticket. I remember being scared of Brixton due to the riots the previous year. All I remember of the gig is how surreal it was and how different it was to the previous gigs I'd been to - Shakin' Stevens and Big Country. Unfortunately, it turned out to be their last gig. So very bittersweet....

I WAS THERE: TIM MARTIN

What can I say? It does stick in the memory. I still have the ticket stub. They came on to 'Take me Back to Dear Old Blighty'. I remember 'Hang the DJ' ('Panic') with a noose spinning above his head and flowers in the back pocket. I think the album was a big influence over me. It changed my mood. Now I look for more positive, simpler sounding things. But that evening, I really thought I was at the centre of the world for those two hours.

1987

CATHEDRAL CLUB

13 FEBRUARY 1987, DUBLIN, IRELAND

I WAS THERE: DES FOLEY

We were approached on Grafton Street by a girl who asked if we would like tickets to see the band recording a TV appearance for a show called *TV Gaga*. It was an invite only audience and I remember we were all in the venue when the band came in and walked right past us all. Morrissey was wearing a denim jacket with a painting of Elvis on the back; they were recording 'Shoplifters of the World Unite'. I managed to get a quick word with Mike Joyce and told him about us getting t-shirts off him at the Stadium gig. He was really friendly and we were so chuffed to get to meet one of the band. At the time they were the most important band for me; everything they did was hugely relevant and we followed them avidly. I heard them first just at the right age I was too young for punk so The Smiths were my year zero for music. Everything changed for me after that.

NEW MUSICAL EXPRESS

JULY 1987, LONDON, UK

SMITHS TO SPLIT

An article in the *New Musical Express* carried the story….

Thorns in sides, anyone?

SMITHS TO SPLIT

THE SPLIT: MICHAEL FARRAGHER

Cathouse Studios in Streatham is where The Smiths ended up recording their last recording sessions. When they were doing the B-side for 'Girlfriend in a Coma', they recorded 'I Keep Mine Hidden' and 'Work is a Four Letter Word' there, in the studios across the road from where we lived. You could see that house from our front room. I was visiting a different sister up in north London, giving them a hand with mending their roof, when I got a call from my sister Rita. She was in Streatham and she said, 'You're never going to believe this but do you know who I've just met? Mike and Andy in the chip shop at the top of the road. I said, "What are you doing in Streatham?" and they made up some story.' They didn't say, 'We're recording.'

So after we knew that The Smiths were in town we were sitting at our front window watching people come and go into the studio. We never actually saw Morrissey or Johnny arrive but we knew that there was something going on there. We wouldn't go over and knock on the door and we weren't going to camp outside. We weren't that kind of fan. But we knew that they were likely to be over there. We did talk to Johnny about this. I've met Johnny since and had a good few chats with him. He told us that because they'd written to us and had our address and knew where we lived, they were considering coming over and knocking on the door. Can you imagine opening the door and Morrissey or Johnny Marr was there? You'd faint. That didn't happen, fortunately. But we saw Chrissie Hynde going in there, and Billy Bragg. We knew people would come to record. And it wasn't really until those B-sides appeared that we realised that that's what they were doing there.

When the split happened, there had been a rumour in the press that all was not well. How we found out about that was that Fred, the guy who lived with Grant Showbiz in the house across the road from us, was in a band called The Impossible Dreamers. He played drums with the band on one of the London gigs when they played 'Draize Train' at either Kilburn or Brixton when they had a second drummer come on. I think the house actually belonged to him. Rita had become friends with Fred and he said to her in the July before the split had been announced, 'I've got an advance copy of the Smiths' new album. Do you want to come over and listen to it?' So she went over on her own - without me - to listen to *Strangeways* in his house two months before it came out and he hinted to her at that point that all wasn't well with the band.

Dear Rita and Michael,
Your support shall always be remembered when we think of the tour. It was long and hard and not always enjoyable. But there were, for me, some joyously tearful moments.
The non-success of "Shakespeare's Sister" is hard to live with. That record meant so much to us. Our days with RT are certainly numbered.
Have you done your second demo yet? The world is waiting.
love at least,
MORRISSEY
XXX

One of the many letters from Morrissey send to Michael and Rita Farragher

Whether he knew they were splitting up at that point, I don't know. I don't think even the band knew that they were splitting up at that point. But he intimated to her that all wasn't well within the Smiths camp. And she came back and she had a copy of the tape which I still have. It has a slightly different mix of 'I Started Something'. We were listening to that for months before the album came out. And then we heard on John Peel that The Smiths had split. It was completely devastating. It was like, 'Is there any way this couldn't be true?' And then we were watching the music press and, 'No, this looks like it's going to be permanent.'

I talked to Johnny afterwards. I met him at a The The gig in around '95 or '96 when they played at the Albert Hall. I went up during the day and Johnny came outside and he was speaking to lots of people. He was on the steps, it was a really lovely summer's day and he sat down on the steps outside and just chatted to us for about an hour. We were talking to him about The Smiths and about other stuff and I said to him, 'How long had you been wanting to leave The Smiths before you did?' He said, 'I wanted to leave after the first album.'

THE SPLIT: MALCOLM GREENLEY

I remember opening the *NME* and seeing the story that they were splitting and thinking, 'Please don't let this be true.' They'd only been around for just about five years by then. It was obviously between Morrissey and Marr and the full truth has never come out yet. I've read several books about them and I think Morrissey must be a very difficult person to work with. I think Marr had had enough.

I don't understand why they didn't get proper management. I remember reading that Johnny would come off stage and there'd be people there with cheque books waiting for him to sign. He was only 21 when that was happening. Morrissey wouldn't speak to people, and if Morrissey wanted rid of somebody out of the Smiths camp he would say, 'He's gotta go' and then Johnny had to do all the dirty work. For someone who was 21 and who just wanted to play guitar and write music that must have been a nightmare. I just don't think Morrissey trusted anybody. When you look at it in that light it's amazing that they lasted as long as they did.

THE SPLIT: CAROLINE ALLEN

I can remember it like it was yesterday. I just happened to be at home one afternoon. We were in the sixth form at school at the time so we had a lot of free periods. *Granada Reports* came on and the woman reading the news just said, 'And we're having reports that Johnny Marr has left Manchester band The Smiths'. I couldn't believe it. It was the worst thing to ever happen to me as a youngster.

THE SPLIT: KEV JONES

Every Wednesday morning it was a bit of a joke at work. 'It's *NME* day is it? There'll be no work for half an hour.' Before I'd opened my copy, someone else had got one and one of the guys I worked with said, 'I think you'd better sit down, Kev. There's some news before you open that.' I remember the headline, 'Smiths to split', I was just a bit gutted, really. I don't think anybody really saw it coming.

THE SPLIT: RITA FARRAGHER

People often asked us if we ever got bored seeing the same band over and over again and I can honestly say, it was never boring. No matter how tired we were, as soon as The Smiths hit the stage we would be mesmerised. We couldn't wait for them to announce dates. They were a brilliant live band and when I have read about how difficult things were behind the scenes during those years I am amazed, because they put on a great show.

Rita Farragher and her brother Michael followed The Smiths around Ireland

We certainly did it the hard way. We were just students and pretty penniless so we looked for the cheapest forms of transport - usually a coach – and collected vouchers to get discounts all the time. Mars Bars did a National Express offer and we collected every wrapper we could to get free coach travel, saving us a fortune. We also hardly ever got a place to stay, sleeping in the coach station or trying to find somewhere open all night where we could safely hang out. We had a few sticky situations!

The last year of The Smiths was all a bit strange. Our dad died, so we missed some things. Then they turned up to record what turned out to be their final recording in the studio on our road. I met Andy and Mike in the chip shop and they seemed very upbeat but when I spoke to Fred, the studio owner, it was clear that all was not well. Shortly after that we heard about the split and it was pretty devastating. To be honest I though at the time that it would just be a break for a while and that we would definitely see them as The Smiths again but then as the years went by and the court case came it was clear that would never happen. I still hope for a Morrissey and Marr reunion at some point.

It was a great way to spend our late teens and it was great to have my brother to share that time with - I would never have done it on my own. I fell out of love with music in general a bit after The Smiths. They remain unmatched for me.

Johnny Marr: People didn't make my life easy after I left the Smiths. I was 24. I think I was expected to stick with the same three geezers until the day I died.

STRANGEWAYS, HERE WE COME

RELEASED 28 SEPTEMBER 1987

Reaching number 2 in the UK album charts, the band's final album was released after they had announced their split.

ITV's flagship arts programme, *The South Bank Show*, was dedicated to The Smiths.

THE SOUTH BANK SHOW

18 OCTOBER 1987, LONDON, UK

I WATCHED IT: STEVE WILLIAMS

The South Bank Show was a big thing for anybody arty at the time, particularly if you were into music or into punk music. It was coming up on the Sunday night and I was really excited to be seeing it, right up to the death of The Smiths. And in the week leading up to it the announcement came that they were splitting up. I'll always remember, on the introduction, Melvyn Bragg saying, 'We've filmed this show but since we've filmed it they've split so we've had to edit it and change it.' I was shocked. I thought, 'This can't really be happening.' It seemed such a strange thing to split up just before they got on the programme when it was all about them. I can't remember how I heard about the split. I can remember friends saying, 'It can't be true. They're the biggest thing around in indie music at the moment. Surely they can't just disappear like that?' But that's what happened.

THE SOLO YEARS

Since the demise of The Smiths, many fans have followed the twists and turns of the former members of the band, and the careers of Morrissey and Johnny Marr in particular. Here are a few of those memories.

1988

VIVA HATE

RELEASED 14 MARCH 1988

After much speculation in the music press about whether the Smiths split was permanent, Morrissey unveiled *Viva Hate*, his debut solo album.

MOZ WASN'T THERE: ROCHELLE D WEISKOPF

I slept in someone's yard for about 10 to 12 hours and about half a mile from the record store where Morrissey was doing a signing. This was when *Viva Hate* came out. We had to get wrist bands showing we were first in line before they would let us in. I'm six people away from the door and so excited. Next thing I know, Morrissey is being hurried out the door because someone ahead of me was talking about The Smiths. I was devastated.

RANK

RELEASED 5 SEPTEMBER 1988

Almost two years after their last live performance, and following the band announcing they were splitting, the live album *Rank* was released. It captured the October 1986 performance at Kilburn's National Ballroom. One title suggestion for the album was *The Smiths in Heat*. The band's 21 song setlist was trimmed to 14 numbers, with 'There is a Light That Never Goes Out' and 'How Soon is Now?' amongst those failing to make the cut. It was a poor memento of an illustrious live career.

The Smiths had not performed live for two years when Morrissey announced a one off show at Wolverhampton Civic Hall, his solo debut. Entry was 'free' except to gain admission attendees needed to wear a Morrissey or Smiths t-shirt. There were rumours that this was a Smiths reunion gig and the venue was swamped with Smiths fans trying to gain access on the night. An estimated 1,500 fans were locked out.

Morrissey: I thought a free concert was a very good gesture. I couldn't think of anyone who'd done it in recent years. I was and still am in a situation where I could sit down with some very heavy money moguls and organise huge tours with highly inflated ticket prices. I don't do that because it's against my nature. So I thought above all people would see a free concert as a very welcome gesture, regardless of who got their sandals stolen or dropped their crisps in a puddle.

CIVIC HALL

22 DECEMBER 1988, WOLVERHAMPTON, UK

I WAS THERE: JOHN TAGGART, AGE 18

I guess every music fan has 'their' band and for me and my siblings, Darrin and Ann-Marie, it was The Smiths. We fell in love with the music, the band and Morrissey. We entered into a world of all thing Smiths. We bought the records on the day they came out. We devoured Morrissey's interviews in the press. We became vegetarians and read the works of Oscar Wild and Shelagh Delaney. But just as our love and devotion for the band hit its peak - disaster! The Smiths split.

John Taggart queued overnight sans sleeping bag for Morrissey's solo debut

We were devastated, and the most gutting thing about them splitting was that we had never got a chance to see them play live. So fast forward to December 1988 when it was announced in the music press that Morrissey was to play his first live solo gig in Wolverhampton. As beautiful fate would have it, it was just a 20 minute train journey away from us in Birmingham. And it was a free gig to those who turned up in a Smiths or Morrissey t-shirt. We were overwhelmed with excitement. At this point it was not certain Morrissey would ever play live again. That excitement quickly turned to anxiety. We knew that we were unlikely to get in by just rocking up on the day. Wolverhampton was going to be invaded by an army of Smiths and Morrissey disciples. If we stood any chance of getting in we needed to camp out the night before. But it was a small price to pay.

Being teenagers - I had just turned 18, my brother 17 and my sister 15 - we were not burdened with any notion of practicality. We arrived at Wolverhampton Civic Hall on the evening before the gig with not so much as a sensible coat between the three of us, never mind a sleeping bag or a blanket. Already a queue snaked around the side of the Civic Hall so we took our place amongst the line of 'rain-coated lovers, puny brothers', all with sleeping bags. We spent a freezing cold December night on the pavement of Wolverhampton with just a few cans of cider to keep us warm. We didn't sleep. We didn't care.

The next day, as predicted, Wolverhampton was invaded by an army of Morrissey-Smiths fans. We took turns to leave our place in the queue to use the toilet in McDonalds, hoping Morrissey would forgive us this transgression. A carnival atmosphere developed throughout the day as the streets of Wolverhampton became a sea of quiffs and flowers.

As the hour of the gig got closer, the atmosphere changed. It was clear that a large percentage of the now thousands of fans surrounding the venue were not going to get in. Police on horses tried to maintain some sort of order as desperation and panic set in. Fortunately our place in the queue was safe as we were hemmed in by barriers that prevented people from pushing in. The feeling of euphoria and relief on finally entering the venue was overwhelming. I have never felt that kind of excitement before or since at any gig in my life.

Inside the venue, football chants of 'Morrissey, Morrissey, Morrissey' drowned out the support band, Bradford. They never really stood a chance. Then, to Cilla Black's 'Love of the Loved' and a confetti of flowers, Morrissey came onto the stage, backed by Mike Joyce and Andy Rourke with Craig Cannon. The only Smiths member missing was, of course, Johnny Marr. This was more than any of us could have hoped for. The first song of the night was the stand out track from the last Smiths album and fan favourite, 'Stop Me If You Think You've Heard This One Before' and the place erupted with sheer joy. This song had never been played live before. Each song played was interrupted by constant stage invasions, with fans climbing onto the stage to embrace Morrissey before being dragged away by security. Morrissey was unfazed and was clearly enjoying being kissed and adored by everyone that made it onto the stage.

There was an electric energy that was palpable. The gig seemed to fly past in a beautiful blur, Morrissey playing a number of new songs such as 'The Last of the Famous International Playboys', until we reached the encore, the magnificent and highly appropriate Smiths song, 'Sweet and Tender Hooligan'. Then it was over. We drifted out of the hall and onto the streets of Wolverhampton, the pavement littered with tearful and dejected fans who hadn't been able to get into the gig but couldn't bring themselves to leave.

I caught sight of my own eyes reflected in a passing bus window. They were shining. There is something about being a teenager and seeing the band or artist you love the most for the first time that is totally transformative.

I WAS THERE: MARK CROOK

Mark Crook thought he was going to be one of the 1,500 locked out of Morrissey's debut solo show

The morning of 22 December 1988 started much like any other. Mom shouting me, soon to be 24 and working in a dead end job in the DHSS, to get up to go to work. However, this wasn't going to be any other day. This was the day Morrissey was starting his solo career at, of all places, Wolverhampton Civic Hall. A free gig no less where entry was down to wearing a Smiths or Morrissey t-shirt. And basically it was The Smiths without Johnny.

Having used all my annual leave up, it was down to my lovely mom to phone in sick for me and she did a fine job. Sorted. The only decision I had to make now was, 'Do I head in to Wolvo later in the day or ASAP?' Despite the bitter cold I decided an early start was the better call, so in my 'What Difference…' t-shirt with oversized jumper and obligatory overcoat, I headed off. After an hour's bus ride I get to the Civic Hall and the queue is about half way round the building at 10.30am. Meeting up with some work colleagues I start to wait out the day, with about eight hours until the doors were due to open.

Thinking back it had been less than five years since my first Smiths gig at Victoria Hall, Hanley on 28th February 28 1984. Visiting a mate who was at North Staffs Poly, it cost £3.50 and exciting as they were, they were developing their popularity, and the audience was far more restrained than later and certainly than this show turned out to be. There were no chants of Morrissey and no made attempts to get on stage to hug Moz in Hanley. I think it's the only time, until bigger venues became the norm, that I heard him sing an entire set uninterrupted.

Anyway, time ticked by. I missed Moz turning up in the vintage bus as I'd gone to get a coffee and something to eat as it was so cold. Story of my life! By about 4pm there were a few thousand there and the police turned up not realising they had a large crowd of 'youths' gathering. Up went crowd control fences and, as it got darker, the crowds started to push further forward. The doors open and I'm thinking, 'Shit, please let me get in.' Slowly I moved closer until I started to hear the words 't-shirt, mate' in broad Black Country accents. I'm really shitting it now, just imagining the 'full' sign going up. Just outside, in the doors, forgetting to pull up my jumper to show my entrance fee. God bless Terence Stamp.

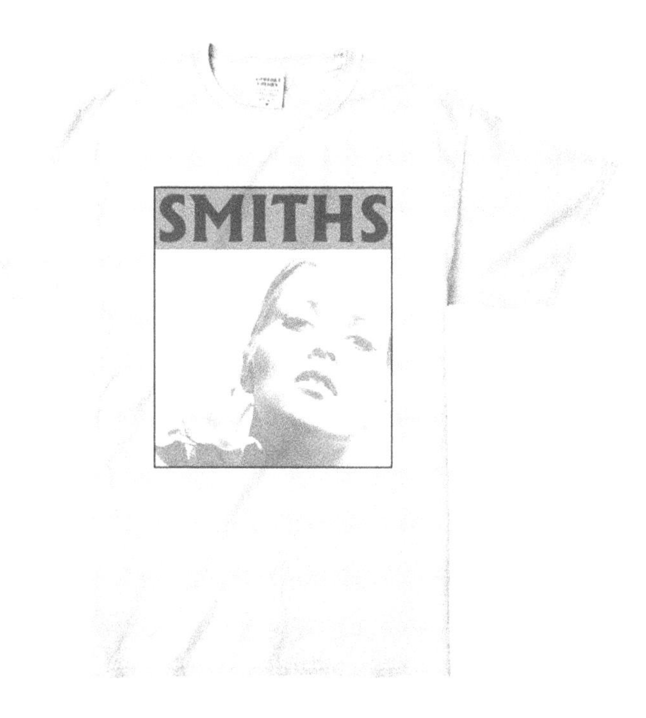

Rumour has it about 1,500 didn't make it in but I'm not sure about that and selfishly I don't care. I was in. I did hear a few windows being put through as some must have tried to force entry. The gig itself, after about 10 hours of waiting, was really short and sweet. And absolute fucking sweaty mayhem. Every time I see a clip on YouTube I just think, 'I was there at the start of Morrissey's solo journey' and I can't listen to 'Sweet and Tender Hooligan' without being transported back to that freezing cold, but hot bouncy night in December 1988 in the Black Country.

And I didn't get found out at work and left for a better career 10 months later.

I WAS THERE: SEAN DONAGHUE, AGE 17

Living in Birmingham made it easy to get to Wolverhampton when it was announced on the radio. I can't remember whether I spent one or two nights camping outside. I was within the first 10 people to get inside and I appear on the *Hulmerist* video briefly coming through the main doors. It's the scene where the doormen are repeatedly saying 't-shirts please'. The doormen must have had no idea what a Smiths t-shirt was as someone I knew managed to get inside with a Billy Bragg t-shirt! Once in I was right up the front next to the girlfriend of the singer from the support band Bradford. Most people know what the concert was like from watching the film *Hulmerist*. What has not been seen is when Morrissey threw the black shirt he was wearing into the crowd. I jumped and caught it whole, pulling it into my chest. Whilst trying to keep this to myself everyone else had other ideas and it was torn from me by everyone around, scenes similar to that of a rugby ruck. In the end I had to let go as it was round my neck and strangling me to

the point of asphyxiation. All I ended up with was a few buttons of the sleeve. I am sure if I had died no one would have cared.

I WAS THERE: NICK TUDOR, AGE 17

Entry was free if you wore a Smiths t-shirt. People had been down there queuing for days but we rocked up a couple of hours before the doors opened and jumped over the barriers about 50 fans from the door! I'm embarrassed by this now but when you're 17 things like this don't matter when it comes to Morrissey. The gig is my favourite one of his that I've been to, not only because it was his first solo one but also because it practically was The Smiths, just without Johnny. I can only use one word to describe it - awesome!

Morrissey shows are electric - religious even - and only a Smiths fan knows or understands this. Out of the 22 Morrissey gigs I've been to (and I know people who've been to a lot more), I've got on stage 15 times. You just have to do it. I've been physically abused by security a good few times, not least in my own town of Bridlington in September 2004 after getting onstage to 'I'm Not Sorry'. I was ushered offstage – quickly!

My most memorable onstage moment was that I was the only one to get onstage at Wembley Arena on the *Kill Uncle* tour. During the last song, 'Disappointed', he actually piggy-backed me and there's video footage of this. I'd got thrown out of Wembley twice trying to make the stage but got back in both times through a toilet window, which is difficult at six foot two!

The last time I saw him was at the Hull Arena in September 2015 and I took my 14 year old son. During the last song, 'What She Said', I lifted my son up and Morrissey shook his hand. My son was stunned at why all these people hugged him after what had happened and I told him that he'd just done at his first gig what these other people had probably not been able to do in 10 or 20 years of coming to Morrissey concerts. I think he got it.

I never saw The Smiths, a failure I'll take to my grave.

I WAS THERE: ANDREW CLEAR

It was me who kicked the windows in at Wolverhampton Civic Hall when Morrissey did his first solo concert. The *NME* headline, accompanying a photo of the broken windows, was 'Sweet and Tender Hooligans'....

I WAS THERE: MICHAEL HOWE

Morrissey said we could shake his hand as long as we didn't pull him off the stage.

I WAS THERE: ANGELA LAMBERT

It was Morrissey's first solo gig. It was supposed to be a farewell Smiths concert. The only band member missing was Marr. Morrissey took his short off and it was ripped to pieces. I managed to get about an inch square of it. I kept that piece of sheer black material for years. Good times for a change.

I WASN'T THERE: RICHARD LAURIE

I was 10 from the entrance when the doors closed at Wolverhampton Civic Hall. I had queued for four hours. My favourite story from that day is of Smiths fans wearing *Meat Is Murder* t-shirts happily accepting ham sandwiches from nurses taking blood donations on the other side of the hall.

I WAS THERE: JUSTIN OSBORNE, AGE 17

First memories for me are watching the classic *Top of the Pops* TV appearances in the mid Eighties of 'William...' and 'Heaven Knows...' I remember sitting around with Mom and Dad with them saying, 'Who the bloody hell is that swinging flowers round with 'Marry me' across his chest?' I was a 15 year old mesmerised kid. I vividly remember buying my first Smiths seven inch, 'William, It Was Really Nothing' soon after from HMV in the Mander Centre in Wolverhampton. It was in the singles box on the counter and it felt like gold dust when I flicked through and found it there. Good times.

Morrissey reads Mia Osborne's letter onstage in Ljubljana, Slovenia in 2015
The family Osborne visiting Salford Lads Club

Me and my wife, both young Smiths fans, slept on the pavement the night before Moz's first solo gig at Wolves Civic. It was my 17th birthday. We now follow Moz around Europe and in 2015 my daughter Mia, who was 14 at the time, got a letter to him on stage in Ljubljana which he opened and put in his jeans pocket - she was thrilled! We are a Moz family.

I WAS THERE: GARY WOODBRIDGE, AGE 14

Sadly I never got to see The Smiths but that's me at the Civic Hall with my mate with Will and about 10 more at our first ever gig. We're all over the *Hulmerist* video. We went the day before and slept on the street around the venue in the queue to make sure we got in. Our parents allowed it mainly because there was so many of us, a couple of us were maybe 16 years old and we could look after ourselves. I was watching from the balcony when Will got on stage. He was maybe the second or third person to do so. I knew I had to or I would never hear the end of it, hence I was straight downstairs to the front and then on stage. I gave Moz a big kiss on the cheek. And I still have a piece of his cardigan. Happy days.

Gary Woodbridge made a brief appearance on stage with Moz at Wolverhampton Civic

I WAS THERE: TOM HICKS

I was 15 at the time of Morrissey's solo concert and was the only Smiths fan amongst my immediate friends. It was my first concert. The school I was at in the West Midlands was called a comprehensive. I still find this baffling - it only lived up to that description in one sense – it was comprehensively uninspiring. They did a proper job of it.

I'd developed a huge interest in music but couldn't find an outlet for it anywhere and certainly not at school. We had a music teacher who used to lock all the instruments away in huge cupboards, ostensibly because he was 'concerned about theft' but I suspected at the time that it was really down to the same mean-spirited outlook that informed 'Rusholme Ruffians'. He had a disdainful approach to all but the most talented of pupils and basically saw us having a future in the factories in the area. The only lessons I remember involved him handing out individual parts of a glockenspiel for us to hit with a small hammer.

Although I lived right next to Wolverhampton and Birmingham, I hadn't reached the age where I was going to gigs, mainly because I couldn't convince people to go. Most of my friends were into football or skateboarding and none of us had any money. The nearest thing to seeing bands for me was to read about them.

In the absence of any real culture, I tended to spend a lot of time in my local library, which had a great music section. The idea that it was free to use and kids were welcome seemed incredible at the time. I also used to use the fantastic reference library in Birmingham, which had an amazing record collection and an inclusive, broadminded approach to educating the public.

It had a liberal collection policy that allowed you to suggest new purchases. You'd fill in a slip suggesting that the library buys a new album and a few weeks later you'd get a postcard through the door to say it was ready for you. For a kid operating on a zero-budget footing it was fantastic.

The library also stocked back copies of *New Musical Express*. It's hard to convey how important the *NME* was at that point – the writing was still of such a high standard and aside from the John Peel show, it was the only way to engage with the best music of the time. I quickly arranged to have it delivered by the newsagent (transferring seamlessly from *Smash Hits*). It used to arrive every Wednesday and it was basically the peak event of each week for me.

The Smiths featured regularly in the *NME* – gig reviews, album reviews and most importantly for me - interviews. For me these were the thing that absorbed me fully into the worldview of Morrissey and Marr. I think more than any other band before or since, The Smiths created their own culture. In interviews they referenced films, music, clothes and of course other bands. For me personally I think they arrived a time when I had a real desire to broaden my horizons and look at new ideas. I never saw them as fey, which was a common misconception. I saw them as having aging mentality, but one that praised intelligence, reading and ideas above all else. These were values that seemed to be discouraged elsewhere, not least at school.

What still stays with me is the strong visual identity that the group, particularly Morrissey, managed to create. It's well documented that Morrissey himself was an uber fan of groups such as The New York Dolls, so perhaps the hours he spent poring over their record sleeves gave him a deep appreciation of the importance of the sleeve as a form of connection with fans. They are still beautiful objects.

Even the cassettes were well thought out! I still have a copy of *The Queen Is Dead* on that format somewhere and the plastic cover was a cream colour that was carefully chosen to match the typeface on the sleeve. I loved how the cover stars ranged from the most famous (Elvis, *Shoplifters of the World Unite*) to the most obscure (Leo Ford, *Hand in Glove*), often with no real context other than Morrissey loved them as people, the films they appeared in or the television series that they graced.

During the build-up to the day of Morrissey's debut solo gig, I was at school and completely unaware that it happening. But during morning break a friend of mine, whose nickname was (and still is) Tot, came to find me. At first I thought he was joking! The idea that Morrissey was nine miles up the road in Wolverhampton seemed pretty unlikely to me. But as Tot spoke, his story seemed to make sense. He told me that his older brother was already in the queue outside Wolverhampton Civic Hall and had been there for hours with a few friends. All we had to do was arrange to get up there and we could meet up with him.

For me there were a few big obstacles to negotiate – the most immediate being that we still had half a day of school to complete. I'd never skived school before – Tot was an old hand – but I was quite conscientious in those days and didn't know what to do. We also had no money and Wolverhampton was pretty much regarded as a no-go area after dark.

One of the upsides was that the gig had been announced as free, as long as you wore a Smiths or Morrissey t-shirt. It may be that Tot knew I was in a good position in that sense (I had a drawer full), so we headed to mine at lunchtime. As far as I remember, I wore a *Hatful of Hollow* t-shirt and I gave him a faded one featuring the This Charming Man cover. Come to think of it, I don't think he ever gave it back to me.

Once we'd scraped some money together we got the bus to Wolverhampton and as we arrived it was immediately obvious that something big was happening. I was used to spotting the occasional Smiths fan in the town where I was from, but the city centre was teeming with people in Smiths t-shirts, badges and, of course, cardigans, flowers, beads and quiffs.

The huge majority were a lot older than us but it kind of felt safe. It was bedlam – the queues were so long and it was easy to see that there were just too many people there – a lot of people toward the back of the queue really had no chance of getting in – the Civic wasn't big enough for his level of fame really.

It took a while to find Tot's brother but we eventually tracked him down. When we did, it caused some friction because clearly everyone behind him had been queuing since the early hours. He quickly dealt with the grumbling by telling them to 'fuck off'. I'm glad he was older and bigger than us. I remember that we spent hours sat on the pavement outside the cold façade of the Civic with no guarantee of being let in or any real proof that Morrissey was even in the building.

The concert itself was amazing as an event. My memories of the music are good but in a way the performance quickly became a side issue. The atmosphere seemed to me to be a mixture of a cup final and the appearance of a holy man. The chants of 'Morrissey, Morrissey, Morrissey…' were lifted directly from the terraces (Ingerland) but the main feeling I remember was a sense of awe in the crowd, mixed with disbelief. 'Is this really happening?'

As the video recording of the concert shows, the performance quickly became an extended stage invasion. I wasn't near enough the front to try to get on stage and I don't think it's something I would have done. But I understood the desire to get nearer Morrissey. I never had the chance to see The Smiths but I'm glad I can say I was there.

What struck me was how respectful it was, people wanted to either hug him or kneel before him. That kind of interaction with performers doesn't happen now really. I think it was so sensitively handled by security.

I didn't get in trouble for skiving school. My Mom was brilliant about it. At that time she was working as a home help and was around at lunchtime when we went to my room to dig out the t-shirts. When I told her what was happening, she was great about - she told us to get carry on and go

to the concert, despite it meaning missing school. I've spoken to her about it since and she has summed it up perfectly – she said she just knew it was important.

Bona Drag was a compilation released on 15 October 1990 featuring an array of Morrissey's songs from his early solo career, most of which had not been released on any previous album. The 14 track album included 'Everyday Is Like Sunday', 'Piccadilly Palare', 'November Spawned a Monster' and 'The Last of the Famous International Playboys'.

On 27 May 1991 Electronic led by Johnny Marr and New Order's Bernard Sumner released their debut studio on the Factory label, which reached number 2 on the UK chart.

Morrissey released his second solo album *Kill Uncle* on 4 March 1991, which included the singles 'Our Frank' and 'Sing Your Life'.

NATIONAL STADIUM

27 APRIL 1991, DUBLIN, IRELAND

I WAS THERE: FERGAL COSGRAVE

I came late to the party and only discovered Morrissey in 1988 when he appeared on *Top of the Pops* singing 'Everyday is like Sunday'. I was immediately intrigued. So for me it started with *Viva Hate* and *Bona Drag* and I worked myself backwards to The Smiths. My aunt - my father's twin sister - lived on Kings Road in Stretford, just 30 doors up from Morrissey. I have seen Morrissey live 30 times, including every time he has played Dublin, the *Boxers* tour in Birmingham in 1995 and the ill fated Bowie tour later that year, his 45th and 50th birthday shows in Manchester, six other Manchester shows and Blackpool during the *Quarry* tour. He never fails to disappoint. His first solo gig in Dublin was at the National Stadium in April 1991 in support of *Kill Uncle*. It was like Beatlemania!

All-day queues for Indie legend

By DERMOTT HAYES

FANS stormed the stage of the National Stadium to touch, hug, kiss and, on one occasion, knock over their idol, singer Morrissey, at the gig on Saturday night.

Daffodils, lupins and geraniums showered down on the Mancunian legend throughout his exciting one hour set.

With both parents hailing from Crumlin, Dublin, it seemed logical to the legendary Mancunian rock singer, Morrissey, to choose Dublin as the first venue for his first live concert in three years.

The former lead singer with '80s Indie legends, the Smiths, disappointed none of the sell-out capacity audience of 2,000 at the stadium.

CAIRD HALL

15 MAY 1991, DUNDEE, UK

I WAS THERE: KATE SULLIVAN, AGE 22

I knew about The Smiths when I was 15 because people at school knew about them. A lot of the girls in my class went to Johnny Marr's primary school in Wythenshawe, so when they first came out and they were on *Look North West* and stuff a lot of the girls at school used to talk about them. I was in sixth form college before I really started liking them so that would be 1983, '84 perhaps, when they were on *Top of the Pops*. But I never saw them because I was in youth theatre and always acting in plays. I was buying the records but I didn't see anyone I liked. I would have liked to see Dexy's Midnight Runners.

I was gutted when they split because I didn't imagine that Morrissey would go on to be as good. But *Viva Hate* came out and it was just a leftover Smiths album as far as I was concerned - The Smiths Mark Two. Not long after, he announced a cluster of dates, or he might have announced one gig in Aberdeen, so everyone rushed to buy a ticket and then a week later he announced a gig in Dundee and obviously you're already thinking, 'Oh well, I'm in Aberdeen, I might as well go to Dundee', and then he announced another one in Glasgow. There were none, apparently, coming up in Manchester. So me and two friends who were very big Smiths fans decided to go to Scotland.

You could only get tickets by phoning up or by post. I was working in my mum's lighting shop on a Saturday when those went on sale. In between serving customers I spent a lot of time on the phone and I managed to get tickets for Aberdeen, Dundee and Glasgow on sequential nights.

I went with my friend Clare, and her best friend in sixth form was Lucette, who was the girl in the 'Every Day is like Sunday' video. Lucette had been part of the Smiths' fan club. She was in the 'I Started Something...' video when they were all on the bikes. The Smiths fanzine had invited people to apply to be in the 'I Started Something...' video. The idea was you had a quiff and you wore a Smiths t-shirt and so you would be a Morrissey lookalike, but it was a mix of women and men. I think she was about 14 or 15 at the time. On the day of filming, she was very intimidated by the fact that Morrissey was there. She was a big fan, but whereas a lot of people were going up to him and going, 'Ooh, Morrissey, I really love you,' she was crippled with shyness and just couldn't bring herself to do it. He came up to her at one point and she ran away. I think he really liked that. So when it came to doing the 'Every Day is Like Sunday' video, he asked for her to be in it.

I had a little Mini at the time, a very old one, and we didn't really know how far away Aberdeen was or even how to get there particularly. And my sister gave me really duff instructions because she told me to go to Scotch Corner and then north from there which isn't really the way you'd go from Manchester. So we set off in the morning and got there really late. We had somewhere to stay booked in Dundee and I think we had something booked in Aberdeen but hadn't paid for it. Or perhaps we were just going to look for something when we got there. When we got to Aberdeen it was just about getting to the concert and being on time.

I've got a memory of quite a nice hall but I don't remember the gig itself. Afterwards, we were parked up outside the back of the venue in the car park across the road. And they were saying, 'Let's hang around backstage and see if he comes out.' So we just got in the car, because it was cold, and waited. The tour bus was there so we were watching the door to see if he came out. We didn't really see him come out and we still don't know whether he did come out of that back door or not. But then the tour bus started to move off.

We must not have had anywhere booked in Aberdeen because Lucette and Clare were saying, 'Let's just follow the tour bus and stay at whatever hotel they stay at,' thinking it was going to be local and that they would go on to somewhere nearby.

But they got on the motorway to Dundee and so were going straight on to where they were playing the next night. So we followed them. And it was really embarrassing because there was a point where there was only the tour bus and us on the motorway and, clearly, we could have overtaken the tour bus at any time and didn't.

We got into Dundee centre and the tour bus was going round and round a bit, and we were going round and round with it, following 50 yards behind, and then the bus stopped and the driver came up to me. So we were stopped because we didn't know where to go and the driver said, 'I take it you're following us?' I thought there was no point in lying because he's seen us behind him all the way from Aberdeen to Dundee so I said 'yes' but as I said 'yes' the other two said 'No! No.' but they realised I'd said 'yes'. And the driver said, 'Do you know where you're going? We're lost.'

And I said, 'No, we're following you' and he said, 'Oh, all right.' So he got back in the bus and off we went again. But then we decided it was super embarrassing because they had definitely clocked us, so it would be super embarrassing to go to the same hotel as them and so we thought we'd just go and find somewhere to stay for the night because we had somewhere booked for the following night.

We really didn't know where we were and ended up in some terrible one way ring road system thing, going round and round in circles. We went over a big bridge a couple of times and were trapped in a loop. Then this car started following us and we were really conscious of it. It overtook us and stopped us and these blokes got out and flashed ID and said they were the police. It was an unmarked police car, but it seemed really dodgy. They asked us, 'What are you doing?' We said, 'We're looking for somewhere to stay' and the policeman said, 'Follow me, I'll take you somewhere.'

We were really, really panicking by this point now. We were thinking they weren't really police officers. We were three young women in a completely alien place with no back up or anything. They took us to a hotel. It wasn't the best of hotels. They walked us into it and checked us in. We were really scared at this point. But the hotel gave us a room for three people. So we piled the chairs in the room up against the door because we thought these blokes were going to return and attack us. It was so scary. But nothing happened.

And we went to the gig the next night. I don't remember much about the gigs. I think he played about an hour in Dundee. His voice was breaking up. We were near the front. Obviously you know where this story is going, with three nights on the run with

Morrissey. It's just not happening, is it? He did do Aberdeen and he did do Dundee, but he went off early in Dundee and cut the show short: 'I'm terribly ill' He had a sore throat. And then he cancelled the Glasgow one.

ROYAL CONCERT HALL

16 MAY 1991, GLASGOW, UK

I WAS THERE: STEVE NASH

I was slightly too young to see The Smiths live. They played my local leisure centre in Newport in September 1986, an infamous gig where Morrissey was pulled off the stage by enthusiastic fans so the gig only lasted about eight songs plus an impromptu 'Draize Train' instrumental before the lights came up so I clearly didn't miss that much. I was still too young to travel from the Cardiff area to see Morrissey's first solo gig at Wolverhampton Civic Hall in 1988. Because Morrissey didn't play any live dates in the intervening period, I had to wait three years until 1991 for my first experience of him live. But even that was delayed.

Morrissey had announced three solo dates in Scotland in May 1991 – Aberdeen, Dundee and Glasgow – and we decided to go to the last of these. My moment had arrived and my brother and I set off from Cardiff extremely early that morning, boarding a train around 6.30am. We had plenty of magazines, books and cassettes for our Walkmans for the eight hour journey. We arrived around 2.30pm and found the venue with its glamorous walkway and steps to the entrance. It was the perfect setting to the perfect occasion. On arrival there was virtually no one in sight, no hard core fans queuing to ensure front row certainty, absolutely nothing. This was simply not what I expected at all. I was anticipating the wild hysteria that I had seen on television from various snippets of

Smiths gigs and the solo Wolverhampton gig.

All of a sudden, a deep Scottish dialect from behind us said, 'It's off.' We turned to see the obvious die-hard Smiths fan from his quiff, Smiths t-shirt and various beads and badges who said, 'He's only just cancelled, lost his voice last night.' At first, my brother and I thought it was a joke but soon I spoke to a distraught fan who had travelled from Germany and he repeated the same story in shock and almost disbelief. 'There is no concert. Morrissey has cancelled. He lost his voice last night.' It was 1991. At this stage, the internet and mobile phone were mere figments of the inventor's development table and there was no way of checking in advance. Yes, we could have phoned the venue but on such a short three night tour, we just assumed it would be going ahead. We were 'truly disappointed'. The gig was re-scheduled for July but we sold the tickets on to try and make some of the money back we had lost.

This was quite a significant event, of course, as it would be the first of the many cancelled Morrissey solo gigs that would follow. It started on the very first solo tour, some without advance warning like this gig and others including Glastonbury, huge USA tours and even the last UK tour due to those alleged 'logistical reasons'.

DOME LEISURE CENTRE

25 JULY 1991, DONCASTER, UK

I WAS THERE: RICH OWEN, AGE 20

I attended a solo Morrissey gig at the Dome in Doncaster. It was a strange old venue. At the end, I was bang smack in the centre when his shirt came off and flying into the crowd. I was in the middle of the scrum and had most of it and fought my way to the exit to find my mates. It was at that point I also noticed how my own shirt (which I had also taken off and tied round my waist was in shreds), so I have always thought that someone, somewhere, has part of my own shirt hung on their wall thinking they have Morrissey's!

Back at home the next day I surveyed my grand prize. I had most of the back of the shirt and a large part of one sleeve and the front. Not exactly the whole shebang, but enough to be proud to keep it and claim my badge of honour. Despite my mother asking me why I had a woman's shirt pinned to my wall, I was a happy young man. In 1995, I moved to the USA so packed many of my belongings in my parent's loft, including the shirt, now folded and packed neatly in a bag, in order to keep it from the damp or mice and retain that sweaty Morrissey aroma that had seem to linger in it. A few years later, I was on the phone to my dad who had informed me of a clear out that had happened to the loft. My heart sank. What clear out? My mum had tried to take my vinyl records to the charity shop claiming it was all CDs these days, but my dad - a collector of lots of old vinyl and gramophone records to boots - fought her off. But then came the admission - there was an old rag in a bag that she chucked out. And that was the end of the Morrissey shirt....

KING GEORGE'S HALL

26 JULY 1991, BLACKBURN, UK

I WAS THERE: DAVID BAMBER

My mate Graham Love was driving and on a very steep hill in Blackburn, he braked a bit late and we ploughed into the back of a stationary car. A great start to the evening. Even worse, it was an off-duty policeman. Things picked up though and the gig was fantastic! I also saw Morrissey at a leisure centre in Chester in 1997 and remember feeling that the end was nigh for his career.

I WAS THERE: DAVID ROUNDELL

My first Moz concert. It was a great concert but very hot. Everyone went to McDonalds round the corner from King George's Hall after it was over. It was full of very sweaty Moz and Smiths-shirted people. Sweat is murder!

HORDERN PAVILION

13 SEPTEMBER 1991, SYDNEY, AUSTRALIA

MOZ WASN'T THERE: MATILDA REID

He cancelled. We had a small baby and we had planned a big night, getting a baby sitter, etc. We were totally oblivious to the situation until we got to the venue. There was a little sign on the door. We sat in the car watching the rain roll down the windscreen, making strange patterns on our skin, trying to think of something else to do.

VICTORIA HALL

1 OCTOBER 1991, HANLEY, UK

I WAS THERE: GRAMP

I've met Mike and had him write a birthday card for my missus. I've seen Moz many times although I missed the free gig in Wolverhampton (my hometown) as didn't have a t-shirt. I was going to borrow one off a mate and went round to his house but he'd gone to see Dio with another mate leaving me with no t-shirt, so no show. But my mates are on the *Hulmerist* video which was filmed at that gig, as is one of my neighbour's son's - a copper!

The first time I saw Moz solo was at the Victoria Hall in Hanley, supported by Phranc. We tailgated the tour bus back to the hotel

NOW HE KNOWS H
JOAN OF ARC FELT

in Cheshire. I didn't get to see him but spied through the gap in the curtains and saw a bottle of Evian on a bedside table.

GLOUCESTER LEISURE CENTRE

7 OCTOBER 1991, GLOUCESTER, UK

I WAS THERE: JAMES BRYANT

I still have my ticket from my first Morrissey gig. What a depressing venue, lining up watching people go in to play badminton or to have a swim. It was amazing to think you could see Morrissey up close and personal and within spitting distance in a leisure centre when his arena tours now sell out online in minutes and you get a seat two miles away from the stage. I honestly thought his music career was coming to an end and I was just glad to have seen him before he retired to a coastal town. I last saw him during the sell out shows at Alexandra Palace, which were huge with different generations of fans. Back in 1991, I thought he'd soon be like a Quentin Crisp character, bringing out strange unpopular volumes of poetry. Never write Moz off.

PAULEY PAVILION, UCLA

1 NOVEMBER 1991, LOS ANGELES, CALIFORNIA

I WAS THERE: ROXANE MARQUEZ

I saw Morrissey two times. The first time, he made an in-person appearance at the KROQ 106.7 FM studios in Burbank. This was in 1990 or 1991. A group of friends ditched school to see him. Next thing you know, we're with about 100 Morrissey fans basically stalking him and the poor guy must've freaked out seeing all these nutty kids. He left the studios through whatever back door they had. The second time was when I saw him at UCLA. There was a riot and the concert ended early. Totally nuts.

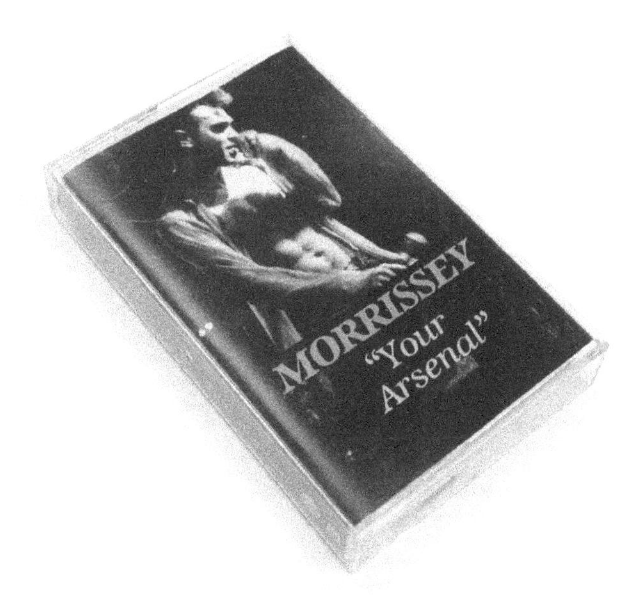

Morrissey released his third solo album *Your Arsenal* on 27 July 1992, which included the hit singles 'We Hate It When Our Friends Become Successful' and 'You're the One for Me, Fatty'.

MADSTOCK, FINSBURY PARK

8 AUGUST 1992, LONDON, UK

I WAS THERE: STEVE NASH

Madstock. It was the triumphant return of Madness after a lengthy hiatus. The setting was highly appropriate and the supports in Ian Dury and the Blockheads, Flowered Up and Gallon Drunk also suited the day. But even someone like myself, who went to see both Madness and Morrissey, which was a bonus of course, felt that Morrissey was not the most natural choice of support. My brother and I travelled on a concert coach trip. Such trips regularly ran from our local record shop and it's a shame such trips are no longer run. As we got to the outskirts of the park, you could see the pubs packed full of skinhead types and fans spilling out of them. You could see the atmosphere before tasting it, on leaving the coach and walking up to the park in the throng of the crowd. You could just detect the air of hostility more and more. It was like walking into a lion's den of trouble.

For most, Flowered Up and Gallon Drunk passed them by although I enjoyed their sets very much. It wasn't until local hero Ian Dury took the stage that more of the crowd filed in and started to pay attention, The Blockheads whipped the crowd into a frenzy and the party had started. After the Blockheads set, I assumed the party atmosphere would naturally continue with a triumphant Morrissey set before the main event of Madness. How wrong I was. Morrissey's set was fast approaching and the huge backdrop of the two skinhead girls appeared along with Morrissey's usual stage set up music, but suddenly the atmosphere took an unexpected turn and got much more hostile. You could hear booing 15 minutes before Morrissey had even appeared. When he arrived

in a half-undone gold lame shirt, hurling an enormous Union Jack flag around, large sectors of the crowd were unimpressed and coins began to fly. I could hear someone near me shout, 'I'm gonna get that bastard.' It wasn't going well but the band ploughed on until several pints and bottles headed Morrissey's way and within half an hour he told the band to stop playing and he swiftly departed.

The plain fact is, despite the considerable in-depth analysis from the *NME* that followed for several years after this gig, Morrissey did get it wrong that day. He may have been a huge fan of ska and skinheads, dressing in his usual quiff, turned-up jeans and Dr Martens boots, but that movement were not a huge fan of him. Morrissey was not to the taste of the ska and skinhead hardcore and he simply wasn't welcome on that stage on that day. The atmosphere completely changed when Madness took to the stage, so much so the large crowd accidentally created a mini earthquake which was felt several miles away during the introduction to 'One Step Beyond' as a result of some very enthusiastic 'nutty' dancing. Needless to say, Morrissey did not appear for the following day's scheduled support slot, which I'm sure was no surprise to anyone.

HMV

14 MARCH 1994, MANCHESTER, UK

I WAS THERE: LISA DAWN ROBINSON

I queued for eight hours to meet Morrissey at Manchester HMV when *Vauxhall and I* came out. I got a hug, a kiss and a squeeze of the waist from the great man. I even made him laugh. One of the best days of my life.

HMV, OXFORD STREET

15 MARCH 1994, LONDON, UK

I WAS THERE: STEVE NASH

On Monday 14th March 1994, Morrissey released what was and still is to many his greatest solo album, *Vauxhall and I*. Several weeks before the record chain HMV announced that Morrissey was to do two record signings, one in Oxford Street in London on the 15th and one in the HMV store in Manchester. At the time, my friend Paul and I were students both studying at university in Leicester but this was big news. Very big - we simply had to be there. It was a huge risk knowing we could arrive only to join the back of a two mile long queue, because the event was free and not ticketed and so there was no knowing how many people may turn up - or if Morrissey would.

We devised a strategy and put it into action. We set off from Leicester coach station taking an all-night 2am service so that we would arrive in London in the early hours. The coach was full and we even had to sit apart. But with trusty Walkman in hand, it was the perfect opportunity for me to listen several times to the one day old *Vauxhall and I*. I'm pretty sure Paul was doing exactly the same thing in his seat several rows in front of me. We arrived at HMV around 7am. It was raining heavily but we simply did not care and our spirits were massively lifted when we saw that the queue was only about 20 deep. We knew that, bar some uncontrolled riot, we were definitely getting in and our dreams of meeting Morrissey were actually going to happen at lunchtime that day.

The early morning passed slowly. First many delivery drivers came back and forth to the many stores on Oxford Street. Then of course the mass of commuters appeared before giving way to the throng of shoppers and sightseers. By the hour the queue grew - at first a few, then a few hundred, then it was clearly a few thousand and by lunchtime it had snaked its way into several side streets. Fortunately the kind employees of HMV had built some indoor railings for the queue and they let us in the store at about 10.30am so we could sit on the carpet. We all began to chat to each other, swap stories about how far we had travelled, previous gigs we had attended, etc. and the atmosphere was rapidly building. Morrissey was due to appear at 1pm and it was fever pitch by midday. Moments before his arrival, we were told he would sign three items each which for a while he did, until the store realised the queue was barely moving so it was swiftly cut to just one item but we were rewarded for our early start by getting three signatures each.

All of a sudden, there he was, just metres away, I began to get nervous just knowing that within minutes I would be stood next to him, hopefully shaking his hand or even speaking to him. I could see Paul was feeling the same. It was almost too much for us and everyone else within view. One by one we watched as fans took their place for their moment of glory, Morrissey dressed in a very smart brown suit jacket with a 'Famous when dead' badge on one lapel. His close friend at that time, Jake, was stood just behind him watching the event unfold. Every so often, Morrissey would turn and have a brief chat with Jake before returning to the job in hand, the signing. It was one place from my turn, my heart was beating fast, my mouth very dry and suddenly there I was, just a table between Morrissey and me, all those years of intense admiration and for a minute of my life, it was my moment in his presence, it was surreal to say the least.

He signed a poster, the *Vauxhall and I* LP and CD. I said I was Stephen with a 'ph'. He said, 'Hmmm, interesting,' with him being with a 'v' of course. I could barely think, let alone speak. I said, 'You're going to get writer's cramp by the end of this.' He laughed and said, 'I will be fine, I'm very strong.' I thanked him for all of his work and how it had related so much to my life and told him I loved him and we shook hands. Yes I touched the great idol. I couldn't resist, I just had to. And then it was Paul's turn and he did very much the same thing. I remember he asked Morrissey if he could liven up his copy of the *Shot* photo book for him. Morrissey said, 'I'll try' before scrawling that famous large signature right across the front in gold pen. Fortunately, we brought a camera so Paul took some photos of my moment and then of course I did the same for his moment.

We had done it. We had met Morrissey, spoken to him, touched him and got his autograph. The euphoria was off the scale. Whilst on the raised platform, I turned and looked out at the scale of the queue. It was as far as I could see snaking out of the store. It was then I noticed the store had built a small area in the front for fans to simply watch the event. I also noticed a TV film-type camera and suddenly realised this event was major as it was being filmed as well. I later discovered it was MTV that filmed the event.

This was of course still pre-internet and mobile phone times, so it was primitive camera and film equipment only. We joined the crowd area and watched others take their turn, hugging him, handing him letters, being totally overcome by his presence. After an hour or so, Morrissey suddenly moved from the table to a huge poster of his face by the side of the crowd area and wrote 'Bigmouth' in huge letters with a black felt pen and the crowd applauded wildly. It was a magical day but it was time for us to head back to the coach station. On leaving the store, we looked left at the queue. We walked up Oxford Street a short way but still could not see the end of it. We had been in the store since the signing started at 1pm and it was 3pm when we left so I somehow think many of those much further down the street may not have got nowhere near the event before Morrissey departed.

Morrissey released his fifth solo album *Southpaw Grammar* on 28 August 1995. The cover photo of boxer Kenny Lane was taken from the April 1963 issue of boxing magazine *The Ring*.

CARDIFF INTERNATIONAL ARENA

27 NOVEMBER 1995, CARDIFF, UK

I WAS THERE: IOAN HUMPHREYS

I did get to see Morrissey supporting David Bowie at Cardiff International Arena on his Outside tour. It must have been one of the early dates as I think Bowie eventually booted Morrissey off the tour.

I WAS THERE: STEPHEN NASH

Morrissey had regularly made his admiration of David Bowie's work very public. So much so, David had covered 'I Know It's Gonna Happen Someday' on his 1992 *Black Tie White Noise* album. In 1995, David had announced a tour to support his *Outside* album. I was a huge Bowie fan so buying a ticket to finally see him live was a dream come true. A few weeks later, Morrissey had announced he was to support David on this tour, which naturally made this gig unbelievably exciting. The gig finally arrived and I took my place in the front row on the barrier but the Morrissey set was not up to its usual brilliance. Obviously it was not his audience but he appeared somewhat fraught and you could detect a certain level of anxiousness. Something just didn't feel quite right. Morrissey did a considerable amount of complaining between the songs and the set was fast paced and short. He said something along the lines of, 'We're sorry but we've been instructed that this will be the final song.'

It later transpired that Morrissey had fallen out with David about the length of his support slot. Apparently it was too long and the Cardiff gig was the final straw for Morrissey so he pulled out of the remainder of the tour, leaving Morrissey fans in Aberdeen the night after as miffed as I had been the night I had travelled all the way to Glasgow in 1991.

On 4 February 2003 Johnny Marr + the Healers released their debut album *Boomslang*. The band featured drummer Zak Starkey and former Kula Shaker bassist Alonza Bevan.

PETÕFI, CSARNOK

5 JULY 2006, BUDAPEST, HUNGARY

I WAS THERE: KATE SULLIVAN

My best Morrissey gig? My Twinnie (he shares a birthday with me) Mark Doyle and I went to see him in Budapest. It was an open air gig in a park and so we wandered up to the park mid-afternoon to see where we were going to be going that evening. There was no one around. There was a little bar next to where the arena was so we stopped and had a drink and then another drink and another drink and then the tour bus must have arrived and then we had another drink and then they started sound checking. So we finished our drinks and we went round to have a look at what was going on. It was quite a small arena with a wooden fence all around it and there were some wooden steps you could walk up and look over the top of the fence. We were pissed. They did three songs and we were stood at the top of these steps, looking over the fence and cheering and clapping. We were the only people there. At one point he said, 'Thank you.' I said, 'There's no way he would have seen us.' But when we were in the venue that night I looked back to where we had been stood and it was really, really close. He definitely saw us. So that was our own little private Morrissey concert.

ECHO ARENA

6 NOVEMBER 2009, LIVERPOOL, UK

HE WASN'T THERE LONG: MARTIN BLENCO

I have two contrasting memories of seeing Morrissey solo as he's cancelled on me a few times. In 2009 my girlfriend and I decided to go and see him at the Britannia Pier Theatre in Great Yarmouth which meant a 200 mile drive from Manchester that afternoon, including several breakneck manoeuvres overtaking tractors and turnip lorries on the A17 on possibly the slowest road in Britain. So there was the triple 'thrill' of almost dying under the wheels of an oncoming two ton truck, the prospect of arriving home to a series of fixed camera speeding tickets and not knowing whether Moz would actually put in an appearance. We arrived on the seafront, met my mates - who couldn't get in without the tickets I had - in front of the pier with its coloured lights glowing in the gathering gloom and got into the crowded bar in time for one quick drink before the great man arrived on stage. I can't remember much about the show but the adrenalin rush of having successfully made it there on time was great. And the memory of that mad dash across the swede fields of England with Kate muttering 'Oh god!' and adopting the brace position every time I overtook a slow moving vehicle will always be with me.

Kate Sullivan got her own private Moz concert when she caught the Budapest soundcheck

We were also at the infamous Echo Arena show. We were about 12 rows from the stage and had a great view. The crowd was convivial. Then some tosser decided to throw a small plastic bottle of water at Morrissey. It was a good shot and glanced off his forehead. He was surprised rather than injured and, after a moment's hesitation, he walked off stage. In the immediate aftermath Boz Boorer, Moz's guitarist, was on stage and trying to identify the culprit, giving the crowd the impression that if they offered the offender up to the stage crew for a good kicking backstage then the show would continue. The crowd did but Moz didn't and 5,000 disappointed but amazingly placid Morrissey fans shuffled out of the Echo Arena.

After working as a prolific session musician, including stints with the Pretenders, Beck, Pet Shop Boys, Billy Bragg, The The, Electronic, Modest Mouse, The Cribs, Talking Heads and Hans Zimmer, Johnny Marr released his debut solo album *The Messenger* on 25 February 2013.

HOP FARM FESTIVAL

2 JULY 2011, PADDOCK WOOD, UK

I WAS THERE: MARK REED

Day two of the Hop Farm Festival. Morrissey is headlining without, as far as I can tell, any real justification for his alleged second Indian summer. His commercial currency after 2004's *You are the Quarry* is long since spent and his fourth greatest hits album – following 2008's *Greatest Hits* with 2011's redundant, pointless and heard-it-all-before *The Very Best Of* - managed to hit the lowly heights of 68 in the moribund charts.

Face it, even from the view of the once-fervent Morrissey disciple – yes, I am one - Morrissey is commercially washed up. Fast entering his second moribund era, he is iconic but not for what he is but what he once was.

So, if you've never seen him before, or are wearing rose-coloured gladioli, you might conceivably think that this is the man at his best. Very far from it. Even in his doldrums of 2001, four years since an album and freewheeling rudderless through a concert existence with no commercial future, Morrissey had with him a supple, strong band he kept, in various forms for 13 long glorious years. Supported ably by Alain Whyte – the finest foil he had in his solo years, Gary Day, and the versatile Boz Boorer, those years were his glory years. The 1991 *Kill Uncle* tour was, and remains, probably his single brightest concert period. The fresh, and ravenous, band – and the reborn, bequiffed indie Jesus, roamed the land and conquered all. The screech and howl of a messanic comeback on that tour has never been accurately captured by anyone, and quite unlike anything I have ever experienced any other time in my life. The band leaped out as hungry tigers, and Morrissey himself preened and shone after a five year exile from the stage.

Now – 20 years after – that band a fading memory and replaced with by and large thumping lumpen American sessioneers, that is a memory. Morrissey, who may very well dump band members at the slightest whim, employs these compliant workers as a backing band: only Boz Boorer – sorely underrated and capable of playing anything but chess – demonstrates any flair or subtlety. Compare tonight's crunching and disturbingly 1976 stadium rock plod through 'This Charming Man' with the original 1983 version. And weep. The subtle dexterity, the deftnes of touch, the class and the verve are all absent.

And there are far too many Smiths songs.

Morrissey now represents a curious demographic: the young idealists have been honed into prime ministers at direct odds with everything Morrissey ever expressed (up to the date of the show, anyway) and shell-fund managers. I bet every politician you hate has a favourite Smiths song. And I bet it's Moz's disturbingly castrated, mogadon-paced, lethargic rendition of 'There is a Light That Never Goes Out', rendered tonight without passion, without pace. Morrissey recites the words, as he has so long for this song, that divorces the song from meaning. It becomes just words, music to be sung along to in a big fat field. The song plods on at half-pace, extended into a frankly tedious coda, as Morrissey climbs down to the crowd and shakes the unwashed flesh.

And there are far too many Smiths songs.

Once upon a time – at the birth of his solo career – when his band were capable and had fire, the renditions of 'London' and 'Shoplifters of the World Unite' were aflame with a righteous reclaiming of the body of work. Now they are tired cover versions. Jesse Tobias, former Red Hot Chili Pepper, crunches big rock riffs as if he were in any band in the world, not gifted with some of the most glorious material ever committed to the human ear. Solomon Walker and his ex-Smashing Pumpkin brother Matt are disposable parts of a rock lawnmower, running through the songs with little fluency. How Morrissey could have chosen these musicians baffles me, unless they were a reasonably good buy. Even on 'Meat Is Murder', which sees the band run from silence to a deafening roar in seconds as the stage is bathed with blood, the song is simply nostalgia and karaoke. Memories of memories. And 25 years since the final Smiths songs, there are few left to contest them.

I spend most of 'Meat Is Murder', whilst the band play in blood-red strobes and Morrissey intones 'Eat – Kill – MURDER', transfixed by the moments where the self-appointed intensity of the moment is broken by a fairground wheel in a dozen shades of orange and green and blue neon unapologetically breaking out from behind the stage every few seconds. 'Eat! Kill!' WHEEEEEEEEEE! 'Eat! Kill! Murd-' WHEEEEEEEE!

Morrissey may sing these songs wonderfully but his career and legacy deserve better than being known as a tribute act to himself. For one who never wants to reform The Smiths, Morrissey's choice of songs belies the fact. Maybe he would have preferred The Smiths to quietly kowtow to his ego: but make no mistake, the 'band' he had that carried him from 1991 to 2004 has been quietly dismantled for cheaper, more pliable alternatives.

Whilst, thankfully, Morrissey has never sought to return to the 'Play An Album In Full' or reformation route, his career has been distinctly nostalgic – it always has been a nostalgia for a mysterious, idealised time of pre-youth, framed before puberty, the world of adults when he was a child, and thus, to an extent, a desire to return and reclaim an innocence – Morrissey has never, thankfully, rested on laurels. Even now, again, without record company backing in a self-funded wasteland waiting for an elusive big deal, Morrissey continues doggedly on clinging to the old ways of sign / deal / album / tour.

But there are too many Smiths songs.

Wonderful as those songs are this band isn't The Smiths and they tackle the songs without flair or attack, turning them into dull cover versions and punctuating a potentially exciting set with the knowledge that you are never more than 10 minutes away from a butchering of a 25 year old song which is inevitably in the wrong key or tempo or bludgeoned with power chords.

After this though, his band ably and wonderfully perform the solo material. Unlike many of his peers, Moz is blessed with an enormous body of work – 11 solo albums and numerous compilations of rarities – though, on the strength of tonight, you may not know it. Some of his finest work is barely referenced, with only one song from most

of his records. Whilst it is a lovely moment for the much under-appreciated 'Alma Matters' to appear again in set lists after an 11 year absence, think about what is excused for his choices – 'The More You Ignore Me', 'Interesting Drug', 'Suedehead', 'Now My Heart is Full'. Can anyone say that 'You're The One For Me, Fatty' is better than these songs? On the other hand, Morrissey opens with 'I Want The One I Can't Have' and from there the Hop Farm crowd is in the palm of his hand – if what you want is a set of memories constructed for singing along to in a big field.

To an extent now, Morrissey is a parody of himself. We all become entrenched with age and, for Morrissey and a fragile ego, the vindication enforce the ego and makes the act to an extent, potentially. To start with, Morrissey's weapon was his intelligence. Now it is fear and withdrawal. No one ever tells Morrissey things are bad ideas and so there is the risk is of a slide into an irrelevancy or a artistic cul-de-sac. Which is why there is a Morrissey song called 'You're The One For Me, Fatty'. But years of being proven largely right, and being the one key cog in the Morrissey industry, have made him, even without being aware, even when being himself, a parody of himself.

His band, meanwhile, perform the solo songs – especially the later ones they have almost entirely written themselves – such as 'You Have Killed Me', 'Irish Blood, English heart', 'First of The Gang To Die', 'I'm Throwing My Arms Around Paris', with no shortage of belief. It's the older songs, the ones they did not write, that sound not quite authentic.

Perhaps tonight, it's that Morrissey knows his competition is fierce. The rest of the bill is the strongest he has headed in his life. 'How the hell do you follow Iggy and The Stooges?' he says. And for the first time, perhaps ever, Morrissey descends from the stage for communion and to press the flesh and shake the hand of his crowd. Normally, to an extent, aloof. Certainly, the stage invasions and euphoria that accompanied the 1991-1995 tours appear to have faded into soft middle age. So instead of the crowd coming to him, tonight – for the first time – Morrissey comes to them: but to an experienced eye, 20 years of Morrissey gigs later, tonight is by no means the man at his best or even close to it. If this is close to anything, it's the wilderness years between albums when all Morrissey was, was having becoming unemployed except for occasional live appearances.

With the legacy of The Smiths a memory of a memory, his solo career at a curious crossroads, his band take his songs, good, bad, ugly – and render them all with the shape of a generic indie thump. Dressed identically, his Sleeperblokes, the gang he desperately wanted when younger, compliantly deliver B-grade mid 90's indieland, filled with enthusiasm and skill but no taste. And the songs! He sings them so beautifully, when he can be bothered. The new material is average – just another three Morrissey songs to join the 250 or so already in existence – sandwiched between a curious mix of album tracks and occasional hit singles. With so many hits – Morrissey has 35 solo singles and another 18 or so as part of The Smiths – it's a choice of songs that sees most of his 2009 era set list junked (only four songs were also performed on his most recent tour) – and whilst you can never please everybody all the time, his sets are perverse and unpredictable. Not helped by a band that mauls classics in different keys or tempos, flattening the glory of 'There is a Light That Never Goes Out' into a huge singalong on a farm and pretending that 'Suedehead' or even 'Something is Squeezing My Skull' doesn't exist.

But Morrissey is iconic now: all he has to do is be, not even do anything, to be Morrissey. Like it or not, he's becoming an elder statesmen, entering a late period irrelevancy, backed by a band terrified of taking risks and terrified of the inevitable sack. But maybe it's time to get off the stage. There's little new left in these old tricks for now. Sack the band. Take risks. Be alive again, Morrissey. You are very good at what you do, but what you do isn't very good anymore.

I WAS THERE: ROBERT NEGRI

I was supposed to see Morrissey at Brixton in July 1991 but got drunk on Grolsch and Southern Comfort at my mate's house and fell asleep in his garden. I was still mangled on my way to the gig so I went home.

I WAS THERE: BRIDGET DUFFY

The Smiths at the Winter Gardens in Margate was my husband's first ever gig. He enjoyed James. I saw that same tour at Birmingham Hippodrome and couldn't wait for James to finish their set as I just wanted to see The Smiths. I went with my friend Lorraine. I wore black Sixties ski pants and a paisley Sixties rave shirt with a boxy suede Sixties jacket. Lorraine and I both thought Johnny was the bee's knees - and I had just gone veggie!

I WAS THERE: ANDY GILLESPIE

I was there when Morrissey showed up at a book signing on Sunset Boulevard for Johnny Rogan, the Smiths biographer.

COPLEY SYMPHONY HALL

10 NOVEMBER 2018, SAN DIEGO, CALIFORNIA

I WAS THERE: CARLOS RODRIGUEZ

I've been a Morrissey fan since the early Nineties and high school. But since my wife got me front row tickets at a Staples Center show a while back for a birthday present, we make the trip whenever he is close. Prior to San Diego we had attended about 10 concerts landing in the front of the pit a good seven times. Like at all Moz concerts, fans reach out and hope to have the opportunity to touch the man's hand, or have a record or an arm signed. I was able to shake the master's hand at show in Santa Barbara, as did my wife. But for the past 30 plus years some fans that take a chance to get closer. At most shows, those who make it get their five second hug and are escorted back to their spot and the show goes on, as at the Tropicalia Festival recently. I tried to get onstage in Reno, Nevada to no avail. I made it on stage and just as I was lifting myself up, security grabbed me.

San Diego ended differently. It was not planned. I just saw the opportunity and took my shot. I made it on stage and past security to hug our beloved Morrissey. On video it looks aggressive but honestly at that moment I was literally beside myself, like an out of body experience. It was a rush of energy that I have never felt before. Granted I am a 40 year old man but that I was able to move that quickly still is crazy to me. I hugged the Master and told him 'thank you' before both of us were grabbed by security. He was smiling and laughing, especially after seeing me headlocked and escorted back to the pit. There was a lot of backlash from fans and news media alike. It got so bad Moz himself came to my defence on Facebook:

'Nobody tried to punch M last night. Morrissey's fans are not malicious. The fans were simply doing what they have been doing for almost 30 years. Trying anything they could do to jump onstage and touch him, or hug him.'

ALBERT HALL

4 SEPTEMBER 2019, MANCHESTER, UK

I WAS THERE: KATE SULLIVAN

In 1989 I was going out with somebody called Neil who lived in a bedsit in Mayfield Road in Whalley Range. Linder Sterling, Morrissey's best mate, lived upstairs. Neil was approached by the BBC arts TV programme *Arena* to see if they could film in his bedsit. They were doing a programme about The Smiths and Neil's bedsit was like Linder's bedsit.

There was a communal postbox. Morrissey quite often used to send postcards to Linder so me and Neil would race down every morning to see if there were any postcards from Morrissey that we could have a look at. These days you'd take a photo of them, of course!

I don't think Morrissey has cancelled on me loads. I think I've had about four cancellations which, given the amount I've been to, I don't think is too bad.

I went to all the gigs on the mini tour of Manchester he did in 2006. I've seen him all over the world. I've been to New York to see him, at Radio City Music Hall twice, and in Budapest and Paris. Why have I fallen out of love with him? The politics and the music really. Things like sending wreaths and condolences to the Krays' funerals. He's just a dick. Nobody who's a decent person thinks the Krays were good. And it's all posturing because I'm sure he doesn't really mean it.

And I don't like the politics and the racism, which I never used to think it was before. I thought he was misunderstood before. All that wrapping himself in the flag thing? I think he was just a bit ahead of his time, because Noel Gallagher got himself into Downing Street by doing the same thing. But it's more the music. Boz Boorer has got to be the worst person to pair up with, to write music with, because the music is so pedestrian. He gets a shit tune off Boz Boorer and then the words he puts to it are really dreadful.

Ringleader of the Tormentors is an absolutely corking album and *You are the Quarry* has got three good songs on it. But that was the last good record he did. The last one (*World Peace Is None of Your Business*) was bloody awful. Although not everyone agrees with me. After seeing Johnny Marr at the Apollo in Manchester, I was telling a friend of my daughter's boyfriend how bloody terrible Morrissey's last album was and she said it was the best album he's ever done.

Johnny's great. He's the music. He's still got it going on, basically. It is a real shame that he and Morrissey aren't paired up. But it's not all Boz Boorer's fault that Morrissey's music is shit. Morrissey's lyrics are also shit now. Seeing Johnny is the only time you're going to hear Smiths songs played properly. Boz Boorer can't do it. Boz Boorer has he difficult bits taped. He's not playing them. He can't play them. When Johnny does 'How Soon is Now?' the hairs stand up on the back of my neck. I never saw The Smiths live so when Johnny plays it now is the only time I'll ever hear it played properly. When Johnny does 'Please Please Please…' I just want to cry.

I WAS THERE: MARTIN BLENCO

After The Smiths split up, Johnny's career has taken various different paths. Although I'd seen Morrissey solo a few times, I hadn't seen Johnny on his own. I did get tickets for Hebden Bridge Trades Club a while back but then found I had to work that evening. I finally got to see him at the Albert Hall in Manchester in 2019. I'd read online reviews that suggested he was doing a clutch of Smiths numbers and that I wouldn't be disappointed. And I wasn't. It was great to hear those songs sounding as fresh and as beautiful as ever.

PAYING TRIBUTE

The Smiths may be no more. Morrissey or Johnny may not be playing your town any time soon. But around the world there are tributes acts to Manchester's finest sons.

Chris stole Morrissey's do not disturb sign from his hotel room door

CHRISTOPHER QUINN FROM CALIGULA BLUSHED, WASHINGTON DC

I was born exactly one week before Johnny Marr on October 24, 1963. I was coming of age when The Smiths hit. I was raised by two older brothers and two older sisters as far as music was concerned. All of them went off in different musical directions. My oldest brother was really into the Allman Brothers, the Doobie Brothers, Steely Dan and Todd Rundgren. My oldest sister was really into Motown, R&B and all the black music at the time. My middle brother was more into Seventies pop like Elton John and Elvis Costello. And the sister closest to me in age was the one who had the biggest influence because she was into David Bowie, Roxy Music and Mott the Hoople. Each one of them gave me something and all of it was based in melodic music. My first visit to England was November 1983 and I realised in hindsight that I narrowly missed seeing *The Smiths* as they were playing in London while I was there. But at the time I was still into heavy metal as I went through a phase in my late teens where it was Judas Priest and Iron Maiden and bands like that. It wasn't until I got home that I happened to catch one of those American radio stations that did this British feature every Friday night and I heard the song 'Heaven Knows I'm Miserable Now'. That was it. Within a month I owned *The Smiths* album and I had a haircut like Morrissey. The music was beautiful.

While I haven't performed it live that many times when I first started doing this, I found 'Heaven Knows I'm Miserable Now' really difficult to do. I'm better at it now. The music is just incredible, the shimmer of the guitars, the words. I never heard anybody sing words like that. And the line that jumps out at you of course is, 'What she asked of me at the end of the day, Caligula would have blushed.' I think I laughed out loud. So I was really, really hooked. And it was funny because I bought the first album thinking I would find the song and didn't. But then I latched onto 'Pretty Girls Make Graves' and 'I Don't Owe You Anything' and 'This Charming Man' and it just grew.

I grew up in Rockville, Maryland, in the suburbs of DC. There was a record store called Yesterday and Today and the proprietor would go on buying trips to the UK three, four, five times a year and come back with all this great stuff. He knew what I liked and he would look out for stuff for me. He turned me on to bands like The Trash Can

Sinatras, That Petrol Emotion and Prefab Sprout.

The UK has a band called The Smyths and their lead singer saw The Smiths. They and we are the only two (tribute acts) that saw The Smiths. I saw them twice in '85, on the *Meat Is Murder* tour, at a theatre in DC which to this day is the greatest live show I've ever seen and then in Philadelphia the following night. I'd became close friends with a young fellow who worked at that record store and he and I and a group of people went down to meet them at the Shoreham Hotel and we found out the room Morrissey was in and I stole his 'do not disturb' sign and got him to autograph it.

When I first tried to set up a tribute act in the Nineties, before the information age, it was very, very difficult to find the right people. DC likes to congratulate itself on being very cosmopolitan and really it's a black hole. Doing a Smiths tribute in DC is the equivalent of being a classical ballerina in Galveston, Texas. I've played DC once, at the 9.30 Club, opening for a Neil Diamond tribute band. That's a pretty prestigious gig and the place was sold out. We got to perform to about 2,000 people.

In the early 90s I was trying to do this with the drummer from Girlfriend in a Coma. But it was one of those things where you could find a bass player but couldn't find a guitarist or you'd find a guitarist but bass players were nowhere to be found.

There was a Smiths/Morrissey karaoke night at this place in Baltimore and I got the report back that there were 120 people there. And we thought, 'If we could put a competent band together we could get twice as many people.' And we did. The first time we played was in October 2006 and we got about 150 people there. We played again three months later and the place was sold out.

I call myself a fan of The Smiths first. I do appreciate Morrissey but I don't think he's done a great album since *Vauxhall & I* and he's starting to get a bit dodgy in the head. I consider it my responsibility to channel Morrissey's moods, his emotions. It's less important that the guitarist wears stripy shirts or the bass player has a blond buzz cut. It's the band's job to nail the songs.

Morrissey cancelled a bunch of shows in the north east in 2007. He played at the Filene Center in Wolf Trap, Virginia and my wife and I went. It was a good show but you could tell he was struggling. The next day I was walking into a client's office when I got a text saying Morrissey wasn't playing the Ram's Head in Baltimore that night and that if we could be in Baltimore by 6pm we were filling in for him. So we did. We were offered as a free consolation. The show had sold out, probably about 1,700 tickets, and about half the crowd showed up to watch us. It was the most amazing thing. We played to 700 to 800 people from all over the world. There were Brits, Aussies and people from the West Coast. Everybody was standing with crossed arms during the first song or two and then they let go and just had a great time.

Afterwards, I sat down on the edge of the stage listening to people's stories for about two hours and the common thread was. 'This is better than a Morrissey show.' That makes you feel good. I think what they're saying is, 'You're giving it all you've got and you play an awesome set.' We're playing all the songs you want to hear. It was such an amazing high, as people were singing the songs back at us. It was almost impossible for me, with my in-ear monitor, to hear myself or to hear the band. That's what you want.

Girlfriend in a Coma split up because I wanted to book more gigs. I don't know how much longer I can do this. Morrissey may be able to keep doing it, but at some point I'm going to lose credibility. Peter Pan may have to grow up at some point.

My by-line is 'Caligula Blushed - there are only two Morrisseys!' Onstage I'll say, 'There are only two Morrisseys and only one shows up.'

All of my kids love The Smiths! My son Sean is an absolute Marr disciple. He met the man himself in October 2018 at the Fillmore. Johnny was really impressed that Sean had earned and saved all of his own money to purchase his own Jaguar, and Sean's already saved another $1,500 with his eye on a Rick. At some point Sean will join us on stage. He's usually at our gigs as backline support to the guitarist. He's not quite ready, but I'm really looking forward to that day.

Caligula Blushed can be contacted via their Facebook page.

EDDIE STEPHENS FROM THESE HANDSOME DEVILS, LOS ANGELES, CALIFORNIA

These Handsome Devils with Eddie Stephens (far right)

Right after the *You are the Quarry* album dropped in 2004, a bunch of mutual friends decided they wanted to do a tribute to The Smiths and Morrissey - two brothers, a cousin, a brother-in-law and me. I was the honorary family member. We're based in LA, which is quite the mecca for Morrissey bands but back in 2004 the only one that was doing it was The Sweet and Tender Hooligans. So we decided to jump on and see what was going to happen. The band's been running for 15 years now.

We were all doing other projects. I'd been a cover band musician my entire career, because I learned very quickly that if I wanted to make money at it and be in my own bed at night, I had to play other people's music. The other guys were doing some original stuff that obviously wasn't really going anywhere, because that's not a very prudent side of the industry anymore. So we all came together to do this one.

We play a minimum of 15 to 20 shows a year, at least once a month. If you don't do enough gigs, you don't remain relevant on the scene. There's at least seven or eight Morrissey/Smiths tributes in LA and you can't go a weekend without a Morrissey event happening somewhere in the general LA area. You really have to play fairly often to stay in people's minds and fresh in their faces and their ears.

We'll go wherever anyone wants to host us and play the proper wage. Mostly it's LA and Orange County, to the south of Los Angeles. We are beginning to stretch out to San Diego, but we haven't travelled out of state, because nobody wants to pay the proper salary. Morrissey bands are starting to pop up more and more all over the United States. There's a new one up in Seattle, Washington and for the Pacific North West, they're going to call there before they call us because quite frankly it's cheaper.

People come on stage. Generally it's more the female clientele than the male. I don't know why. Maybe they have more cojones? When we do our big shows, we'll get the gladioli. There's a huge flower district in downtown LA where you can get them all the time and they're really cheap. So we'll buy bunches of gladioli and toss 'em out. We give them to people in the audience, which they absolutely love. Doing a tribute show, we're trying to create this illusion of a Morrissey/Smiths show. When Morrissey does his solo shows, the band will be in matching outfits while he wears what he wants. We'll do that too. It's all part of the illusion, and people get lost in that illusion and they'll do their part, jumping on the stage or throwing undergarments on stage. If the show goes well, usually something like that does happen. Not as often as you might think – or desire – but it does happen.

We have two guitar players that we use live. One does more Johnny Marr stuff and the other does the Boz Boorer stuff. They don't always play a Rickenbacker but they do try to emulate the tone. They are trying to recreate the sound, like I am as the bass player in the group. We're all doing our bit to create the audio illusion as well as our front man creating the visual illusion.

I don't usually play with a pick but when we do a lot of Smiths material I have to, because Andy did. Being the bass player playing the Andy Rourke stuff is just so much fun. It's not a gig that you do and fall asleep on, because he played so much and his parts were so intricate.

I have a couple of theories on why there are so many Morrissey tribute bands when Morrissey himself is still performing. I don't know if you've looked at his set list latterly, but he plays a lot of his new stuff and a lot of his really obscure stuff. He doesn't play a whole lot of the Smiths stuff because of the break up. I prefer the 'William, It was Really Nothing', 'Barbarism Begins at Home' really die-hard Smiths stuff that you'll never hear live again. Even when Johnny Marr goes out he doesn't play a whole bunch of the Smiths stuff that you want to hear.

One of the marquee gigs that my group has is a local swap meet, which doesn't sound like it should be a marquee gig, but it's the mecca for tribute bands in LA. We do three one hour sets, all Morrissey or Smiths and no repeats. So people are getting at least 50 different songs from us every time we play there. And people hear those songs that they really want to hear and that they know they're otherwise never going to hear live again. So that's one side of it, the variety.

The other side of it is that Morrissey has quite the reputation for cancelling. I have friends who went to his Paso Robles, California show in 2017. It was an outdoor show.

The opener went on and it was as cold as shit, like 47 degrees Fahrenheit. Everybody's waiting for Morrissey to come on and all of a sudden this lady comes on over the PA and says the show's cancelled. And it was because the heater on stage was broken, so Morrissey wouldn't go on. There was a mixed bag of reactions to that. Some were like, 'Poor Morrissey. I hope he doesn't get sick.' And others were like, 'Fuck this guy, that's fucked up. We're out of here.'

We don't cancel because the heater didn't come on. We still go out there and play. We don't cancel because of whatever unknown reason. We still go out there and do the show. So I think people enjoy that when they make plans to come see a Morrissey tribute they know the show is going to happen, outside of a death. They appreciate the non-cancellation factor.

These Handsome Devils can be contacted via thesehandsomedevils.com

---

STEVEN AND FRASER FROM FRANKLY, THE SMITHS, UK

Our first public performance was actually as a duo. Steven and Fraser (our Morrissey and Marr) performed a short acoustic set of The Smiths songs at a charity night in Edinburgh called Maladjusted in May 2017, and then later that year we played our first full band show at The Glad Cafe in Glasgow. We sold out the venue and have been going from strength to strength ever since.

Frankly, The Smiths

We got together thanks to Fraser's persistence! He had been trying to form a Smiths tribute band for a number of years, with our drummer, Gary, actually attending the very first rehearsals which auditioned some unsuccessful Morrisseys. After putting the idea to bed for a couple of years, Fraser then put out a hopeful advert on Gumtree not expecting much, but both Gary and Steven responded. After an incredible rehearsal they firmly cemented their places in the band. Dean our bassist then joined a little bit later thanks to bumping into Fraser on the street! Fraser and Dean both knew one another already as they have mutual friends. After a quick catch up Fraser asked Dean if he would be interested in rehearsing with the band and the rest as they say is history.

Fraser is a music graduate and has been in a number of bands since the age of 18.

Dean is from a music background as well and has played bass in a few Glasgow-based bands. Gary's job is as a wedding band drummer so he constantly absorbs and plays music too. Steven was a Smiths tribute band singer in waiting. As a massive fan of The Smiths and Morrissey's music and with a powerful stage presence and singing voice, he is a natural at keeping the audience captivated and believing that they are at an actual Smiths gig.

All of the band except Dean were already hardcore Smiths fans. Dean didn't become as obsessed as the rest of us until he learned Andy Rourke's incredibly intricate basslines!

To contact Frankly, The Smiths visit their Facebook page.

PAUL BLAKE FROM VIVA MORRISSEY, UK

I began advertising for band members in 2007 and we played our first show, under our previous name, Ambitious Outsiders, later that year. I hadn't realised how much of a handicap it was going to be that our name didn't have the 'instant artist recognition factor', for want of a triter term, but it quickly became apparent that we may need to be more obvious in our choice of name were the band to survive. I certainly never started this band to get rich. I just wanted to go out and sing these fantastic songs to other people who might like them too.

Paul Blake is Viva Morrissey

The audience at tribute band shows is mainly people who tend to only know the most popular songs, although it is quite a broad church, including people who loved The Smiths the first time around but maybe fell away somewhere between then and now, to younger people who have discovered Morrissey and The Smiths through older siblings, or even their mothers and fathers.

We've played in some of the same cities and towns where Morrissey draws thousands of people to his shows, and we've struggled to get 100 people along to ours. Part of the reason for this may be the misconception that we only play Morrissey's solo material, when in actual fact half of our set is made up of songs written by Morrissey/Marr.

I love all the songs, and they're all a joy to play. We always move the set around for each concert, and we're continually adding songs to our repertoire, so it never gets stale or uninspiring. Morrissey rarely plays many of his more well-known songs, so even the more knowledgeable members of our audience are happy to hear us play some of those, but I always find room for a few songs that perhaps an audience wouldn't be expecting to hear, simply because they're songs I particularly want to sing.

Why a tribute to Morrissey rather than The Smiths, particularly given he's still touring? Apart from that voice and those lyrics? Because he's such a singular artist and utterly unique in terms of his personality and character, despite my best efforts.

There are innumerable things that elevate him above most other singers/lyricists. It's not simply about personal taste when we speak of the true innovators, the pantheon of greats who altered the landscape and will forever stand the test of time.

Morrissey changed the lexicon of popular music, altered the very language used in popular songs and brought a strand of social realism to pop lyrics which hadn't been seen before and he deserves to be mentioned in the same breath as Elvis, Dylan, Bowie, Johnny Rotten, John Lennon and the handful of others who quite literally changed the world.

I was always frustrated by the fact that Morrissey's career, post-The Smiths, seemed to be treated as little more than a footnote to the work he did with The Smiths, with only a handful of solo tracks played. Also, it never really worked for me when they did play Morrissey songs, as I don't recall the Smiths ever playing Morrissey's solo material, and so the whole thing lacked authenticity. I'd often thought it would be great if someone would focus on the present day Morrissey, and perform a contemporary Morrissey set, which always includes much loved Smiths classics anyway, and as no one came along, I decided to do it myself. I realise that there are those who don't consider 'tribute' bands to be 'real' bands, but I think of us, in relation to Morrissey, as the same play, but with a different cast, that's all. It's me. It's Morrissey. What a combination!

We tend to average one or two shows per month during the course of a year, zigzagging our way up, down, and across the UK.

Viva Morrissey can be contacted via Facebook

GRAHAM SAMPSON FROM THE SMYTHS, UK

We got it from Mike Joyce's very own mouth that we're Smith not Smythe. 15 years ago we were rehearsing for our first live show in April 2004. We were all Smiths fans who were original musicians getting a little too old in the music industry – we were in our late 20s. Rather than quietly going away, we decided we

The Smyths with Smiths and Morrissey creative collaborator Stephen Street

wanted to carry on playing live. Doing this was really borne out of a passion to take the songs that we love by a band that we love and to see what we could do.

Some bands are timeless. The music of The Smiths will always prevail. I felt that back in the day, buying their records as a teenager and going to see them. They've got a fantastic rhythm section, they've got the guitar hero and they've got the enigmatic frontman. And then there's the other element, which is Morrissey's lyrics, that speak of the human condition and which are timeless. People will always be in love, out of love, happy, sad, feel despair. And Morrissey has an ability to forensically take apart and expose those things in lyrics. All the ingredients were set in stone for their brilliance.

It was 'What Differences Does It Make?' when I suddenly thought, 'Now I see what people are going on about.' That's when the penny dropped for me. And then you go back and discover the earlier singles and you realise there's something very special about this band. In 100 years' time that music is still going to speak to how humans love and hate and the passions that they have.

I saw them twice in 1986. The London Palladium was a great night. I'd been into people like Gary Numan and David Sylvian and Japan. I was living in Stevenage and it was just a train ride into the capital with friends. We had a pint in Soho and then a walk around the corner. We were in the first or second row of the balcony so great seats.

I remember loving the pomp around the arrival because three tracks were played before The Smiths took the stage. They were like three intro tunes. There was Klaus Nomi's 'Death', which Morrissey has subsequently used, followed by 'Why Don't Women Like Me?' by George Formby and then into Prokofiev and 'Dance of the Knights' and the big bright lights behind the drum kit. Then I remember Morrissey strolled onstage with his 'The Queen Is Dead' sign and on the reverse it said 'Two light ales please', which I thought was very, very funny.

I liked the show enough to immediately the following Saturday go back into London to the Stargreen box office for the next show that I knew The Smiths were playing, at Brixton Academy. I went to my girlfriend's house the night before – we were both going to the gig – and she said, 'The Smiths gig is cancelled. Johnny Marr's had a car crash.' She'd been listening to Kid Jensen, or possibly Janice Long.

Johnny Marr: I'd been out with Mike and his girlfriend and I went to take Mike home... The car went completely out of control, then bounced off a couple of walls and ended up in the middle of the road. I jumped out and saw that the car was completely squashed. I couldn't believe that I was still alive.

I think we had to reapply for tickets. My friend said, 'Do you want a ticket?' You could get them straight away or you could get them in two weeks. It wasn't like it is now where you have 15 seconds to try and get a ticket. So I found myself at what has turned out to be one of the most famous gigs in rock history.

I remember saying to my friend Paul, who I was with, 'It's just the simplicity of The Smiths that I absolutely love, the unfussiness.' The Smiths didn't need all the stage effects because they had the songs. And the gig ends, and of course with The Smiths you knew you were only six or seven weeks away from the next single and only 15 weeks away from the next album and you're looking forward to going to see them this time next year somewhere else. But it just never came to pass.

Simon, our bass player, had been in a tribute band to the Beautiful South and The Housemartins and that had been very successful. And he'd formed an early version of The Smyths while he was at university in Newcastle. They ended up supporting Dodgy in one of the three shows they played. Simon and Chris, who helped found the band but who has moved on to other things, had the idea of forming a tribute to The Smiths and having some fun and Chris said to Simon, 'Do you know a Morrissey?' My voice is nothing like Morrissey's but there's something in my voice that allows me to get in that same tone.

Our audiences? We get grandparents with grandchildren. We get fathers with sons and daughters. We get a real cross section and it speaks to the nostalgia market. People who are reliving, rekindling a moment. It speaks to those people who weren't there at that time but wished that they had been and who are getting a chance to hear the songs off the turntable.

There was a jam tribute called The Jamm, with two Ms, who were very much a role model for us. We looked at the sorts of venues they were playing, the venues that weren't already occupied by another tribute band. Then we were getting the festivals. Then we got the Academy Group venues. It just rolled and rolled. Then we got Glastonbury. We're in a fortunate position where we get more enquiries that we can actually fulfil. So if we play 80 shows a year we'd have had a demand to play 120. And there's some that we just can't play. We lived through it and I think we're a band that absorbed The Smiths. We experienced it first time.

We knew what it was to be a teenager who was a Smiths fan, and going to school and talking to others about The Smiths because you'd just seen them on *Top of the Pops*. Teenagers are impressionable and you get influenced by your heroes. We had such proximity to our heroes and that rush of excitement that we almost absorbed something from the time that you take onto stage with you which I think gives us an authenticity that younger tribute bands won't have.

We didn't have a pitch. We just approached venues that didn't have a Smiths tribute and said, 'Would you be interested in a show?' and we built it that way.

Morrissey was interviewed on Radio 4's *Front Row* about 10 years ago and was asked about a reunion and he said, 'No, I'm not that person any more.' And as the years have gone on I think that's more true. It could have happened. But it appears that that ship has sailed. But life is full of surprises.

The Smyths can be contacted via thesmyths.net. Details of Graham's other band can be found at beautifulmechanica.com

RAVI MARR FROM THE SONS AND HEIRS, NEW YORK, NEW YORK

The Sons and Heirs in action

I was born in 1975 so hadn't quite attuned my listening tastes to where they were going at the age of 10. I grew up near New York. I was listening to Billy Joel and playing piano. I remember hearing The Smiths at high school through friends and, listening to WDRE, the first song I remember hearing by Morrissey on WDRE was 'My Love Life'. I saw Morrissey at Madison Square Garden in 1991 on the first solo tour, having barely listened to his music. I was 15, 16 and completely awestruck at what I was seeing. Years later I became friends with Spencer Cobrin, who was in Morrissey's band during the Nineties. He was in his early 20s and only a few years older than me at that point. He said he was totally terrified playing that Madison Square Garden show. His parents had flown in from London and he'd never played an arena like that in the United States before! He's since sat in on a few of our shows.

I had been trained in piano but bought a guitar off a neighbour. I never took lessons. I started teaching myself by playing along to records. I learnt with The Sex Pistols, then The Cure and REM and then I started playing along to The Smiths. Listening to the multi-tracked guitar orchestrations by Johnny Marr is when I really, really fell in love with the band. It was a combination of sitting there and figuring out all the parts on the recording of 'Heaven Knows I'm Miserable Now' and going down to Bleeker Bob's in New York and buying my first Smiths live bootleg of The Smiths, a show they played in Amsterdam in '85. I'll never forget putting that bootleg on and listening to 'Heaven Knows I'm Miserable Now' and just totally losing it when I heard what was happening. I'd assumed that was a heavily overdubbed part in the studio but when I listened to the live recording it was, 'Wait a minute, he's playing all the parts at the same time!' It was that moment when I found what I felt for me personally was the top of the mountain as a guitar player. And that's where I wanted to go one day.

My original college band was called Charming, which name was definitely inspired by The Smiths. The college newspaper wrote about us and, as our records went out in the indie-pop community, I often got compared to Johnny Marr in my guitar playing. But by 2006 my original band had run its course. We had put out three records over about 10 years, were living in different cities and there was just no way to keep the momentum up and keep going with it. We weren't playing out, and I had fallen into a pretty productive full time career, writing music for television commercials. Because I was writing a lot of music on a daily basis I didn't really miss that part of being in a band. But I really missed being on stage and being in a room with other musicians.

My wife, in her infinite wisdom, said, 'Go find another band.' So I went on craigslist and typed 'Marr' in the search bar thinking, 'Maybe there's a band looking for a guitar player with that influence,' and came across a post from a singer looking to put together a Smiths tribute band. An email exchange developed between the singer and three other musicians. The bass player and drummer had already played together in a band. We agreed to learn four songs, including 'Still Ill', 'There is a Light That Never Goes Out' and 'This Charming Man', and meet up.

We got together and the singer, who had posted on craigslist, was a really nice guy and very enthusiastic but absolutely not up to the job. Listening to him sing was like listening to your friend next to you at the concert singing along. Everything was in sync rhythmically speaking but there was no pitch. Morrissey doesn't use a lot of pitches but you have to have the few that he does use.

I was walking back to the subway when I got a call from the bass player and drummer and they said, 'Hey, we don't think that's really going to work with that guy but we sounded good playing together. We should actually do this.' So we diplomatically let the singer know how we felt it went and we advertised ourselves for a singer and that's how we met Ronnie. Ronnie showed up and we knew that it was going to work. And that's how The Sons and Heirs was formed.

We're fortunate to own the New York City market as a Smiths tribute act. There's been a couple of other one off things that have happened over the years but we've developed our community and built our fan base in New York. We'll play on average between six and 12 shows a year. We play on a pretty regular schedule every three months or so in New York and other shows develop more organically. We've made our way down to Philly a bunch of times, to Virginia, we've been up north to Boston once and then we've played a couple of flyaway shows over the years. We were brought over to Tel Aviv about five years ago by a promoter who's a huge Depeche Mode fan and does a big Depeche Mode boat party every year in New York. And the next day we got a tour of the local sites from the person who runs the Morrissey fan club in Israel and who'd given Morrissey and his band the same tour when they came over. We've gone over to LA a few times. We've played the Smiths and Morrissey Convention once and we also played a big show at the House of Blues with The Sweet and Tender Hooligans, who were very gracious in bringing us over to put together a big show for the two of us. We've played Nashville. We've played Austin.

The tribute band world is friendly but competitive in a territorial sense. We're friendly with other bands but we don't really want them visiting New York any more than they really want to us trying to play their home cities. We just try to focus on our area and our relationships. That's usually how shows come about.

Everybody has a different approach to the idea of what a tribute band should be. The people who follow us appreciate the way we think about it and the work we put into making it as close as possible to seeing The Smiths in the Eighties and how, beyond our singer, all of us really work at our sound, our equipment and how we present ourselves on stage to try to honour what those four guys were when they got together.

The largest demographic of our audience is people in their 40s and 50s now but we have a lot of younger people. Sometimes it depends on which part of New York City we're playing. It's really funny how that works but if we're playing in Manhattan we might be more likely to run into people who are visiting from the UK or ex-pats, and if we play in the Park Slope area of Brooklyn we get a lot of people our age in their 40s, and who probably have babysitters to get to the show. And then if we play in Williamsburg that crowd tends to be younger and we get a lot of musicians and people who play different kinds of music but who are really big fans of what The Smiths did, or quote them as influences.

I've seen Morrissey eight times over the years. I've not been faithful enough to get to every single tour when he's come through New York. But I've seen him every other tour or so. The most recent time was in May 2019 when I had tickets to see him on Broadway. And we've done a few after parties for his shows. One of our first after parties, which was one of our biggest early shows, was when he cancelled a Madison Square Garden show about a day before. There were still people getting off the train near Madison Square Garden who hadn't gotten the news yet. We had already been booked to play about eight blocks away at 11pm or midnight. So we went down with some flyers for our show and said, 'Hey, go get dinner and then come back to our show. It's free!' We had about 700-800 people at BB King's that night. People were really appreciative that they'd come all the way into New York City – in some cases they'd come in from other countries – and still had something to do.

I saw Johnny with The Healers in the very early 2000s, before The Sons and Heirs started. Ronnie and I figured out later that we were both at that show, standing about 10 feet apart, but we hadn't met each other yet. That night I had a Charming CD with me and after they got off stage I put it on Johnny's pedal board, thinking he might pick it up and listen to it. I don't know what I was thinking.

I've seen him on almost all of his most recent tours, including in New Haven in May 2019. He's getting better as a front man on each tour and on each record.

I don't think he'll ever be the lyricist that Morrissey is and nor is he trying to be.

But seeing him play The Smiths with his band is the ultimate fan experience because the room is usually so loud singing every word of the song and at the top of their lungs you barely care what his voice sounds like. It just becomes a space for fans to sing along and love those songs. To hear those parts played the way they were written is amazing. He's a really terrific performer and his band is super tight.

I've got to meet him after shows twice and had brief conversations with him and he's really a super nice guy. The last time he came through we talked about his signature Jaguar model, one of which I own, and we talked about what he did to redesign that instrument. Another time we talked about running the New York marathon because we've both done it. He said, 'Nice trainers', using the British parlance for sneakers!

There was a period after The Sons and Heirs started where I saw Morrissey a couple of times but I found the shows really frustrating. I almost didn't enjoy them because whenever he'd start playing The Smiths it would feel like his band is just not doing this material justice. I'd always felt that way but after the first few years of The Sons and Heirs, I knew what it was like to actually play that music on stage the right way and I was thinking, 'Let me get up there. Let me get on there and play that part.'

My eyes are very open about Morrissey being a difficult guy to work with on the business end and creatively, and I know it might change my relationship to him and his music and perhaps not in a positive way, but that's a risk in any situation. If I could get 10 of my best seconds of video on YouTube to him one day, if that's what he wanted, I'd do it for the experience of playing the kinds of shows that he plays. Playing with him would be amazing, but I'd also like to show my love for that material and to share that with fans. I don't think it will ever happen, mostly because I don't think that that's how he views what he wants to do as an artist. I don't think he wants to recreate The Smiths on stage.

But if he ever decided that he wanted to present that material the right way from a guitar perspective I would drop what I was doing and everybody in my life would understand. If I got a call from Morrissey saying Boz Boorer was leaving and asking me to join his band and go on the road with him for 12 months then I'd absolutely do it, in a heartbeat.

To contact The Sons and Heirs go to thesonsandheirs.com

RANDOM ENCOUNTERS

I WAS THERE: GRAHAM WEAVER

I once followed Morrissey up Oxford Street.

I WAS THERE: PETER ROWE

I bought *Rank* the day it came out but was too late to see The Smiths. Like many I'm struggling with Morrissey nowadays. His framed record just came off the wall

I WAS THERE: MICHAEL INGLESON

I was too young to see The Smiths but have seen Moz a handful of times. One time in Hull I saw two massive blokes in their 40s fighting over the shirt he threw into the crowd. It ended with a head butt.

I WAS THERE: MICHAEL GILHAM

The Smiths were one of my favourite bands through my last couple years of high school and into college but I have only seen Morrissey live. I have many rewarding gig experiences. For one of the Alma Matters tour gigs, being a broke postgrad 20 something without a car and living with my mom and her husband in their North Arlington townhouse, I rented a minivan and drove a number of like-minded acquaintances up to Glen Burnie, Maryland. The venue was a banquet hall-like place called Michael's Eighth Avenue prompting Moz, upon taking the stage, to greet the crowd with, 'Welcome to the Bar Mitzvah'. It was on this tour that I first heard them perform Smiths songs and they performed 'Paint a Vulgar Picture' at this show.

The Smiths and their iconoclastic singer changed my life. The music and Steven's words opened up my world and expanded my mind. Being so removed from the press coverage of the band and Mozza's ensuing solo career, none of this was anything to do with Steven's sexuality, or lack thereof. It wasn't until I'd been listening to Morrissey for years that I realised he was almost certainly not heterosexual. For me, it was all about the music and those inimitable lyrics. I can recall on more than one occasion driving in the car listening to 'This Night Has Opened My Eyes' and getting chills. This is how powerful some of The Smiths' songs are for me. Likewise, I've had the same sensation when listening to certain songs in Morrissey's solo oeuvre, eg. 'Now My Heart Is Full', 'Lost' or 'Speedway'. I've never had time for people that called The Smiths 'depressing' 'mope rock'. Moz has had his demons but any morose content in his songs was almost invariably in conjunction with Mozza's uniquely supreme wit.

I have never seen Morrissey do a bad gig.

HE WASN'T THERE: NED P CANNON

I once turned up for a Smiths gig in New York which was cancelled because Morrissey was stung by a bee.

I WASN'T THERE: IAN NESBITT

Sadly I never saw The Smiths. I was due to see them supporting Altered Images at the Hammersmith Palais but apparently their van broke down and they couldn't make it!

I WAS THERE: CARL HINDE

I saw them quite a few times. The first time was Newcastle in 1985 I saw the last gig in 1986. I was also in the audience for their final live performance on *The Tube.* I also saw Morrissey's first live solo gig at Wolverhampton. I have a pic of us in *No. 1* magazine at the Liverpool Royal Court gig for Liverpool City Council, *With Love from Manchester*. I had to sleep rough in Liverpool that night as I couldn't get home and I had no money for digs.

I WAS THERE: STEPHEN GILBERT

They were my favourite band as a teenager. People said they were depressing but I was in love and never got the whole depression thing. The guitar work is just amazing and I suppose with Morrissey being a bit odd it appealed to the alternative youth of the day! I still want 'There Is a Light That Never Goes Out' played at my funeral.

Peter McDermott's 'There is a Light' tattoo

I WAS THERE: PETER MCDERMOTT

I got a tattoo a few years ago 'There Is a Light, That Never Goes Out'. This song has been my favourite from the moment it was released. The lyrics are so great. I want 'There is a light that never goes out' written on my headstone when I die.

I WAS THERE: STEVEN WRIGLEY

'Shakespeare's Sister' had just been released and we were out in this naff local restaurant in Saddleworth, where I grew up. Pat Phoenix, the cover star from the picture sleeve of the single, was at the next table with her actor partner, Tony Booth. I thought, 'I'm just going to nip home, get the single and she can sign it.' And then I thought, 'That's a bit naff. I can't do that' so I didn't.

She must have been fairly ill because she died not long after, and then I was thinking, 'I really wish I'd got her to sign it.' I was at university at the time but it was the holidays. My dad was working at a hospital, doing a painting job on Oxford Road in Manchester, and I must have said I was bored because he said, 'Right, you can come and help me do this painting job.'

The hospital was next door to the Holy Name Church on Oxford Road and it was Pat Phoenix's funeral that day. So of course I'm going, 'Fucking hell, this is brilliant. My two favourite things – Morrissey and Corrie!' (UK TV soap opera *Coronation Street*). That was one of the reasons I loved The Smiths and Morrissey, because those were the things that he was into - the Sixties and the kitchen sink dramas and Albert Finney and all the rest of it. I was going out for ciggie breaks and I said to my dad, 'Everybody's arriving so I'll be back in half an hour. I'm just going to watch to see if Morrissey's here, and the Corrie people.' We were stood at these barriers at the entrance to the church and Morrissey arrived. Next minute, all these other guests had arrived and it was just about to start when they suddenly opened up the barriers and said, 'Right all you lot – inside the back of the church.' And I thought, 'Well, I'm not missing much. I'm only missing a bit of painting.' So I went in with my overalls covered in paint.

They had jazz bands and it was a real celebration of her life. I could see that Morrissey was quite a few rows ahead of me and I thought, 'How can I get up there? I know, I'll go and take communion. So then I can walk around and if there's any spare seats where he is, I can go and plonk myself down next to him.' That was my plan. By the time I'd got round and done communion, coming back there wasn't anywhere. But I made sure I walked past him, right next to Morrissey.

Coming out afterwards I thought, 'I'll see where he goes.' So we're coming out of the church and there were loads of Smiths fans outside by that time. They were filming people leaving the church and Julie Goodyear, who played Bet Lynch on *Coronation Street*, was being interviewed outside and I just walked past her straight across camera. On *Look North West* that night, you could see me going past. I wasn't thinking about the television cameras. I was just thinking, 'Morrissey, Morrissey, Morrissey.' He was outside and he wandered up the road and he signed a few autographs and stuff like that but I didn't have anything with me.

I moved to London in 1988. The first thing I did was get a job application off to Rough Trade. After a few months I actually got a job in their distribution factory at King's Cross. Being a Smiths obsessive I thought, 'Oh, Morrissey's still bound to pop in now and again.' I thought that even though The Smiths had finished and of course he did pop in a couple of times. By then everybody was a bit too cool for school at Rough Trade. But word got round that I was a big fan so every time he was in the building people would come and find me and go, 'Morrissey's in. He's upstairs. Go and hang round the doorway. He's going to be out in whatever time.' But I'd heard the stories of how he could be a bit dismissive and I thought, 'I don't want to spoil it.'

Jo Slee was still working at Rough Trade. It was her birthday. We'd been invited to her party, which was just a little pub in King's Cross. I was thinking, 'Morrissey will be coming to this which'll be great. This is my big chance to meet him.' One of the guys I knew at Rough Trade played in Luxuria, Howard Devoto's band, and they'd toured the states with Morrissey. He said, 'I know Morrissey. I can introduce you' and I thought, 'This is it!'

For some reason we decided to go out at lunchtime and we got pretty drunk. All sorts went on at Rough Trade - drugs and all sorts, all day every day – so we were drunk at lunchtime. I don't think we did much work. And then at five o'clock we all piled down the pub and then about eight o'clock Karl, who played bass with Howard Devoto, said, 'Right, we'll all go to this party.'

By this time I was literally paralytic. I think the excitement of it all was part of the problem. We were in this little club where this party was and Morrissey arrived. We were actually in the same little room. He had a Stetson on and he was chewing gum and he looked really tall. He looked like a real pop star, whereas when I'd seen him in Manchester a couple of years before he was in his jacket and jeans and looking like he always looked. So we get a drink and we get another drink and then Karl says, 'Come on then, I'll introduce you.' By this stage I could hardly walk. So we went up to him and Karl said, 'This guy Stephen just wants to say hello…' and I took a step forward and was just about to shake his hand and say something when I almost tripped.

I staggered over to one wall about two metres away to hold myself up and then I pushed myself off that wall and went flying across the room to the other side and managed to just about stray upright. Then I staggered back to the back wall and just about made it back to Morrissey and fell on my knees at his feet.

All I remember is looking up and Morrissey was looking down at me with a look of utter disgust. I've never seen anything like it. He must have thought, 'Who is this absolute drunken person?' I said, 'hi' and he just walked off. It was the biggest anti-climax of my life. I was just mortified. Karl said, 'You're unbelievable.'

Johnny Marr: Everything that I was doing in The Smiths I can do now; but there's things that I do now that I wouldn't have had the skill or the mindset to do in The Smiths. I would never have been able to stand in front of a 70-piece orchestra and play to thousands of people, for example. So it's all good. I'm happy with how things have turned out.

Morrissey: I would rather eat my own testicles than reform The Smiths, and that's saying something for a vegetarian.

Drawing by Lee Thacker

WHAT DIFFERENCE DOES IT MAKE?

When I said I was going to write a book on The Smiths, a number of people who might have contributed a memory of seeing them live declined to do. Their reasoning was that they found recent endorsements by Morrissey of right wing groups abhorrent.

Of those who did share memories with me, more people volunteered opinions on Morrissey's political statements than I have included in this book. I felt it would skew the focus of the book to include all the comments people made on Morrissey's politics. But I also felt it was wrong to leave them all out.

Some people were angry at Morrissey. Most were just sad that he no longer seemed to speak for the outsiders that his lyrics once spoke so eloquently for, and to. No one who offered an opinion on Morrissey's right wing leanings expressed any sympathy for them.

Richard Houghton
Manchester
August 2019

ACKNOWLEDGEMENTS

This book would not have been possible without the help of everyone who contributed a memory and I'd like to place on record my thanks to all of them, but particularly Simon Wolstenholme, whose memoir *You Can Drum But You Can't Hide* is a must read for any Smiths fan, and Lee Thacker, illustrator extraordinaire, whose Peel-inspired book on the Festive Fifty is available at

http://www.lulu.com/shop/lee-thacker/the-festive-fifty-an-illustrated-memoir/paperback/product-11605351.html.

I'd also like to thank the following for permission to quote from their publications or blogs - Karren Ablaze, *The City is Ablaze*; Martin Whitehead, *The Underground*; Stuart Edwards, blackcountryrock.co/2015/0522/with-love-from-manchester; Photographer Mike Powell, michaelpowell.com; Colm O'Callaghan, The Blackpool Sentinel, https://theblackpoolsentinel.wordpress.com/2017/08/04/the-smiths-in-cork-1984/; Peter Smith, https://vintagerock.wordpress.com/2014/03/30/red-wedge-tour-newcastle-city-hall-31st-january-1986/; Neil Ward, UEA Vice-Chancellor, 'The Smiths 14 February 1984: a belated review'.

And the following Facebook page administrators for their kind support for and promotion of my appeal for Smiths fans to get in touch: Ben Darnton from Guildford Past and Present; Aberdeen Music; Paul from Decade 77-87 – A Grown Up Disco; Davie Kirk from The Westway Kilmarnock Music Society; Nick Boldock from Hull Music Archive; James Bruce from Colchester Music; Luke Gilligan from Classic Dublin Gigs; William Wycherley (@MorrisseyIndeed).

I'd also like to thank Lou Duffy-Howard and Jeremy Kidd of The Red Guitars (https://www.redguitars.co.uk/); Billy Bragg; Roger Denton, for his loan of Johnny Marr's *Set The Boy Free* and for the early and relentless exposure to The Smiths; Sharon Watters, Steve Catterall, Joseph Kelly, Martin Mullaney, Ken Sweeney, Gavin Underhill, Dave Stan, David Manning, Peter Lindsey-Jones, Anthony Jackson, Brian Parkyn and Nuan Butcherd and Sam O'Daniel of yourolderbrother.com

Copies of Stephen Wright's iconic photographs from the Salford Lads Club are available at www.smithsphotos.com

Finally, I'd like to thank Neil Cossar and Liz Sanchez at This Day In Music Books for their support, my son Bill for undertaking the additional domestic duties that enabled me to get this book finished (and for passing his degree) and Kate Sullivan for the peace, love and understanding.

If you have a memory of a Smiths show or of any other act from the last 50 years I'd love to hear about it at iwasatthatgig@gmail.com.

THE
WEDDING
PRESENT
sometimes
these
words
just
don't
have
to
be
said

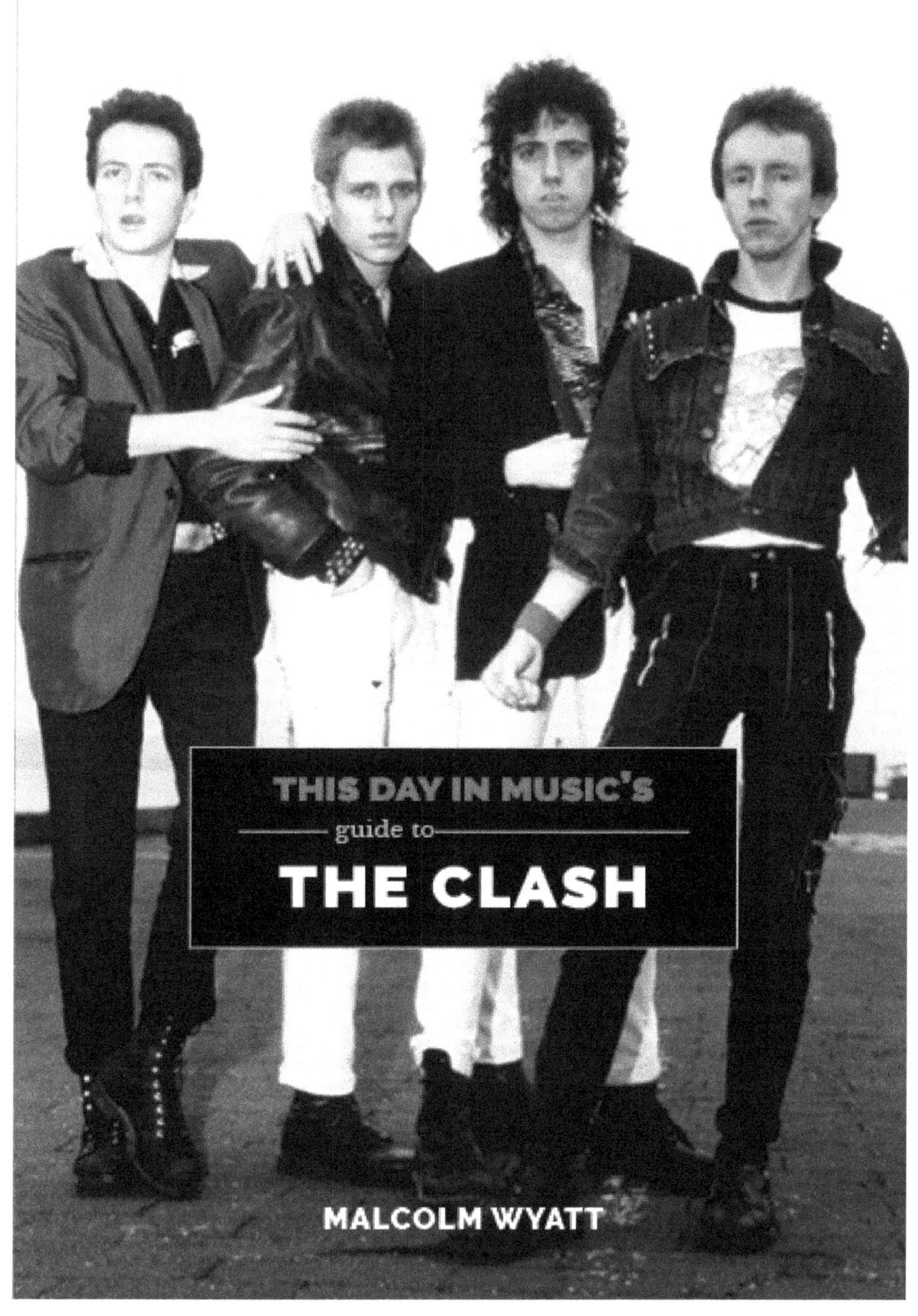
THIS DAY IN MUSIC'S
guide to
THE CLASH
MALCOLM WYATT

Lightning Source UK Ltd.
Milton Keynes UK
UKHW020708220522
403340UK00003B/353